UNIVERSITY COLLEGE
WINCHESTER

Martial Rose Library
Tel: 01962 827306

1 5 FEB 2007

2 6 JAN 2012

To be returned on or before the day marked above, subject to recall.

THE CATHOLIC CHURCH AND CATHOLIC
SCHOOLS IN NORTHERN IRELAND

The Catholic Church and Catholic Schools in Northern Ireland

The Price of Faith

MICHAEL McGRATH

IRISH ACADEMIC PRESS

DUBLIN • PORTLAND, OR

First published in 2000 by
IRISH ACADEMIC PRESS
44, Northumberland Road, Dublin 4, Ireland
and in the United States of America by
IRISH ACADEMIC PRESS
c/o ISBS, 5804 NE Hassalo Street, Portland, OR 97213–3644

website: www.iap.ie

British Library Cataloguing in Publication Data
McGrath, Michael
The Catholic church and Catholic schools in Northern Ireland: The price of faith
1. Catholic schools – Northern Ireland – History – 20th century   2. Education and state – Northern Ireland   3. Catholic schools – Northern Ireland – Administration
I. Title
371'. 0712'416'0904

ISBN 0–7165–2651–4

Library of Congress Cataloguing-in-Publication Data
McGrath, Michael
The Catholic Church and Catholic schools in Northern Ireland. The price of faith / Michael McGrath.
    p.   cm.
Includes bibliographical references and index.
ISBN 0–7165–2651–4
1. Catholic Church—Education—Northern Ireland—History—20th century.   2. Catholic schools—Northern Ireland—History—20th century.
3. Educational law and legislation—Northern Ireland.   4. Church and state—Northern Ireland.   I. Title.
LC506.G72N676 2000
371.071'2416—dc21   99–31405
                                                                                                    CIP

Typeset in 10.5 pt on 13 pt Palatino by
Carrigboy Typesetting Services, County Cork
Printed by Creative Print and Design, (Wales), Ebbw Vale.

*This work is dedicated to the memory of my father
Dr Michael McGrath*

Jesus said to her 'I am the resurrection and the life, he who believes in me, though he die, yet shall he live, and whoever lives and believes in me shall never die. Do you believe this ?'

John 11, 25 and 26

Contents

Acknowledgements

Most academic books are private affairs, but I cannot end my long voyage without thanking those who have helped me along the way.

Firstly, I wish to thank Professor Brendan O'Leary for supervising the doctoral thesis which forms the basis of this book. I also wish to thank John Barnes and Professor Patrick Buckland for their dedication is acting as my examiners. I would also like to thank Andrew Beh, Steve John, Scott Kelly and Brendan O'Duffy for all their help over the past few years. I must also thank Linda Longmore of the *Irish Academic Press* for all her hard work in helping me transform my thesis into the work you are about to read.

I also wish to thank the staff of the British Library of Political and Economic Science at the London School of Economics, the British Library in London, the Northern Ireland Public Record Office in Belfast, the Catholic Central Library both in London and in Dublin, the Linen Hall Library in Belfast and the library staff at the Queen's University of Belfast for their constant attention and assistance. I have made many demands, not all of them reasonable, over the past five years, and they have always responded with kindness and enthusiasm. I also wish to thank the staff at the Bishop's Palace in Belfast who were so friendly during my search of the diocesan archives.

Finally, I thank my family – my mother, my brother Damian, and my sisters Catherine and Brenda – for their support over the past five years. I hope that they, if no one else, will feel that all my labours have been worthwhile.

Abbreviations

ACT	All Children Together
CCMA	Catholic Clerical Managers Association
CCMS	Council for Catholic Maintained Schools
EMU	Education for Mutual Understanding
DCDA	Down and Connor Diocesan Archives
DENI	Department of Education for Northern Ireland
INTO	Irish National Teachers' Organisation
NIO	Northern Ireland Office
PRONI	Public Record Office of Northern Ireland
SACHR	Standing Advisory Commission on Human Rights
SDLP	Social Democratic and Labour Party
UEC	United Education Committee

Foreword

This very important study prompts major questions of political and historical analysis. The Roman Catholic Church and its ancillary institutions, and their relations to political power, are now rarely the subjects of detailed research by historians, sociologists and political scientists. This is strange given that the Church was one of the first successful trans-national, international and indeed global institutions, and that it has been the longest running organisation of the modern Occident. Indeed it has been an amazingly hardy survivor, a long-lived multi-national enterprise and pioneer of a range of managerial and bureaucratic techniques – including the subordination of conscience and intellect to other-ordained rules, the papal-line. As an organisation it exemplifies, *par excellence*, the routinization of charisma. Sometime the sovereign, sometime the joint sovereign of Christendom, the Church is older than all the states of the world, and has outlived an astonishing range of empires and more recent ideologies. Its very name reflects its claim to the legacy of the greatest empire of European history, with which it made its first political accommodation.

Students of statecraft and of management have much to learn from the history of the Church – a subject too important to be left to the in-house and partisan concerns of its theologians, or the pieties of its tenured staff, and too interesting to be left to the abuses of its religious competitors. Students of nationalism also have much to learn from the history of the Roman Catholic Church. It is a testing site for the power of nationalism as a principle of political and indeed moral authority. Roman Catholicism, like Islam, has never, in principle, been national, either in form or content. It is declared to be universal, catholic, and cosmopolitan: unlike its Judaic predecessor it claims that it is not the religion of a people, but of all peoples. Its sacred language, the language of Rome, was at once a language of power and mystery but also a language to unify its diverse officials – its priests, nuns, monks, abbots, bishops and monsignors – enabling them to transcend their parochial, or ethnic identities. In fact, the first nations of European history to be called such were the students of Catholic universities organised in clubs, or halls of residences, in rough correspondence with their students' geographic origins and mother-tongues. Like their patron the Church, the universities recognised these harbingers of national difference and managed them, but they aspired to create a transcendent integrated identity out of them – a Latin-literate clerisy with supreme loyalty to the Church of Christ and his apostles' successors on earth rather than to the nation or local kings. The effort was made to strip the clerisy of local particularisms notably through such radical innovations as the requirement that senior management positions would be confined to celibates, those who would break with hereditary commitments to family and tribe – an innovation eased by the creed's deep fear and hatred of sexuality, especially female sexuality as Dr Uta Ranke-Heinemann has reminded us.[1] The Church, in short, has been for much of its history a much more successful multinational *Internationale* than those organised by socialist or communist parties.

In principle, one might therefore expect organised Catholicism, especially at the highest clerical level, to be anti-nationalist – loyal to Rome rather than to home. And, in considerable measure so it has been, and, at a doctrinal level, so it will always be. The Church's successive leaders struggled with the emerging European State in early modern Europe. They sought to protect their organisational and decision-making autonomy, above all their powers of appointment, from merely national statal interference. Where the Church lost these contests national Protestant churches took over its local branch offices in concert with impious princes – the most locally interesting nation-alisation without compensation was the formation of the appropriately named Anglican church – facilitated by the difficulty an English king was having with his Spanish wife. Where the Church won these contests it nevertheless often had to compromise, as it had originally with Constantine, and let the local organisations acquire a limited national coloration or patronage – 'Gallican' compromises that were despised by the hard-liners, those loyal to supreme papal authority on the other side of the Alps, the aptly named 'ultramontane'.

Gallican deals were one thing: necessary side-payments, mostly within the aristocratic class, to preserve the universal church. Protestants were more serious, heretical rivals, both to hierarchy and to the ordered religious regulation of politics, and dangerous facilitators of individualism – even if they did not always practice it. But the Church's worst enemies were yet to come, the secularists. The Church famously feared Jacobins, and their liberal and socialist associates, as kindred spirits. Jacobins, liberals and socialists were rightly seen as the nationalisers and secularisers of education. As nationalisers and as democrats they sacralised the people's will – rather than God's, or the Pope's – a blatant form of self-worship that Durkheim helps explain but the Church regarded as idolatry. And as secularisers the Jacobins and their allies demanded that the state (and sometimes private entrepreneurs) should take-over education, nationalise it, sometimes in every sense of that word, and expel the superstition-mongering cosmopolitan clerics that were not properly national, not fully loyal, because, after all, they were subordinate to Rome.

That, however, has been only one side of the story. While the Church has been cosmopolitan by disposition its adherents have not, and everywhere it has proselytised, the Church accommodated ethnic, religious and national pasts that were not of its making. In Ireland the Church had, so it was later claimed, saved civilisation, or at least the civilisation of Rome and Greece as filtered by the Christian censors.[2] It had successfully evangelised amongst the Gaelic natives before the first Anglo-Norman conquests of the twelfth century – though their pagan traditions and cults were tacitly adapted in the Irish version of Romanism. At least one of its Popes legitimated, or was held to have legitimated, the Anglo-Norman conquest of Ireland. The pre-Reformation Church in Ireland catered to an ethnic and linguistic colonial dual society, one with considerable signs of assimilation (of the settlers by the natives), and reflected these divisions within its ranks and organisation. But after the Reformation the Church found itself an alien power within the English empire, as the Church of the natives and the old settlers but not of the new settlers; and it was an alien power tacitly and explicitly allied to England's major competitors, Spain and France. The historian Hugh Trevor Roper puts these developments pithily,

> 'Why was Ireland so sensitive an issue in English politics? It was, of course, our postern gate through which foreign enemies – first the Spaniards, then the French – sought to attack us. It was to us what Poland was to Prussia once Prussia was strong and Poland weak; and through fear we treated it similarly: colonisation, expropriation, discrimination, partition. The response too was similar: exasperated nationalism inflamed by religious difference, religious difference inflamed in turn by awakened nationalism.'[3]

After the Reformation and Counter-Reformation, and leaving aside complicated tales which found the Pope temporarily allied with the Dutch Protestant King William and organiser of the *coup d'etat* of 1688, the Roman Catholic Church in Ireland was outlawed, and its adherents, mostly the natives with a leavening of the 'old English', were the targets of 'penal laws' that, amongst other things, were not designed to assist a good Catholic education. The precarious survival of organised Catholicism in these circumstances was remarkable, and the reality and myths of the martyred church and nation did much for the subsequent convergence of Catholicism and Irish nationalism. Indeed the ethnic identification of the native Irish with the Church was, so to speak, an equal and opposite reaction to the penal laws.

Within two centuries of the passage of these laws the Catholic Church in Ireland was to be remarkably powerful, more powerful and rigorous than it had ever been in regulating its flock, organiser of the religion of the island's majority, the natives, and in charge of much of the island's education and social services. What explains the nineteenth century comeback of the Roman Catholic Church? In a phrase, the conjunction of British imperial policy and Catholic opportunity. It was also aided by the repercussions of the Famine, that brutal moderniser of Ireland. Politics was, however, primary. The threat of Jacobinism, manifest in the United Irishmen, and in nineteenth century republicanism, concentrated English and Papist minds. The British state in Ireland abandoned the attempt to Anglicise the native Irish through mere coercion. It would collaborate with the Catholic Church – it would be given permission to pacify and civilise the native Irish, most importantly in education and social welfare.[4] The Protestant state of the United Kingdom of Great Britain and Ireland, having failed to pacify Ireland through centralised policing, Protestant education and subsidised emigration, tolerated and eventually supported the Catholic Church in Ireland: Catholics had restrictions on citizenship and property rights lifted after the 1770s, were emancipated in 1829, and had the Anglican Church (the so-called Church of Ireland) disestablished in 1869.[5] The investment in reform was partly repaid: the Church would significantly assist in creating a Catholic rural bourgeoisie with a stake in the imperial order; and the Church would regularly counsel against insurrectionary secular republicanism.

The Church that would do so was built by Cardinal Paul Cullen, an ultramontanist who tempered the Church's policy to Irish circumstances, and who brought with him from Rome the distinctly puritanical version of Catholicism now associated with Irish Romanism. The Church had followed an astute collaboration, obtaining control of schools in Ireland that had been intended to be non-denominational, and it was vigorously critical of militarist republicanism, but Cullen knew there were limits to effective collaboration. The Church could not become enthusiastically in favour of the Union of Great Britain and Ireland without endangering its ethnic base – whose political leaders minimally favoured repeal of the union and home rule. So the Catholic Church resisted the British state's offer to subsidise its clergy, and Cullen opposed 'current endowment', the British state's remarkable proposal to establish both the Catholic Church and the Anglican Church of Ireland. Cullen worked instead for no established church in Ireland rather than two – although Vatican policy of the time held that the separation of church and state was an evil. Cullen's reconstruction of an autonomous, centralised and re-invigorated Church between 1849 and 1878 put a major road-block in the path of British nation-builders in Ireland, secured the Church's ethnic base, and gave it an organisational penetration of native civil society that would not diminish until the 1970s. The Church would have been entirely content with home rule – as it was it had to cope with the unexpected victory of militant republicanism between 1916 and 1921 before, as usual, making an accommodation with the new powers that were.

As Dr McGrath's book goes to press the remarkably long nineteenth century of Irish Catholicism is surely ending. The Republic of Ireland and Catholics in Northern Ireland are secularising fast, though not at the same pace as in Quebec in the 1960s. Native priest and nun production rates are respectively low and negative. The Papal visit of 1979, when half of Ireland's Catholics turned out to see him somewhere, will be seen in retrospect as the last moment of its moral hegemony. The Church's austere, indeed wintry reputation, is now deeply damaged by scandals, both financial and sexual. It does not have the work force to run its core let alone its ancillary organisations, and is slowly beating retreats – ceding power to lay Catholics in hospitals, charities and schools. The ambitious no longer pursue a churchly career as a first or second choice. Modernization is working its normal impacts – albeit with a long delay that can largely be attributed to the Church's successful accommodation with Irish nationalism. The Church is now becoming a mere interest group, with special influence over the politics of the body – over public policy debates on birth-control and abortion – though it has lost its war of position on abortion and looks set for further defeats.

It is against this backcloth that Dr McGrath's book should be read: a book about times past that has compelling intellectual and public policy interest. The *Catholic Church and Catholic Schools in Northern Ireland* will establish itself as the opening reference for anyone interested in the history of the Roman Catholic Church and Catholic Schools in Northern Ireland between 1920 and 1993. Dr. McGrath's book is a scrupulous investigation, based on primary, governmental, and diocesan archival sources, of a much neglected subject: the relations between the Roman Catholic Church, the Northern nationalist community and the state of the United Kingdom, during both the Stormont era (1921–72) and that of direct rule (1972–).

Dr. McGrath tells the tale as one of incremental gains by the Church, staving off threats to its control of its own educational institutions in the 1920s, gradually extracting a greater degree of public funding of Catholic schools, and in 1993 full funding for Catholic schools was achieved – though not entirely because of the Church's efforts as we are told. McGrath notes that the price of financial success has been the loss of clerical control within the Church's own educational bailiwick: 'Catholic clerics have surrendered power within Catholic schools, but to Catholic parents, Catholic teachers and DENI officials rather than to Unionist politicians' (p. 244). The other price of success over the long run was that Catholics in Northern Ireland had inferior physical accommodation in their schools, and, in the early days, teachers who were paid less than their colleagues in the state/Protestant sector. The Catholic community paid a further price for its autonomy in education, a 'double burden', paying taxes for schools they did not use, and making voluntary contributions towards their own. Dr. McGrath rightly draws attention to the difficulties in establishing the educational, credentialist and labour-market damage that Catholics experienced in consequence – but no one disputes that there was some.

Dr. McGrath suggests in his conclusion that Catholic schools were vital in preserving both the Catholic and nationalist identity in Northern Ireland. The first claim is almost true by definition; the second is less evident. The Protestants of Northern Ireland, in the main, as the 1920s controversies showed, did not want secular or integrated education: and it is difficult to imagine any successful integration project, whether pan-Christian or pan-British, at that time. Moreover, Catholic schools, as Dr. McGrath shows, and as I can testify from personal experience, were not, in the main, vigorous stalwarts of Gaelic and republican culture – indeed they have become more so after the events of 1969 than they were before, accommodating rather than leading their flock's ethno-national sentiments. Under the system of control, organising the majority and disorganising the minority, that the Ulster Unionist Party ran between 1921 and 1969, the Catholic Church was both a site for autonomous education and social and political activity by nationalists, and a mechanism through which unequal relations between Catholics and Protestants were preserved. Under the system of direct rule, which was not, as Dr. McGrath shows, as magnanimous in its educational largesse as is sometimes suggested, the Church has become less important in the politics of a community that has broken free from unionist domination and has its own authentic political parties and autonomous civil society. Compared with the 1920s the nationalist identity of northern nationalists is now at least as vigorous, overt and obvious, whereas their Catholic identity is much less vigorous, overt and obvious – a change which suggests that Catholic schools are now less effective at producing Catholics than they once were. Whether the schools were, and are, the principal aquaria of nationalist sentiments may legitimately be doubted, but that they played some role in the communal, collectivist and moralising character of northern nationalism cannot.

The Church's schools place in the new political system agreed on April 10, 1998 remains to be confirmed, not least because it is uncertain whether the Good Friday Agreement will be implemented. That Agreement does, however, suggest a clear possible future for Northern Ireland's educational system, at primary and secondary levels.[6] Power-sharing, proportional representation and veto rights are the key governmental principles in the new consociational political system to which the parties agreed, and the public endorsed, for the internal politics of Northern Ireland. The parties and their publics did not, however, agree to any new model of integrated education, though they did not oppose it in the Agreement. By implication the principal parties will maintain the new system of equal funding of all systems, Catholic, state/Protestant, and the small integrated sector. This principle of educational autonomy is part of all known consociational systems. It suggests a future for Catholic schools in Northern Ireland as part of the mechanism through which nationalists protect and express their identity – and it suggests that they will become more nationalist, less Catholic and more secular in character, driven by the material and educational priorities of an emancipated laity (in continuation of existing trends). But whatever their future Dr. McGrath's book will be the reliable guide to their past.

BRENDAN O'LEARY
Professor of Political Science, LSE
London, England, Summer 1999

REFERENCES

1. Uta Ranke-Heinemann, *Eunuchs for the Kingdom of Heaven: Women, Sexuality and the Catholic Church* (London: Penguin, 1990), trans. Peter Heinegg.

2. The most recent and extremely popular statement can be found in Thomas Cahill, *How the Irish Saved Civilization: the Untold Story of Ireland's Heroic Role from the fall of Rome to the Rise of Medieval Europe* (New York: Doubleday, 1995).

3. Hugh Trevor Roper, 'The Lost Moments of History', *New York Review of Books*, 27 October 1988.

4. This is the theme of Tom Inglis's book *Moral Monopoly: the Catholic Church in Modern Irish Society* (Dublin: Gill and Macmillan, 1987)

5. John Whyte, *Church and State in Modern Ireland* (Dublin: Gill and Macmillan, 1979) is a scrupulously reliable guide to the political history of church-state relations in Ireland.

6. For further analysis see Brendan O'Leary 'The Nature of the British-Irish Agreement' *New Left Review* (1999) 233: 66–96.

CHAPTER ONE

Introduction

This is a tale of one of the most profound forms of power; the power to fashion fundamental values and beliefs in schools. The central purpose of this book is to examine the efforts of the Catholic authorities[1] to improve the funding conditions for Catholic schools in Northern Ireland, and to measure their success during the four major contests which led to the Education Acts of 1930, 1947 and 1968 and the Education Order of 1993. The book also assesses the scale of the financial and educational price paid by Northern Ireland's Catholics to maintain a network of autonomous Catholic schools.

The principal conflict between the Catholic authorities and the Northern Ireland government centred upon clerical efforts to extract higher rates of public funding and the politicians' attempts to exert an influence within Catholic schools. The clergy refused to abandon clerical control, and the politicians refused to grant Catholic schools increased funds without obtaining some influence for the education committees established by the 1923 Education Act. The dilemma troubling the Catholic authorities after 1923 was whether to accept a degree of political influence in exchange for improved rates of funding, or maintain a principled resistance to state influence which would exact a severe financial burden upon the Catholic laity and, eventually, condemn many Catholic children to a second-class education.

'THE POWER OF CATHOLIC TRUTH'

Pope Pius XI defined the demands of the modern Catholic Church in the Papal encyclical *Divini Illius Magistri* of 1929:

> Letters, the sciences, the arts, so far as these are necessary or useful to Christian education and to her whole work for the salvation of souls, are fostered by the Church, and she founds and maintains her own schools and institutions for the teaching of all subjects and for the imparting of every degree of knowledge.[2]

1

The following year an influential Catholic academic, Professor Timothy Corcoran of University College Dublin, outlined the consequences of the Pope's guidance for Ireland's Catholic schools:

> The school chapel, the classroom altar will be the powerhouse of Catholic education within the Catholic school. Power will be transmitted from that centre of energy over the closely textured cable of Religious Instruction . . . It will be distributed in various ways, according to subjects, according to types of education, according to age and outlook of students. But for the realisation of Catholic education the power of Catholic truth, supernatural in its whole content, must penetrate every branch of study.[3]

The Catholic authorities insist upon a pervasive religious atmosphere within Catholic schools to promote 'the power of Catholic truth'. Therefore, they demand control of all aspects of the school, including the vital issue of teaching appointments, and they consider the most effective means of exercising this authority is for the parish priest to serve as the sole manager of the local school.

Their control of schools is clearly considered to be vital to the eternal interests of the Catholic Church, and has been the policy of Catholic bishops throughout the world for centuries, but the Catholic authorities in Northern Ireland were not only motivated by doctrine in their opposition to greater state influence within Catholic schools. The intense animosity between nationalist Catholics and unionist Protestants in the early 1920s ensured that the Catholic authorities feared for the future of Catholic schools managed by education committees, particularly after the government addressed Protestant clerical fears that 'nationalist' education committees would control the education of Protestant pupils by manipulating the boundaries to ensure that all eighteen committees contained a unionist majority.

EDUCATION REFORM

Catholic doctrine on the role of the clergy in education clashed profoundly with the devolved government's ambitions for Northern Ireland's elementary schools[4] in the early 1920s. The clerical manager was to be supplanted by local education committees which would supervise, coordinate, rationalise and modernise elementary education. The new government, following the course outlined by reformers during the final years before partition, embarked upon a fundamental reform of the structure of education. Ministers were partly motivated by concerns for the future of Northern Ireland's Protestant schools, but they were also eager to apply the principles governing education policy in England and Wales to underline their attachment to the rest of the United Kingdom.

The 1923 Education Act sought to encourage a transfer to education committee control by inflicting financial penalties on existing 'voluntary'[5] schools. Teachers' salaries, the largest item of any school's budget, were fully paid from public funds along with half the cost of heating, lighting and cleaning schools, but there would be no funds for building or renovating voluntary schools. The government was determined to establish 'local democratic control' of Northern Ireland's elementary schools.

The conflict surrounding the 1923 Act appeared to be similar to the struggles the Catholic Church waged – and usually lost – throughout Europe in the late nineteenth and early twentieth centuries. This fundamental conflict between the sacred and the profane was to be blunted by the success of the Protestant clergy in establishing effective control of public elementary schools during the 1920s. The 'secular' and 'civic' features of the 1923 Act were diluted to accommodate the Protestant clergy.

The Price of Faith demonstrates that the distinction between voluntary and public elementary schools in Northern Ireland became essentially a contrast between Catholic and Protestant schools by 1925, and this difference was underlined by the 1930 Act. Also, this book shows that Northern Ireland's voluntary grammar schools – an element of the voluntary sector that contained a significant number of Protestant schools – enjoyed preferential treatment after 1947. Education policy was not simply a question of 'local democratic control'. Partisan motives influenced the decisions of ministers, though not always the Minister of Education.

PROTESTANT CLERICS AND NATIONALIST POLITICIANS

The relative success of the Catholic authorities' campaign after 1925 to temper the penalties imposed by the 1923 Act was influenced by two major factors; the scale of concessions to the Protestant clergy, and the response of Nationalist politicians to the Catholic authorities' uncompromising stance.

The success of the Protestant clergy in establishing effective control of education committee schools greatly influenced the prospects for the Catholic authorities' campaigns. In 1930 the obligation placed upon teachers in public elementary schools to teach 'simple Bible instruction', and the right of Protestant clerics to half of the seats on the school committee and a quarter of the seats on the education committee, eased the task of the Catholic authorities. The removal of this obligation in 1947 weakened the scope for compromise with the government, and only the Cabinet's decision to allow Protestant clerics to enjoy considerable power in the new secondary intermediate schools secured a grant increase for voluntary schools.

After 1947 Protestant clerics played a marginal role, because all their major demands had been satisfied by the end of the 1940s. They were minor figures in the debates leading to the 1968 Education Act and the 1993 Order, and their silence during these major education controversies was a significant handicap for the Catholic authorities. The absence of an assertive campaign by the Protestant clergy partly accounts for the relative failure of the Catholic authorities in recent decades to ease the burden of voluntary status.

The Catholic authorities were able to mobilise the Catholic laity in support of their campaigns during the first half of the century, but there has been a waning of deference in recent decades. In the early 1920s and in 1930 the Catholic populace was prompted to attend public meetings in support of clerical demands, but there were no major public protests surrounding the 1947 Act. The impact of social change and a gradual rise in affluence amongst the Catholic laity led in 1967 to a cool response to the Catholic authorities' rejection of the government's proposals for a revised form of school committee. This initial hesitancy gravely weakened their campaign against the Education Bill, and eventually led to their acceptance of the government's scheme. Since the late 1960s the Catholic populace has been reluctant to offer unconditional support for clerical control, and this ambivalence also explains the failure to secure improved funding conditions from the British government until 1993.

Nationalist politicians were also ardent defenders of clerical interests during the first half of this century. Their loyalty partly arose from the power of the Catholic authorities as an interest group within nationalist politics, but most Nationalist MPs were also devout Catholics who were willing to defer to the clergy on 'religious' issues such as the fate of Catholic schools.

Nationalist MPs were absent from the Northern Ireland Commons until the 1925 elections, but after 1925 they were enthusiastic allies.

The success of 1930, when voluntary schools gained half of all capital costs, partly arose from the Nationalist Party's intensive parliamentary campaign, and in 1947 the persistence of Nationalist MPs also provided valuable support. The attitudes of Nationalist politicians also gradually shifted away from deference in the two decades after the Second World War. The initial ambivalence of the Catholic laity in the autumn of 1967 was reflected in the speeches of some Nationalist MPs. They eventually supported the Catholic authorities, but only after the initial condemnation was tempered by compromise. The Catholic authorities' problems with the political leaders of Catholic opinion persisted after the abolition of the devolved government. Since 1972 nationalist MPs at Westminster have been reluctant to raise funding issues, despite the success of their occasional interventions.[6]

Catholic teachers, though reliant upon the Catholic clergy for their jobs, have also recently adopted a more independent attitude. In 1930 the leader of the Irish National Teachers' Organisation (INTO) joined the delegation organised by the Catholic authorities to the Minister of Education, but by 1967 INTO welcomed the government's proposals for reform.

This ebbing of support has coincided with the advent of a new and profound threat to clerical control of Northern Ireland's Catholic schools. The last twenty-five years have been dominated by the Catholic authorities' efforts – occasionally bolstered by Protestant clerics and unionist politicians – to defend the principle of segregated schools from the interest groups promoting 'integration' as one of the answers to Northern Ireland's problems.

'SHARED SCHOOLS'

The Catholic school claims to confer religious knowledge and encourage enthusiasm for the faith without political repercussions, but the consequences of Catholic education in Northern Ireland pose major problems for the Catholic authorities because, as Dominic Murray notes in his study of two segregated schools:

> The church sees religion as the most important aspect of life. In addition, Catholic education is an essential element in the development of the child. On the other hand, there exists a Christian awareness of the social implications of separating children at an early age in a province where religious conviction is perceived as a cultural or political statement.[7]

The Catholic authorities have faced a challenge to the principle of separate Catholic schools, with some observers highlighting segregated schools as a major source of animosity and conflict. One of the architects of Northern Ireland's education system, Sir Robert Lynn, claimed:

> I think the greatest curse that ever befell this country of ours was when it was decided to establish denominational schools . . . I sincerely hope for the day when Protestant and Roman Catholic will sit together in the same school, and learn the same lessons, and if we do that . . . I think we will get rid of a good deal of the bitterness that has done so much harm to the whole of this island.[8]

The purpose of integration for many unionist politicians was simply to absorb Catholic schools into the state system and the Catholic authorities could easily discount such criticisms. The integration campaign of the past twenty-five years can be less easily dismissed because Catholic parents have played a leading role in the campaign and opinion polls have consistently shown the majority of Catholics supporting integration. Also, the two major nationalist parties – the Social Democratic and Labour Party (SDLP) and Sinn Féin – and the INTO have been reluctant to challenge the principle of integration, though often casting doubt on the prospects for success.

The integration campaign enjoyed marginal success until it secured a powerful convert in the 1980s. In 1972 the British government assumed direct responsibility for Northern Ireland's schools, but only in the late 1980s were British ministers convinced that conflict could, eventually, be eased if Catholics and Protestants were educated in the same schools. As Osborne, Cormack and Gallagher note:

> To observers outside Northern Ireland the existence of a segregated education system where most Protestants and Catholics are educated in separate schools represents an obvious mechanism for the continued social divisions which provide the basis for prejudice and violence to flourish and be replicated across the generations.[9]

This book emphasises how the integration campaign now poses the most significant challenge to clerical authority within Catholic schools – a threat exacerbated by the Catholic authorities' isolation in their defence of segregated education.

'THE ENEMIES OF ULSTER'

Séamus Dunn argues that education in Northern Ireland possesses important political and national ramifications:

> The survival of any community depends on how successfully it initiates its young into its beliefs and habits. It is for this reason that the control of education is so often a matter of passion and conflict, and that religions and churches are likely to be deeply involved in the battles . . . Education has been perceived, and often specifically designed, as an agent of cultural and political power.[10]

This fusion of religion and politics, or the confusion between the two issues, influenced education policy in Ireland for centuries and still wields a profound impact in Northern Ireland today. Catholic schools in Northern Ireland are not only religious redoubts; they are also viewed as nationalist bastions. A principal charge by some unionists against Catholic schools was their cultivation of Irish nationalism. Two distinctive features of Catholic schools – Gaelic language teaching and Irish history classes – attracted the attention and the hostility of unionist politicians. These two subjects were thought to generate Irish nationalist sentiment, the antithesis of the principles of loyalty to the Empire and the Crown which the government was determined to cultivate within public elementary schools. Fifty years of devolved government offered numerous examples of unionist antagonism:

> The only people interested in this language [Gaelic] are the people who are the avowed enemies of Northern Ireland.[11]

> Many of the 25,000 people who voted Sinn Féin in the recent Mid-Ulster election have been educated by this money . . . this Government should not approve of financing the enemies of Ulster in that way.[12]

> Children in Roman Catholic schools are taught a hatred of everything that we hold dear in this country of ours.[13]

> The school must have interfered in the teaching of the children, grinding into them not to stand when the National Anthem was played.[14]

The Cabinet was less troubled by these 'national' aspects of Catholic schools than their supporters on the backbenches or in the Orange Halls. The Gaelic language continued to be taught in Northern Ireland's schools, despite campaigns in the early 1930s and the 1950s, and the delicate topic of history teaching only became a major issue during a brief spell in the 1950s. Also, the government did not promote an assertive patriotism until the 1930s, and this campaign was motivated by threats from within the unionist electorate rather than antipathy towards Catholic schools. Some politicians on the periphery of Ulster Unionism emphasised the cultural threat posed by Gaelic and nationalist Catholic schools, but these were secondary problems for ministers and senior Ministry of Education officials.

Many Catholic clerics were clearly enthusiastic advocates of Gaelic culture, but these features of Catholic schools were also a useful device to promote loyalty amongst the nationalist elements of the Catholic laity. The 'national' question and the fate of Catholic schools appeared to be closely bound in the twentieth century and the Catholic authorities exploited this link to their advantage. The SDLP and Sinn Féin both emphasised the significance of Gaelic language teaching in Catholic schools during the last major reform of Northern Ireland's education system in the late 1980s, and the concession by the Department of Education of Northern Ireland (DENI) on the role of Gaelic within the new core curriculum was their only significant success.

'DRAMATIS PERSONAE'

The cast of characters for this book is modest because Northern Ireland's education policy developed within a small community of politicians, clerics and civil servants. Northern Ireland contains six Catholic dioceses, but only the Archbishop of Armagh, the Bishop of Down and Connor and the Bishop of Derry exercised a significant influence upon clerical strategy.[15] Also, Northern Ireland's voters never elected more than a dozen nationalist MPs to the Northern Ireland Commons, and many of these MPs either abstained on principle or simply did not bother to attend parliamentary sessions. The government and the Catholic authorities therefore never dealt with more than a handful of nationalist MPs.

The Prime Minister, the Minister of Education and his senior civil servants obviously played an important role in deciding education policy during the fifty years of devolved government. The evidence suggests that Ministry of Education officials were intent upon establishing amicable and constructive relations with the Catholic authorities, and the Minister invariably followed the course set by his officials. This 'Ministry view' was countered by three major 'unionist' influences – the thirty backbench Unionist MPs in the Northern Ireland Commons, the leadership of the Orange Order and leading clerics of the three major Protestant denominations. All three groups, to varying degrees, favoured resistance to the Catholic authorities' demands.

The close association between Unionist MPs and the Cabinet ensured that ministers were constantly aware of backbench opinion, and the evidence from their speeches indicates that they were invariably less accommodating than their leaders towards Catholic interests. The backbenches were influential, but they were not dominant. The Cabinet often led and their supporters would, sometimes reluctantly, follow their lead. In 1930 and 1947 concessions to the Catholic authorities caused unrest within Unionist ranks, but Craig and Brooke were able to overcome this opposition and impose their decision on the party. The limits of the party leadership's control of their followers were amply demonstrated less than three years later when a backbench insurrection led to the downfall of Northern Ireland's most liberal Minister of Education.

The Orange Order's interventions were fitful, but, as the events surrounding the 1925 Act demonstrated, they were influential in determining the course of events.[16] The Order's perspective on education matters broadly followed the course of Unionist MPs, who, almost without exception, would be leading members of the Order. The close ties between the Unionist Party and the Orange Order did not temper the Order's conspicuous lack of deference towards the government, and there were many occasions after 1921 when individual lodges would be critical of education policy.

The Protestant clergy were more industrious in attempting to influence education policy, but they were also more ambivalent in their opposition to the Catholic authorities' demands. They concentrated upon securing concessions within the schools managed by the education committees rather than blighting the prospects for their Catholic counterparts. These efforts to secure control of the education of Protestant pupils invariably aided the Catholic authorities' efforts to improve their position,[17] but since 1947 they have been peripheral players. They were largely silent during the debates surrounding the 1968 Act and the 1993 Order,[18] and some Protestant clerics are now critical of a perceived neglect of their interests by both the British government and Ulster's unionist parties.

The outcome of the Catholic authorities' campaign was usually governed by the ability of the Minister of Education to convince his Prime Minister and his Cabinet colleagues to defy the traditional, almost instinctive, antagonism of many Ulster unionists towards concessions to the Catholic minority. The role of the Prime Minister was pivotal in determining the success of the Ministry's efforts to promote a durable settlement with the Catholic authorities, and the actions of Northern Ireland's three major Prime Ministers – James Craig, Basil Brooke and Terence O'Neill – offer intriguing contrasts. Craig (1921–1940) and Brooke (1943–1963) confronted their own MPs, and some of their ministers, to fashion a compromise with the Catholic authorities in 1930 and 1947. O'Neill (1963–1969) enjoyed a reputation as an accommodating liberal, but without ever granting benefits for the Catholic minority. The evidence of the 1968 Education Act indicates that, even after they accepted the principle of school committees, the Catholic authorities were offered a relatively harsh settlement by O'Neill and his Cabinet.

The public, particularly parents, played virtually no role in the course of events until the late 1960s, and remain a minor actor today. The first significant indication of the potential impact of Catholic public opinion came in the autumn of 1967 when lay Catholics appeared reluctant to respond to Philbin's condemnation of the government's proposals. Also, nationalist politicians, alert to the views of their electorate, have responded to the 'Gaelic revival' in the nationalist areas of Belfast and Londonderry, and Catholic voters' approval for integration has influenced both the SDLP and Sinn Féin.

The Orange Order, Protestant clerics, Unionist MPs, Catholic clerics and nationalist politicians all competed for influence, but the British government consciously played a minor role. The evidence contained in the Public Record Office of Northern Ireland (PRONI) archives indicates that the primary concern of the British government was to avoid any involvement in Northern Ireland's affairs. In 1925 the Home Office in London was unsettled by Craig's decision to compromise with the Protestant critics of the 1923 Act, but five years later the Home Secretary refused to act against a more denominational Act.[19] British inertia reached its zenith in 1945, when British ministers and civil servants vigorously discouraged the Northern Ireland Cabinet from disturbing the 1930 settlement of compelling teachers to provide 'simple Bible instruction' in education committee schools.[20]

British ministers and civil servants may have been eager to evade their obligations, but after 1972 they assumed direct responsibility for Northern Ireland's schools. The DENI now enjoys greater powers than the Ministry of Education ever possessed during the fifty years of devolved government, with the Education and Library Boards which replaced the education committees in 1972 under its effective control. The reluctant player is now the dominant force, and this book will also explain why the Catholic authorities have failed to promote their interests within the power structures created since 1972.

SOURCES

This book relies upon five major sources; the public papers available in the PRONI,[21] the archives of the Catholic diocese of Down and Connor, the annual Reports of the Ministry of Education and other official reports by both the Northern Ireland and Westminster governments, two Northern Ireland newspapers, and the records of debates from the Northern Ireland House of Commons, the Northern Ireland Senate and the Westminster House of Commons from 1972.

The Ministry of Education files and the Cabinet Papers in the PRONI provide valuable insights into the deliberations of the devolved government. This book dedicates considerable attention to the major education laws of 1923, 1930 and 1947, and the PRONI files reveal interesting evidence of disputes within the Cabinet. The PRONI files are also particularly effective in illustrating the role of senior Ministry of Education officials such as Lewis McQuibban, Bonaparte Wyse and Reginald Brownell. The efforts of these three officials, who led the Ministry from 1921 until the late 1950s, to fashion an agreement with the Catholic authorities only fully emerges from a study of the PRONI archives.

One notable feature of the PRONI archives is the absence of correspondence with Catholic clerics. The Ministry and Cabinet Office files contain copious evidence of negotiations with the Protestant clergy, but the Catholic authorities make only fleeting appearances. The records of meetings with Catholic clerics, mostly arising from Samuel Hall-Thompson's six years as Minister of Education in the late 1940s, offer meagre evidence for answering many important questions. Clerical archives, therefore, are vital for a fuller understanding of their education strategy.

The three clerics who served as Bishop of Down and Connor from 1915 to 1982 – Dr Joseph MacRory, Dr Daniel Mageean and Dr William Philbin – all led the defence of Catholic education interests. Therefore, the Down and Connor Diocesan Archives' education files offer a number of rewarding insights into the Catholic authorities' deliberations. MacRory burnt his private papers for the years from 1915 to 1928, momentous times for Catholic education, before he left for the Archbishop's Palace in Armagh, but the files for the 1930s and 1940s are a lucrative source for policy discussions amongst senior Catholic clerics. The diocesan files reveal a clerical leadership often uncertain of its strategy, always wary of compromise, and usually despondent about the eventual outcome.[22]

The most valuable official publication during the fifty years of devolved government was the Ministry of Education's Annual Report, and this book appears to be the first methodical attempt to extract information from these Reports and other official documents. The book also employs Parliamentary Questions in the Northern Ireland and Westminster Commons, and the findings of the Standing Advisory Commission on Human Rights' study of Northern Ireland's schools in the late 1980s, to assess the financial and educational contrast between voluntary Catholic schools and the education authorities' schools.

Newspapers offer an interesting public comparison to the confidential and often ambiguous minutes of Cabinet Room discussions and official files. The *Belfast Telegraph* and the *Irish News* often illuminate the material in the PRONI files and the diocesan archives. The *Irish News* is a particularly useful source because the paper's editorials, leading articles and letters invariably offered uncritical support for the Catholic authorities. The paper may often have been no more than a propaganda sheet for the Catholic authorities, but careful study offers an appreciation of the subtle shifts and variations of clerical tactics. The importance of the media was underlined in the autumn of 1967 when the *Irish News* published a number of articles and letters critical of Bishop Philbin's rejection of the government's White Paper – criticism which one Nationalist MP later claimed explained the government's reluctance to compromise.[23]

The *Irish News* also reveals evidence of discord within the Unionist Party not available from either the debates in the Northern Ireland Commons or the PRONI files. The *Belfast Telegraph* illustrates Protestant and unionist opinion, and offers evidence of divisions within the nationalist community neglected by the *Irish News*. Newspapers also serve as a vital source for recent developments because the thirty year exclusion rule denies access to the relevant PRONI and diocesan files.

The limitations of parliamentary democracy in Northern Ireland during the fifty years of devolved government should not be under-stated, but the Northern Ireland Parliament provided a forum for both nationalist and unionist discontent. Nationalist MPs were more than simply parliamentary attendants for the Catholic authorities, but they were close allies during the major campaigns, and their speeches during these crucial debates often disclosed the concerns and under-lying strategy of the Catholic authorities. Also, sustained 'Orange' campaigns in the Northern Ireland Parliament often compelled the Ministry to change its course. A reading of the Northern Ireland Hansard often provides answers to questions not fully explained by the PRONI files.

THE PRICE OF FAITH

The Price of Faith offers a clearer understanding of issues not fully explored by previous studies of Northern Ireland's education system. Professor Donald Akenson provided an excellent account of the conflict between the devolved government and the Protestant clergy in *Education and Enmity: The Control of Schooling in Northern Ireland 1920–50*. Akenson, however, concentrates on the success of the Protestant clergy in securing control of the education committees' schools. Also, his work was published in 1973, and a substantial amount of public archive material is now available.

Mary Harris and Sean Farren have both studied the history of Catholic education in Northern Ireland with *The Roman Catholic Church and the Foundation of the Northern Irish State 1912–1930* and *The Politics of Irish Education 1920–1965* respectively.[24] However, Harris' distinguished work concentrates upon the first decade of devolved government, and education is only one issue of her book. This book encompasses the history of Catholic schools in Northern Ireland from 1921 to the present day. Farren explores the relationship between culture and education in both the Irish Free State and Northern Ireland until 1965 whereas this book concentrates upon developments in Northern Ireland, and emphasises the importance of prosaic questions such as funding policy and the cost of maintaining autonomous schools.

The Catholic authorities in Northern Ireland recognise the vital importance of maintaining clerical control of education because the most effective means of fostering devotion to the Catholic faith, and loyalty to the doctrines of the Church through the generations, appears to be the education of the Catholic child within a school system operating under the control of the clergy. Also, the struggle to preserve this autonomy offers important evidence of the state of community relations during the last seventy years. As Cormack, Gallagher and Osborne note:

> The Department of Education in Northern Ireland occupies a distinctive place in terms of the general relationships between the government and the Catholic community. Throughout the period since the creation of Northern Ireland, the most significant social institution over which the Catholic community has exercised control, principally through the Catholic Church, has been the Catholic education system.[25]

This book argues that Northern Ireland's education system was a consequence of the inability of the first devolved government and the

Catholic authorities to fashion a compromise in the early 1920s. The government was determined to reform Northern Ireland's education system, but it failed to appreciate the Catholic authorities' fears of the education committees which meant that their compromises with the Protestant clergy later in the decade remained an unacceptable solution for senior Catholic clerics. The Catholic authorities were solely concerned with the issue of clerical control. The 'power of Catholic truth' could, they contended, only be 'safe' within a school solely supervised by the clergy. Therefore, they resisted all calls for a dilution of clerical authority until changes within the Catholic community compelled a more accommodating approach by the 1960s.

Catholic clerics and Unionist politicians suffered the consequences of living on the 'narrow ground' of Northern Ireland, and clashes of outlook and philosophy, rather than the simple issue of discrimination, offer a clearer explanation for the course of events outlined in this book.

CHAPTER TWO

Lord Londonderry's
Godless schools

The first quarter of the twentieth century was a time of profound upheaval in Ireland, but these years brought only modest change to Irish schools. The two campaigns for political and education reform led to intriguing contrasts. The nationalist revolutionaries of Sinn Féin demolished the Union, but preserved the education structures inherited from the British government and deferred to the traditional powers of the Catholic authorities. Ulster's unionists, struggling to maintain the constitutional status quo, were enthusiastic advocates of recasting the education system.

The Catholic authorities were determined to preserve the considerable advantages extracted from the National Board after seventy years of struggle, and vigorously disputed the reform campaign. In the Irish Free State clerical power was undiminished after partition, but in Northern Ireland the government's determination to reform the elementary education system along English lines clashed with the resolve of the Catholic clergy to preserve their influence.

The Catholic authorities, opposed to any dilution of clerical power and wary of alienating a militant nationalist electorate, refused to cooperate with the devolved government's education scheme and the new system was fashioned solely by Northern Ireland's unionist and Protestant majority. The 1923 Education Act aimed to establish 'local democratic control' of education through local education committees, but the Protestant clergy were eventually allowed to retain effective control of the education of Protestant pupils. After 1925 Catholic schools were confined to voluntary status, unable to enjoy the considerable advantages of the new 'public elementary' schools.

NATIONAL SCHOOLS

In October 1900 the Irish Catholic bishops met in Maynooth to declare:

> the system of National Education has itself undergone a radical change and in a great part of Ireland is now, in fact, whatever it is in name, as denominational almost as we could desire . . . and thus it has come, in a great part of Ireland, to be a help rather than a hindrance to the Church.[1]

By 1900 there were only two significant influences in Irish education policy; the Treasury and the Catholic authorities. As Akenson notes:

> At century's end national education was ostensibly under the control of the commissioners of national education, but actually dominated by the proclamations of the Roman Catholic hierarchy, and by the English treasury.[2]

This 'ideal' system was not granted immediately to the Catholic authorities, but was gained over seven decades by a long and arduous process of incremental victories. The National Schools system was gradually amended from a non-denominational scheme into a network of denominational schools which would satisfy the most wary Catholic cleric.

John Coolahan offers the clearest summary of the principles framed by the Chief Secretary for Ireland, Lord Stanley, in 1831:

> he proposed a government appointed mixed denominational board comprised of men of high personal character, including individuals of exalted station in the church. This board was to exercise complete control over schools erected under its control. A main aim of the system was to unite the children of different denominations and so applications for aid from mixed denominational groups were to be especially favoured. Local funds had to be forthcoming for the aid of teacher salaries, the cost of furniture and maintenance, while the school site and one third of the building costs should also be provided by local sources. Schools were to be open for four or five days each week for literary instruction while separate religious instruction could take place on the remaining one or two days. The Board was to have complete control over textbooks used, and by means of inspection, ensure that regulations were enforced.[3]

The creation of the National Schools was an implicit recognition of the failure of the Protestant mission in Ireland. In the first decades of the nineteenth century Ireland was inundated with evangelical Protestant groups attempting to convert Catholic children in the classroom, but the Catholic authorities, eventually, convinced most Catholic parents to withdraw their children from these 'Bible schools'.[4] The defeat of the 'Bible schools' and the Kildare Place Society led the new Whig government to offer a compromise to the Catholic authorities which finally abandoned the official campaign to convert the Catholic Irish to the Protestant faith.

The change was not as dramatic as Protestant critics and Catholic supporters claimed in the decades after 1831. The National Board preserved the privileged position of the Church of Ireland by granting three of the seven seats to Anglicans and only two seats to Catholic commissioners to represent the overwhelming majority of potential National School pupils.[5] Also, the Lord Lieutenant of Ireland presumed that the Duke of Leinster would only serve as an honorary president of the National Board with the Church of Ireland Archbishop of Dublin, Richard Whatley, acting as 'the invisible president of the board'.[6] Therefore, the British government hoped that Irish education would continue to serve British and Protestant interests.

The Catholic authorities were apprehensive, fearing either 'secular' education or a resurgence of Protestant proselytism, but, in contrast to their successors ninety years later, they chose to cooperate with the Whigs' scheme. This decision can be explained by three major differences between Ireland in 1831 and Northern Ireland in 1921.

Firstly, in 1831 the Catholic authorities were unable to offer their laity a realistic alternative to the British government's proposals. As late as 1824 only 423 of Ireland's 11,000 schools were administered by the Catholic authorities.[7] The teaching orders such as the Sisters of Mercy, the Irish Christian Brothers and the Presentation Sisters could educate only a small minority of Catholic children. The initial success of the 'Bible schools' highlighted the threat from another concerted official campaign if the Catholic authorities failed to offer Catholic parents opportunities to educate their children. Sir Robert Peel, no friend of the Catholic Irish, told the Commons in February 1816 that 'the greatest eagerness and desire prevails, among the lower orders in Ireland, for the benefits of instruction'.[8] The Catholic authorities could not afford to alienate Catholic parents anxious for their children to gain the advantages of a decent education.

Also, the 'hedge schools' educating most Catholic children in the first decades of the nineteenth century were not supervised by the Catholic clergy. They were autonomous schools maintained by the teachers who offered religious instruction, but who were often 'products of educational incest, men trained in hedge schools to teach in hedge schools'.[9] Therefore, the Catholic authorities did not influence the appointment or training of the overwhelming majority of teachers educating Catholic children. In December 1831, only three months after Stanley announced his plans for National Schools, James Doyle, the Bishop of Kildare and Leighlen, claimed Stanley's scheme 'will aid us in a work of great difficulty, to wit, that of suppressing hedge schools, and placing youth under the direction of competent teachers, and of those only'.[10] In 1922 the Catholic authorities enjoyed the benefits of nearly a century of extensive funding by the National Board, with a comprehensive network of Catholic schools throughout Ireland and their own Catholic teacher training colleges.

Secondly, in the early decades of the nineteenth century the Irish Catholic Church was emerging from an era of persecution which had only recently tempered to mere discrimination, and bishops were still struggling to exercise effective authority over the local clergy.[11] By 1922 the Catholic authorities exercised a profound influence over the lives and beliefs of the Catholic masses, and the threat of an outbreak of lay disloyalty, such as the presence of Catholic children in 'Bible schools', was modest. The rise of Ultramontane Catholicism, the social changes wrought by the Famine and the impact of Cardinal Cullen upon Irish Catholicism all ensured that the Catholic authorities in the 1920s could be confident of securing the support of the Catholic laity. The Catholic authorities were closely tied to the political notables of nationalist Ireland, both moderates and radicals, and the politicians governing the twenty-six counties of the Irish Free State were avowedly loyal to the Catholic faith. The Catholic authorities in 1922 could be more confident of asserting their authority over the Catholic laity than their predecessors nine decades before.

Finally, in 1831 the National Schools could be interpreted as evidence of compromise by a Whig government sympathetic to Irish Catholic aspirations after nearly fifty years of Tory rule. In 1922 Northern Ireland's Catholics were reluctantly accepting the reality of partition, and the devolved government appeared hostile to the religious and cultural values of the nationalist minority. Catholic confidence in the government was sadly absent during the bitter and fearful early years of devolved power.

The Catholic clergy, encouraged by the endorsement of Archbishop Murray of Dublin, swiftly accepted the National Board's guidelines. One thousand priests applied to the National Board within the first four years to finance their schools,[12] but this initial enthusiasm could

not conceal serious disagreements. The Irish Christian Brothers withdrew their schools from the control of the National Board in 1836,[13]
and by the end of the 1830s the National Schools question was causing
profound dissension amongst senior Catholic clerics.

The major protagonists were Murray and Archbishop MacHale of
Tuam, whose opposition to cooperation with the British government's
education schemes began in the early 1820s when he was still a student
at Maynooth.[14] The two archbishops waged their struggle in the Dublin
press with thinly disguised pseudonyms until the Papacy intervened to
attempt to resolve the conflict. The Vatican edict of 16 January 1841
failed to settle the dispute, ruling 'that no judgement should be
definitely pronounced in this matter, and that this kind of education
should be left to the prudent discretion of each individual bishop'.[15]

The Papal decision of 1841 was viewed as a success for the moderates,[16] but by the end of the decade the bishops were less accommodating. In 1850 Article I of the Synod of Thurles' decree began:

> The prudent course of proceeding which the holy see has followed
> in regard to the system of national education, on which it refrained
> from pronouncing definitively, we think we should also follow.
> However, we deem it to be part of our duty to declare that the
> separate education of catholic youth is, in every way, to be preferred
> to it.[17]

This notable change was not caused by fears that the National Schools
were subverting the Catholic faith, as the local clerical manager had
proved to be an imposing obstacle to any proselytising designs by the
National Board. The Catholic authorities were more assertive because
the developing strength of the Church's organisation in Ireland, the
prevalence of Ultramontane theology in Rome[18] and the intense
alienation from the British government wrought by the Famine
allowed them greater scope to confront the National Board. The
National Schools debate was conducted in theological terms, but the
central question was the political issue of whether the Catholic
authorities could, and should, challenge the British government for
control of the schools.

Stanley's initial outline for the National School envisaged a non-
denominational structure, but, as Hislop explains, 'it was obvious that
any generally acceptable educational scheme would have to recognise
the realities of denominational control'.[19] Ireland was a devout land in
the nineteenth century, and remains conspicuously religious today.
Therefore, 'secular' education was simply unacceptable to the over-

whelming majority of the populace. The Northern Ireland government was to face a similar problem in the 1920s when 'Lord Londonderry's Godless Schools' were criticised by both Catholic and Protestant clerics. In 1831 the British government partly recognised these denominational realities by appointing five clerics to the seven seats of the first National Board, but the next fifty years were to witness the gradual surrender of state authority in Ireland's schools.

The principles guiding the National Schools were not contained in statute law, merely in a letter from Lord Stanley to the Duke of Leinster asking him to be president of the National Board and in subsequent rulings by the Board. The scheme was therefore pliable, allowing the Commissioners to amend the 'constitution' of National Schools without awkward scrutiny from Parliament. The devolved government in Northern Ireland, in contrast, was constrained both by the education laws passed by the Northern Ireland Parliament and by the Government of Ireland Act of 1920 which, ministers and officials believed, restricted their scope for denominational concessions to both the Protestant and Catholic clergy.[20]

The National Schools system's adaptability was exploited by the Catholic authorities, and they pursued their objectives with a relentless determination. The Catholic authorities' efforts wrought considerable change by the end of the century, but they were not solely responsible for the segregated schools bequeathed to the governments of Northern Ireland and the Irish Free State.

'The errors of popery'

Protestant clerics were the sharpest critics of the new system during the 1830s and 1840s, mainly because they recognised the National Schools as a significant obstacle to their efforts to convert Catholic children in the classroom. As a Church of Ireland petition of 1835 stated, 'the System as far as they are concerned is a conspiracy between its supporters and the Roman priests, to keep the light of God's word from ever shining upon a Roman Catholic child'.[21] Protestant clerics contested the right of the Roman Catholic priest:

> to make use of the schoolrooms for the purpose of teaching the peculiar dogmas, the superstitious rites, the intolerant sentiments, the blasphemous fables, the dangerous deceits, and, in a word, all the errors of popery.[22]

Archbishop Whatley favoured participation, but the majority of the Church of Ireland clergy refused to cooperate with the Whigs' scheme.

Anglican clerics petitioned Parliament for state funds to provide an alternative to the National Schools while they waited for the return of their traditional allies, the Tories. They were to wait nearly ten years, only to be abandoned in November 1842 when Peel, reluctantly, decided to persevere with the National Board.[23]

Many Church of Ireland clerics chose not to rely upon the return of Peel, who had abandoned Protestant Ireland before by accepting Catholic Emancipation. They founded the Church Education Society in 1839 to continue their proselytising efforts outside the scope of the National Board.[24] The Society enjoyed the financial support of affluent Protestants, and by the middle of the century was supervising nearly 1,900 schools for over 120,000 pupils.[25] After 1850 the Society's fortunes declined as the determination of Irish Anglicans to sustain such an extensive system wavered, and in 1860 Archbishop Beresford of Armagh urged his clergy to cooperate with the National Board.[26]

The waning influence of the Church Education Society[27] left the British government and the Catholic authorities as the only major actors in Irish education in three of Ireland's four provinces, but Ulster's Protestant clerics secured popular support to challenge the National Board.

The Presbyterians of Ulster were both more radical and more success-ful than their Anglican counterparts in amending the founding prin-ciples of the National Board. Ulster's Presbyterians were determined to secure a central role for religion within the schools attended by their children, and in January 1832 the Presbyterian Synod met in Cookstown to declare 'in a Christian country the Bible, unabridged and unmutilated, should form the basis of National Education'.[28] Ulster witnessed a series of mass meetings against the National Schools, protests which occasionally degenerated into violent assaults on National Schools and National School teachers.[29] The National Board, opposed by most Church of Ireland clerics, was anxious to secure some Protestant support for the National Schools, but the majority of the Synod demanded unacceptable conditions and the initial dialogue ended without an agreement. The financial burden of providing their own schools eventually moderated the Presbyterian tone, and the Synod drafted a more accommodating proposition which, after prolonged discussions, formed the basis of an agreement with the National Board in 1840.[30]

The compromise allowed 'Presbyterian' National Schools to pro-vide religious instruction at any time during the school day, withdrew the special visiting rights for the clergy of other denominations and demanded only that the children of other denominations be allowed to leave during religious instruction, rather than insisting upon the National Board's initial policy of compulsory exclusion. These concessions were the first substantial amendments to Stanley's initial design, and they arose from the persistence and the militancy of Ulster's Presbyterians rather than the obduracy of the Catholic authorities.

A century later Protestant clerics opposed a similar scheme for non-denominational schools in Northern Ireland, and they too eventually fashioned a denominational education system to accommodate their interests. The contrasts between the policies of the National Board and the Northern Ireland Ministry of Education are also notable. In the 1830s the Catholic authorities accepted Stanley's scheme, but the Protestant clergy refused to cooperate. The response of the National Board was to allow sufficient amendments to the founding principles to allow some Protestant clerics to participate. In the 1920s the Ministry of Education was faced by the resolute opposition of both Catholic and Protestant clerics, but once the suspicions of the Protestant clerics were eased Catholic schools remained outside the scope of the public system.

The Catholic offensive

The Catholic authorities seized the opportunity offered by the National Board's concessions to the Presbyterian Synod to gradually expand their influence within 'Catholic' National Schools. Akenson claims 'the Catholic prelates' aggressiveness was reinforced, rather than extinguished, by their being rewarded with a concession almost every time they attacked the commissioners of national education',[31] but the British government's options were severely limited in the aftermath of the Famine. One of the few measures available to bolster its standing amongst the Catholic majority was to accept the Catholic authorities' education demands.

The Catholic authorities launched an intense campaign against the National Board in 1859, and the Irish Chief Secretary Edward Cardwell responded by offering ten of the twenty seats on an enlarged National Board to Catholic representatives.[32] Four years later the bishops issued another challenge by refusing to employ graduates of the National Board's model schools, and the British government sought a new settlement by establishing an inquiry – the Powis Commission – to once more study Ireland's schools.[33] The seven Catholic and seven Protestant members of the Commission accepted the denominational reality of Irish education by recommending further changes to the National Board's regulations to allow for the full development of segregated schools. The Powis Commission did not partition Ireland's children into segregated schools, but only underlined an existing preference for denominational schools. Auchmuty notes that 'for some time it had been realised on all sides that the policy of non-denominationalism was a failure', and though the National Board was instructed in 1831 to favour joint applications from Protestant and Catholic clerics, by 1850 3,418 of the 4,547 National Schools, three quarters of the total, were managed by a solitary cleric. Fifty years later, 7,636 of 8,684 schools, nearly ninety per cent of all National Schools, were 'clerical' schools.[34] The growth of clerical management also led to a decline in the number of schools educating both Catholics and Protestants. In 1867 most Irish schools contained children of both major religions, but by the outbreak of the Great War only a quarter of Ireland's elementary schools were attended by children of another faith.[35]

The Powis Commission of 1870 was a major success for the Catholic authorities, but they were to wait more than ten years before events at Westminster allowed the National Board to follow the Commission's advice.[36] The general election of 1880 returned the Liberals to power, and satisfying the Catholic authorities' education demands allowed Gladstone to placate an influential element of Irish society without the extensive constitutional changes that threatened to fracture his Cabinet.[37]

In December 1880 the National Board finally allowed National Schools to be used for religious worship and allowed religious emblems to be constantly displayed in classrooms. The Board also confirmed that the ritual of the sign of the cross, a distinctly Catholic gesture, was not a violation of the regulations. The 'Land Campaign' and the disruption of the House of Commons by Irish Nationalist MPs brought further success in 1883 when the National Board suspended its regulation denying teaching posts in National Schools to members of religious orders.[38] The culmination of the Catholic authorities' campaign came later the same year when the National Board sanctioned denominational teacher training colleges.[39]

After 1883 the Catholic authorities could place clerics in the classroom and also ensure that lay teachers were trained under their control. The power to appoint teachers was a vital means of maintaining clerical influence, but the Catholic authorities were also anxious to ensure that all prospective candidates were instilled with Catholic religious values before they embarked upon their teaching career. Catholic teachers were graduates of Catholic schools, but the teacher training college was also a formative influence. Clerical control of teacher training, therefore, granted the Catholic authorities monopoly control of all aspects of Catholic education. Catholic and Protestant clerics were united in their determination to maintain their influence over the training and the appointment of teachers,[40] and the creation of denominational teacher training colleges also allowed the Protestant clergy to intensify their control of Protestant schools.

Education reform was not the prerogative of the Liberals. The Conservatives, traditional allies of the Protestant Irish, also sought to appease the Catholic authorities with the Intermediate Education (Ireland) Act of 1878. The Act employed the interest from the monies saved by the disestablishment of the Church of Ireland in 1869 to fund a modest network of intermediate schools,[41] and the benefits of this Act appear to have been enjoyed almost exclusively by the Catholic middle class. In 1881 there were an equal number of Catholic and Protestant pupils studying at intermediate schools, but by 1911 there were three times as many Catholics as Protestants.[42] O'Buachalla claims that the 1878 Act 'did little to improve . . . secondary education in Ireland',[43] but the evidence suggests that the Act widened the scope for Catholic participation in intermediate education. The 1878 Act was a notable achievement for the Catholic authorities because almost all Catholic intermediate schools were supervised either by the clergy or religious orders, and it supplied funds by granting awards for examination results without surrendering significant influence within the schools to the Intermediate Board.

The Catholic authorities' decision to accept the Whigs' offer in 1831 and seek to expand clerical influence within the National Schools proved to be an astute choice. They sought assurances from the National Board that the integrity of the Catholic faith would not be challenged in the classroom, and the only practical way of securing this guarantee was for the Board to allow the Catholic clergy to supervise the schools attended by Catholic children. The local priest was, therefore, able to control Catholic schools while most of the cost of the schools was borne by the taxpayer. As Auchmuty states:

> The duty of the State to provide education for all was balanced against the claim of the Church to control all such education . . . The only power exercised by the Board was through the handling of the financial weapon, in every other respect the authority of the local clerical manager and of the Bishops of the diocese was of more importance. Such a situation had not been the original aim of the National Board, but it had to give way before the organised might of the Irish Roman Catholic Church.[44]

The Maynooth Synod of 1900 marked the pinnacle of clerical authority within Irish Catholic schools because the early years of the twentieth century witnessed a new threat to the Catholic clergy's role in Catholic schools. The belief that the involvement of local councils would improve the quality of education had governed education policy in England since 1870 and education reformers were eager to export these principles to Ireland.[45]

The secular threat

Education policy in Ireland and England followed broadly similar paths throughout most of the nineteenth century but English schools followed a new course in the final quarter of the century, a course which contrasted sharply with the spirit and practice of the National Schools. In 1870, the year of the Powis Commission's report recommending a consolidation of clerical influence within Irish schools, the Education Act introduced a significant role for local government in education in England and Wales.

The local authorities, to fulfill their obligations under the Act and to fund the extension of elementary education to ever larger numbers of children, were allowed to levy a rate to finance the building of new schools and making improvements to existing schools.[46] The independent sector was unable to cope with the demand generated by the 1870 Act and the Compulsory Attendance Act of 1880 which demanded an elementary education for every child from the age of five until ten, and the number of voluntary schools dwindled during the final decades of the nineteenth century. In 1880 four out of every five elementary schools in England and Wales were administered by churches and other charitable bodies, but by 1900 less than half of all pupils were being educated in these schools.[47]

The Catholic authorities recognised the approaching threat and launched a resolute defence of the rights of clerical managers. They refused to consider any change to the structure of Irish education, opposing the 1892 Compulsory Attendance Act as a violation of parental rights because they feared Catholic schools would be unable to satisfy the needs of all Irish Catholic children.[48] In 1898 their response to the first tentative proposals for reform was unusually strident:

> the men who seek to weaken or destroy this just and necessary control of the priest over the Catholic schools of his parish must be regarded as hostile to religion and undisguised enemies of the Catholic Church.[49]

The first overt official criticism of clerical influence came in September 1902 when the Resident Commissioner of the National Board, William Starkie,[50] addressed a meeting of the British Association in Belfast. He outlined the reformists' arguments and claimed the local cleric was the major obstacle to reform:

> the majority of managers are quite indifferent to education . . . in many cases the schools are left well-nigh derelict . . . This neglect is demoralising to the teacher, but its ruinous effects are most discernible in the material condition of the schools . . . in return for the absolute power over school and teacher with which managers insist on being invested, they contribute nothing in very many cases where help is most needed.[51]

The Catholic authorities responded to Starkie's speech the following month by forming 'An Association of Clerical Managers of Schools'[52] and launched a concerted offensive against Starkie.[53] The campaign failed to deflect the reformers, and when the Chief Secretary for Ireland, George Wyndham, confirmed in the House of Commons that the government was dedicated to reforming Irish education the Catholic authorities prepared for a long and demanding conflict.[54] The Conservative government[55] collapsed in the final months of 1905 before Wyndham could act, but the Catholic authorities could not expect a more accommodating approach from the Liberals, traditional allies of Irish nationalism.

In January 1906, as the Liberals relished their landslide victory over the Conservatives, Bishop O'Dwyer of Limerick warned of the persistent threat to Catholic education:

> Complete popular control is the watchword of the Liberals on the schools question. They make no secret about it. Every one of them is pledged to it. That means complete Protestant control of Catholic schools. The Borough Council of any English town can then turn out the nuns and priests and put in declared infidels, Agnostics, or members of any Protestant sect to teach Catholic children.[56]

The Conservatives and the Liberals both favoured change, and Wyndham's successor, James Bryce, was equally determined to pursue reform.[57] The Catholic authorities were isolated because, as Titley states, 'British political opinion was united on this question. The model of education forged in 1870 and refined and modified in 1902 was to be transferred to Ireland if possible'.[58] Nationalist MPs had opposed the 1902 Education Act, which widened the powers of local

government in education in England and Wales, as a menacing portent
of the future for Irish schools, but they were a peripheral minority at
Westminster.

The Liberals attempted to entice the Catholic authorities to accept
an element of local accountability in exchange for increased funding
for Catholic schools, but they would not compromise. As Cardinal
Michael Logue, Archbishop of Armagh, explained in his Lenten
Pastoral of 1907:

> one of the chief duties of the Catholic pastor is that of watching over
> the education of the children of his flock, especially in the primary
> schools, where their character is formed. It is a duty which the
> pastors of the Church cannot shirk, a right which they cannot
> abdicate. It is a mission given neither to elective bodies, not to
> County Councils, not to local bodies: nor, as far as Christian
> education is concerned, even to the democracy.[59]

Irish education for the next decade was paralysed, while British and
unionist criticism of the poor state of Irish education was countered by
charges of inadequate funding from nationalist politicians and Catholic
clerics. The impasse lasted until 1918 when the reformers secured a
significant success. The British government established two committees;
the Molony committee to investigate intermediate education and the
Kilanin committee to examine elementary education.[60] The committees'
reports were to form the basis of the final British attempt to reform
Irish education; the Education Bill of 1919.

The Bill was a precursor of Northern Ireland's Education Act of 1923,
aiming to create a single Department of Education, county education
committees and local rate funding for education.[61] The government was
careful to preserve the school manager, but Titley rightly terms the Bill
as 'the thin end of the wedge of popular control'.[62]

The Catholic authorities employed every device to defend their
interests, even collaboration with the radical insurgents of Sinn Féin.
In 1907, the Catholic authorities had opposed the Irish Council Bill
because the Bill proposed a Department of Education that would
threaten clerical autonomy.[63] However, in 1919 they exploited Irish
nationalist sentiment, gathering strength since the Easter Rising, to
link the national question to the defence of clerical control of Catholic
schools:

> The penal days are supposed to have passed. But this is the
> Department that is to control the books and curriculum of the

schools, to regulate the positions and salaries of the teachers, and have its way, perhaps, on the managerial question. It means Irish education in foreign fetters.[64]

In February 1920 Logue intensified the campaign against the Bill by calling for churchyard protest meetings by the fathers of Catholic schoolchildren on Passion Sunday. The protests proved to be an impressive display of Catholic resolve,[65] and when the Irish Secretary James Macpherson retired his successor abandoned the struggle.[66] The defeat of the Education Bill blunted the offensive against the National Schools, but the Catholic authorities could not be confident of overcoming the powerful coalition ranged against the autonomy of the clerical manager. The long-term future for clerical control of Catholic education in Ireland appeared bleak by 1920.

Education reformers in Ulster

Ulster's unionists played a prominent role in the campaign for education reform. Belfast's Corporation had been developing municipal amenities in the final years of the nineteenth century, and after 1902 the city's unionists were eager to emulate their counterparts in England and Wales who were providing rate aid for schools.[67] The rapid growth in Belfast's population in the final quarter of the nineteenth century highlighted the problems facing the city's schools[68] and led to two major initiatives for reform.

In the final years of the century, William Walker, an independent Labour councillor, led a campaign for democratic accountability for the education system in Belfast. He secured the support of the Belfast Trades Council for his views, but his efforts to convert the Irish trade union movement to the cause of reform floundered at the 1907 Irish Trades' Union Congress. Catholic delegates, wary of antagonising the Catholic authorities, preferred to avoid discussing clerical management of schools, and Walker was to remain an isolated figure within the Irish trade union movement.[69]

Walker's efforts amongst trade unionists were complemented by another education reformer, the distinguished Belfast surgeon Dr William McKeown. He launched the Educational Reform Association[70] in February 1903 to challenge clerical power in Irish education.[71] The following month McKeown's inaugural lecture criticised clerical influence on school attendance committees, and claimed that the churches and clerical managers were primarily responsible for the defects of Irish education.[72] McKeown drafted a model education bill that offers a useful guide to the ideas motivating Ulster's education reformers in the early years of the twentieth century. A department of education would supervise intermediate, technical and university education while elementary education was to be the responsibility of directly elected education authorities. The proposed bill also attempted to reduce clerical influence by prohibiting clerical teachers in public schools.[73]

McKeown carefully apportioned blame to both Catholic and Protestant clerics, but the prohibition against clerical teachers was a greater threat to clerical interests in Catholic schools than in Protestant schools, where few clerics served as teachers. Also, there were no Catholics on the Association's executive committee, an absence explained by claiming that 'a fear amounting to terror exists of the consequences of opposing the Hierarchy'.[74] McKeown and his followers, despite their efforts to attract Catholics, offered an essentially unionist prescription for the ills facing Irish education. The influence of the Educational Reform Association ebbed after McKeown's death in July 1904, but the Association provided the first significant outline and structure for the principles which eventually appeared in Northern Ireland's Education Act of 1923, the foundation of Northern Ireland's education system.

The problems facing Protestant school managers in Ulster ensured that reform would appeal to Ulster's unionists. In 1918 Hugh Pollock, president of the Belfast Chamber of Commerce and later Northern Ireland's first Minister of Finance, claimed that the commitment to find a third of the costs of new schools was too great a burden for the Protestant clergy.[75] Holmes agrees that 'there was undoubtedly truth in the Catholic allegations that the Protestant churches in Belfast had failed to meet the obligations to provide for Protestant children'.[76] The poor state of Belfast's Protestant schools was underlined in 1918 when the city's unionists vainly sponsored a Bill to create an education authority and provide rate aid for elementary schools.[77]

Bonaparte Wyse, Secretary of the Ministry of Education from 1927 until 1939, explained to a colleague in 1929 that the Catholic laity were willing to fund the clerical manager, but 'the Protestant people, as a rule, see little need to make these sacrifices in order to keep the clergymen in control'.[78] The Catholic authorities were swift to note Protestant reluctance to fund their schools, and in December 1919 they claimed that the Education Bill was designed to ease the problems of Ulster's Protestant schools:

> these semi-independent Irish Boards are to be swept away and replaced by a British department at the instigation of an intolerant

minority in one angle of the country, who demand that others should be taxed with them to do what they, like their poorer neighbours, should long ago have done voluntarily for themselves.[79]

Bishop Joseph MacRory of Down and Connor disputed Protestant and unionist claims that Catholic schools were in a poor condition,[80] but the evidence indicates that Catholic schools in Ulster were also not prospering in the final years before partition. The 1901 census found that almost twenty per cent of Ulster's adult Catholics were illiterate while less than ten per cent of the province's Church of Ireland congregation and only five per cent of Presbyterians were unable to read. Ten years later the contrast was even more notable, with Catholic illiteracy more than double the rate for the Church of Ireland and five times the scale of Presbyterian illiteracy.[81]

The British government sought to transplant English principles to Ireland but, as Holmes states, 'there was no real prospect of reforming Irish education along English lines, as there was very little demand for unsectarian education.'[82] Protestant and Catholic clerics were both hostile to non-denominational education, but the strident opposition of the Catholic authorities allowed Protestant clerics to enjoy a dignified silence. This silence was misinterpreted by unionist politicians as tacit consent for the basic principles of reform, and the consequences were to dominate education policy in Northern Ireland throughout the 1920s.[83]

The creation of the Irish Free State in 1922 preserved the Catholic clergy's custody of Catholic education in twenty-six of Ireland's thirty-two counties, but after 1921 the leaders of the new devolved government in Northern Ireland consciously imitated British developments. Catholic clerics remained adamantly opposed to any dilution of their authority within Catholic schools. The government and the Catholic authorities were braced for a brutal collision.

EDUCATION REFORM

Any study of the formative years of Northern Ireland's education system must recognise the ferocity of the antagonism between the Protestant majority and the Catholic minority in the early 1920s. As Harris states:

> The period between the foundation of the state and the introduction of Londonderry's education bill was one of intense animosity between Catholics and Protestants. The large number of Catholic deaths during the pogroms, the activities of the security forces . . .

served to reinforce Catholics' belief that the state was hostile to their interests. On the other hand, IRA activity, and the boycott of the state by Catholics in general and teachers in particular reinforced the view of Catholics as disloyal and subversive.[84]

The new government consciously chose to embark upon the sensitive task of education reform in such a belligerent atmosphere when in September 1921 it established a committee to:

enquire and report on the existing organisation and administration of the educational services in Northern Ireland, and to make such recommendations as may be considered necessary for the proper coordination and effective carrying out of these services.[85]

The committee, chaired by Robert Lynn, the Unionist MP for West Belfast and editor of the staunchly unionist *Northern Whig*, was directed to undertake a comprehensive investigation and devise a draft scheme for the new system, but unionists already possessed a detailed plan for reform before the Lynn committee began its deliberations. The basic structure of the proposed system was fashioned in the summer of 1921 by a 'Belfast coordination conference'. The recommendations fore-shadowed the new education law:

the establishment of a single ministry of education responsible to parliament; creation of local education authorities on English lines; instigation of a requirement that county councils and borough councils levy rates to aid education; and introduction of a policy whereby the ministry of education and the local education authorities would be jointly responsible for the building and enlargement of schools.[86]

Akenson claims that 'underlying the readiness of Ulster Unionism to introduce local control of state educational institutions was their desire to keep in step with the English',[87] but the principal reason for the Unionists' support for education reform was the failure of Ulster's Protestants to pay for their own schools. They were determined to employ public funds to resolve the crisis, and once they secured their own devolved government there was no prospect of the Catholic minority thwarting education reform.

The Catholic authorities could expect only a perfunctory discussion followed by a revival of the British government's proposals of the final years before partition – proposals which many unionist candidates had already promised to support during the elections for the first

Northern Ireland House of Commons in the spring of 1921.[88] Therefore, when Northern Ireland's first Minister of Education, Lord Londonderry, invited Logue to nominate four representatives to Lynn's committee[89] the Cardinal's answer was predictable:

> I regret I do not see my way to nominate members of the Commission on education which Your Lordship proposes to appoint. I should be glad to cooperate in any effort for the improvement of education, but judging from the public utterances of some members of the Belfast Parliament and their sympathisers, I have little doubt that an attack is being organised against our Catholic schools. I fear that the Commission proposed by Your Lordship, I am sure with the best intentions, will be used as a foundation and pretext for that attack.[90]

Londonderry was deeply offended by Logue's reply,[91] and convened a Cabinet conference to discuss the Cardinal's letter. He later wrote to the Lord Lieutenant Lord Fitzalan:

> It is naturally very disheartening to me at the outset to meet with such a refusal to cooperate on the part of so important a section, and I regret that I fail to understand the objection raised. A minority report as well as a majority report could quite well have been made, and I need hardly say that it is very improbable that I shall be biassed in framing my measure by any prejudice.[92]

Dunn claims Logue misunderstood Londonderry's intentions in 1921,[93] but Logue was limited by his role as guardian of the eternal interests of the Church. He could not place his trust in the integrity of a single transient politician, even if he believed Londonderry was acting 'with the best intentions'. Catholic bishops are rarely adventurous and Logue, eighty years old and suffering failing health, was unlikely to be attracted by Londonderry's promises to embark upon a bold departure.

Londonderry's suggestion of a minority report was also unlikely to appeal to the Catholic authorities, because a Catholic minority on the Lynn committee would not divert the government from the course set by the British government and many unionist politicians since the beginning of the century. The Catholic authorities *may* have secured a minor advantage by presenting their case for denominational education to the rest of the Lynn committee and using the minority report as a treatise for Catholic education. Also, the presence of four Catholic representatives on the committee *may* have diminished the obvious chasm between Protestant unionist and Catholic nationalist perceptions of education reform, but these must be no more than optimistic speculations during daunting times for cooperation and compromise in Northern Ireland.

An alternative to full participation might have been available to the Catholic authorities. In 1918 Belfast's Chamber of Commerce organised a conference which led to the 1919 Education Bill. The Catholic authorities did not send delegates, but they sent observers,[94] and this may have been a viable option for Logue and his colleagues. The evidence indicates that Londonderry, though not perhaps the rest of the Cabinet, was eager to involve the Catholic authorities. There was no reason why the Catholic authorities could not have maintained discreet contact with Londonderry who, the PRONI files suggest, enjoyed cordial relations with senior Catholic clerics.[95] The advantages to be gained from a detached role rather than abstention would *probably* have been marginal, but the Catholic authorities do not appear to have explored this possibility.

The Interim Report of the Lynn committee stated:

> We have throughout been careful to keep in mind and to make allowance for the particular points of view of Roman Catholics in regard to education, as far as known to us, and it has been our desire to refrain as far as we could from recommending any course which might be thought to be contrary to their wishes.[96]

Unionist politicians were fully aware of 'the particular points of view of Roman Catholics in regard to education' after two decades of resolute opposition to reform, and a handful of Catholic representatives would not prevent the committee 'recommending any course which might be thought to be contrary to their wishes'.

The boycott of the Lynn committee has been viewed by two distinguished historians, Professor Donald Akenson and Professor Patrick Buckland, as a pivotal error by the Catholic authorities. Akenson claims:

> In all probability the refusal of the Roman Catholic authorities to join the Lynn committee was the single most important determinant of the educational history of Northern Ireland. By refusing to sit they surrendered their last shred of influence at the very time when the basic character of Ulster's educational development was being determined. From the recommendations made by the Lynn committee emerged the principles of all later developments.[97]

Buckland agrees:

> As regards education, the beginning of discrimination was facili-
> tated by Catholics themselves. The refusal of the Catholic hierarchy
> to nominate representatives to the Lynn Committee . . . meant that
> the committee, which presented the most detailed articulation of the
> reform ideas that had been discussed by educationalists in Ulster
> since the end of the First World War, was dominated by Protestants.
> Although it claimed to have borne Catholic interests in mind, its
> educational assumptions were inevitably framed according to those
> of the Protestant churches.[98]

Farren is correct to note that Akenson and others have been 'harsh in
their judgement of the Catholic Church'.[99] Akenson and Buckland
overstate the significance of the Catholic authorities' absence from the
Lynn committee. Akenson is correct to note that the Catholic authorities enjoyed no more than a 'shred of influence' by the autumn of 1921,
because Catholic education interests were irrelevant to the majority of
the Lynn committee. Logue was exaggerating when he claimed 'I have
little doubt that an attack is being organised against our Catholic
schools',[100] but the Lynn committee was unlikely to sustain the status
quo.

Also, the Lynn committee did not determine 'the basic character of
Ulster's educational development'. Buckland is more accurate when
he terms the Lynn committee 'the most detailed articulation of the
reform ideas that had been discussed by educationalists in Ulster since
the end of the First World War'. Dunn, who claims that 'the Catholic
Church made a serious error in refusing to be involved with the work
of the committee', also states that any Catholic members of the Lynn
committee could not have prevented the committee proposing significant reform.[101]

The intense violence of Northern Ireland's first traumatic year exacerbated the distrust between the two communities, and there was no
prospect of reasoned dialogue between Catholic and Protestant representatives on the delicate topic of education, or any other subject, in 1921.[102]

The partiality of Lynn only emphasised the futility of Catholic
participation. Rafferty is guilty of overstatement when he claims Lynn
was 'an ardent extremist whom even Sir James Craig regarded as a
fanatic',[103] but Akenson acknowledges that the Unionist MP for West
Belfast 'was not altogether open-minded or tactful in matters involving the cultural patterns of Roman Catholics'.[104] Farren also claims that
Lynn was 'particularly hostile to the Roman Catholic Church's claims
on education'.[105] Lynn supplied two notable examples of his views
during the debates on the Education Bill:

> If I were an enemy of religious instruction in the schools I think I would find the best argument in the fact that the Roman Catholic Bishops have controlled religious education for over thirty years, and if one wants to find the result of religious instruction they have only to read the last Lenten Pastorals, which point out that really what has been bred all over Ireland in recent times is a race of murderers. It does not lie in the mouths of the Roman Catholic Bishops to criticise the noble Marquess and to say that he has got no religious convictions. I would rather share in the religious convictions of the noble Marquess than share in those which have resulted from the training of these people in the past.[106]

> There are two peoples in Ireland, one industrious, law abiding and God fearing, and the other slothful, murderous and disloyal.[107]

Lynn must be viewed as an inept choice as chairman if the government wished to involve the Catholic authorities in the work of the committee.

Logue's decision to boycott the Lynn committee was essentially a refusal to cooperate in the elimination of the clerical manager, but the Catholic authorities were also aware of the political implications of cooperation with the new government. The Kilanin and Molony committees of 1918 both threatened the role of the clerical manager, but the Catholic authorities appointed representatives to these committees.[108] Logue's refusal in 1921 was also a political decision to demonstrate to Northern Ireland's Catholics that he was not recognising a government implicated in the mistreatment of Catholics by unionist vigilantes and the Ulster Special Constabulary.

Ireland's Catholic clergy were traditionally conservative, but in the early 1920s they imitated the militant mood of the Catholic minority illustrated by the defeat of the Nationalists by Sinn Féin in the 1918 Westminster elections, the 1920 local government elections and the first elections for the Northern Ireland Commons in 1921. The Catholic authorities in Ireland favoured participation in the parliamentary process and during the 1918 elections, when the issue divided the Nationalists and Sinn Féin, many clerics spoke against abstention.[109]

Accommodation and participation proved to be unsustainable as the Anglo Irish War raged throughout 1919 and 1920, and the electoral fortunes of Sinn Féin reached their zenith in the summer of 1921. In the twenty-six counties of 'Southern Ireland' Sinn Féin candidates were returned unopposed in every seat except the unionist bastion of Trinity College Dublin,[110] whilst in Northern Ireland Sinn Féin polled nearly twice as many votes as the Nationalists despite their rivals' conversion to abstention.[111] The Catholic authorities abandoned their traditional preference for moderate nationalists, and Sinn Féin enjoyed unprecedented clerical support. The party's candidates in West Belfast, East Belfast, Queen's University and Down, where de Valera's nomination papers were signed by the Bishop of Dromore, were nominated by clerics.[112] In May 1921 Sinn Féin eclipsed the Nationalists, and the Catholic authorities adapted to the climate by avoiding direct public recognition of Northern Ireland. The following month Logue refused to attend the opening ceremony for the new Northern Ireland Parliament,[113] but Londonderry's invitation to the Lynn committee was the first significant challenge.

The Catholic authorities demonstrated their opposition to the Northern Ireland government, but teachers in many Catholic schools were more forthright in their resistance. A third of Northern Ireland's elementary Catholic schools repudiated the Belfast government and collected their salaries from the Provisional Government in Dublin.[114] Also, twenty-three Catholic secondary schools refused to test their pupils with the Ministry of Education's examinations.[115] Buckland claims 'the Catholic clergy fully endorsed this boycott',[116] and Akenson states:

> It is hard to tell whether the clergy or the teachers were more important in instigating and maintaining the non-recognition campaign. The clerical managers tended to be more discreet in their statements than did the teachers, but not necessarily less important; given the absolute control by the clergy over local primary schools, it is certain that the non-recognition policy could not have been effected without their tacit approval.[117]

In February 1922 MacRory claimed 'I have issued no instruction, whether public or private, to either managers or teachers. I think it is better to leave the matter to themselves as for the present at any rate it is a political rather than a religious issue',[118] but others claimed he approved of the boycott. Two emissaries from Dublin visited Northern Ireland early in 1922 to muster support for the campaign. They met John Duffin, a Belfast teacher:

> When I inquired as to the attitude of the clerical authorities I was informed that a number of managers favoured this move and that no manager had objected to his teacher taking this step, and that the Bishop likewise favoured the move otherwise the managers would not have agreed to it. When questioned as to whether Dr MacRory or any of the managers had made a public statement on the matter or had to their knowledge written a private letter to anybody which

would bear out their statements they were not, they said, in a position to go further than to state positively that many managers and some bishops among whom they mentioned Dr MacRory approved of the suggested non-recognition of the Northern Government and of the acceptance of their teachers' salaries from the Dublin Department.[119]

The envoys were unable to substantiate their claims of support from MacRory, and the attitude of senior Catholic clerics to the boycott remains unclear. The first Secretary of the Ministry of Education, Lewis McQuibban, offers the most realistic assessment of the Catholic authorities' role in the boycott:

> One can understand, even if one does not agree with, the attitude of the Church in this matter. The Church whatever its sympathies have been, or may be, could in the circumstances hardly be expected to make a pronouncement which, for political reasons, its own adherents might consider themselves satisfied in disregarding. In all fairness it may certainly be assumed that the Church left a complete measure of freedom to the responsible manager. There is, I glean, a general feeling amongst the Managers that, if at all possible, a settlement should be arrived at. Amongst the teachers the desire for a settlement is not quite so far advanced.[120]

The Catholic authorities did not prohibit the teachers from protesting against the government. However, McQuibban viewed the fact that two thirds of Northern Ireland's Catholic elementary schools recognised the authority of the Ministry of Education as evidence that the Catholic authorities were neither orchestrating nor fully endorsing the campaign.[121]

Catholic teachers were more hostile than the Catholic authorities to the new devolved government, but they were also more accommodating towards the Ministry of Education's plans for reform. The largest teachers' union – the INTO,[122] failed to condemn the 1919 Education Bill, provoking bitter criticism from Catholic clerics,[123] and the annual conference of the northern section in March 1923 also highlighted the INTO's equivocal attitude to reform. The chairman of the conference, the general secretary – a TD from the Irish Free State – and the president of the union all welcomed the Education Bill. The conference was presented with a resolution from the union's leadership:

> That we, the teachers of Northern Ireland, associated with the Irish National Teachers' Organisation, hereby approve of the main

principles of the Education Bill now before the Parliament of Northern Ireland. We see in this Bill provisions for the education of the children and young people of Northern Ireland of a wise, just and generous nature, and we earnestly hope that Parliament and the public may support the Minister of Education in carrying through and making effective the proposed legislation. We desire to congratulate the Minister of Education and the Cabinet of Northern Ireland in their statesmanlike efforts to give the children in this province such a charter of educational promise and opportunity.[124]

The resolution did not meet with universal approval. A teacher from Belfast spoke of the threat of 'Godless schools' and another delegate proposed that the conference add 'legislation of such a character as to be acceptable to every section of the community' to address the Catholic authorities' concerns.[125] The amendment was eventually accepted, but another suggestion to delay debating the motion was rejected after a substantial minority of the meeting threatened to resign from the union if the motion was not discussed. The conference only avoided a schism by passing the motion and studying the Bill in a private session.[126] There can be no doubt that a significant number of Catholic teachers supported reform in the early 1920s, and the presumption that Catholic clerics could dictate to teachers on all issues is seriously questioned by the teachers' boycott and the events at the 1923 conference.

The government adopted a conciliatory approach to the teachers' boycott. Northern Ireland's first Prime Minister, Sir James Craig, urged Londonderry to reach a reasonable settlement with the rebellious teachers after the collapse of the boycott in the autumn of 1922 because he believed a discreet agreement would aid the Cosgrave government in its struggle with the republicans.[127] Londonderry obviously heeded his Prime Minister's advice because by the end of the year the administrative and technical questions arising from the boycott were resolved without embarrassment or publicity.[128] Also, in June 1922 the Dublin government organised examinations for secondary schools in Northern Ireland, and the Cabinet allowed the exams to be held without penalising the participating schools.[129]

The Catholic authorities' boycott of the Lynn committee did not appear to antagonise the Ministry of Education. Londonderry's letter to Fitzalan indicated disappointment rather than indignation, and McQuibban appeared to appreciate the political constraints upon the Catholic authorities' relations with the devolved government in Northern Ireland's first years. The boycott of the Ministry of Education by a third of all Catholic teachers was a more profound challenge than Logue's refusal to appoint representatives to the Lynn committee, yet the episode ended without significant repercussions. Londonderry remained on good personal terms with senior Catholic clerics[130] and the resolution of the teacher training issue in the spring of 1925 demonstrated that the Ministry and the Catholic authorities were capable of developing an amicable *modus vivendi* despite the boycott of the Lynn committee.[131] Also, by the autumn of 1923 the government was more concerned by their relations with the Protestant clergy.

Unionists, Protestants and the Education Bill

The determination of Londonderry and his officials to pursue their version of education reform was illustrated by the fate of the Lynn committee's recommendations on the vital issue of religious instruction in schools to be controlled by the new education committees. The committee's Interim Report of June 1922 recommended that 'Class One' schools, that is schools transferred to education committee control or built by the committees, should provide religious education for an average of half an hour each day, and presumed that 'a common Scripture programme will be agreed upon for the religious instruction of children belonging to all Protestant denominations'.[132]

The committee members were to be disappointed in February 1923 when the Education Bill was published, explicitly prohibiting the education committees from providing religious instruction in their schools.[133] The Bill provoked bitter criticism from Lynn. He complained to Londonderry that the proposed law was a radical change from the contents of the Interim Report, and threatened opposition both to the Bill and to the government:

> Had I known that you intend to introduce such a Bill I should have entered the strongest protest at the time. Frankly, I was horrified when I read the Bill, and I know that my feelings will be shared by every friend you have in Ulster. It is an essentially bad Bill and I believe that it is quite impossible to get it through Parliament. Indeed, if it became law it would put back education in Ulster for half a century . . . regardless of the consequences I am determined to fight this Bill line by line and page by page, and I can see there is a grave danger that the resulting fight will mean the destruction of the Government.[134]

Londonderry was conscious of the threat posed by Section 5 (1) of the 1920 Government of Ireland Act which stated: 'in the exercise of their power to make laws under this Act the Parliament of Northern Ireland shall not make a law so as to either directly or indirectly establish or endow any religion'.[135] He feared the attentions of the Judicial Committee of the Privy Council, which ensured that no Act of the Northern Ireland Parliament violated the 1920 Act, if he followed the committee's advice.[136] The purpose of the 1920 Act was to insulate British politics from the Irish question, and the subsequent history of Northern Ireland's devolved government was to highlight the reluctance of the British government to become embroiled in the region's affairs, but in 1923 the fear of the Privy Council was a genuine concern for ministers and civil servants. Therefore, Londonderry refused to follow Lynn's advice for a tacit recognition of 'Class One' schools as Protestant schools.

Londonderry and his officials would not be diverted by unionist politicians and Protestant clerics on the Lynn committee, and any Catholic representatives on the committee would have been even less successful in defending clerical control of Catholic elementary schools. The devolved government would not please their political friends, and they were unlikely to offer similar concessions to their political adversaries.

In October 1923, Dr Hugh Morrison, Unionist MP for the Queen's University of Belfast, claimed Lynn 'turned right about face and supported a Bill that was in direct conflict with his own report on the most vital and important question', but Lynn immediately countered by asserting that 'the Bill conforms in almost every particular with that report, and therefore I do not see how I turned right about face'.[137] Lynn was less than forthright with the House because, despite his threat to 'fight this Bill line by line and page by page', he fully supported both the Education Bill and the government during the prolonged parliamentary debates. Lynn may have been placated by assurances from Londonderry, his officials or possibly his Cabinet colleagues that the Act would allow Protestant clerics and Protestant teachers *de facto* powers to provide religious instruction. Also, he may have recognised the futility of opposing the Cabinet, and preferred to be silent to avoid embarrassing the government.

Lynn's protests were a minor problem for Londonderry in the final months of 1922. He expected some Unionist MPs to argue for a more 'secular' education system during the forthcoming debates on the Education Bill. This view was endorsed by the Parliamentary Secretary for the Ministry of Labour, John Gordon, who stated 'there is a wide feeling against clerical control' and the Minister of Finance,

Hugh Pollock, also maintained that 'provided the right of entry is given, the Protestant clergy generally will welcome the opportunity to transfer'.[138] Pollock's remarks are particularly interesting because within six months he was negotiating with senior Protestant clerics to amend the basic principles of the Act.[139] In the summer of 1923 he offered concessions to the Protestant clergy, but in the final weeks of 1922 he viewed the right of entry into public elementary schools to be the only significant issue. Protestant clerics did not raise any concerns about the fate of religious education while unionists were campaigning for education reform during the final decade before partition.[140] Ministers, therefore, felt confident that the Protestant clergy would accept the principles of education reform.

Education policy throughout the first thirty years of the devolved government was dominated by the efforts of Protestant clerics to enhance their influence within the education committees' schools. Thus, it is both surprising and intriguing to note the silence of the Protestant clergy during the debates of the Education Bill. The need to maintain the unionist coalition during Northern Ireland's critical early years may partly account for this silence, but the Protestant clergy themselves exploited this fear of dissension in 1925 to extract concessions from the devolved government.

No definitive answer can be offered to explain the behaviour of the Protestant clergy in 1922 and 1923 other than a gradual recognition that the government, particularly Londonderry, would not allow the education committees' schools to remain overtly denominational schools. The Lynn committee's Interim Report offered Protestant clerics nearly all their major demands, and Londonderry's refusal to implement the committee's recommendations only emerged in the first months of 1923.[141] So, until they realised that Londonderry would not follow the course set by the committee there was no reason for Protestant clerics to oppose the government or the Bill.

The publication of the Bill provoked outrage from Lynn, but the rest of the Unionist Party appeared to welcome the proposed new law. The debates on the Education Bill concentrated on the poor state of the region's schools and teachers' salaries rather than the role of the clerical manager or the place of religious instruction in the curriculum.[142] Londonderry's speech moving the First Reading of the Education Bill in the Northern Ireland Commons included only half a column on religious instruction, which he began by stating: 'I refuse to look upon this as either difficult or dangerous'.[143] Also, the occasional references to 'clerical' issues were distinctly unsympathetic to the

Protestant clergy. The Unionist MP for Londonderry, Sir Robert Anderson, called on the government not to defer to denominational interests.

> *Anderson* Let me . . . hope . . . that the Bill will not establish itself as absolutely denominational in character. While I consider it is not possible at the moment to get away from denominational education –
>
> *Hon Members* Why not ?
>
> *Anderson* I hope the Bill will be built up on such lines that eventually we can have a system of education under which the youth of the country can be educated together, irrespective of creed, or class, or party.[144]

During the same debate the Unionist MP for Fermanagh and Tyrone, William Coote (who was to protest in October against education committees employing teachers 'who burned the Bible'),[145] advised the government:

> to bring in a Bill that will cut out all sectarian education whatever. They ought to bring in a truly national system of education. Let them bring in some formula that will honour God and acknowledge God in the school . . . If any Church wishes to teach a dogma let there be some facility by which that Church may teach that dogma, but the teachers should not be made the servants of any particular Church.[146]

Another Unionist MP, Samuel McGuffin of West Belfast, also called on the government to maintain the principles of the Bill:

> If you are going to teach piety in the school, then by all means let us have it and plenty of it. If you are going to teach theological dogma, eschew it. It has done nothing but harm in our midst, and I am afraid it will multiply trouble for us in the future.[147]

Notably, Lynn was the only speaker to highlight the potential problems for the government:

> I do think there is a strong feeling in Ulster in favour of teaching the simple principles of the Bible in our National Schools, and I see nothing that would cause greater trouble for the Ministry than the suggestion that we should go to what some people foolishly call a Godless school.[148]

Lynn was cautious, but even he added 'there will be no trouble, at any rate so far as the Protestant churches are concerned, with regard to religious teaching'.[149] Unionist MPs united behind Londonderry's vision for Northern Ireland's elementary schools in the spring of 1923. A significant measure of education reform in Northern Ireland was inevitable once the British government resolved to partition the island, and the final outcome was always likely to bear a close resemblance to the 1923 Act. The Education Bill debates did not anticipate the troubles ahead for Londonderry and his colleagues as Unionist MPs eagerly supported the 1923 Act, confident that the Act would herald a new era of efficiency and progress.

The 1923 Act

The 1923 Education Act was a comprehensive measure[150] that sought to refashion Northern Ireland's education system along English lines. The Act created three classes of elementary schools, each enjoying differing levels of financial assistance from the government and the education committees established by the Act. Teachers' salaries in all three classes of school were paid by the Ministry, but the scale of funding for building new schools or substantial renovations and the payments for heating, lighting and cleaning schools varied according to the degree of control exercised by the education committees.

The first class of schools were either those built by the education committees or former voluntary schools transferred to the education committee's control by the trustees of the school. These schools were fully maintained by public funds in exchange for managerial control by the education committee and were known as public elementary schools.[151] The 1923 Act explicitly stated that the education committee, though obliged to allow access to denominational religious instruction, was not to provide religious instruction in these schools, and the Act also insisted that no religious tests were to be applied to teachers in public elementary schools.[152] These two clauses, Clause 26 and Clause 66(c), were to be the focus of Protestant clerical agitation against the Act, but they attracted only slight attention during the passage of the Bill.

The second class of schools were commonly known as 'four and two' schools. The school's management committee comprised four members chosen by the trustees of the school and two representatives of the education committee. The 'four and two' schools were viewed by the authors of the 1923 Act as a just compromise between the concerns of the clergy to maintain the distinctive character of their schools and the need for the education committees to supervise the spending of public monies. The 'four and two' schools were highly successful in England and Wales, but only prospered in Northern Ireland in the late 1920s and the early 1950s when Protestant voluntary schools adopted 'four and two' status before transferring to education committee control. In 1968 the Catholic authorities accepted a revised version of the 'four and two' principle – the 'maintained' school.[153] Maintained schools comprise the overwhelming majority of Catholic schools in Northern Ireland today. The original design, however, was rejected by the Catholic authorities in 1923.[154] The managers of 'four and two' schools collected half the school's maintenance costs, and were entitled to claim, though they were not guaranteed to receive, half of the costs for capital projects.[155] The financial conditions for 'four and two' schools were not as favourable as those available to public elementary schools, but they were preferable to the terms offered to the third class of school, the voluntary schools.[156]

The vast majority of Northern Ireland's two thousand elementary schools in 1923 were classed by the Education Act as voluntary schools. These were independent denominational schools, usually managed by the local priest, vicar or minister. Every major denomination in Ireland devoted substantial sums to the maintenance of their own schools during the nineteenth and early twentieth centuries, and clerics were reluctant to surrender such a heavy investment to the new education committees. Teachers' salaries were paid by the Ministry of Education, but voluntary managers received only half of the costs of heating, lighting and cleaning and no funds to build or renovate their schools because:

> We think that if possible all schools should be under the local com-
> mittee, and that inducements should be offered to bring this about.
> It would be inequitable to afford out of public funds the same degree
> of aid to schools which adopt only a modified form of local control,
> or none at all, as to those which are completely handed over.[157]

The amount of money parishes needed to find to pay for their schools, known as the voluntary contribution, imposed by the 1923 Act was not an exacting burden. Teacher's salaries accounted for three quarters of the regular costs of schools,[158] so the 1923 Act exerted a gradual rather than a dramatic impact upon voluntary schools. The absence of capital funding would effect only a minority of voluntary schools and finding the cost of repairs and half the costs of heating, lighting and cleaning would not compel most voluntary schools to transfer. The prospect of a large number of Protestant schools retaining voluntary status for some time after 1923 may partly account for the reluctance of the Ministry of Education to deny all forms of public funds to voluntary schools, but the decision to concentrate the voluntary contribution on capital investment and general maintenance costs may have arisen from Ministry officials' preference for incremental rather than extensive and immediate change.

The Ministry's funding strategy was probably influenced by the dire financial and administrative problems facing the devolved government in the early 1920s. Ministry of Finance officials would not have relished the prospect of immediately assuming responsibility for Northern Ireland's two thousand elementary schools. Therefore, the voluntary contribution was not severe enough to prevent most voluntary school managers maintaining their autonomy in the early 1920s. The government sought a gradual drift rather than an avalanche of transferred schools, all demanding investment from meagre resources. The decision not to pay repair costs would also have encouraged gradual change, persuading the more derelict schools to abandon voluntary status whereas most schools would survive without funds for capital and repair work until they were ripe for renewal. The only financial advantage for many schools in the early 1920s would be half of the costs of heating, lighting and cleaning the school – an insufficient incentive for most Protestant clerics.

The government was determined to replace existing denominational schools with larger, better equipped schools. A constant feature of education policy in Northern Ireland after 1921 was the determination of the Ministry of Education to amalgamate small schools into larger and, they presumed, more efficient schools supervised by the local education committees. As early as 1924 the Ministry was advising education committees to be relentless in their pursuit of amalgamations:

> It cannot . . . be too often urged on the regional education committees, in whose hands the matter will in future largely lie, that no more potent means of raising the efficiency of elementary education throughout the Province will be found than the provision, especially in urban centres, of well equipped central schools, to take the place of existing accommodation.[159]

The impact of this policy was to determine relations between the devolved government and the Protestant clerics, because the authentic purpose of the 1923 Act was to address the crisis facing Protestant schools in Northern Ireland. The National Board allowed each denomination to construct its own schools, and by the beginning of the twentieth century Ireland was littered with a host of small schools, particularly small Protestant schools. Scotland, with more than 600,000 pupils possessed only 3,500 schools whilst Ireland's 500,000 pupils attended more than 8,500 schools.[160] In 1929 the Parliamentary Secretary to the Ministry of Education, John Robb, bluntly admitted to the Commons that the government was unable, and unwilling, to maintain all the denominational schools created by the National Board.[161] Ministry officials viewed many of Northern Ireland's small schools as both too expensive to maintain and a major obstacle to education reform because the solitary teacher was often unable to teach the range of subjects considered necessary for a modern education.[162]

The Ministry was determined to recast Northern Ireland's elementary education system because, as the Interim Report of the Lynn committee explained:

> there are areas, generally, though not exclusively rural, where there has been, owing chiefly to the spirit of denominationalism, an unnecessary multiplication of small schools . . . These small schools have never been justifiable on educational or economic grounds.[163]

The committee proposed that 'the Ministry should have power to amalgamate primary schools where necessary, regard being had to the needs of the Roman Catholic and Protestant communities'.[164] After 1923 there would no longer be Catholic, Church of Ireland, Presbyterian and Methodist schools; only Catholic and Protestant schools. Disputes between the various Protestant denominations were minor issues for the government, because it was determined not to allow troublesome diversions from the central task of renovating Northern Ireland's Protestant schools.

The Protestant clergy secured 'simple Bible instruction' in public elementary schools and effective control of the appointment of teachers, but they were unable to resist the Ministry's tenacious ambition to amalgamate and modernise elementary schools. The Cabinet responded to clerical and 'Orange' agitation for a central role for Protestantism within public elementary schools, but ministers were impassive to calls to preserve small and deteriorating schools. The Ministry was determined to bring these schools, however reluctantly, into a modern and efficient era. Catholic schools, in contrast, were to remain in their nineteenth century condition.

'The lambs of their flocks'

The Catholic authorities' view of education reform was explicitly stated by Cardinal Logue in his address of 27 February 1920 to his bishops calling for protests against Macpherson's Education Bill. The Cardinal declared that the only acceptable school for the Catholic authorities was one in which Catholic children were:

> educated as faithful Catholics in a Catholic atmosphere, and under the care and direction of their pastors, whose strict right and leading duty it is to watch over, direct and safeguard the religious education of the lambs of their flocks. We are convinced that the enactment of the measure would deprive the Bishops and clergy of such control of the schools as is necessary for that religious training of the young which Leo XIII declared to be a chief part of the care of souls.[165]

The Cardinal was restating the Church's principles on Catholic schools, consistently maintained since the Synod of Thurles in 1850, of exclusive clerical control unfettered by state or parental involvement. Therefore, when Northern Ireland's six Catholic bishops published a statement at the end of March 1923 few were surprised by their objections to the Bill. Their pronouncement may have been prompted by the publication of the final version of the Bill, but they were also reacting to events at INTO's northern conference. The Catholic authorities clearly needed to assert their authority within Catholic schools after the INTO conference, and three days later the six bishops published their statement.

The northern bishops' declaration, compared to earlier pronouncements on education issues, was a restrained document. They offered an objective assessment of the rules for religious instruction in public elementary schools, without the vitriolic abuse which was to characterise the Protestant clerical campaign against the 1923 Act:

> What the Education Bill now before the Parliament of Northern Ireland proposes to do for religious instruction in elementary schools is to afford opportunities if they be desired, for such education in a school outside obligatory hours.[166]

The Catholic Church was universally hostile to any expansion of the state's role in education, but the bishops, as Ulster Catholics, were also deeply suspicious of the education committees which would directly manage public elementary schools. Local councils in Northern Ireland were viewed as Orange bastions, and in many areas they were bulwarks manufactured by the Leech Commission, a committee established in 1922 to eradicate the nationalist local councils in the vulnerable border areas. The Commission left Northern Ireland's nationalists with only two of the region's seventy-two local councils,[167] and Akenson notes the influence on education developments:

> This cynical manipulation of the instruments of local government by the Protestants has important implications for the development of educational institutions in Northern Ireland, because it confirmed the Catholic clergy's fear of any educational ties with local government agencies.[168]

The bishops linked the creation of the education committees to the actions of the Leech Commission, once more identifying the political grievances of the nationalist electorate with their own concerns for the fate of Catholic schools. The most strident paragraph of the document was reserved for the political threat to the autonomy of Catholic schools:

> Certainly if recent legislation abolishing Proportional Representation and rearranging the Local Government Board areas, thereby ousting Catholics from the representation, is to be taken as an indicator of what we may expect the outlook is of the gravest character for our people. The provided schools are impossible for our children. Schools managed at present are to be stricken with poverty . . . and the little to be gained by forming school committees on the English model in an Ulster environment may be dearly bought.[169]

The potential control of Catholic schools by the education committees was the central concern of the Catholic authorities, and their fears were confirmed by evidence that the unionist majorities on some of the eighteen education committees were manufactured to safeguard Protestant interests.

The education committees

The Ministry of Education archives in the Northern Ireland Public Record Office contain a draft proposal for twenty-three education committees with estimates of the numbers of 'RCs' and Protestants in each area. The original scheme anticipated nine areas where Catholic voters outnumbered Protestants with a further two areas vulnerable to an eventual Catholic majority. The Cabinet was therefore faced with the prospect of eleven 'nationalist' and only twelve 'unionist' committees.[170]

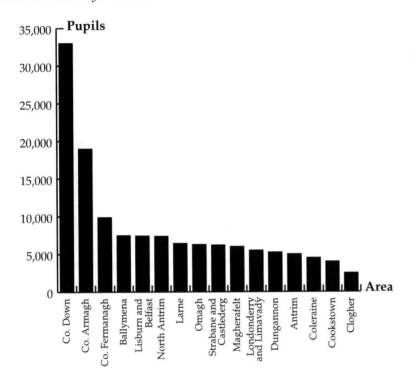

Figure 2A. Pupils in education committee areas in 1927

The presence of the draft proposal in the Cabinet Papers indicates that Londonderry intended to present the scheme to the Cabinet, however the Cabinet minutes do not contain any references to the plan. The evidence suggests that Craig refused to present the scheme to the Cabinet and insisted upon a more arbitrary design. The Ministry's initial plan emphasises the resolve of Londonderry and his officials to develop a constructive relationship with the Catholic authorities, though Catholic clerics would probably also have resisted lay Catholic intervention in Catholic schools. The draft version of the education committee boundaries would have posed awkward questions for the Catholic authorities. A number of 'Catholic' education committees would have offered a significant challenge to the Catholic authorities' refusal to participate in the new system, but the government saved them from this dilemma.

The final version created only eighteen education committees, and every committee was controlled by unionists with a safe majority.[171] The boundaries for the education committees were not included in the

Education Act, an unusual omission as the creation of these committees was the central purpose of the law. Londonderry claimed this was a minor detail,[172] but the delay was to allow for an apportionment that would ensure a unionist majority on every committee. As late as March 1924, more than a year after the Northern Ireland Parliament passed the 1923 Act, the boundaries outside Belfast and Londonderry were still unclear. Londonderry claimed 'each county will probably contain two or more regional areas, but it may comprise a single such area only, since the system is as elastic as possible'.[173] The Ministry exploited this flexibility to fashion a partisan structure after the rejection of the initial scheme.

Figure 2A highlights the vast contrasts between the numbers of pupils served by each education committee.[174] Antrim's 30,000 school pupils were administered by five education committees whilst 32,000 children in Down were governed by a single education committee. Armagh and Fermanagh were also managed by a single education committee. Fermanagh's 9,000 pupils may have merited only one committee, but Armagh's 18,000 pupils probably required more than a single county committee, especially as the largest of Antrim's five education committees – Ballymena – supervised only 7,000 pupils and Clogher in Tyrone contained less than two thousand pupils. County Londonderry's three committees and Tyrone's five committee were conspicuously small, with none responsible for more than 6,000 pupils. Antrim and Tyrone are Northern Ireland's largest counties, but geography alone cannot explain these variations.

Akenson notes that the Ministry ignored the Lynn committee's recommendations to duplicate existing local government structures and claims 'it is impossible to understand why these departures were made from the Lynn plan'.[175] The evidence from the PRONI files suggests that the principle of local control was compromised to preserve unionist control of every public elementary school in Northern Ireland.

The decision to ensure that every committee was governed by a unionist majority ended any faint hopes of the Catholic authorities cooperating with the education committees, but ministers were not solely motivated by simple prejudice. They could not attempt to satisfy Catholic concerns without alienating their own Protestant supporters, because the fear of 'nationalist' education committees was a significant obstacle to the transfer of Protestant denominational schools.

In June 1923 Professor William Corkey, later to lead the Protestant clerics' opposition to the 1923 Act, sent an account of a meeting of

Presbyterian clerical school managers to the Secretary to the Cabinet, Sir Wilfred Spender:

> The ministers from the Border and the city of Derry stated that they could not conscientiously transfer a school and the ministers present pledged themselves to stand with their Border brethren until the difficulty had been remedied. There seems to be no *via media* between Regional Committees which must be Roman Catholic in many areas and local management committees, one or the other must appoint teachers, and in many districts the Protestant schools would come under Roman Catholic management if Regional Committees are adopted.[176]

Protestant clerical fears were not confined to fundamentalists such as Corkey. The Church of Ireland Archbishop of Armagh, Charles D'Arcy, wrote to Craig to complain that the Education Act would lead in South Armagh to education committees:

> which will be actively Roman Catholic, probably composed exclusively of R.C. priests (so far as the locally elected are concerned). The same methods of education which have worked havoc in Southern Ireland will prevail.[177]

Lynn was also alarmed by the prospect of 'Catholic' education committees supervising Protestant schools, claiming that 'the Catholic Regional Committees will act tyrannically in their appointments to schools attended by a large majority of Protestant children'.[178] Protestant clerics would not be satisfied by Farren's claims that 'the few nationalist controlled committees would be more than likely to respect the wishes of local Protestant communities given that Catholic schools would not be subject to any interference at all in the matter of teaching appointments'.[179] They would view the prospect of 'Catholic' education committees as the most significant threat to the future of their school.

These anxieties were only partly eased by the machinations of the Leech Commission, and Protestant clerics were not only troubled by the threat from the local Catholic bishop. In 1928 a senior Ministry of Education official, Dr Henry Garrett, visited every education committee in Northern Ireland. He found many Protestant clerics still fearful of a 'Catholic' local education committee gaining control of Protestant schools, but he also noted that Protestant clerics were concerned by the prospect of other Protestant denominations gaining control of their schools.[180] The Church of Ireland bishop for Derry explained to Garrett that one of the major concerns of the Church of Ireland clergy was the fear of Presbyterians appointing teachers to transferred Church of Ireland schools.[181]

A settlement between Protestant clerics was therefore vital for the success of the government's reforms. The Lynn committee offered an optimistic solution to the Ministry's dilemma:

> It became apparent during the course of our inquiry that there is a marked tendency towards unity among the Protestant denominations on the subject of religious instruction. In these circumstances, and having regard to the modification of the managerial system which will result from the introduction of local administration of education, we feel sure that the amalgamation of small schools . . . will be facilitated rather than resisted.[182]

The Presbyterian churches and the Church of Ireland remained suspicious despite the Lynn committee's solution, concerned by the prospect of losing control of 'their' children in the amalgamated schools. In 1923 they proposed that the head teacher of all public elementary schools should be of the same denomination as the majority of the school's pupils and teaching appointments should also reflect the denominational blend within the school.[183] Londonderry refused to endorse such a plan, but in 1934 Ministry officials discovered that Down's education committee was asking all candidates for public elementary school teaching posts to state their denomination.[184] In the 1930s almost all Catholic teachers graduated from either St Mary's college in Belfast or St Mary's college in London, a fact that would be clearly stated on any application form. The education committee was thus probably attempting to establish the *Protestant* denomination of graduates of Stranmillis college in Belfast to satisfy local Protestant clerics.

The Protestant clergy were as hostile as their Catholic counterparts to surrendering their schools, in which many of their parishes had invested so much money and effort, without firm guarantees of the maintenance of their Protestant character. In contrast to the Catholic authorities they chose to wrest concessions from the government which would enable them to enjoy the financial benefits of transferred status without conceding effective control of the school to the education committee. Education policy in Northern Ireland during the first decade of devolved government was to be dominated by these efforts to increase their influence within public elementary schools.

'English speaking and Protestant children'

Irish schools played a central role in the centuries after the Reformation in the British government's attempts to assimilate the Gaelic, Catholic

Irish into the United Kingdom. As Auchmuty states 'for two hundred and fifty years it was the dual purpose of education in Ireland to turn out English speaking and Protestant children.'[185] The British government was only partially successful because, though it secured only a modest number of conversions to the Protestant faith, the Gaelic language 'had ceased to be the national language' by the middle of the nineteenth century.[186]

Akenson asserts that the National Board members 'were not hostile to the Irish language so much as unaware of it', and claims that Gaelic was only discussed twice during the first forty years of the National Board. Akenson understates the partiality of the National Board, because on both occasions the request to teach Gaelic was refused. Also, a senior inspector argued for the use of Gaelic in Gaeltacht areas in the 1850s, but his proposals were repeatedly ignored by the Board.[187] Farren claims that 'the official attitude to Irish tended to be quite hostile'[188] and quotes another Board inspector who revealed a sharp hostility to the language:

> The partial use of the native tongue as a living language may gratify our pride and recall pleasing associations in the history of our ancient nation . . . {but} . . . the substitution of English in its stead will henceforth be a measure, though far from being a main cause, of the improved civilization and higher social condition in the south and west of Ireland.[189]

Education officials may have been obstructive, but Catholic clerics also failed to promote the language during the first forty years of the National Board despite their success in establishing clerical control of most National Schools.

The advent of the 'Gaelic Revival' began to influence education policy by the final quarter of the nineteenth century, and the National Board responded by doubling the fee it paid to the schools for Gaelic teaching in 1879.[190] The National Board was more amenable, but clerical apathy towards Gaelic was underlined when only one hundred schools adopted the language as a subject for the curriculum.[191] By 1900 the Catholic authorities were also adapting to the prevailing nationalist mood, calling for Gaelic to be taught in all schools in the Gaeltacht areas, and the following year Cardinal Logue supported the Gaelic League's criticisms of the Intermediate Board.[192] In 1908 more than 3,000 Irish schools were offering Gaelic classes to their pupils.[193]

The clandestine government formed by the first Dáil in January 1919 did not contain an education minister, but in October J. J. O'Kelly, a leading member of the Gaelic League, was appointed to promote the development of the language in schools through the new ministry for Irish, Aireacht na Gaelige. Nearly a year later the second Dáil appointed O'Kelly as education minister.[194] Therefore, from the outset the leaders of Sinn Féin viewed education primarily as a means of establishing an Irish Gaelic nation, and it was to be the dominant theme of education policy in independent Ireland until the 1960s.[195]

In 1922 the report of the Irish Free State's National Programme Conference stated:

> One of the chief aims of the teaching of history should be to develop the best traits of the national character and to inculcate national pride and self respect . . . the Irish race has fulfilled a great mission in the advancement of civilisation and that, on the whole, the Irish nation has amply justified its existence.[196]

The education policies of the two polities created by partition were motivated by contrasting and contradictory aims and convictions. In Northern Ireland the devolved government, the Ministry of Education and the education committees expected public elementary schools to foster loyalty to the Empire and to the Crown, whilst in the Irish Free State the government and the Catholic authorities launched an ambitious project to create a new generation of Gaelic speakers. The Irish Free State's government was faced by a small and passive unionist minority, but the devolved government in Northern Ireland was challenged by a substantial and militant nationalist minority determined not to share the government's ambition for a 'British' education system.

Gaelic embodied the Irish nationalist values unionists were determined to escape,[197] but the devolved government was surprisingly accommodating towards the language in 1921. The Lynn committee advised the Ministry of Education to cease paying additional fees for Gaelic teaching in the third and fourth standards, but schools would continue to receive special grants for Gaelic classes beyond the fourth standard. Also, the Ministry provided subsidies for teachers to study at Irish language summer schools,[198] and the Lynn committee recommended the appointment of an 'Organiser of the Irish Language' to promote the language.[199]

The committee's moderation was not a unanimous decision, because two members drafted a reservation to the final report objecting to the proposal for an Organiser and to special payments for Gaelic classes. William Miller and Dehra Parker, the latter later to serve as Parliamentary Secretary for the Ministry of Education, stated:

> We have no objection to anyone who wishes learning the Irish language, but we most strongly object to the minds and brains of our children being burdened with such useless work; and we have a still stronger objection to the teaching of that language being paid for out of the public purse. If parents wish their children to learn Irish or any other useless language they should pay for it out of their own pockets, but it should not be a charge upon either the tax or rate-payer.[200]

Lynn, though chairman of the committee, also spoke against the language during the debates on the Education Bill:

> None of these people who take up Irish ever know anything about it. They can spell their own names badly in Irish, but that is all. I do not think it is worth spending money on.[201]

A common theme amongst unionist critics of Gaelic language teaching was to emphasise the futility of learning Gaelic, but the Unionist MP for North Belfast, William Grant, offered stark evidence of the attitudes of many unionists:

> the people who are most in favour of that particular language do not take their seats in this House, and I think during their absence we ought not to make any provision for that particular matter.[202]

The Ministry of Education responded to these criticisms by rejecting the Intermediate Board's examinations because the papers granted excessive importance to Gaelic,[203] and by allowing the post of Organiser of the Irish Language to remain vacant (though the nationalist boycott may have prevented the Ministry appointing a suitable candidate).[204] Also, McQuibban favoured the mutual exclusion of Gaelic and history, because the subjects in Catholic schools were 'likely to have a bias of a very considerable kind'.[205]

Farren claims that 'no account was taken of the general cultural values and practices of the Catholic–nationalist community. This failure further served to bear out some of Cardinal Logue's fears that the committee would be inimical to Catholic interests'.[206] This assessment appears harsh as the Lynn committee did not advocate the abolition of the grants, and the Ministry's circular of April 1923 allowed ninety minutes each week for Gaelic classes.[207] The opponents of Gaelic scored a few successes in the early 1920s, but the language remained an approved subject for any school in Northern Ireland.

The cultural and national clash between Irish nationalism and Ulster unionism was not an intense collision for either the Catholic authorities or the devolved government. 'Fenian' elements within Northern Ireland's Catholic schools were secondary issues for Unionist politicians and civil servants during the first decade of devolved government. They were more concerned by the fate of the entire structure of the education system which was suffering a sustained assault from their erstwhile allies the Protestant clergy.

The 1925 Education Act

The principal objective of the 1923 Education Act was to encourage the various Protestant denominational schools to integrate in larger, better equipped and more efficient schools by providing the incentive of full funding for cooperation and the penalty of no capital funds if clerical managers insisted upon retaining their autonomy.

The advantages of transferred status failed to attract the overwhelming majority of Protestant clerics, and the Ministry's Report for 1923–24 noted:

> exception has been taken by the Protestant Churches to the clauses relating to the facilities for religious instruction in elementary schools under public management and to the appointment of teachers in these schools. It may be expected, therefore, that there will be a certain hesitation and consequent delay on the part of these religious bodies before any general transfer of voluntary schools to the local authorities takes place.[208]

The Ministry's Report only noted the defiance of the Protestant clerics. The opposition of the Catholic authorities to the Education Act was not mentioned, evidence that as early as the summer of 1924 the Ministry abandoned any hope of negotiating with the Catholic authorities. The Ministry officials' lack of interest in the fate of Catholic voluntary schools was probably understandable because they were encountering severe problems in convincing Protestant clerics to cooperate with education reform. By 1925 only ten of Northern Ireland's two thousand elementary schools had transferred to the control of the education committees.[209]

The Ministry of Education may have preferred a gradual transfer of Protestant schools, but the government's education reforms faced an inglorious collapse without swift action to resolve the problem. Londonderry and his officials were faced with the obdurate resistance of both Catholic and Protestant clerics to the 1923 Act, and within two years they conceded to Protestant clerical claims.

'The whole differences on the education question . . . ' Lynn told the Northern Ireland Commons in March 1924, '. . . narrow themselves down to two points, simple Bible teaching in the school, and Protestant teachers for Protestant children'.[210] Protestant clerics argued that the only effective guarantee of both Bible instruction and Protestant teachers in public elementary schools was for the clergy to retain control of teaching appointments, and they began their campaign for a revision of the 1923 Act as early as the summer of 1923 with a series of meetings with the Minister of Finance, Hugh Pollock.[211]

The discussions with Pollock led to a tacit understanding that Protestant clerics would be able to operate an informal religious test for candidates for teaching posts.[212] Therefore, within the first six months of the Act the Protestant clergy extracted from a government minister – though not from Londonderry – a tacit recognition of their rights in public elementary schools.

These concessions failed to satisfy many Protestant clerics because they were determined to gain official, legal recognition of their role within public elementary schools. The loss of clerical support for the government was surprisingly swift. Archbishop D'Arcy, who was urging caution and patience in December 1923, was calling for an amending Act by March 1924.[213] Also, the three major Protestant denominations – the Church of Ireland, the Presbyterians and the Methodists – responded to the Ministry's strategy of financial coercion in December 1924 by forming the United Education Committee of the Protestant Churches (UEC) to campaign for changes to the 1923 Act.[214]

Londonderry was dismissive of the Protestant clergy's determination to maintain control of their schools and their ability to amass support within the Unionist Party. In October 1923 he told his Cabinet colleagues that 'he did not . . . consider that the agitation on this question was really of a serious character, but thought it was largely manufactured by certain interested ecclesiastics'.[215] The lack of political support for the Protestant clerics' campaign appeared to be confirmed three weeks later when William Coote, who advised Londonderry in February not to allow teachers to be servants of the clergy, secured only the vote of Dr Morrison for a motion critical of the Act.[216] The UEC was able to collect more political support during 1924, but Londonderry remained vehemently opposed to the Protestant clerics. In December 1924 he wrote to Craig:

> they persist in circulating deliberate falsehoods . . . they continue to urge upon us to produce an amending bill for which there is no

necessity whatsoever nor do I believe that there is any genuine backing in the Six Counties.[217]

The question of the scale of popular support for the Protestant clergy's campaign is difficult to assess. The Education Bill did not appear to provoke public concern that the proposed law would undermine the Protestant faith, and the failure of Coote's motion in October 1923 indicated that the Unionist Party was impervious to clerical agitation. There was to be a significant change though in the final months of 1924 when the UEC greatly strengthened their position by securing the support of leading figures in the Orange Order. The Belfast Grand Lodge voted at the end of January 1925 to support the clerical campaign, and two leading figures within the Order – Sir Joseph Davison and John Drennan – attended the meeting in Stormont Castle on 6 March which settled the issue in favour of the UEC.[218] The influence of the Orange Order within the Unionist Party was, and remains, considerable, and the success of the UEC in binding the Order to their campaign was a significant factor in its victory in March 1925. The conflict, as Farren notes, was to 'demonstrate the strength of traditional Protestant beliefs in Northern Ireland and the capacity of the Protestant churches to act just as vigorously as the Catholic Church had a few years previously when it had judged it necessary to do so in order to protect its own interests'.[219]

The UEC was also fortunate to exploit the opportunity provided by Craig himself in the spring of 1925. Craig called an election to underline opposition to any significant changes in Northern Ireland's border arising from the deliberations of the Boundary Commission. Unionists viewed the issue as vital for the future of Northern Ireland, and Craig was obviously unwilling to threaten unionist unity by confronting both the Protestant clergy and the Orange Order in the vulnerable weeks before the election.

Akenson argues that the UEC campaign was 'an unmistakable political threat to Sir James Craig'[220] and Farren claims the dispute 'threatened to undermine or at least seriously impair its capacity to govern and, thereby, to pose a question mark over the very existence of Northern Ireland itself'.[221] These claims appear exaggerated, and it is doubtful whether the government was genuinely alarmed by the UEC in the spring of 1925. Some Protestant clerics may have been prepared to risk losing Fermanagh and most of Tyrone for the sake of greater clerical control of public elementary schools, but few members of the Orange Order would sacrifice land in exchange for guarantees that Protestant clerics – rather than the unionist politicians on the local education committee – would appoint teachers.

Craig had already demonstrated greater willingness than Londonderry to accommodate the Protestant clergy,[222] and he compromised in the spring of 1925 because the difference between the UEC's claims and the concessions already conceded by Pollock in the summer of 1923 seemed too insignificant to justify a major clash with the Protestant clergy. Craig could be reasonably confident that the Unionist Party and, eventually, the Orange Order would support the Cabinet, but any contest with the UEC would generate unnecessary aggravation within the Unionist Party and sour relations with the Protestant clergy at a delicate moment.

Also, the Protestant clergy held a significant advantage over the government in the struggle for control of public elementary schools. The government recognised that Protestant clerics were entitled to assurances that the Protestant religion would be preserved in the new schools, and the UEC presented itself as an authority on what constituted sufficient guarantees. The claim by the general secretary of the Ulster Teachers Union in April 1924 that 'the teachers will do their duty . . . as zealously in the future as they have done in the past'[223] implied that an obligation to provide some form of religious instruction existed, and neither the teaching unions nor the government could challenge the UEC's claims to define the nature of the guarantees that there would be religious instruction for Protestant pupils in former Protestant schools. Religious instruction in schools was clearly a 'clerical' issue, and was accepted as such by the government as early as the summer of 1923 after Pollock's discussions with the UEC. Catholic ministers in the Irish Free State were not the only set of Irish politicians to defer to clerics on distinctly 'clerical' issues.

Londonderry was resting in London after a bout of influenza, possibly a 'diplomatic' illness, when the delegation from the UEC and the Orange Order met Craig to discuss a settlement. He cabled his approval of Craig's attempt to remove the 'two red rags' of Bible instruction and the education committee's control of teaching appointments in public elementary schools,[224] but he warned Craig that the accord offered only a truce in a prolonged struggle:

> feel sure you are certain to adopt the right course but am bound to utter warning that our opponents want religious education provided and compulsion of teachers. If they give up these am certainly willing to agree with your compromise . . . I regret necessity for

taking this course on the Bill as I am convinced that the battle is only postponed.[225]

A Bill allowing education committees to provide the Protestant formula of 'simple Bible instruction' in public elementary schools was hastily passed through the Northern Ireland Parliament in the final days before the dissolution.[226]

The 1925 Act arose from the failure of the Ministry of Education to convince the overwhelming majority of Protestant clerics to accept the 1923 Act. The capacity of most Protestant clerical managers to sustain their independence was questionable, but Craig could not afford the immediate political damage caused by an alienated and resentful Protestant clergy. The coincidence of the conversion of the Orange Order into enthusiastic advocates of clerical interests and the advent of the 1925 election should not obscure the enduring factors behind the compromise of March 1925.

Londonderry attempted to steer a course between the Protestant clergy and the Judicial Committee of the Privy Council, but after the British government refused to intervene to prevent the abolition of proportional representation for local government elections in 1922, its reluctance to become entangled in Northern Ireland's affairs was obvious to both ministers and clerics. Therefore, the Ministry needed only to satisfy the demands of the Protestant clergy, and as early as the summer of 1923 they secured an assurance from Pollock that Protestant clerics would exercise effective control of teaching appointments in 'Protestant' public elementary schools. The fundamental principles of the new system were firmly established by the autumn of 1923, and the UEC's success in the following decade was the inevitable and logical consequence of the decision to allow the Protestant clergy a dominant role in public elementary schools.

Londonderry wrote in March 1924:

> if there has been one thing for which the people of Northern Ireland have looked as compensation for the imposition upon them of a form of self government which they never desired, it is the reform of the system of public education in the Province.[227]

Northern Ireland's first Minister of Education was certainly enthused by the idea of fashioning a progressive, efficient and modern education system. The two thousand denominational schools managed by local clerics were to be replaced by large, modern and efficient schools under the supervision of the new education committees, because 'it must be confessed that we have outgrown a system of private management'.[228] The Ministry's strategy of rationalisation and modernisation was dependent upon the cooperation of the clerical managers, particularly Protestant clerics. Londonderry's hopes that 'a better understanding of the Act will convince the Churches that their fears are founded upon misapprehension'[229] were shown to be hopelessly misplaced by a Protestant clergy determined to instil denominational principles in the new public elementary schools. Dr Morrison claimed in June 1924 that Londonderry was a half Englishman who did not understand Ulster,[230] and the evidence of his five years as Minister of Education indicates that he had failed to grasp the dynamics within Ulster unionism, or the limitations of creating an education system without the conspicuous consent of the clergy.

Akenson portrays the 1925 and 1930 Acts as fundamental departures from Londonderry's original Act,[231] but Londonderry disagreed with the UEC's methods rather than their objectives. He was concerned by the possibility that the Lynn committee's recommendations, if translated into law, would violate the 1920 Act, but he also wished to ensure that Protestant children received regular Bible instruction. In January 1924 he claimed that 'Religious Instruction is safe in Ulster so long as the people of Ulster remain religious people and so long as the churches maintain their influence over her people'.[232] The UEC was unimpressed by Londonderry's guarantees and unconcerned by the legal implications of compulsory Bible teaching, and though Londonderry argued that religious education within public elementary schools was the responsibility of the clergy, the UEC demanded 'simple Bible instruction' from the teachers. Unionist MPs, despite their enthusiasm for Londonderry's proposals during the passage of the Education Bill, abandoned the 1923 Act after the Orange Order entered the debate on behalf of the Protestant clergy.

The new law caused disquiet in Whitehall. The Governor of Northern Ireland, Lord Abercorn, informed Craig that only the British government's reluctance to embarrass the government during an election campaign prevented the Home Office from delaying the Bill, and he warned him that the Bill might yet be considered by the Judicial Committee of the Privy Council.[233] The London government expressed its concerns, but British ministers eventually opted to evade their obligations under the Government of Ireland Act of 1920. The 1925 Act was never challenged in the courts or examined by the Privy Council.

Craig was not to be troubled by the London government, but his Minister of Education was sowing confusion in the aftermath of the election by claiming that because the Government of Ireland Act superseded every law of the Northern Ireland Parliament, the 1925 Act was no more than a superficial change to the 1923 Act. The UEC was, understandably, disappointed and demanded further discussions with the government. Craig urged Londonderry to reach a compromise before the 12 July commemorations offered the Protestant clergy an opportunity to embarrass the government, and a settlement was eventually reached between the UEC and the Ministry of Education a week before the 'Twelfth' celebrations.[234]

The government capitulated to the Protestant clergy in March 1925 despite Londonderry's appeal to a Unionist MP the previous month: 'I look for the support of members of Parliament generally, who after all, in so far as they passed the Act with practically unanimity, are as responsible to the constituents for the Act as I am'.[235] Londonderry found his education policy, so eagerly sanctioned by the Unionist Party in 1923, abandoned by the spring of 1925, and the following January he resigned as Minister of Education.

Londonderry's warning to his Prime Minister in March 1925 proved to be perceptive because the 1925 Act failed to satisfy the radical elements within the Protestant clergy. The UEC renewed its call in the late 1920s for 'simple Bible instruction' to be compulsory in all public elementary schools, and for teachers in these schools to be compelled to provide the religious instruction.[236] Londonderry hoped the Protestant clerics would be satisfied with *de facto* denominational schools, but the UEC refused to be pragmatic, and insisted upon absolute guarantees that Londonderry, wary of Section 5 of the 1920 Act, was reluctant to grant. This conflict between practical politicians and bureaucrats and idealistic clerics had been the central education issue since 1923. It was to continue to dominate education policy until the 1930 Act finally created a system of public elementary schools which was, to quote the Catholic bishops at Maynooth in 1900, 'as denominational almost as we could desire' for Protestant clerics.

CONCLUSION

The Catholic authorities' success in establishing their control of Catholic National Schools was their most significant political accomplishment of the nineteenth century. The century began with

Catholic bishops writing to their Church of Ireland counterparts for permission to establish schools,[237] and ended with Catholic clerics enjoying comprehensive authority over a vast network of Catholic schools funded by the British government. All aspects of the school were supervised by the clergy as the local priest appointed the teachers and the Catholic teacher training colleges ensured a supply of 'reliable' Catholic teachers. As Farren notes: 'the outcome was a system that became more and more explicitly denominational over the course of the following decades'.[238]

The new century brought fresh challenges. Titley and Akenson provide an extensive account of the Catholic authorities' opposition to education reform, but both understate the political and religious implications of lay control. The evidence from Northern Ireland, where the devolved government abandoned the 1923 Act after just two years in favour of a system of 'sound denominational education' that allowed Protestant clerics most of the powers they enjoyed under the National Board, indicates that many education reformers in Ulster were not disputing clerical control of schools, only *Catholic* clerical control. The Catholic authorities and their nationalist allies were able to thwart the British government's plans for reform, but after 1921 the devolved government was determined to follow the course of education reform adopted in England and Wales.

The Catholic authorities' boycott of the Lynn committee prevented them presenting the case for denominational schools, but their opposition to the central tenets of reform was already known to ministers and officials. A Catholic presence on the Lynn committee was unlikely to preserve clerical interests because the devolved government was dedicated to substantial reform, outlined in the Education (Belfast) Bill of 1918 and refined by the 1921 conference. The Catholic authorities may have been able to play a peripheral role by not waiting until the final publication of the Education Bill in 1923 before commenting on the committee's proposals, but they remained wary of any formal contact with both the Lynn committee and the devolved government.

The Catholic authorities were also unable to cooperate with the nascent Ministry of Education without testing the loyalty of many of Northern Ireland's Catholics who supported Sinn Féin in the 1921 elections. The intense political violence afflicting Northern Ireland limited their scope for cooperation, and senior Catholic clerics were unwilling to follow a different course from their nationalist allies for such meagre prospects of success.

Akenson claims that 'it was the partisan religious arrangements and not the recommendations for the involvement of local authorities in controlling primary schools which made the Lynn report a partisan document'.[239] However, the Leech Commission and the Cabinet, by ensuring that all eighteen education committees were controlled by unionists, gravely undermined any prospect of the Catholic authorities allowing the education committees an influence within Catholic schools in the immediate aftermath of the 1923 Act.[240] Catholic clerics were distrustful of the education committees, but they were no more suspicious than the Protestant clergy who had less to fear from 'local democratic control' by unionist politicians.

The Ministry's initial proposals for the education committees would have presented a difficult challenge to the Catholic authorities, enticing some Catholic schools to consider either transfer to 'Catholic' education committees or accepting 'four and two' school committees. Craig ensured there was no such dilemma, and the final version appeared to confirm Catholic clerical and nationalist fears of partial treatment by the devolved government. In the spring of 1924 ministers ensured that public elementary schools might not become fully 'Protestant', but would be completely 'unionist'. The government's concessions failed to satisfy the Protestant clergy. As Farren notes:

> they were to prove just as capable as the Catholic Church of protecting their interests whenever they perceived them to be endangered by a political power and, as events in the 1920s were soon to demonstrate, it would matter little that that power would be both Protestant and unionist.[241]

The manipulation of the education committee boundaries, as well as the limited role of the clergy within the proposed public elementary schools, explains the Catholic authorities' fears by looking beyond the legal texts of the major education laws to examine the practical realities governing Northern Ireland's education system.

Education in Ireland has been strongly influenced by ethnic and national implications since the time of the Reformation, and after 1921 the new governments in both the Irish Free State and Northern Ireland aimed to consolidate distinctive political and national values within the education system.

The most obvious contrast between Catholic and Protestant denominational schools was their differing attitudes towards the Gaelic language. The 'Gaelic Revival' of the late nineteenth century had become an integral element of Irish nationalism by the time of partition, and a significant minority of Northern Ireland's schools offered the language. The devolved government, despite its resolute opposition to the republican government of the Free State, preferred a cautious approach. The government sanctioned the post of Organiser of the Irish Language, although their liberalism was tempered by leaving the post vacant, and retained the special grants for Gaelic classes inherited from the National Board.

The Ministry, ignoring the advice of some members of the Lynn committee and of Unionist MPs, did not wage a 'cultural revolution' against the Catholic minority. The Cabinet limited the opportunities for Gaelic teaching, but Farren appears harsh when he claims the Ministry did not further limit Gaelic classes because of 'the fear of provoking greater opposition from the Nationalist community'.[242] The special grants survived for more than a decade, and Ministry officials also resisted the efforts of unionist MPs for an official course for Irish history.

The 1925 Act only modified Northern Ireland's education system because, as Akenson notes, 'the plain fact was that the Lynn report favoured granting similar religious rights to two distinct classes of schools, but proposed to finance fully only the Protestant schools'.[243] Londonderry refused to accept the Lynn committee's *explicit* endowment of Protestantism, but only in preference for an *implicit* acceptance that Protestant schools would transfer to the control of the education committees without any threat to their distinctive Protestant character. Public elementary schools became 'denominational in all but name, at least for the Protestant community'.[244] The differences between the UEC and the Ministry of Education revolved around legalities rather than practical politics because the Ministry expected some form of Bible instruction for Northern Ireland's Protestant pupils.

Buckland contends:

> Carefully devised as it was, the 1923 act completely underestimated the determination of the churches to maintain their control over education. Despite their theological differences and mutual detestation, Protestant and Catholic clergymen shared remarkably similar educational principles. Both believed that children should be taught by teachers of their own denomination; that children should attend schools with their co-religionists; and that religious instruction should be woven into the curriculum . . . They would have nothing to do with what they called Lord Londonderry's 'Godless' schools and successfully demanded instead both state money and independent control of teaching appointments to ensure sound denominational education.[245]

Buckland rightly notes the common purpose of the UEC and the Catholic authorities, but the UEC's success allowed Protestant voluntary schools to transfer to the control of the education committees without endangering the religious ethos of the school. This was an advantage denied to Catholic voluntary schools, both by the unionist majorities on every education committee and by the conditions for 'simple Bible instruction' in public elementary schools, and led to 'a pernicious double standard in Ulster education'.[246] The dilemma facing the Cabinet in the spring of 1925 was whether to persist with their vain efforts to attract the Catholic authorities or satisfy the fears of the Protestant clergy who appeared willing, in principle, to transfer their schools. Ministers, naturally concerned for the fate of Protestant schools, opted to search for a compromise with the Protestant clergy.

As Farren notes:

> The Protestant churches in Northern Ireland were not, as churches, acting out of character in opposing the terms of the Act. What they displayed was the same apprehension that any other church or similar group would have displayed at the idea of no longer being in full control of religious instruction.[247]

Londonderry, as Dunn claims, hoped that public elementary schools would eventually educate both Catholics and Protestants, but the Catholic authorities could never trust the education committees with their schools – especially on the vital issue of teaching appointments. Also, the ease of the UEC's victory in the spring of 1925 underlined the weakness of the Ministry when confronted by an orchestrated 'Orange' and Protestant clerical campaign. There was no guarantee that Londonderry or his successors would be able to resist the 'Orange' elements within the Unionist Party and defend the Catholic authorities' interests.

After 1925 there were three education systems in Northern Ireland; a Catholic voluntary system, a declining Protestant voluntary system, and an expanding network of state schools managed by the education committees and Protestant clerics. The 1925 Act marked the end of the first phase of Northern Ireland's education system; after the 1925 election Nationalist MPs took their seats in the Northern Ireland Commons and the Catholic authorities began their struggle for improved funding conditions for Catholic schools. Their success, and their failure, will be the central theme of the forthcoming chapters.

CHAPTER THREE

Sound denominational education

The 1930s were dominated by the economic depression which struck Northern Ireland's feeble economy and raised unemployment to unprecedented levels by 1935.[1] The early 1930s were menacing times for the Catholic minority; the rising tide of unemployment and poverty in an area already enduring the lowest standard of living in the United Kingdom aggravated strife between the unionist and nationalist communities. The 'Outdoor Relief Riots' of October 1932, when Protestant and Catholic unemployed workers rioted for three days, underlined the potential threat to the Unionists from a destitute Protestant working class, and they responded with a campaign against 'disloyalty' to sustain the troubled Unionist coalition. In July 1933 the Unionist MP Basil Brooke announced to an Orange Order meeting that he did not employ any Catholics on his estate, and advised his audience to follow his example and only give jobs to 'Protestant lads and lassies.'[2] Craig refused to condemn Brooke, who joined the Cabinet the following year as Minister of Agriculture.[3]

The Unionists' efforts to portray the Catholic minority as the major threat to the welfare of northern Protestants were aided by the defeat of the Cummann na nGaedheal government in the 1932 by de Valera's 'slightly constitutional'[4] Fianna Fáil.[5] Also, the immense celebrations surrounding the Eucharistic Congress of 1932 in Dublin embodied a triumphant Irish Catholicism which provoked a violent reaction from some northern Protestants.[6] The persistence of the depression intensified sectarian animosity, and in the summer of 1935 the worst riots in Belfast since the early 1920s left eleven dead and over five hundred injured.[7]

The severity of the economic depression also generated an embittered atmosphere between nationalist and unionist politicians after the gradual improvement evident in the late 1920s. In May 1932 the Nationalist leader, Joseph Devlin, led his contingent of MPs out of the Commons following a dispute with the Speaker and he was never to return, dying in January 1934. T. J. Campbell succeeded Devlin as MP for the Central seat in Belfast and as leader, but the party soon lapsed into apathy. In the 1933 elections, twenty-seven of the thirty-six Unionist MPs were elected without a challenge, and nearly two thirds of all seats were won without a contest.[8] Nationalists were either officially elected as abstentionists or they simply stayed away from the Commons, and by the late 1930s only Belfast's two nationalist MPs were frequent visitors to Stormont.

The economic upsurge generated by the war with Germany eventually ended the depression, but the 1930s emphasised how Northern Ireland remained a bitterly divided society. The successes of the Catholic authorities during these troubled years is testament to their persistence, and the integrity of moderate unionists within the devolved government.

'THE CATHOLIC CLERGY ATTACK'

The Catholic authorities were eager for compromise by the autumn of 1923. The defeat of the republicans in the Irish Free State's civil war and the consolidation of the devolved government in Northern Ireland encouraged a return to the traditional preference for participation. Their appeal to nationalist politicians and Catholic voters came in a statement in October 1923 objecting to the abolition of proportional representation for local elections, the refusal of the Ministry of Education to allow segregated teacher training colleges, and the government's insistence that all teachers – including Catholic clerics – swear an oath of loyalty to the Crown. They concluded one of their sharpest criticisms of the Unionist government with a disguised call for traditional constitutional nationalism when they declared: 'The time has come for our people to organise openly on constitutional lines and resolve to lie down no longer under this degrading thraldom'.[9]

The Catholic authorities' condemnation of 'this degrading thraldom' could not disguise their retreat, and Farrell argues that the principal motive for the Nationalist Party's decision to take their seats in the Commons after the 1925 election was the Catholic authorities' demand for nationalist politicians to defend their education interests:

> The one area where Craig's government had acted with a fair degree of impartiality had been education . . . The Lynn committee recommended the establishment of a system of state schools where there would be no religious instruction and no account would be taken of

religion in appointing staff . . . The Catholic Church, which had always insisted on religious segregation in schools and its own complete control of the education – and hopefully the attitudes – of its members, was alarmed. The new proposals threatened its power. The Northern bishops contacted Devlin and the Nationalists, and in October 1923 called on them to take their seats in the Northern parliament to defend Catholic interests. If the bishops had to choose between accepting the Northern state and losing their schools then they were going to keep their schools.[10]

Farrell assumes that 'no account would be taken of religion in appointing staff' in public elementary schools, but many Unionist local councils were partial when choosing candidates for most local government posts, and Farrell has been one of the most persuasive critics of this treatment of the Catholic minority. Many education committees would be tempted to appoint 'loyal' teachers in their schools, especially after the 1922 boycott revealed the depth of republican sentiment amongst Catholic teachers.

Farrell suggests that the Catholic authorities were faced with a realistic choice between accepting partition or seeking to protect the most important autonomous Catholic institutions in Northern Ireland. Michael Collins, Eamonn de Valera and a host of militant nationalists failed to incorporate Northern Ireland into the Irish Free State, and Cardinal Logue and his colleagues – simply by denying recognition – were unlikely to succeed where bolder men had already failed. They adopted a realistic and pragmatic course in October 1923 when they asked Nationalist politicians to reconsider their boycott. Partition was an irrefutable fact by the end of 1923, and the new leaders of the Irish Free State were too engrossed in the problems of establishing their own state to pay close attention to the fate of Northern Ireland's Catholics. There was no imminent prospect of an end to partition and the bishops, following their naturally conservative impulses, attempted to compromise with the new government.

The Nationalist Party also accepted the need for participation, and the 1925 election witnessed the most intensive clerical intervention of the twelve elections to the Northern Ireland Commons. Priests chaired candidate selection and campaign meetings,[11] one priest resorted to soliciting for votes in his Sunday sermon[12] and eleven Nationalist candidates were nominated by priests.[13] In contrast to 1921 no Republican was nominated by a Catholic cleric.[14] Archdeacon Neil Convery of Belfast spoke at an election meeting for Devlin in West

Belfast. His speech, later to appear as an advert for the Nationalists in the *Irish News,* offers an example of the importance the Catholic authorities attached to their approval of nationalist politicians:

> Not alone the people but the priests are engaged in this National struggle. The names of four reputed priests to Mr Devlin's nomination papers . . . are sufficient guarantee of the position Mr Devlin occupies in the minds of those *fitted to judge his merits as a Catholic and Nationalist representative.*[15]

This assertive clerical campaign encouraged a dramatic change in the fortunes of the two nationalist parties. In 1921 Sinn Féin won over 100,000 votes, but four years later their republican successors secured a mere 20,000 votes and just two seats while the Nationalists won over 90,000 votes and ten seats.[16] The Treaty schism and the defeat of the insurgents in the Irish Free State's civil war severely weakened the Republicans, but clerical support provided a significant advantage for the Nationalists in 1925. Buckland and Farrell, an improbable combination, both claim the Catholic authorities' support for the Nationalists was motivated by their concern for their education interests,[17] but the obvious failure of the Republicans by the spring of 1925 also left them with no feasible alternative to accepting the status quo of partition.[18]

The Nationalist success of 1925 doubtless aided the Catholic authorities in their future campaigns but, before the first Nationalist MPs appeared in the Commons in the spring of 1925, the Catholic authorities waged a successful campaign to defend one of the most significant achievements of their prolonged struggle against the National Board; the right to train the teachers for Catholic schools.

Teacher training

The most obvious disadvantage of the 1923 Act centred on the scale of the voluntary contribution from parishes, but the principal education question for the Catholic authorities during the first years of devolved power was the fate of denominational teacher training colleges. Londonderry's only reference to the Catholic authorities during his speeches on the Education Bill was to mention their refusal to accept integrated teacher training colleges,[19] and the statement of March 1923 against the Bill dedicated nearly a third of the document to teacher training.[20] Bishop MacRory's Lenten Pastorals for 1923 and 1924 mentioned only the threat of mixed teacher training courses at Queen's University Belfast when discussing education,[21] and the following year he referred to 'the vitally important question of training Catholic teachers in excluded Ulster'.[22]

The supervision of teacher training is a vital means of sustaining clerical authority because, as Corcoran noted, 'the most essential issue in the Catholic nature of Catholic Schools is full Catholic control of the choice of teachers'.[23] The prolonged struggle waged by the Protestant clergy to secure control of Stranmillis college highlighted the importance they also attached to clerical control of teachers' training.

The Ministry failed to reach an agreement with the Irish Free State's Department of Education to train its prospective teachers and resorted to organising courses at the Church of Ireland's training college in Dublin until the new college at Stranmillis was opened in the autumn of 1923. The college agreed to accept the Ministry's conditions for training the students in March 1922, graduating sixty-one students in 1923 and twenty-seven students the following year.[24]

The Catholic authorities' insistence upon sexual and religious segregation raised major problems for the Ministry of Education.[25] The Ministry funded the training of Catholic women at St Mary's college in Belfast after the college abandoned its boycott in October 1923,[26] but officials argued that the small number of male Catholic trainees did not justify a separate college. One solution was to send the Catholic men to train in the Irish Free State, where Protestant students were training at the Church of Ireland's college in Dublin, but the Catholic colleges refused to accept candidates without the approval of the Irish Free State's Department of Education.[27]

The teacher training issue was not just creating problems for the Ministry of Education, because Catholic students were willing to study in the government's new training college at Stranmillis. Londonderry told the Commons in April 1923 that more than a third of the applicants for training at Stranmillis college were Catholics.[28] Harris notes that one hundred and thirteen of the Catholic applicants were women who were entitled to study at St Mary's college, but an equally striking fact was that most of the male applicants – forty-six of ninety-one – were also Catholics.[29] This enthusiasm certainly disappointed the Catholic authorities, but the Protestant clergy were also concerned by the prospect of substantial numbers of Catholic graduates of Stranmillis, excluded from Catholic voluntary schools, seeking work in public elementary schools. In February 1924 the Secretary to the Cabinet, Sir Wilfred Spender, wrote to McQuibban to ask whether Catholic teachers were being employed in Protestant schools. McQuibban replied that the question left him 'breathless' and explained 'even if it were the case it would not be the function of the Ministry to raise objections'.[30]

McQuibban dismissed Spender's query, but Protestant clerical fears that a substantial number of Catholic trainee teachers would study at Stranmillis greatly strengthened the Catholic authorities' case for a compromise. They eventually secured an agreement in January 1925 which sent the Catholic male students to an English Catholic teacher training college, St Mary's college in London, at the expense of the Ministry of Education.[31] The official announcement of these sensitive arrangements was delayed until after the March 1925 election, when Lynn challenged the decision as a violation of Section 5 of the Government of Ireland Act,[32] and the importance of the teacher training issue to the Catholic authorities was underlined by the reaction of their nationalist allies. Five days later, during the next sitting of the Commons, Devlin of West Belfast and Thomas McAllister of Antrim became the first Nationalist MPs to swear the oath and take their seats.[33] Wyse may have been unduly optimistic when he claimed 'Roman Catholic male teachers are brought up in surroundings conducive to promote breadth of view and loyalty to the Empire',[34] but the compromise allowed the Ministry to settle its most significant dispute with the Catholic authorities during the early 1920s.

THE 1930 EDUCATION ACT

The Catholic authorities were anxious to replenish the decaying stock of Catholic schools and grasped the opportunity offered by the resurgence of Protestant agitation against the 1923 Act in the late 1920s to demand concessions for their own schools. The refusal of Armagh's education committee to incorporate a pledge to provide Bible instruction in the deeds of transfer for Protestant schools provoked a second campaign from the UEC in 1929.[35] The Protestant clergy – as Londonderry warned they would in March 1925 – demanded compulsory Bible instruction in public elementary schools and that teachers be required to teach these classes. The government abandoned its initial defiance and granted most of the UEC's demands in the final weeks before the May 1929 elections,[36] prompting the Catholic authorities to present their own demands.

The Catholic bid for improved funding began in August 1929 with a private letter from Archdeacon John Tierney of Enniskillen to Lord Charlemont, Londonderry's successor as Minister of Education.

Tierney's confidential diplomacy failed to provoke a response,[37] so the Catholic authorities changed their strategy to launch a concerted public campaign. By January 1930 MacRory, now Archbishop of Armagh, was in determined mood:

> While palatial schools costing hundreds of thousands of pounds are being erected within the Six Counties, schools of which Catholics cannot avail on account of conscientious reasons, yet with trifling exceptions, no money has been spent on the building and enlargement of Catholic schools since the Belfast Parliament came into existence . . . Cannot the Belfast Government allow us to have our fair share of money for building and enlarging schools on terms that were allowed by the British Government ? One thing is certain, we cannot go on as present. Public money is being poured out on the buildings of schools, and Catholics are getting practically none of it.[38]

The bishops issued a similar statement on 17 February demanding relief for Catholic schools,[39] and the traditional St Patrick's Day celebrations a month later were dominated by demands for improved funding.[40] The Catholic authorities fully exploited their ability to concentrate the efforts of the Catholic community upon a single issue, employing every device to present their case. As Akenson notes, 'a year previously it had been the Protestant clerics who had been attacking the ministry of education most fiercely, in 1930 it was the Roman Catholics who were fighting hardest'.[41] Two vital groups – Nationalist politicians and Catholic teachers – were fully mobilised by the Catholic authorities for their campaign.

Devlin's first education speech during the debate of the Ministry of Education's Estimates in May 1925 was notable for ignoring funding questions.[42] However, the following year's debate provoked sustained criticism from Patrick O'Neill of Down, Devlin and McAllister,[43] and in March 1927 O'Neill moved a motion calling for the restoration of the funding policies of the National Board.[44] The prolonged debate allowed Nationalist MPs to display their concern for Catholic schools.[45] O'Neill led the Nationalist campaign during the Estimates debate in May 1927,[46] but twelve months later only Cahir Healy of South Fermanagh spoke against the Estimates.[47] In March 1929 O'Neill, the Nationalist MP for Aramgh John Collins, Devlin and Healy returned to the offensive with bitter speeches against Ministry policy,[48] and in June 1929 O'Neill claimed the poor state of voluntary school buildings was the principal issue facing the Ministry of Education.[49]

Nationalist attendance at the Northern Ireland Parliament was erratic during the late 1920s, but every Nationalist MP and Senator attended the delegation to Charlemont on 1 April led by Bishop Bernard O'Kane of Derry. Also, the Second Reading of the Education Bill on 9 April was one of the longest sessions of the House of Commons and attracted a record number of MPs.[50] Devlin paid his first visit to the Commons since the 1929 election to speak in the debate, and the entire Nationalist party met for two hours the previous day, missing the annual debate of the Education Estimates, to discuss their strategy.[51]

Nationalist MPs also underlined the importance of the funding issue by bluntly threatening another boycott if the government failed to address their grievances. The Nationalist MP for Mid Londonderry, George Leeke, claimed that a refusal to address Catholic claims would raise the threat of abstention once more. Devlin lamented that 'for four years I did not come here and I was fairly effective. For four years I have been here and I am absolutely ineffective'.[52] Devlin's attitude to participation, however, had been starkly different only a week before when he told Charlemont that 'the Catholics did not wish to repeat the fiasco of 1923; they wished to establish peace in educational matters'.[53] Devlin probably understated his commitment to abstention in 1921 to appease Charlemont, and he was an abrasive opponent after the failure of these initial discussions, but the 1930 campaign illustrated the potential advantages to the Catholic authorities of a band of loyal Catholics MPs. As Akenson notes:

> Neither in the debates in the Commons nor in the arguments outside were the Catholic clerical leaders let down by their lay allies. In the Commons Joseph Devlin was persuasive, amusing, vitriolic by turns; and outside the *Irish News* poured forth a torrent of propaganda which often became sheer invective.[54]

The Catholic authorities were also aided by the attitude of the Catholic teachers. The INTO was an overwhelmingly Catholic and nationalist union by the end of the 1920s after most Protestant teachers left for the Ulster Teachers' Union,[55] and there was no repeat of the events at the union's 1923 conference. The INTO President, Eugene Carraher, was a member of the delegation to Charlemont on 1 April[56] where he pledged the union's support for Catholic clerical management and insisted that 'the question of school buildings is the most pressing need in the Irish educational world today'.[57] In 1930 the INTO was an asset rather than a liability for the Catholic authorities in their struggle to preserve clerical control of Catholic schools.

The government's concessions to the UEC, the enthusiasm of Nationalist MPs and the support of the major Catholic teaching union greatly enhanced the prospects for the Catholic authorities in the spring of 1930, and the Cabinet was also concerned by the threat of intervention by the Home Office in London.

The 1925 Education Act provoked unease in Hillsborough and Whitehall, and the government's fears were exacerbated when the British general election of May 1929 led, eventually, to a Labour government.[58] The Conservatives were the Unionists' traditional allies, challenging the authority of Parliament and condoning the threat of armed revolt in the summer of 1914 to defend the Union, but the Labour Party was disinterested in such constitutional questions.[59] These fears were apparently confirmed at a meeting in London in November 1929 when a senior Home Office official, Sir John Anderson, claimed that 'Bible teaching . . . would certainly be regarded by Roman Catholics as unacceptable and constituting a preference in violation of Section 5 of the Government of Ireland Act'. Anderson advised Charlemont and Wyse that the British government would refer the matter to the Judicial Committee of the Privy Council if 'substantial representations were received against it from responsible parties in Northern Ireland'.[60]

The Catholic authorities were probably unaware of Anderson's comments, but they exploited the possibility of an appeal to the Privy Council. The Nationalist Senator T. J. Campbell mentioned the Judicial Committee during the visit to Charlemont[61] and, only days before the vital Second Reading of the Education Bill, Bishop Daniel Mageean of Down and Connor intensified the threat of a legal challenge:

> we shall be forced to find in the highest court in the Empire whether the endowment of Protestant schools is in harmony with that Constitution. We are confident of the result.[62]

Wilson argues that the Catholic authorities did not appeal to the Judicial Committee because they feared the committee would rule against any form of state funding for voluntary schools.[63] However, the evidence suggests that they were warned by the London government that any appeal was both unwelcome and likely to fail. The Home Secretary, J. R. Clynes, wrote to Devlin on 15 April thanking him for sending him a copy of the Education Bill, but added:

> I can only say at the moment that I had not lost sight of the provisions of Section 51 of the Government of Ireland Act, but that there does not appear to me to be any ground at present for invoking them.[64]

The British government's strategy in 1930 can only be explained by their determination to avoid becoming entangled in Northern Ireland's education controversies, and the most politic course appeared to be to discourage both parties from adopting a belligerent stance. The evidence suggests that this was a shrewd policy, as Anderson's warning and Clyne's letter probably induced a less implacable approach from the Cabinet and the Catholic authorities.

Charlemont presented proposals in November 1929 and February 1930 to encourage Catholic clerical managers to accept school committees. He sought to prevent education committees denying funds to 'four and two' schools, and to limit the education committee's role in the appointment and dismissal of teachers.[65] Charlemont's inducements failed to tempt the Catholic authorities,[66] and when the Cabinet confirmed its earlier decision to grant concessions only on the basis of 'four and two' committees the issue, once more, was deadlocked.[67]

A settlement appeared impossible until 22 April when Mageean, possibly encouraged by Clyne's letter to Devlin, offered a compromise which edged the Catholic authorities towards accepting 'four and two' committees. Mageean proposed a revised form of 'four and two' committee which would only be responsible for the school building and general maintenance while the power to determine the school's curriculum and teaching appointments remained with the clerical manager.[68] This astute proposal was both an offer and a challenge to the Cabinet.

Mageean posed a difficult question for Charlemont and his colleagues, because public elementary schools only enjoyed greater levels of funding for construction and general maintenance costs. The 'four and two' committee should, Mageean contended, only be responsible for these issues. The Ministry and the education committees would be liable for the maintenance of the school's buildings, but the central questions of curriculum and staffing would remain the responsibility of the Catholic clergy.

Protestant clerics were attracted to Mageean's proposed committee because they too viewed the control of teaching appointments as vital for the preservation of clerical influence within public elementary schools.[69] The Protestant clergy's insistence upon the school committee, where the local cleric would exercise a predominant influence, playing a significant role in the appointment of teachers was as important as 'simple Bible instruction' in the conflict between the UEC and the Ministry of Education.[70] The threat of a compact between the Catholic authorities and the UEC, despite their common interests, should not be overstated.

The UEC was dedicated to amending the conditions for public elementary schools rather than allowing Protestant schools to retain their voluntary status. The only evidence from the PRONI archives of concerted action by Protestant and Catholic clerics occurred in Fermanagh in October 1926 when twenty-eight voluntary managers approached Charlemont to urge him to persuade the education committee to provide free school books for voluntary schools.[71] The Ministry's officials may have been justified in fearing such an alliance, but the evidence suggests that the Catholic authorities and most Protestant clerics were pursuing their objectives by sharply differing methods.

By the end of the first week in May the three deaneries of Down and Connor, representing the Catholic clergy from every parish in the largest diocese within Northern Ireland, endorsed their bishop's proposal – though insisting that 'all matters relating to religious teaching, including the selection of the teacher, shall be subject to the control of those who represent Church interests'.[72] The Catholic authorities appeared to be willing to accept 'four and two' committees, but on conditions that would both undermine 'local democratic control' and appeal to many Protestant clerics. The government, therefore, faced the prospect of the Catholic authorities forging an alliance with disaffected Protestant critics of the 1923 Education Act, and acted swiftly to separate Protestant and Catholic clerics.

Craigavon, in another surprising development, announced that the government would offer an unconditional grant of fifty per cent of capital costs for voluntary schools, and that these funds would be available from the Ministry of Education rather than the education committees.[73] The Cabinet's decision to compromise appears both surprising and unnecessary. The 'ill-tempered'[74] debates of the Education Bill did not suggest that the government would yield to nationalist agitation, and its response to British pressure was confined to Charlemont's proposals to diminish local education committee control within 'four and two' schools. The Catholic authorities were not expecting concessions. MacRory told Mageean in the middle of April 'it doesn't look very promising',[75] and Tierney also wrote of the interview with Charlemont on 1 April:

> when we came away from that interview there was little hope that there would be any concession whatever. The Bishop of Derry was quite convinced that the Government and Ministry were adamant.[76]

The decisive Cabinet meeting of 7 May viewed the reports in the *Irish News* of the clerical conferences as important developments,[77] but these gatherings were standard devices employed by the Catholic authorities, and few observers of Northern Ireland would be surprised by the clergy's support for their own bishop's scheme. The government had been indifferent to such protests in previous years, and would be so again after 1930.[78]

The government may have adopted the traditional British practice from the nineteenth century of offering concessions to both the Catholic and Protestant clergy, and preferred to offer this compromise from a position of strength at the beginning of May rather than during the passage of the Education Bill. However, concessions to voluntary schools at the beginning of the year would have avoided the rancour which dominated the spring of 1930. Nationalist MPs and the nationalist press would certainly have maintained their opposition to partial funding, as they did after Craigavon's announcement of 8 May,[79] but the government's response to the Catholic authorities' demands contrasts sharply with their swift surrenders to the UEC in 1925 and 1929.

The decision of 7 May remains difficult to explain without questioning the government's appetite for converting Catholic schools to 'four and two' schools. The Ministry of Education never anticipated significant numbers of Catholic schools transferring to the control of the education committees because, as Charlemont explained to his colleagues:

> No well-informed person acquainted with the mentality of the Irish Roman Catholic clergy ever expected to see them transfer their schools, more especially to local committees bound to be predominantly Protestant.[80]

Charlemont posed an awkward offer to the Catholic authorities with his proposals for changes to the 'four and two' school committees, but this strategy was abandoned after Mageean responded with his own perplexing challenge. Mageean's offer was a genuine attempt to accommodate ministers' insistence upon public representation in exchange for public funds. They were given an opportunity to demonstrate that they were not aiming for control of Catholic schools, but they insisted upon the clerical manager surrendering his most significant power – the right to appoint teachers.

The government's decision in May 1930 may also have been motivated by the financial implications of accepting Catholic schools as 'four and two' schools. Charlemont presented a paper to the Cabinet only four days after Mageean's speech in which he outlined the potential costs of granting 'four and two' status to Catholic schools. The Ministry's inspectors found eighty 'unsuitable' Catholic schools catering for nearly 8,000 pupils with a further 14,000 pupils in nearly two hundred 'fairly suitable' schools, and Ministry officials calculated that the average cost of new accommodation for each pupil would be £30.[81] The 1923 Act did not determine the scale of capital funding for 'four and two' schools. The precise liability was therefore uncertain, but the combined agitation of Catholic and Protestant clerical managers might raise grants above the traditional rate of two thirds of capital costs, requiring more than £400,000 of public money. The Ministry eventually spent less than £128,000 on new voluntary schools and a further £37,000 improving existing voluntary schools during the 1930s.[82]

The government's scope for compromise is obviously open to question, but Craiganon was probably close to the truth when he claimed that 'the Government can go no further. We have gone to the very limit'.[83] A prominent lay Catholic wrote to Mageean to recount a conversation with a senior government official who claimed that Craigavon was concerned by the attitude of the Unionists in the Senate.[84] Craig may have overstated the threat to Unionist Party unity, but events in the Commons underlined the disquiet within Unionist ranks. Only twelve Unionists MPs, including eight members of the government, supported Craig's concession, and Nationalist MPs saved the measure by remaining in their seats rather than voting against the government.[85]

The government's concession to the UEC was a major factor in explaining the success of the Catholic authorities' campaign in 1930, but senior Catholic clerics and their Nationalist allies were indifferent to the Protestant clerical agitation against the 1923 Act. As Devlin explained during the Second Reading of the 1930 Education Bill:

> Catholics do not in the least degree object to what you are doing in the building, extension, and lighting and cleaning of schools for the Protestant children. They do not object to your making provision to meet the conscientious convictions of the Protestant population . . . But they do claim, and claim emphatically and justly, a similar right for themselves.[86]

The Nationalist MP for South Armagh, Joseph Connellan, also paid tribute to the role of the Orange Order 'for insisting upon the retention of religious education in the schools with which the members of the Order were concerned'.[87] The compulsion of teachers in public elementary school to teach 'simple Bible instruction' also did not disturb Catholic clerics who viewed the teaching of religious instruction to be the primary task of teachers in Catholic schools. In 1932, when the governors of Stranmillis college resigned after the government increased Protestant clerical representation on the governing board, Devlin told the Minister of Education:

> I have no complaint to make about any concessions he has made to the Protestant churches. We are distinctly denominationalists. We have never departed from that position, and we have no right or desire to interfere with the system of education of our Protestant fellow countrymen.[88]

The Catholic authorities and the Protestant clergy were united in their belief in the vital importance of religion, and their own central role, within elementary schools, but there were profound theological differences on the role of 'simple Bible instruction'. Distinct classes could not satisfy the Catholic authorities' demands for an education permeated by a Catholic ethos which Church doctrine considers to be central to the religious development of the Catholic child. Also, religious education based only upon the Bible – even a version of the Bible sanctioned by the Papacy – was neither sufficient nor compatible with the central tenets of Catholic teachings. As Mageean explained:

> We cannot transfer our schools. We cannot accept simple Bible teaching. I wish to emphasise this point. Simple Bible teaching is based upon the fundamental principle of Protestantism, the inter-pretation of sacred Scriptures by private judgement. According to Protestants that is a rule of their Faith, and we Catholics cannot accept schools in which our children are to be, from their earliest years, taught the first principles of Protestantism.[89]

Healy and James McCarroll, the Nationalist MP for Foyle, County Londonderry, faithfully followed their bishops' lead in disputing the assumption that 'simple Bible instruction' could be acceptable to Catholics:

> Simple Bible instruction . . . does not satisfy our requirements. It is a formula that apparently satisfies the Protestant managers. Catholics, on the other hand, must insist, as a matter of conscience, upon their children receiving a religious instruction in schools under the direction of the Church.[90]

> Catholics cannot accept simple Bible teaching. They cannot at all accept the Bible as the rule of faith. Catholics are not forbidden to read the Scriptures but our case is that the Bible is not the only source of faith. It is a dead letter calling for a divine interpreter.[91]

The 1930 Act ensured that education committee control remained manifestly unacceptable to the Catholic community. A less blatantly

'Protestant' network of public elementary schools may have raised doubts amongst the Catholic laity that the cost of the voluntary contribution was a reasonable price to pay for clerical authority within Catholic schools, but the concessions to the UEC in the spring of 1929 rescued the Catholic authorities from such problems. The 1930 Act isolated Catholic schools as voluntary schools while the remaining Protestant voluntary schools were able to transfer to education committee control. The concept of 'simple Bible instruction' distinguished Protestant and Catholic schools, and by the end of the decade the terms voluntary and public elementary schools were tantamount to Catholic and Protestant schools.

'Medieval determination'

Akenson recognises that the 1930 Act discriminated against Catholic schools, but he also argues that the Act was a spurned opportunity:

> the Catholic authorities could have gained increased educational grants for Catholic children without endangering the Catholic control of the schools – if the clergy had been able to transcend their medieval determination to control the schools singlehandedly and had been willing to enter into partnership with the Catholic laity in controlling schools through newly-restructured school management committees.[92]

Akenson is correct to note that senior Catholic clerics were prepared to impose the burden of the voluntary contribution upon the Catholic laity to maintain their control of Catholic schools, and the evidence from the diocesan archives for Down and Connor indicates that they were reluctant to pursue the issue of full funding because of the potential threat to their authority, but he overstates the prospects for a durable agreement in 1930. Akenson asks: 'why did the Catholic clergy refuse to enter under the 'four and two' schemes?' and claims to be unable to provide a convincing answer.[93] A memorandum from Mageean written in 1946[94] offers an illustration of the fears of senior Catholic clerics:

> If they succeed in getting us to accept the Four and Two committee what will be the extent of their victory? Will they have taken control of the school from the Pastor at one sweep? Possibly not. It may be that in most instances the Pastor will still control his school in fact while the Committee will remain a nominal and harmless enough body. But even if this should prove to be the case (and in certain areas of the Six Counties one could have reasonable fears that the

Four and Two Committee will not be so workable) the Government will have scored a major victory. They will have substituted for the School Manager a School Committee – however harmless its composition and activities. From their point of view any subsequent step, as for example to change the form and composition of the Committee to increase its powers at the expense of the Pastors, should present less difficulty and be less radical in appearance than the change from Manager to Committee which they now seek to effect. The thin end of the wedge will have been inserted and it will only require gradual and scarcely perceptible pressure over a period of time in order to have the schools run by a Committee with effective state control.[95]

Akenson states that the Catholic authorities' 'unnecessary insistence on maintaining their sole clerical prerogatives in the management of primary schools hurt the Catholic children of Northern Ireland, for it perpetuated the usage of inadequate and outmoded school facilities'.[96] The Catholic authorities certainly cannot be excused from some responsibility for the burden of voluntary status, which an independent study in the 1990s found to still be a notable disadvantage for Catholic pupils.[97] However, a lifetime in the upper echelons of the Irish Catholic Church did not encourage a daring and innovative approach while their experience of the education committees in the 1920s did not inspire confidence in the possibility of an amicable settlement.

The education committees, Akenson claims, had 'no choice but to support financially according to very strict standards, the local transferred and provided schools in both daily expenses and capital expenditure',[98] but some Catholic managers faced severe problems collecting heating, lighting and cleaning grants, underlining their fears of unjust treatment from the education committees.[99] The 1923 Act granted voluntary schools half of the funds for heating, lighting and cleaning the school from the education committees, but these payments were a constant source of conflict between Catholic clerical managers and the education committees. Reginald Brownell, Wyse's successor as Secretary of the Ministry of Education, later claimed that the education committees disputed applications presented by Catholic voluntary managers whilst the managers of Protestant voluntary schools faced few problems collecting their grants. The Ministry often intervened to ensure the education committees fulfilled their obligations,[100] and in December 1944 they recognised that 'the arrangement has not always worked satisfactorily', conceding that many voluntary schools were cleaned by teachers and pupils.[101]

In October 1938, when senior Catholic clerics were discussing further assistance for voluntary schools following the 1938 Education Act, Mageean wrote to Tierney to recall the struggle of 1930:

> No one knows better than Mr Wyse how difficult it would be to get a grant of any kind for schools under Catholic Clerical Management from the Education Committees. He admitted to me himself that the reason behind the Section of the 1930 Act dealing with grants for Voluntary Schools was to make it possible for these schools to get grants: if it depended on the good-will of the Regional Committee they would get none, and therefore it was enacted that the Ministry itself should make the grants directly.[102]

Akenson also claims that the Catholic clergy would have been able to provide Catholic denominational teaching after 1930 if they had entered 'the rough and tumble of Ulster politics' and used the transfer deeds to guarantee Catholic denominational religious instruction for every former Catholic school.[103] The behaviour of Armagh's education committee in the 1920s emphasised the reluctance of local politicians to allow clerics, even Protestant clerics, to define their powers within public elementary schools and there was no obligation upon the education committees to accept schools offering for transfer.

The 1930 Act aimed, in the words of a Unionist MP, 'to make sure for all time that simple Bible instruction shall be given to our Protestant children in our Protestant schools'.[104] The UEC would only be satisfied with such absolute guarantees, but Akenson expected the Catholic clergy to entrust Catholic schools to education committees which, in the words of the bishops' statement of October 1923, were 'animated by the dominant spirit towards Catholics'.[105] In 1929 the Minister of Labour, John Andrews, was insisting upon 'the need for a guarantee of security that Protestant transferred schools shall not in any circumstances get under Roman Catholic control'.[106] Catholic clerics were as concerned as their Protestant counterparts to ensure that their schools did not fall under the influence of their rivals, and the education committees simply could not be trusted not to abuse their powers. The *Irish News* noted in November 1933 that only three of the thirty-seven members of Down's education committee, one of the ten attendance officers and none of the committee's administrative staff were Catholics.[107] Clearly, the education committees did not enjoy the confidence of most Catholics in Northern Ireland, and the government conceded a major Catholic demand when Craigavon stated that the capital funds would be paid by the Ministry of Education rather than the education committees.

Buckland recognises that the 1930 Education Act was 'the effective endowment of Protestantism'.[108] Akenson also notes that 'the 1930 act redefined the religious nature of the transferred and provided schools so as to preclude any Catholic school manager who had a strict sense of the law from transferring his school',[109] but he offers alternatives to the Catholic authorities' 'medieval determination' to maintain clerical control of Catholic schools. Buckland also adds, 'had the clergy been willing to share control with the laity and bend the law a little, they could have worked the system to their own advantage'.[110]

None of these options guaranteed that Catholic schools would not suffer Mageean's 'gradual and scarcely perceptible pressure' from the education committees, and the fate of the religious instruction clauses in the 1923 Act illustrated the possible threat. The 1923 Act prohibited the education committees from providing religious instruction in public elementary schools, but this law was amended within two years to allow religious instruction and was capsized in 1930 to compel 'simple Bible instruction' in public elementary schools.[111] The collapse of Londonderry's plans for non-denominational schools, though welcomed by the Catholic authorities, could not inspire confidence in the government's ability to confront Unionist, Protestant clerical and Orange Order hostility to the autonomy of Catholic schools.

Also, the power to appoint teachers, so vital for the Catholic clergy's control, was not secured by the 1930 Act. The school committee was entitled to send three names to the education committee, but there was no guarantee that the unionist majorities on the education committees would not exploit their powers to appoint Protestant applicants. Unionists would be tempted to appoint unionists as a form of patronage[112] and to prevent 'republicans' teaching in Northern Ireland's schools. The Catholic authorities could not rely upon the Ministry's officials to support Catholic school committees against the education committees, and both the law and the realities of political power in Northern Ireland favoured the right of the education committee to the final choice of teachers in public elementary schools.

Any assessment of the Catholic authorities' success in 1930 must consider their objectives. Akenson claims 'the precise nature of the Catholic demands is unknown',[113] and there was certainly some confusion amongst the Catholic authorities and nationalist politicians. In January 1930 MacRory asked for 'our fair share of money for building and enlarging schools on terms that were allowed by the British Government', because Catholic schools deserved 'corresponding concessions'[114] following the government's surrender to the UEC. Catholic clerics were reluctant to pursue the cause of equal treatment with the public elementary schools because, as Tierney explained to Mageean in November 1929, full funding 'if granted would deprive us of our moral right to ownership of the schools'.[115] Tierney's letter to Charlemont the previous August asked only for the restoration of the National Board's rate of two thirds of capital costs[116] and, a week after the Second Reading debate, the President of Maynooth, James MacCaffrey, wrote to Mageean:

> if they say that we are asking for more than the Protestant – viz, the retention of the managerial system together with full grants for building repairs etc, in a word ownership of the school . . . I should be inclined to admit that there is something in that contention.[117]

Healy and Devlin called for full funding of Catholic schools,[118] but some Nationalist politicians were also demanding only two thirds of capital grants. O'Neill's motion of March 1927, the most significant nationalist parliamentary offensive against the 1923 Act in the 1920s, proposed only that Catholic voluntary schools be allowed the grants available from the National Board.[119] The evidence from the Down and Connor Diocesan archives and the PRONI archives indicates that the Catholic authorities, eventually, aimed for a restoration of the funding policies of the National Board. Therefore, the concession announced by Craigavon in May 1930 granted the Catholic authorities three quarters of their former rate of capital funding.

The 1930 campaign centred upon the scale of capital funding, but the Act did not address the issue of repairs. Tierney explained to Mageean in May 1930 that capital grants concerned only a few Catholic schools, but repairs were a constant problem for all clerical managers,[120] and the leading Nationalist Senator, T.J. Campbell, called the cost of repairs 'a vexatious burden' in the Senate in April 1931.[121] MacRory later claimed that 'had there been any desire to give general assistance it might have been done by contributing towards repairs, but that, it appeared, would not be entertained by the Government'.[122]

Mageean was still complaining to Charlemont more than four years later that 'the refusal of a grant towards maintenance I could never understand, and has proved an insupportable burden to our Managers',[123] but by the middle of the decade the wretched economic climate limited Charlemont's scope for offering more public money, even if the political will existed within the Cabinet to assist voluntary schools.

The Catholic authorities were certainly culpable if they thought maintenance and repair costs were important issues in 1930, because they only discussed the scale of the capital grant and the influence of the education committees with Charlemont and Ministry officials. The prospect of significant funding for repairs was remote as Ministry officials would not abandon one of their most effective forms of financial coercion against Protestant clerics, especially after the 1930 Act allowed voluntary schools half their capital costs. The Ministry was determined to maintain a clear distinction between the funds available for voluntary and public elementary schools to entice Protestant clerics to transfer their schools.

PROTESTANT SCHOOLS

In 1924 the Ministry of Education's Report outlined the official version of the problem facing Northern Ireland's schools:

> The Ministry has followed a consistent policy of amalgamating small and unnecessary schools during the past year . . . Owing to the past conditions of education in Ulster it is notorious that schools have been unnecessarily multiplied in rural areas as well as in urban centres and both on grounds of economy and efficiency a centralisation and a rearrangement of educational machinery are eminently desirable and long overdue.[124]

The evidence from the Ministry's Reports indicates that public elementary schools enjoyed a considerable advantage over their voluntary counterparts throughout the late 1920s as the education committees and the Ministry attempted to refashion Northern Ireland's education system by amalgamating schools to eradicate the small denominational schools they considered such an obstacle to efficiency. The education committees spent more than £500,000 providing 55 new schools with nearly 18,000 places and nearly £200,000 renewing and improving nearly 200 transferred schools by the end of 1931.[125] The committees were clearly following the Ministry's advice by investing in large new schools and renovating existing schools[126] and, by the end of 1931, the average number of pupils in a 'provided'[127] school was 276 in contrast to 134 in a transferred school, 124 in the few 'four and two' schools, and a mere 90 pupils in voluntary schools.[128]

The tale of capital spending for voluntary schools in the 1920s is swiftly told, because they received no capital funds during the 1920s and no new voluntary schools were built between 1923 and the early 1930s.[129] Many Protestant pupils shared the disadvantages of voluntary

status with their Catholic counterparts, but the advantages of transferred status were only enjoyed by Protestant pupils.

The Ministry's Reports for the 1920s are littered with references to
the contrast between the condition of voluntary and public elementary
schools, particularly in Belfast. The Report for 1923–24 noted that the
Belfast education committee 'is taking most energetic measures for the
provision, with the least possible delay, of the new schoolhouses
which have been so urgently required in Belfast'.[130] Two years later the
Report declared that 'there can be nothing but praise and congratu-
lations for the Belfast Education Committee upon the manner in which
they attacked their task'.[131] The Ministry commended Belfast's education committee for its enthusiasm,[132] but many Protestant clerical
managers were unable to maintain their schools without the financial
advantages of transferred status. The Ministry concentrated its efforts
on the city throughout the 1920s. By the end of 1931 they had spent
nearly £350,000 providing new accommodation for more than 10,000
pupils in the city compared to £200,000 for less than 8,000 pupils in the
rest of Northern Ireland.[133]

In Belfast the principal reason for the high rate of transfers was the
need for public funds to refurbish the city's Protestant schools.
Unionists had identified the plight of Belfast's Protestant schools as an
urgent problem during the First World War when they sought to
introduce rate funding and an education authority for the city with the
Education (Belfast) Bill of 1918.[134] The Interim Report of the Lynn
committee restated the problem facing the city's schools:

> it is now estimated that at least 12,000 children of school-going age
> are without school places. Of the places available (about 60,000) a
> large proportion are in schools which are unsuitable and unsanitary,
> and which ought to be disused at the earliest possible moment.[135]

The Protestant clergy's anxiety was highlighted in April 1923 when
Archbishop D'Arcy of Armagh urged Craig to reform Belfast's schools
while retaining the status quo for the rest of Northern Ireland.[136]
Londonderry responded to these concerns by introducing education
reform in Belfast and Londonderry city on 1 October 1923 – twelve
months before the rest of Northern Ireland. The Ministry's officials
were eager to confront the grave difficulties facing the city's schools
which were overcrowded 'almost to the point of danger'.[137] By the end
of 1927 forty-two per cent of Belfast's Protestant voluntary schools had
transferred to the city's education committee with a further fifteen per
cent negotiating conditions for transfer with the education committee.[138]

The Report for 1927–28 claimed that 'the financial disability attaching to the voluntary system is small', but continued:

> The Education Act has already proved its value in the improvements which have been made in the schools transferred to the regional education committees and in the provision of new schools by these authorities. In Belfast, the transfer of a school means an immediate improvement in the building equipment, heating and cleaning. Elsewhere . . . the committees . . . aim at reaching a high standard in buildings and equipment.[139]

The following year's Report contrasted the two classes of elementary schools. 'In nearly every case', the Report stated, 'in which schools have been transferred the committees have done or are doing a great deal towards rendering the accommodation and equipment adequate and suitable', but 'the majority of voluntary schools are still unsuitable and ill equipped. Many are barely tolerable and several are so poor and so incapable of being brought up to modern requirements that their replacement is a matter of urgency'.[140] The Ministry's Report for 1929–30 maintained the theme of the poor state of voluntary schools:

> The condition of the majority of the voluntary schools tends to contrast more and more unfavourably with that of the provided and transferred schools, and even of those which have come under the management of 'four and two' committees. There is no perceptible general improvement of the voluntary schools to enable them to keep pace with their more fortunate fellows, nor is any general improvement to be hoped for.[141]

The Ministry's Reports should not be interpreted as impartial accounts. The Ministry was determined to construct a new education system based upon a smaller number of large schools, and was anxious to promote the virtues of transfer to the Protestant clergy while highlighting the problems of voluntary schools. The Ministry's efforts, combined with the obvious attractions of transfer, encouraged more than 400 schools to become public elementary schools by 1930. Public elementary schools were now educating more than 70,000 pupils – nearly half of Northern Ireland's Protestant pupils.[142]

The 1930 Act was designed 'to make the provided and transferred schools safe for Protestant children'[143] but the Ministry's statistics indicate that the 1930 Act failed to encourage the transfer of Protestant schools.[144] In 1926, ninety-three schools transferred to the control of the education committees, and the following year they were joined by at least one hundred and twenty schools.[145] The rate of transfers settled at around eighty schools for the next two years before falling to fifty-one schools in 1930.[146] The Ministry's Report suggested that this decline was probably caused by clerical managers awaiting the outcome of the UEC's negotiations with the government, but in 1931 the number of transfers fell even further to just thirty-one schools.[147] The Ministry claimed to be negotiating with the managers of 80 schools at the end of 1931, but these discussions were obviously protracted because in 1932 the education committees gained an additional forty-nine schools, and the following year they were joined by just thirty-six schools.[148] After a brief rise to forty-nine schools in 1932 (which was less than half the rate of transfer for the four years before the 1930 Act), the number of transfers declined until a mere sixteen schools opted to transfer in 1936.[149] The evidence contained in Figure 3A indicates that the 1925 Act rather than the 1930 Act was the most significant incentive for the Protestant clergy to transfer their schools.

The majority of Northern Ireland's Protestant pupils were attending public elementary schools by the end of 1930,[150] but the Ministry's Report for 1932–33 noted:

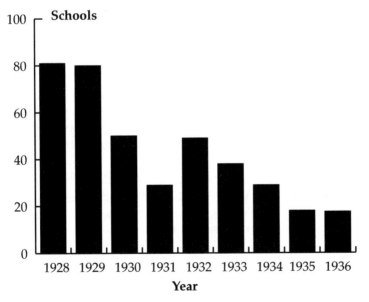

Figure 3A. Transfer of schools 1928–1936

> It is much to be regretted that voluntary managers in the north west of the Province do not take more advantage of the system of transfer. It is the considered policy of Roman Catholic managers to retain their schools as voluntary schools, but it was thought that the objections of other religious denominations to transfer had been removed by the Act of 1930.[151]

Three major factors explain the reluctance of Protestant clerics in the western counties to transfer to the education committees.

Firstly, the problem of low or falling pupil rolls facing the clerical managers of many rural schools posed fewer problems, and required less public funding, than the gross overcrowding suffered by their urban colleagues. The burden of voluntary status for many schools was restricted to finding half the costs of heating, lighting and cleaning the school and maintaining the structure of the building. Thus there was only a slight incentive to transfer in many rural areas.

Secondly, rural clerical managers suspected, rightly, that transfer would eventually lead to amalgamation with other schools. Protestant clerics would be compelled to share the patronage of control with the education committees and former clerical managers from other transferred schools. Therefore, many 'redundant schools'[152] remained outside the scope of the education committees to avoid closure. Akenson is critical of the Catholic clergy's 'medieval determination' to maintain their control of Catholic schools which 'hurt the Catholic children of Northern Ireland',[153] but many Protestant children also suffered in dilapidated schools in the 1930s simply to preserve their local clergyman's prestige and influence within the parish.

Finally, the distinction between urban and rural schools does not fully explain the variations in the scale of transfers at the end of 1934 illustrated in Figure 3B. The only explanation appears to be the Protestant clergy's distrust of Catholic education committees, a fear recognised by Dr Garrett during his tour of the education committees in the late 1920s.

Belfast enjoyed the highest rate of Protestant pupils in public elementary schools, but Armagh's education committee, the committee responsible for the crisis which culminated in the 1930 Education Act, supervised nearly eighty per cent of the county's Protestant pupils. Also, eight of every ten Antrim Protestant pupils attended public elementary schools along with two thirds of Protestant pupils in Down.

The western counties offered a notable contrast. Fermanagh's education committee was responsible for less than a third of the county's

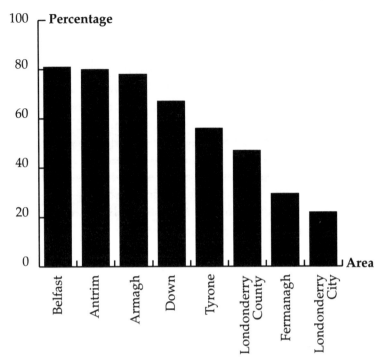

*Figure 3B. Percentage of Protestant pupils in
public elementary schools in 1934*

Protestant pupils, the three education committees for County London-derry managed the schools attended by just over forty per cent of the county's Protestant pupils, and in neighbouring Tyrone a small majority of Protestant pupils were attending public elementary schools.[154]

Belfast's education committee was the most vigorous of Northern Ireland's eighteen committees,[155] but urban congestion did not always provoke an energetic response from the local education committee. Londonderry's committee was responsible for less than a quarter of the city's Protestant pupils as the city's Catholic majority could only be governed through electoral malpractice. The fear of the Catholic electorate eventually overcoming the Corporation's machinations, and Protestant schools falling into the hands of a 'Catholic' education committee, discouraged most Protestant clerics from transferring their schools.

The variations illustrated in Figure 3B indicate that many Protestant schools were not sufficiently dilapidated to require immediate transfer, even after the 1930 Act addressed all the major concerns of the Protestant clergy. The reluctance of many Protestant schools in the west to transfer indicates that for a substantial minority of schools the voluntary contribution was a tolerable burden, and many Catholic schools probably faced similar circumstances. The cost of voluntary status was an acceptable price for the autonomy of their schools for many Catholics during the first two decades of devolved government, but this should not obscure the notable differences in the scale of investment for public elementary and voluntary schools during the 1930s. Catholic schools gradually descended to second-class schools as the education committees and the Ministry of Education invested in the new class of public elementary schools.

'A CRUSHING BURDEN'

Any analysis of the development of public elementary and voluntary schools after the 1923 Act must assess the relative condition of Catholic and Protestant voluntary schools in the final years of the Union. The evidence is conflicting, allowing for only tentative conclusions.

In 1913 a Protestant clerical delegation presented a petition to Belfast city council calling for rate aid for the city's schools. A nationalist councillor dismissed their claims, declaring that 'the Catholic population had sufficient school accommodation, built in recent years at the cost of £180,000 to the Catholic people; and he recommended that the Protestant denominations should take up the matter of school buildings in the same spirit'.[156] A major theme of the Catholic authorities' response to the campaign for education reform in the early twentieth century was to emphasise the reluctance of the Protestant denominations to fund their own schools. Clerical opposition to education reform obviously encouraged nationalist politicians to highlight the quality of Catholic schools, but unionist politicians also believed that Catholic schools were in a decent condition in 1921.

The devolved government's first Minister of Finance, Hugh Pollock, claimed at a Cabinet meeting in February 1923 that Catholic schools had received substantial sums from the National Board, and 'made a far greater use than other denominations of these State grants'.[157] Pollock's claim does not suggest that Catholic schools enjoyed an advantage over their Protestant counterparts in the final years of the

National Board. The Catholic community, by raising the necessary sums to refurbish their schools, were simply more determined to provide their own schools. In contrast to Northern Ireland's education system after 1923, there was no covert distinction between the two communities, because the National Board's funds were equally available to both Catholic and Protestant schools.

In August 1918 the Belfast School Attendance Committee published the results of a survey of the number of pupils and the places available in the city. The committee concluded that there were 17,061 pupils and only 12,700 places in the city's Catholic schools whilst 50,170 Protestant pupils were being educated in schools capable of holding only 44,350 pupils.[158] The Protestant deficit was larger – 5,820 rather than 4,361 – but there were 138 children for every 100 places in Catholic schools and 113 children for every 100 places in Protestant schools. Catholic schools in Belfast appeared to be suffering greater overcrowding than the city's Protestant schools. Protestant clerics and Unionist politicians were more forthright in their criticisms of the condition of many schools, but the statistical evidence indicates that Catholic schools were also encountering difficulties by the end of the First World War.

The 1920s proved to be a stagnant decade for voluntary schools. Public elementary schools, though educating only a minority of Northern Ireland's pupils, enjoyed a virtual monopoly of capital investment between 1923 and 1930.[159] The education committees built 73 new schools for more than 22,000 pupils, a sixth of all Protestant pupils, by the end of 1933 at a cost of nearly £700,000 and spent a further £250,000 improving and expanding transferred schools.[160]

An initial wave of investment enabled the Catholic authorities to build eight voluntary schools for just over 3,000 pupils with a grant of £50,000 by the end of March 1933.[161] By the spring of 1933, therefore, voluntary schools gained just £50,000 for 3,000 places whilst public elementary schools enjoyed nearly £1 million of investment for more than 22,000 places. The statistics contained in the Ministry's Reports also allow for a comparison of the numbers of new places, and the amounts spent on providing those places, for public elementary and voluntary schools in the 1930s. The figures indicate that the 1930 Act only tempered the disadvantage suffered by voluntary schools.

Between 1 January 1933 and 31 December 1938 more than 19,000 new places were provided by the education committees whilst between 1 April 1933 and 31 March 1939, a roughly contemporary six year period, the Ministry of Education funded less than 5,000 new places for voluntary schools.[162] The Catholic portion of the elementary school populace rose to thirty-eight per cent by 1938,[163] but Catholic schools received less than a quarter of the new places created for elementary schools in the 1930s. The evidence also underlines the persistence of the disadvantage.

The government never provided less than 2,000 new places each year for public elementary schools or more than 2,000 new places for voluntary schools. Also, the scale of investment in public elementary schools steadily increased after 1933, yet the number of voluntary school places declined in the final years of peace. In 1938 the Ministry funded fewer than 500 places while the number of new public elementary places rose beyond 5,000.[164] As Figure 3C shows, the gulf between the investment in voluntary and public elementary schools not only persisted, but was widening by the end of the 1930s.

The Ministry's financial statistics underline the significant advantage for public elementary schools. By the outbreak of war in 1939 the education committees had invested more than £1,800,000 in capital projects for public elementary schools in comparison to just over £160,000 for voluntary schools – a mere one twelfth of the combined

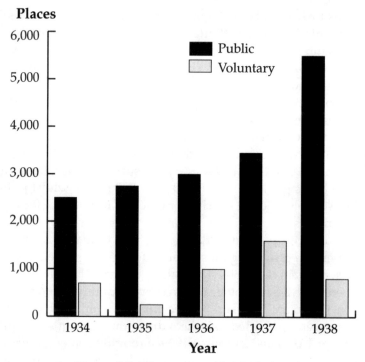

Figure 3C. Elementary school places 1934–1938

total.[165] Also, Catholic schools did not gain all of the funds available for voluntary schools. The Ministry paid nearly £143,000 to voluntary schools by May 1936, but only £120,000 to Catholic voluntary schools and nearly £5,000 of the £20,000 spent on 'four and two' schools was allocated to Protestant schools.[166] Protestant voluntary schools would gradually transfer to the control of the education committees, and be supplanted by modern schools fully funded by the education committees. For this reason the education committees did not sanction any new Protestant voluntary schools between 1923 and 1939.[167] The future for Protestant voluntary schools lay within the public elementary sector, and the Ministry would not allow Protestant schools to avoid their fate by providing capital funds.

Total capital spending on Catholic voluntary schools, both from voluntary contributions and public funds, amounted to only one sixth of the public monies invested in public elementary schools. The Ministry's financial statistics also confirm an advantage for public elementary schools after the 1930 Act, with voluntary schools receiving only one ninth of the available funds for building and renovating schools between April 1933 and March 1939.[168]

The Ministry appeared to be maintaining rather than developing the network of Catholic schools inherited from the National Board. In April 1930 Charlemont's memorandum to his colleagues outlining the condition of Catholic schools on the eve of the 1930 Act found seventy-nine 'unsuitable' schools educating 7,737 pupils.[169] The Ministry funded 7,983 new places by the end of 1939,[170] remedying only the most urgent problems facing Catholic schools at the beginning of the decade.

The costs of general maintenance for voluntary schools were also met by voluntary contributions. The Ministry did not provide statistics to allow for a definitive estimate of the cost of heating, lighting and cleaning voluntary schools during the 1930s,[171] but an article in the *Irish News* in November 1933 claimed that Catholic schools had spent £36,500 since 1930 on maintenance costs in addition to £52,800 on capital projects.[172] Thus, the statistics quoted in the *Irish News* article indicate that maintenance costs for Catholic schools probably amounted to roughly £12,000 each year. The evidence is scanty but, as Tierney explained to Mageean in May 1930, repairs and general maintenance were a problem for almost all schools. An annual figure of £12,000 for general maintenance costs does not appear to be an excessive estimate.

The 1923 Act allowed voluntary school managers to claim half of the costs of heating, lighting and cleaning their schools from the education committees, but Brownell claimed in 1945 that some voluntary schools were denied these grants by the education committees.[173] The Ministry's White Paper of December 1944 also admitted that many voluntary pupils and teachers were cleaning their own classrooms.[174] This financial liability may have been marginal, and the use of pupils to clean schools may not have constituted a notable educational or financial penalty, but the fact that some Catholic children had to do so must be viewed as evidence of petty bias against Catholic schools.

Despite the evidence from the 1918 survey by the School Attendance Committee, and a decade without capital funding, some Catholic clerics in the early 1930s claimed that many Catholic schools, particularly in Belfast, were in good condition. In February 1930 Tierney addressing the local branch of the National League,[175] declared that 'the Catholic population in Belfast was well provided with very excellent schools'.[176] Tierney may have been far away when he pronounced on Belfast's schools, but as a major figure in the Catholic authorities' campaign in 1930 he was probably aware of the state of the city's schools. Also, in April 1930 Mageean stated that Belfast's Catholics needed only three or four schools for between 700 and 900 pupils,[177] and the following June MacRory claimed 'Catholics would get very little money under the new arrangement, for they needed comparatively few new schools, having built in the past according as they became necessary'.[178]

The decision by senior Catholic clerics to emphasise the quality of Catholic schools when negotiating with the government for improved funding conditions appears difficult to explain, but the Catholic authorities faced a dilemma when discussing the state of Northern Ireland's Catholic schools. The Catholic clerics responsible for local schools would obviously urge senior clerics to emphasise their difficulties, but highlighting the failings of Catholic schools might tempt Catholic parents to send their children to public elementary schools. Nationalist politicians faithfully followed the example of the Catholic authorities, highlighting the exacting burden of the voluntary contribution rather than dwelling on the educational costs. The penalty of voluntary status for the Catholic authorities and nationalist politicians was purely a financial one. There was to be no discussion of the possible damage to the quality of education available to Catholic children.

Nationalist politicians and Catholic clerics may have evaded the issue, but the Ministry of Education recognised that Catholic schools required greater investment. In July 1935 the Parliamentary Secretary to the Minister of Education, John Hanna Robb, stated 'it would appear from the reports of the Ministry's inspectors that there is a large number which urgently require attention'.[179] Four years later Robb, now Minister of Education, presented a memorandum to his Cabinet colleagues outlining the state of education in the aftermath of the Education Act of 1938. £2 million had been invested in public elementary schools, but 'in comparison the managers of voluntary schools have done little in the way of building new schools or improving existing schools and as a result the condition of many of the voluntary schools is very unsatisfactory'.[180]

Robb included Protestant voluntary schools in his comments, but by 1939 the vast majority of voluntary schools were Catholics schools.[181] Robb was attempting to extract funds for voluntary schools from a reluctant Cabinet and may have exaggerated to emphasise his point, but the memorandum must also be viewed as further evidence that the Ministry of Education considered the condition of many Catholic schools to be 'very unsatisfactory' by the outbreak of war in 1939.

'SEDITIOUS TEACHING'

In 1923 the Final Report of the Lynn committee recommended that 'all State-aided schools should aim at cultivating a spirit of respect for the law, and obedience to constituted authority, and no aid should be given or continued to any school in which principles are inculcated subversive of the authority of the State'.[182] The importance of elementary schools promoting the distinctive unionist values of loyalty to the Crown, the Union and the British Empire became a constant theme of the debates of the Education Bill:

> We are awaiting a Bill that will not satisfy any particular denomination, but will be truly national in all its aspirations, and truly British in all its history and outlook.[183]

> it is the object of the people of Northern Ireland to apply to the children such education as will make them become good citizens of the British Empire.[184]

> I think it is important that children should at an early age be taught the duties of citizenship and patriotism to the Empire.[185]

> I gave instructions that 'God Save the King' was to be taught and sung regularly in the school. I think we should have a flag pole and put up the Union Jack.[186]

Londonderry's deputy, Robert McKeown, confirmed the government's intention to cultivate these values:

> The one thing that the Ministry has in mind is to turn out good and loyal citizens – citizens who will respect the flag. That is the intention of the Ministry, and we would not be faithful to our principles if we did not do it.[187]

The importance of generating 'good and loyal citizens' was swiftly relegated to a minor issue by the UEC as it embarked upon a sustained campaign against the 1923 Act. The dominant themes for most unionists in the 1920s were the role of the Protestant clergy and 'simple Bible instruction' within public elementary schools; only when these questions were settled could unionist politicians address their own political interests. The issue they embraced was the flying of the Union Flag.

'Put out more flags'

In June 1931 Belfast's education committee resolved that the Union Flag was to be 'recognised as a necessary part of the school equipment' in all public elementary schools, and the following year the committee progressed from *allowing* flags and flagpoles to *insisting* that all public elementary schools in the city fly the flag.[188]

Belfast's education committee was finally responding to the advice of William Miller and Dehra Parker in their supplement to the Final Report of the Lynn committee:

> The curse of this country has been in the seditious teaching which its children have been so long receiving, and loyalty to their Mother country has never been systematically brought before them. If it is considered expedient and necessary to fly the flag of State from the schools of Canada and the United States, is it even more necessary to do so in Northern Ireland? In our opinion not only should the flag be flown over every State-aided school but even the youngest children should be assembled at very frequent intervals and taught to salute the flag, thus inculcating loyalty in the children and preparing the soil in which the seeds of Civics, as they grow more advanced, could be planted.[189]

Belfast's education committee's initiative prompted a campaign from other education committees for flags and flag poles. In November 1932 Dungannon's education committee closed all public elementary schools for the visit of the Prince of Wales and it ruled that 'all schools wholly or partially funded by the education authority' should fly the Union Flag.[190] In August 1934 Larne's education committee requested the Ministry's permission for all the committee's schools to fly 'the emblem of the Empire', and in December Magherafelt's education committee wrote to the Ministry with similar demands. The Ministry was reluctant to sanction such spending, but eventually approved both applications.[191] Also, every education committee spent considerable amounts of public money providing souvenirs for King George V's Silver Jubilee celebrations in 1935.[192] The education committees' patriotic enthusiasm contrasted with the apparent apathy of the former Protestant clerical managers, because the education committees also provided flags and flagpoles for many transferred schools built before 1921 where local clerics had not invested in a flagpole for the Union Flag.[193]

The education committees did not insist upon every public elementary school flying the Union Flag until the early 1930s, ten years after the advent of devolved power. This delay was not simply caused by the Protestant clergy's education problems distracting unionist politicians. In November 1927 the education committee in Belfast, where the Unionist Party faced a challenge from the Northern Ireland Labour Party (NILP) and assorted independent unionists, resolved to buy the Union Flag for every *new* public elementary school 'for instruction in Citizenship', but there was no response from the other seventeen education committees to Belfast's initiative.[194] Belfast's decision of June 1931 provoked an enthusiastic response, but the nadir of an economic depression was an inappropriate moment for spending public monies on flag poles and souvenirs. The flag campaign obviously involved considerable expense to purchase flag poles and flags, yet less than eighteen months later Belfast's Board of Guardians provoked the worst riot in Belfast since the early 1920s by refusing to increase the rates of unemployment relief.[195] The timing was prompted by the electoral challenge posed by the NILP and assorted populist unionists who once more threatened the dominance of the Unionist Party.

Also, it is notable that the flag campaign did not encompass Catholic voluntary schools. Dungannon's education committee's resolution of November 1932 called for 'partially funded' schools to fly the flag, but the education committees concentrated on public elementary schools, where almost every pupil was a Protestant. The aim of the flag campaign was to counter a potential electoral threat rather than antagonise the nationalist minority by insisting upon displays of loyalty to the Crown. Government ministers certainly played a disreputable role in souring community relations in the early 1930s, but the flag campaign did not provoke a reaction from nationalist politicians or Catholic clerics.[196]

The Catholic authorities may have been convinced of the integrity of Charlemont and senior Ministry officials such as McQuibban, Wyse and Brownell, but the Ministry was often prey to the more 'Orange' elements within the Unionist Party. The inability of Ministry officials to prevent such superfluous spending at a time when teachers' salaries were reduced by 7.5 per cent[197] underlined their weakness against concerted unionist agitation (The fate of Gaelic language grants in the early 1930s, just as the education committees were embarking on their campaign to install flags in every public elementary school, only emphasised the limits of Charlemont's power to thwart the 'Orange' unionists.)

'Erse'

The Christian Brothers

The Ministry's treatment of the Irish Christian Brothers in the 1920s underlined its efforts to accommodate Catholic and nationalist senti-ment within the education system. The Catholic authorities refused to accept the 1923 Act's conditions for transfer to either education committee control or 'four and two' committees, but the Ministry secured a significant success when the Irish Christian Brothers agreed to create 'four and two' committees for their eight schools.

In July 1925 the Order's leaders approached the Ministry to discuss the possibility of easing their severe financial problems by accepting 'four and two' status.[198] McQuibban and Wyse visited the Order the following month, but they found four major obstacles to closer relations with the Ministry of Education. The Brothers wished to publish their own books and train their own teachers, and McQuibban and Wyse noted both the conspicuous presence of religious emblems in the schools and the hour of Gaelic teaching each day as significant problems.

A Ministry inspector studied the Order's books and found both the religious and 'national' features unacceptable. The inspector objected to the denominational prayers and the reference to Mary as the 'Mother of God' in the Order's religious education texts – he found one page to be 'disgraceful'. Many of the Order's history books were also viewed as unsuitable, particularly their treatment of the 1641 rebellion.[199]

Wyse, despite the inspector's criticisms, recommended further dis-cussions with the Order. He recognised that the Christian Brothers' schools were viewed by many unionists as 'hotbeds of sedition', but he believed the Order's leaders were willing to compromise.[200] Wyse's optimism initially proved to be misplaced, as in March 1926 McQuibban told Charlemont that 'it is evident that, unless there is a change of spirit . . . the Christian Brothers' Elementary Schools are not fitted to come into connection with the Ministry'.[201] Wyse's confidence was finally vindicated in May when two senior Brothers met Charlemont to discuss terms for transfer. The Order's leaders accepted the Ministry's books for use in their schools, and from 1 April 1927 the Christian Brothers' schools were operating as 'four and two' schools.[202]

The Christian Brothers episode highlighted the cultural implications of education committee control of Catholic schools. The PRONI files contain no references to the Order's fears of the education committees, and the financial arrangements also appeared to be secondary issues compared to the problems surrounding the Order's books and the presence of religious emblems within the schools. The religious symbols the Christian Brothers viewed as essential for their religious work, such as a crucifix, a font of holy water and religious placards, were judged to be unacceptable by the Ministry's inspectors. Wyse instructed the school to remove all these symbols, and the Order consented with the exception of the crucifix. Londonderry insisted on the removal of the crucifix, but Charlemont later allowed the school to retain its sole religious symbol.[203]

The response of Wyse, a Catholic, and Londonderry, probably the most liberal minister in Craig's first government, to the presence of such standard Catholic emblems underlined the scale of the chasm between the devolved government and the Catholic authorities on the nature of religious practice within elementary schools. Protestant clerics were satisfied with regular 'Bible instruction' classes, but the Catholic authorities insisted that the Catholic faith permeate every aspect of a Catholic school to preserve 'the power of Catholic truth'.[204] These evident and conspicuous symbols provoked discontent, as highlighted by Dominic Murray's study of a Catholic and Protestant primary school in the 1980s. A Protestant teacher recounted to Murray his impressions of a visit to a Catholic school; 'It's hard to escape the view' he claimed 'that a special show is being put on for our benefit . . . They must know that these are the very things that we object to, yet still they are flaunted everywhere'. It should also be noted that Murray found many Catholic teachers hostile to the neighbouring Protestant schools' use of the Union Flag.[205]

A minor campaign against Gaelic in the late 1920s prompted a Ministry circular of March 1928 which limited the scope for Gaelic teaching, but even these restrictions were insufficient for some unionists. An obscure organisation called the Loyalty League declared that the funding of Gaelic was 'equal to subsidising an anti-British and disloyal faction, whose politico religious activities are subversive of Ulster Protestantism'.[206] The Secretary of the League wrote to Craigavon in July 1928 claiming that 'the language is of no practical utility, but may be of much value to incipient traitors, as a means of fomenting trouble'.[207]

This campaign against Gaelic also failed to abolish the grants because Ministry officials succeeded in convincing Charlemont and his colleagues that the language was an irritant rather than a profound challenge. Also, as Wyse explained to a colleague in June 1928, 'it was clear that any proposal to prohibit it altogether would give certain parties an opportunity of raising a grievance and at the same time intensify the desire of a section of the people to apply themselves to its study'.[208] The Loyalty League was a peripheral body within Ulster Unionism, but the Ministry was to struggle to deflect such resentment from more influential quarters by the early 1930s.

The bitter atmosphere of the early 1930s led a renewed campaign against 'Erse' in March 1933 led by the Unionist MP William Grant. Grant was swiftly joined by the independent unionists Thomas Henderson and John Nixon.[209] The first offensive against the grants for Gaelic teaching in the early 1920s highlighted the futility of learning the language, but Grant was more honest when he simply stated 'the only people interested in this language are the avowed enemies of Northern Ireland'.[210] The second major campaign, like the first, met no challenge from Nationalist MPs. Devlin led the Nationalist contingent out of the Commons in May 1932 following a dispute with the Speaker,[211] leaving the case for the grants to Robb. He fared poorly in the Commons against such determined criticism.

Charlemont opposed the suspension of the payments, claiming that the abolition of grants for junior classes had been followed by a revival in Catholic schools. Grant payments trebled between 1927–28 and 1932–33 when eighteen per cent of all elementary Catholic pupils were being examined in the subject.[212] Charlemont appeared unsympathetic to the language, preferring to maintain the Ministry's strategy of obstruction, because, as he explained to Craiganon, 'it is quite impossible that anyone could learn Irish from two half hours per week'. He argued that the abolition of the grant could lead to an explosion of interest amongst Catholics in which 'the very dogs of Belfast – at any rate, the Falls Road dogs – will bark in Irish'.[213]

The Ministry's claims that prohibition would only encourage the language should not be viewed as conclusive evidence that Ministry officials shared Grant's and Henderson's antipathy for Gaelic. Ministry officials recognised that the language was the proverbial red rag to many unionist bulls, and their aim was to limit the restrictions upon the language. Senior officials probably advised Charlemont to emphasise the futility of restricting the language, rather than appeal for respect for Gaelic cultural values, to convince his colleagues to retain the grants.

Charlemont's arguments, and the high marks for the schools' Gaelic teaching from the Ministry's inspectors,[214] failed to persuade the Cabinet. The following week Robb informed the Commons that the payments for Gaelic were to be terminated from the end of the school year. He also announced that the post of Organiser of the Irish Language, vacant since 1921, was to be abolished. These announcements were greeted with cheers from Unionist MPs, with the Grand Master of the Orange Order, Sir John Davison, declaring that 'the teaching of Irish has been largely a matter of political propaganda, and of disloyal propaganda at that'.[215]

The fate of the grants underlined the potential threat from greater state influence in Northern Ireland's Catholic schools. Three MPs compelled the government to abolish the grants, against the advice of the Minister of Education, after just five weeks of campaigning in the Commons. This defeat of the Ministry of Education emphasised the fragility of any settlement between the Catholic authorities and a government apparently unable to withstand a sustained challenge from the more intolerant elements within Ulster Unionism.

The 'particularly petty decision'[216] to abolish the language grants may be explained by Craig's 'almost indecent degree of political timidity'.[217] However, his principal political task was to preserve the unity of the Unionist Party, especially when the depths of an economic depression threatened to expose fractures in the unionist coalition. Wilfred Spender claimed in 1927 that the most effective means of extracting concessions from the government was 'to make yourself unpleasant and then interview the Prime Minister',[218] and the critics of the Ministry's Gaelic policy adopted a similar course. The involvement of the two independent unionists, Henderson and Nixon, only exacerbated Craig's problem, because he could not appeal to party unity to deflect the campaign. Finally, the absence of Nationalist MPs undermined the prospects for preserving the grants. Craig and his ministers were unlikely to protect a grant that Nationalist MPs themselves were unwilling to defend in the Commons.

Gaelic antagonised numerous Unionist MPs, but the language attracted minor interest in most Catholic schools. Ten thousand children were learning the language in 140 Catholic elementary schools at the end of 1933.[219] Therefore, eighty per cent of Catholic schools were not offering the language and less than one Catholic pupil in seven was studying Gaelic.[220] Also, the abolition of payments, contrary to Charlemont's prediction, *did* undermine interest in the language. The numbers studying Gaelic fell by more than a thousand by the end of 1936.[221]

The problems of learning a 'foreign' language at such a young age partly accounts for the lack of interest in Gaelic in Catholic elementary schools, because Gaelic was popular in Northern Ireland's Catholic secondary schools. In 1933, 1,225 of the 3,732 pupils sitting the Secondary School Certificate Examinations were entered for the Gaelic exam.[222] The precise number of Catholic secondary school pupils is unknown, but it is unlikely that Catholics comprised significantly more than one third of secondary school pupils.[223] This prevalence of Gaelic in secondary schools was probably not motivated by 'Fenian' sentiment. There were practical reasons for graduates of Catholic secondary schools learning a language that was an entry requirement for the civil service and almost all public sector posts in the Irish Free State. Few parents would wish to exclude their children from working for one of the largest employers on the island of Ireland.

A large number of Catholic teachers were also learning to teach the language. At St Mary's in London, despite Wyse's hope that their stay in London would 'promote breadth of view and loyalty to the Empire',[224] thirty-three of the forty-four students from Northern Ireland were learning the language, whilst in Belfast fifty-three of St Mary's college's seventy-two graduates studied Gaelic.[225] The fact that eighty per cent of Catholic schools did not offer the subject did not discourage the majority of Catholic trainee teachers from studying Gaelic, because the ability to teach Gaelic was an essential qualification for any teacher hoping to work in the Irish Free State.

The rest of the 1930s formed a relatively calm interlude. The Nationalist MPs drifted back to the Commons, but only Campbell raised the issue of the Gaelic grants as a 'hardy annual' almost every March until the outbreak of war.[226] Clerical interest in the loss of the grants was also negligible[227] whilst the Ministry's threat to amalgamate adjacent girls' and boys' elementary schools in the autumn of 1934 provoked a fierce response.[228] Clerical rather than 'national' issues still dominated the debate surrounding Catholic schools in the 1930s.

Gaelic enjoyed a modest revival at the end of the decade. By the end of 1940, 11,570 pupils were studying Gaelic, rising three years later to over 12,000 pupils.[229] Unionist opponents of the language also revived their interest, and in 1942 Davison wrote to the Prime Minister, John Andrews, asking for Gaelic to be prohibited in all schools. Andrews sought the advice of Robb, who tartly replied that 'the choice is for them, and is part of that freedom of the individual for which we profess to be fighting this war'.[230]

The Ministry of Education convinced the Cabinet, even when led by such an intolerant figure as Andrews, that the prohibition of Gaelic would be both unjust and unwise. Gaelic in Catholic schools remained a nuisance rather than a threat for most Unionist MPs, and the meagre interest amongst Catholics themselves, even after the revival of the early 1940s, did not appear to warrant a sustained offensive against the language.

THE 1938 EDUCATION ACT

The evidence shows that voluntary schools continued to suffer a profound disadvantage in the 1930s, but the 1930 Act heralded nearly fifteen years of relative calm for Northern Ireland's schools. The Catholic authorities and nationalist politicians, though still dissatisfied by the failure to provide two thirds of the costs of capital projects or any public funds for repairs, appeared to accept the 1930 Act. There were few lengthy and bitter education debates in the Commons in the 1930s.

Nationalist MPs raised the issue during the annual debate on the Ministry of Education's Estimates, but the criticism was only an item on the list of nationalist grievances until 1938 when the government introduced an Education Bill to raise the school leaving age to 15 years.[231] The economic situation remained dire, but the Cabinet was determined to emulate the British government's Education Act of 1936. The Bill would clearly place greater demands upon Catholic elementary schools and in July 1938 a delegation from the Catholic Clerical Managers' Association (CCMA) visited the Ministry to complain of the 'great difficulty' collecting the voluntary contribution and bid for financial assistance.[232]

Nationalist politicians once more offered ardent support to the Catholic authorities. The Nationalist leader, T.J. Campbell, bluntly stated during the Second Reading of the Bill 'this latest burden is rubbing salt into the sores and wounds . . . of the Catholic people of Northern Ireland'. He called for the Ministry to follow the course set by the London government by providing additional public funds to assist voluntary schools to fulfill their new responsibilities.[233] The 1936 Act granted voluntary schools seventy-five per cent of the total costs of new buildings with only the minor condition that the trustees allow religious instruction for other denominations.[234] The Catholic authorities, with no more than a handful of Protestants in Catholic schools, were obviously eager for similar treatment.

Robb was sympathetic to the CCMA's demands. He told his colleagues that the underlying purpose of the 1923 Act was to allow voluntary schools the same scale of funding as the grants from the National Board. The 'four and two' committees had failed to serve this purpose, and he proposed allowing the education committees to provide a sixth of the cost of capital spending for voluntary schools, thus raising the capital grant to the traditional rate of two thirds of the total cost.[235] The CCMA countered with a proposal for a two-thirds grant direct from the Ministry, and the two parties appeared to be approaching a settlement. Robb was amenable to a compromise, and in May 1939 he wrote:

> I believe that if a reasonably suitable standard of school accommo-
> dation throughout Northern Ireland is to be attained and maintained,
> some amendment of the present system of grants towards the cost of
> erection, improvement and equipment of schools is essential.[236]

Negotiations continued during the first half of 1939 on the vexed issue of the education committees' role in Catholic schools, but the Cabinet refused to consider any new arrangement with the Catholic authorities. The discussions were postponed for a year in June 1939,[237] and three months later the outbreak of war ended all hope of a new settlement.[238]

The role of the education committees within Catholic schools was once more the decisive issue. The education committees probably justified clerical fears, but their potential for limiting investment in voluntary schools was constrained by the Ministry providing seventy-five per cent of the capital grant. Education committees were thus obliged to supply a sum equal to one third of the Ministry's grant to the voluntary schools, allowing Ministry officials to set the amount of public money given to voluntary schools. Robb offered a reasonable agreement to the Catholic authorities in 1938 without insisting upon 'four and two' committees, one of the few occasions when the 'four and two' question was only a minor problem.

The Catholic authorities almost gained two thirds of capital funding in 1938, which would have satisfied the aspirations of many senior Catholic clerics in 1930. An uncompromising persistence had been successful in past contests, but such obduracy proved an unfortunate choice once the outbreak of war in 1939 ended all hopes of reform. The Catholic community was to wait nearly a decade before the capital grant was increased to sixty-five per cent, slightly below the two third rate offered in 1938, and only in 1968 did the capital grant rise above the amount offered to the Catholic authorities in 1938.

Farren claims that nationalist criticism 'had become almost ritualistic',[239] and by 1942 even a Nationalist MP referred to their protests as a 'hardy annual'.[240] The coming of peace was to end such complacency, as education returned to the forefront of political debate in Northern Ireland.

CONCLUSION

The contest for improved funding in 1930 was the Catholic authorities' most successful campaign during the fifty years of devolved government. They exploited the opportunities available in 1930, employing every asset in the Northern Ireland Parliament, the *Irish News* and public meetings to present their case.

The events surrounding the 1930 Act demonstrated the importance of concessions to the Protestant clergy and the resolute support of nationalist politicians. The obligation upon teachers in public elementary schools to teach 'simple Bible instruction', and the guarantees of seats on both the school committees and the education committees for the Protestant clergy, allowed moderates within the Cabinet and the Ministry of Education to argue for a compromise with the Catholic authorities. These arguments were strengthened by the assertive campaign of the Nationalist Party.

Senior Catholic clerics could be satisfied with their success against the 'Orange' elements within the Unionist Party who were opposed to any accommodation with the Catholic clergy. After 1930 voluntary schools secured two thirds of the previous rate for capital funding. Only the Catholic authorities' distrust of the education committees in 1938 prevented Catholic clerical managers receiving the traditional two thirds grant of the National Board, which was also the rate available to their clerical colleagues in the Irish Free State.

The conflict in 1930 centred on the questions of finance and control, with the government consistently demanding greater influence for the education committees and the Catholic authorities resisting the involvement of education committees in Catholic schools. The *Irish*

News summary of the Ministry of Education's Report in February 1932 typified the nationalist minority's view of local councils and the education committees when it stated 'the County Councils are simply Orange lodges and Freemason lodges, who will not give a Catholic, no matter how qualified, any job for which there is a Protestant candidate'.[241] Catholics feared that any Catholic school supervised by the education committees would suffer a similar preference for Protestant teachers.

The government initially adopted a liberal attitude towards the Gaelic language by preserving the special grants for Gaelic classes and creating the post of Organiser of the Irish Language. This liberalism was only diluted by ministers' fears of independent unionists during the depression and the absence of Nationalist MPs to counter the 'Orange' offensive against the language grants in 1933. The grants were abolished, but Gaelic was still available in any school in Northern Ireland willing to teach the language.

The conflict surrounding the Gaelic language was a tepid struggle for most nationalists and unionists. Farren overstates the hostility to the language when he claims 'official attitudes towards Irish had been anything but sympathetic from the very establishment of the ministry. Only the fear of provoking greater opposition within the nationalist community had prevented the ministry from taking more radical measures to curtail the teaching of Irish'.[242] The Ministry placed only minor obstacles in the way of the language and most Catholic elementary schools, regardless of the special grants, preferring not to teach Gaelic. The loss of the grants did not provoke a significant reaction from either the Catholic authorities or Nationalist politicians. The grants were mentioned in the Commons, but only as one article on a list of grievances.

The other major 'national' issue of the 1930s – the flag campaign – was also a minor affair. The timing of the campaign was partly determined by the electoral threat of independent unionists and the NILP as the economy disintegrated in the early 1930s and it was also the first 'unionist' education issue to attract widespread interest. Education policy in the first decade of devolved government was dominated by the struggle of the Protestant clergy to gain effective control of public elementary schools. The 1930 Act resolved all their major problems, and Unionists were keen to emphasise loyalty to the Union and the Empire, issues which had been important during the debates of the Education Bill in the autumn of 1922.

The antagonisms of the early 1930s only underlined the truce reigning for most of the 1920s and 1930s. Gaelic was unpopular amongst unionists, but few within the Unionist Party consistently campaigned against the language, and this minority only overcame the Cabinet's apathetic support for the language grants when the Unionist Party was susceptible to defections to the right. 'Gaelic' Catholic schools were always vulnerable to the 'Orange' elements within Ulster Unionism, but they suffered surprisingly few defeats after 1933.

The burden of voluntary status in the seven decades after the 1923 Act was a blend of financial and educational disadvantages, and in the late 1920s the financial cost of the voluntary contribution was relatively slight, confined to only half the cost of heating, lighting and cleaning the schools and the cost of repairs. An *Irish News* article indicated that the annual voluntary contribution towards internal maintenance costs after 1923 was £12,000. However, the claims by a senior Ministry official in the 1940s, and the statement in the 1944 White Paper that voluntary schools were not receiving their share of internal maintenance grants,[243] also implied that the cost to the Catholic community of heating, lighting and cleaning their schools was more than £12,000 each year. Therefore, during the sixteen years from 1923 to 1939 the costs of internal maintenance was probably close to £200,000.

There was no voluntary contribution for the cost of new voluntary schools in the 1920s because there were no new voluntary schools, but after 1930 the Ministry paid nearly £160,000 for capital projects. Thus, Northern Ireland's Catholics found nearly £160,000 to build new schools, bringing the total voluntary contribution before 1939 to more than £350,000, and this figure does not include the cost of repairs to school buildings. The price of autonomous Catholic schools between the wars translates to nearly £10 million in 1996 prices, a substantial sum during an era of economic hardship. This sacrifice only maintained the condition of Northern Ireland's Catholic schools, because the number of new places created after 1930 almost corresponds to the Ministry's estimate of the number of Catholic pupils suffering unacceptable conditions in the spring of 1930.

The educational cost of voluntary status during the first two decades of devolved government is difficult to assess, but there is no evidence of a significant deterioration in the quality of education provided in Catholic schools. In October 1935, Ministry officials drafted a list of 'condemned' schools which found 131 very unsatisfactory schools, and of these 56 were Catholic schools, only marginally above the proportion of Catholics in the elementary school populace.[244] So, twelve years after the 1923 Act the condition of Catholic schools appears to have been broadly similar to that of Protestant voluntary schools. The most significant disadvantage arose from the lack of improvement for Catholic schools at a time when the education committees invested nearly £2 million renewing public elementary schools. Voluntary schools were to languish as second-class schools compared to the 'palatial' public elementary schools.[245]

CHAPTER FOUR

Palatial schools

Victory and peace in 1945 brought their own problems for the devolved government in Northern Ireland. The Cabinet decided, after some initial doubts, to follow the course set by the Labour government in London and introduce profound changes to the welfare system. The hope of maintaining parity with the rest of the United Kingdom only partly explains why the Unionists, traditional allies of the Conservatives, emulated the Labour government's social reforms. Northern Ireland was not immune to the shift to the left evident in the rest of the Europe at the end of the war. The NILP won more than 66,000 votes in the 1945 elections, compared to less than 20,000 votes in 1938, and independent labour candidates won more than 47,000 votes, in contrast to less than 5,000 votes seven years before. The presence of five 'labour' MPs in the Commons offered a warning to the Unionist Party that it could not rely upon the politics of the border to preserve its dominance.

The fifteen years after 1945 witnessed significant social and economic progress, but the political atmosphere for most of the 1950s was poisoned by the events surrounding the decision of the Dublin government to withdraw from the Commonwealth and declare the Free State to be a republic in 1949. Brooke, following Craigavon's example in the aftermath of the Free State's 1937 constitution which proclaimed sovereignty over the whole island of Ireland, called an election. The major political parties in the Free State announced their intention to aid the nationalists in the forthcoming election, and a collection outside every Catholic church in the Free State funded the campaigns of a record number of nationalist contests.[1]

Brooke seized the opportunity to assail the NILP for its tepid support of the Union and scored the greatest success for the Unionist Party since 1921. Unionists gained four seats, increased their share of the vote and eliminated the NILP in the Commons. Brooke's objective was to counter the threat from the NILP, but the 'Chapel Gate' election also soured relations between nationalists and unionists for nearly a decade.

Many nationalists once more opted for abstention and in 1955 two Sinn Féin candidates were elected to Westminster, gaining the largest republican vote since the early 1920s. The leadership of the IRA mistook this disillusionment for positive support for a republican insurgency and launched 'Operation Harvest' in the winter of 1956. The damage to community relations was lessened only by the abject failure of the IRA's campaign, but internment and the extensive use of the Ulster Special Constabulary ensured that tensions persisted until the end of the decade.

The Catholic authorities were fortunate that the government reformed the education system before the 1949 election, and that the Minister of Education during this vital period was the most liberal minister in the government. He secured increased funding for Catholic schools despite the opposition of most of his colleagues. After 1949, the revival of traditional antagonisms was reflected in the appointment of the most illiberal of Northern Ireland's twelve education ministers, and the 1950s proved to be difficult times for Catholic schools.

EDUCATION REFORM

The settlement with the Catholic authorities hastily outlined by Craig in May 1930 brought fourteen years of peace until the government published *Educational Reconstruction in Northern Ireland* in December 1944.[2] The document provoked an intense conflict within the Unionist Party which eventually led to the resignation of the Minister of Education, threatened Basil Brooke's position as Prime Minister[3] and caused trouble for the Cabinet until the late 1950s.[4] The White Paper was the devolved government's response to the British Education Act of 1944 and, though ministers were reluctant to follow the 'reforming zeal'[5] of the British government, they eventually opted for a substantial reform of Northern Ireland's secondary schools. The most significant long-term aim of the White Paper was the creation of a network of new secondary intermediate schools[6] and the expansion of the existing grammar schools with a sharp division between 'primary' and 'secondary' education from the age of eleven.

The Intermediate Education Board's report for 1920 plainly stated that 'the whole edifice of secondary education in Ireland is toppling to destruction' and warned 'if something is not done immediately to place Irish secondary education in the position of financial equality with that of Great Britain, it is impossible to see how the complete disruption of the system can be avoided'.[7] The first Parliamentary

Secretary to the Ministry for Education, Robert McKeown, confessed to the Commons in 1921 that 'secondary education was handed over to the Northern Parliament in a condition which is absolutely and undoubtedly deplorable'.[8] However, the next twenty-five years saw only marginal progress as clerics and politicians concentrated upon Northern Ireland's elementary schools. In 1939 there were less than 15,000 secondary school pupils in Northern Ireland's seventy-five secondary schools, and only nine of these schools were managed by education committees.[9]

The White Paper proposed free education in the new secondary intermediate schools whilst the Ministry would provide sufficient scholarships for grammar schools to ensure 'no Ulster child who is deemed fitted to profit by attendance at a senior secondary school shall be denied access to such a school by reason of his parents' inability to defray the cost'.[10] The White Paper also proposed lowering the age of compulsory attendance from six to five years and raising the school leaving age from fourteen to fifteen years, with further powers to raise the age to sixteen years.[11]

Education was to play a key role in the emergent social welfare system, so the education committees were to be responsible for a variety of new services such as free medical and dental treatment, daily meals and milk for all schoolchildren. The government aimed to ensure that these additional tasks were accomplished by replacing the eighteen education committees with eight education authorities. Belfast, Londonderry City, Armagh, Down and Fermanagh all retained their existing structures, but the numerous committees in County Londonderry, Tyrone and Antrim were replaced by county education authorities.[12]

Ministry officials had been dissatisfied with the performance of the smaller education committees since the 1920s. In 1933 they attempted to amalgamate the committees in Antrim and Tyrone, but the opposition of local Unionist notables, concerned at the potential loss of patronage to a county committee, frustrated their plans.[13] In July 1944 the Minister of Education, Colonel Samuel Hall-Thompson, outlined the Ministry's criticisms of the education committees:

> An experience of twenty years has shown the Ministry of Education that these small Regional Education Committees are, in many cases, more a hindrance than a help to education . . . Many of their members are persons of very limited education themselves, out of touch with modern educational theory and practice and taking no real interest in anything connected with education except the conserving of the rates and the appointment of teachers in local schools.[14]

The education committees in Antrim, Londonderry and Tyrone struggled to develop elementary schools in the 1920s and 1930s, and they appeared incapable of building a network of new secondary schools. There were no ulterior political motives for this reorganisation as all the education committees in Antrim, Londonderry and Tyrone remained 'safe' for Protestant children. The restructuring appeared to be based solely on the Ministry's preference for fewer education committees and offered the first evidence of the Ministry's more assertive approach. Education reform was to provoke severe discord within the Unionist Party, but the smaller education committees perished without complaint from Unionist MPs.[15]

Reconstruction would clearly be expensive, and a substantial number of the proposed new schools would be Catholic voluntary schools. The government offered to ease the burden of voluntary status by granting sixty-five per cent of all capital costs, as well as the full cost of heating, cleaning and lighting the schools, but only for 'four and two' committees because 'the Government are satisfied that . . . it will be necessary to provide increased financial assistance to the voluntary manager; they are equally satisfied that where additional assistance is given the principle of representation must be observed'.[16]

These proposals charted a similar course to developments in England and Wales, and attracted few protests from Unionist MPs. However, two measures of particular importance to politicians and clerics – the abolition of the obligation upon teachers in the new 'county' schools[17] to teach 'simple Bible instruction' and the Cabinet's decision in March 1946 to raise the grant for voluntary schools to sixty-five per cent without demanding a 'four and two' committee – provoked a profound dispute within the Unionist Party. The conflict was so intense that the newly elected MP for Bannside, Captain Terence O'Neill, found the education debate to be 'the sole topic of conversation' when he arrived at Stormont in November 1946.[18]

The 'conscience clause'

The government's decision to follow the trends set by the 1944 Education Act raised the tender subject of religious education in 'county' schools. The 1944 Act directed every primary and secondary school in England and Wales to begin the day with 'an act of collective worship',[19] and the Cabinet realised that the Protestant clergy would seek a similar condition in Northern Ireland's forthcoming law.[20] The Protestant clerical campaign initially centred on the fate of religious instruction in secondary schools,[21] but in the summer of 1944 a new problem arose to overshadow all other issues. Hall-Thompson informed his Cabinet colleagues that the Attorney General, John MacDermott, was insisting upon a specific reference in the White Paper prohibiting the use of public funds for any religious service; a demand that challenged the right of the Northern Ireland Parliament to compel teachers to teach 'simple Bible instruction' in public elementary schools.[22]

MacDermott's decision left the Cabinet facing the unpalatable prospects of alienating powerful Protestant clerical interests, risking the Education Bill being ruled *ultra vires* by the Judicial Committee of the Privy Council, or having their own Attorney General refuse to grant a certificate for the Bill.[23] MacDermott suggested approaching the Home Office for an amendment to the Government of Ireland Act to avoid a potential confrontation, and his colleagues eagerly followed his advice.[24]

Protestant clerics were naturally angered by the threat to a central tenet of the 1930 Act, and Hall-Thompson met nine senior Protestant clerics in July 1944 to ease their concerns. He found them in a belligerent mood. 'The discussion', he told his colleagues, 'was at times very confused and, once, rather heated. Irrelevancies were dragged in and I had some trouble to persuade the deputation to discuss the draft clauses sensibly'. Hall-Thompson only pacified the clerics with the promise of an amendment to the 1920 Act.[25]

MacDermott's departure in November 1944 did not ease the government's problem as William Lowry swiftly confirmed his predecessor's opinion:

> Prophecy as to the result of litigation is notoriously hazardous – even more so than the outcome of horse racing – but as at present advised my opinion is that paying for Bible instruction out of public funds is and would be *ultra vires*.[26]

The government's chief law officers were no longer willing to sanction Craig's settlement with the Protestant clergy and the Orange Order of 1930,[27] and the government attempted an uneasy compromise. The White Paper promised that 'the school day shall begin with collective worship on the part of the pupils', but also stated that, though the government was confident that teachers were 'only too glad to exercise the high privilege of promoting the spiritual welfare of their pupils', the Government of Ireland Act prohibited any religious test for teachers in public elementary schools.[28]

The promise of an amendment to the Government of Ireland Act had appeased some senior Protestant clerics,[29] but the government's problems deepened early in January 1945 when the Home Office refused to consider an amending law.[30] The central purpose of the 1920 Act was to isolate Northern Ireland from British party politics, and politicians and officials in London were determined to maintain a discreet distance from any potential controversy. Also, with the Germans still in the Low Countries and Parliament considering the first elements of a massive legislative workload for the new welfare system, the British government was troubled by more important problems than the fate of 'simple Bible instruction' in Northern Ireland's schools.

In contrast to 1929, the Home Office was actively discouraging Brooke and his colleagues from changing the law. In October 1944 the Permanent Secretary of the Home Office, Sir Alexander Maxwell, told Ministry of Education officials that he considered MacDermott was imposing unnecessary restrictions upon the devolved government.[31] The following January the British Attorney General, Sir Donald Somervell, also argued that the Free State Agreement Act of 1923, the British Empire's settlement with the Irish Free State, allowed Irish clerics to maintain effective control of their own denominational schools. Somervell felt the devolved government could adopt a similar approach without provoking any objection from the London government.[32]

The threat of intervention by the Home Office was a constant concern for politicians and civil servants in almost every ministry in Northern Ireland, but the evidence from the 'conscience clause' conflict of the 1940s highlights, once again, the reluctance of politicians and civil servants in London to become entangled in Northern Ireland's affairs. Two other major interests, the Ministry of Education and the Catholic authorities, were not interested in the fate of the compulsion clause in the 1930 Act.

Hall-Thompson and the Ministry's officials preferred to maintain the status quo on the practical grounds that the 1930 Act had not aroused objections from either the Home Office in London or teachers in Northern Ireland.[33] Hall-Thompson even threatened to send the Education Bill to the Judicial Committee of the Privy Council for its ruling if the Attorney General refused to grant a certificate.[34]

The Catholic authorities were enthusiastic advocates of 'sound denominational education'. They regarded Catholic religious teaching to be the primary task of a Catholic teacher in a Catholic school, and no Catholic cleric would favour undermining a teacher's obligation to provide religious instruction – even Protestant religious instruction – in public elementary schools. Catholic clerics were dedicated to retaining a central place for religion in Catholic schools, and any drift towards greater secularism in Protestant schools would be unwelcome.[35] Also, the insistence upon teachers providing 'simple Bible instruction' in public elementary schools strengthened the Catholic minority's grievance against the 1930 Act. A more secular system for the new county schools would undermine their arguments for more public money for Catholic schools.

The Cabinet faced widespread opposition within the Unionist Party whilst Catholics in Northern Ireland, and politicians and civil servants in London, were indifferent to the fate of Protestant teachers in public elementary schools. The government's critics were aware of the British government's lack of interest,[36] yet when the Cabinet discussed the outcome of the London meeting on 18 January 1945 Brooke and his ministers confirmed their previous decision to insist upon the removal of the compulsion clause.[37] A few days later Lowry's statement in the Commons, described by the *Irish News* as 'one of the most remarkable issues in the history of the Six Counties as a separate entity',[38] capsized the 1930 Act with a speech that was severely criticised by senior Unionist backbenchers such as the former Prime Minister, John Andrews, and the former Chief Whip, Lord Glentoran. Protestant clerics were also angered by Lowry's statement and William Corkey, brother of Hall-Thompson's predecessor, revived the United Education Committee to counter the latest threat to Protestant clerical interests.[39]

The government's decision to abolish compulsion appears to be one of the most striking mysteries of education policy in Northern Ireland. The PRONI files do not offer any clear evidence to explain the Cabinet's decision to confront the UEC in January 1945, but its determination may partly be explained by the Protestant clergy's pursuit of another, greater objective.

Secondary schools

There were two key issues for the Protestant clergy in 1945; the 'conscience clause' and the role of the Protestant clergy in the proposed secondary intermediate schools. The 'conscience clause' dominated the education debate throughout most of 1945, but by the winter of 1945 the influence of the Protestant clergy within the proposed secondary intermediate schools emerged as the principal question for the UEC. The Cabinet initially offered it a third of the seats on the school committees,[40] but the UEC demanded the rights it already enjoyed in public elementary schools.

The role of Brooke was vital in determining the outcome of the contest with the UEC in 1945 and 1946 because he adopted a surprisingly harsh attitude towards the Protestant clergy. Brooke claimed to his colleagues in October 1945 that the Protestant clerics were not contributing to the new schools, and were therefore not entitled to claim management powers. He also told his colleagues that he opposed surrendering effective control of secondary intermediate schools to the Protestant clergy because he considered them to have been poor managers of public elementary schools.[41]

Protestant clerics were to be denied the powers they already enjoyed on the school committees of 'provided' public elementary schools – schools built entirely from public funds – so the objections of the Ministry and the Cabinet to the Protestant clergy playing a similar role in 'county' secondary intermediate schools appeared to the UEC to be both irrational and unreasonable. The principle of allowing the Protestant clergy a significant influence in the education of Protestant children, regardless of any financial commitment, had been conceded in 1925 and underlined in 1930. Once more, ministers appeared to be defaulting on the promises of their predecessors.

The determination of the Ministry and the Cabinet to resist these claims was certainly undermined by the 'conscience clause' dispute. The UEC argued that the aim of the 1930 Act had been to make public elementary schools 'safe' for Protestant children by granting the Protestant clergy significant powers within the schools and by ensuring that 'simple Bible instruction' was provided in every public elementary school. The 'conscience clause' removed one of the two securities of the 1930 Act. For this reason, the presence of the Protestant clergy was vital for the preservation of the Protestant faith within the secondary intermediate schools. The government's prolonged negotiations with the Protestant clergy finally led to a settlement in March 1946, when the Cabinet granted them half of the seats on the proposed secondary intermediate school committees.[42]

The Protestant clergy were more pragmatic in 1946, but this pragmatism arose from their comparative lack of influence upon government policy and the failure to secure the support of the Orange Order. Corkey revived the UEC to preserve the 1930 settlement – and ultimately he failed – but the 1947 Act was not, despite the strident protests of the UEC, a major defeat for the Protestant clergy. They were rewarded with effective control of the new county secondary intermediate schools in exchange for accepting a 'conscience clause' that was not used by a single teacher during the first seven years of the 1947 Act.[43]

The UEC and Hall-Thompson both accepted a reverse on one issue to pursue a more important objective. The UEC abandoned the compulsion of teachers for influence in the new secondary intermediate schools that would ensure Protestant teachers would be responsible for educating all Protestant pupils, not simply those in primary schools. Hall-Thompson also employed concessions to the Protestant clergy to secure improved funding arrangements for Catholic schools. It was no coincidence that the Cabinet meeting of 28 March 1946, which approved the settlement with the UEC, also agreed to Hall-Thompson's proposal to increase the capital grant for voluntary schools to sixty-five per cent without insisting upon 'four and two' committees.[44]

'An intolerable burden'

Education reform was also posing severe problems for the Catholic authorities. Bishop Neil Farren of Derry warned Catholics of the approaching threat as early as January 1944:

> we may be prepared that some attempt will be made to destroy our educational system in this area before the war is finished or immediately afterwards, and it may be incumbent on us as Catholics to rise up and protest . . . in a very determined way.[45]

The Catholic authorities recognised that the Catholic community would struggle to fund its own network of secondary schools,[46] but their problems were greatly eased in March 1944 when Lieutenant Colonel Samuel Hall-Thompson succeeded Robert Corkey as Northern Ireland's fifth Minister of Education. Hall-Thompson was a liberal by the undemanding standards of Ulster Unionism in the 1940s, and his moderation was eventually to cost him both his ministerial post and his seat in the Northern Ireland Commons.[47] His major contribution on behalf of Catholic schools was to increase the capital funding grant for voluntary schools from fifty per cent to sixty-five per cent in 1947. The 'conscience clause' controversy arose from the determination of two successive Attorney Generals, the Prime Minister and the majority of the Cabinet to amend the Education Act of 1930, but the increase in the capital grant was almost solely due to Hall-Thompson's persistence.

Hall-Thompson was eager for a settlement with the Catholic authorities, and in May 1944, only two months after his appointment, he initiated a series of meetings with the leadership of the Catholic

Clerical Managers' Association (CCMA) to explore the possibilities for an agreement.[48] The Catholic authorities were concerned by the scheme for nursery schools,[49] the fate of 'Catholic Religious Instruction' in the proposed Technical Schools, and the risk of discrimination against Catholic pupils for grammar school scholarships,[50] but the scale of the capital grant and the conditions for any increase eclipsed all other questions.

Hall-Thompson rejected the CCMA's claim for a seventy-five per cent grant, but told the delegation he was prepared to consider the possibility of sixty-five per cent grants without a 'four and two' committee.[51] Six weeks after his first meeting with the CCMA he told the Cabinet that the insistence upon the 'four and two' committee, was futile, and recommended an unconditional sixty-five per cent capital grant to voluntary schools, along with full funding of heating, lighting and cleaning costs.[52] Hall-Thompson was ready to abandon the 'four and two' committee, but he failed to convince his colleagues. The Minister of Labour, Harry Midgley, and the Minister of Health, William Grant, who led the campaign against the grants for Gaelic in 1933, opposed Hall-Thompson. Brooke, fearful that further concessions to voluntary schools would discourage Protestant clerical managers from transferring their schools, preferred to postpone a decision.[53]

In October 1944 Hall-Thompson renewed his efforts to persuade his colleagues to compromise. Brooke was now prepared to abandon the 'four and two' committee, but the Cabinet would not relent on the issue of public representation.[54] Hall-Thompson met the leaders of the CCMA the following week. The leader of the CCMA delegation, Dean MacDonald, bluntly told him 'if the additional financial assistance which they had been led to believe would be given was not forthcoming the Bishops would not cooperate in the new system'.[55] The CCMA delegation clearly believed that Hall-Thompson would be able to convince the Cabinet to accept a sixty-five per cent grant for voluntary schools, and MacDonald was naturally disappointed. Hall-Thompson's failure, after allowing the CCMA delegation to believe he would be able to persuade his colleagues, illustrated his political naïvety and confirms Akenson's opinion of him as 'an idealist in educational matters, who was not politically astute'.[56] Six months later the bishops exploited Hall-Thompson's error to ask:

> Why did the Ministry of Education go back on their own suggestions, utterly inadequate and unjust though they were, those suggestions that were made in advance to the various parties

> interested? Can it be that the White Paper does not represent the legitimate judgements of the Ministry and the Government of Northern Ireland has once again surrendered to the threats of those brewers of bigotry who . . . have brought so much misery on the land we love.[57]

The discussions with the CCMA reached an impasse after the disappointment of October 1944, and the publication of the White Paper in December diverted attention to the 'conscience clause' conflict. The Catholic bishops waited until the Lenten Pastorals of February 1945 to offer their interpretation of the White Paper. MacRory was concerned by the 'vast additional expenditure of money that will be required in order to carry out the suggested changes', but added that 'I object to it far more on spiritual grounds because it proposes to continue what I regard as the utterly unjust treatment of a large portion of the population of the Six Counties on account of their conscientious convictions'.[58]

Mageean provided the most extensive analysis of the White Paper, dedicating more than half of his address to the White Paper and the Church's doctrine on education, but Bishop Farren offered the most forthright response when he stated 'the bald fact is that we are being penalised because we are Catholics'.[59] The following month a collective statement by the six northern bishops presented their formal opinion of the Education Bill. The Bill, they declared, was 'inimical to Catholic interests' and would:

> impose an intolerable burden on the Catholic community, and in a few years it will make it impossible for Catholic citizens to live normal Catholic lives, in accordance with the teaching and legislation of the Church, in the Six Counties.[60]

The bishops highlighted their opposition to the 'four and two' concept so popular amongst Unionist politicians, and concluded with a firm resolution to maintain their autonomy: 'we have had control of our Catholic schools for over one hundred years, and whatever the action we may be driven to take we are determined to maintain it'.[61]

Brownell

Senior Ministry of Education officials thought, surprisingly, the bishops' statement offered the possibility of a compromise. The Secretary of the Ministry, Reginald Brownell, wrote to the Secretary to the Cabinet, Robert Gransden, claiming that a leading member of the CCMA was hoping to lead a moderate element within the clergy. He thought an offer of seventy-five per cent capital funding (the grant available to most voluntary schools in England and Wales), with 'four and two' committees would attract many Catholic clerical managers. Brownell also favoured an agreement with the Catholic authorities:

> the Roman Catholics will not cooperate in reconstruction and as they are almost 40 per cent of our school population our reconstruction will not succeed without their help. Personally, I have no doubt whatever that they have a justifiable grievance and taking the larger view I do not think that it is good for Northern Ireland that the grievance should be allowed to exist.[62]

Government policy in the Ministry of Education, as in all other ministries, was influenced by relations between politicians and officials. The evidence available in the PRONI archives indicates that senior Ministry officials pursued a 'liberal' attitude towards the claims of the Catholic authorities compared to the views of most Unionist MPs and many Unionist ministers. Reginald Brownell maintained the tradition of 'liberal' Ministry officials reaching back to McQuibban in 1921.

Brownell gained experience of education issues during a spell in the Egyptian civil service before Lord Charlemont brought him from the Ministry of Commerce to be his Private Secretary in January 1926.[63] He eventually succeeded Wyse as Secretary in 1939,[64] and after 1944 his moderation complemented Hall-Thompson's liberal approach. Patrick Shea writes of the 1947 Act: 'for that comprehensive Act alone, the names of Brownell and Hall-Thompson are worthy of an honourable place in the history of education in Northern Ireland'.[65] Hall-Thompson collaborated closely with Brownell during his six years as Minister because they shared a determination to resolve the Ministry's differences with the Catholic authorities.

In contrast, Brownell enjoyed poor relations with Hall-Thompson's less accommodating successor, Harry Midgley. Midgley's biographer claims that 'Brownell's formal bureaucratic approach was totally at odds with Midgley's impetuosity and impulsiveness'.[66] He quotes as an example their first meeting when Brownell showed Midgley a list of the Ministry's senior civil servants. Midgley asked for their first names, but Brownell replied that he did not know their first names because 'we don't go in for that sort of thing here'.[67] Personal differences may partly account for the conflict between the two men, but Midgley's problems with Brownell primarily arose from his most senior civil servant's tolerant attitude towards Catholic schools.

Patrick Shea, a Catholic civil servant in the Ministry of Education, provides a portrait of Brownell as 'ambitious, energetic and intense; a moody man whose sternness was relieved by a rich vein of dour humour'.[68] Shea recounts his interview for a job in the Ministry. Brownell and Shea vigorously debated the merits of the Catholic authorities' education policy, but at the end of the interview Brownell offered Shea the post.[69]

In October 1945 Brownell sent a memorandum to Hall-Thompson which claimed to offer an interpretation of Northern Ireland's education system from the viewpoint of the British Home Secretary, Chuter Ede, a former teacher.[70] Brownell did not claim prior discussions with Ede, nor that he was writing on the Ede's behalf. The memorandum was simply an attempt to present *his* personal interpretation of Northern Ireland's education system.[71]

Brownell claimed there was clear evidence that some Catholic clerical managers were not gaining the full grants for heating, lighting and cleaning their schools. Payments were delayed for Catholic managers whereas Protestant voluntary managers faced few problems collecting their money. Also, the provision of scholarships by the education committees was a constant source of conflict, with Ministry officials often intervening to ensure that the education committees allocated the grants fairly. Brownell concluded with as stern a condemnation of the education committees and the 1930 Act as any issued by nationalist MPs or senior Catholic clerics:

> He will have no difficulty in proclaiming that the Ulster system constitutes an offence against the spirit and the letter of the Government of Ireland Act – that it endows Protestantism and denominationalism, that it imposes a disability on the Roman Catholic and that it discriminates against the individual who contemplates becoming a teacher.[72]

In March 1946 Brownell questioned the need for education committee representation on voluntary school committees as a consequence of grants from the Northern Ireland government. Thus, the most senior Ministry official supported one of the Catholic authorities' most significant objections to the government's education policy after 1947 – the right of the education committees, rather than the Ministry of Education, to be involved in Catholic schools.

Brownell proposed abandoning the 'four and two' principle and raising the offer to voluntary schools from sixty-five per cent to seventy per cent of capital costs. Brownell also noted that the Cabinet was demanding a third of the seats on the school committee for the education committee in exchange for paying sixty-five per cent of the capital costs, but the 1930 Act allowed the education committees only a quarter of the seats on the school committees of public elementary schools.[73] The following July he claimed that the Protestant clergy's call for a dominant role in all local education authority schools, including technical schools, constituted the endowment of Protestantism. The education authorities, he contended, would be surrendering effective control of all their schools to the Protestant clerics thus demolishing the concept of 'local democratic control' so cherished by Unionist politicians.[74]

Hall-Thompson began his ministerial career in the spring of 1944 searching for an accommodation with the Catholic authorities but he was to suffer a series of defeats during the next two years, reverses which would lead many politicians to abandon their campaign or leave the government. Hall-Thompson persevered, and this persistence was partly due to the encouragement of his most senior official.

The 1947 Act

Brownell and Hall-Thompson renewed their search for a compromise with the Catholic authorities and met a delegation of Catholic clerics led by Mageean and Farren at the end of September 1945 for further discussions. Hall-Thompson explained to his Cabinet colleagues that 'the chief point they made – and they made it very plainly – was that under no circumstances would the Roman Catholic Church agree to establish '4 and 2' Committees for their schools.'[75] Hall-Thompson persevered despite his earlier defeats, highlighting the contrast between the Cabinet's treatment of the Protestant clergy and their Catholic counterparts:

> the more that concession is made to the Protestant Churches on the question of religious instruction and representation on the management committees of local authority schools the greater will be the complaint of the Roman Catholics that Protestantism is being 'put on the rates' and 'endowed' and that discrimination is being exercised against them.[76]

Hall-Thompson also mentioned the threat of an appeal to the Judicial Committee of the Privy Council:

> there was some force in their contention that the grants for voluntary schools should be more generous than those indicated in the

White Paper and feared that unless schools under Roman Catholic management were assisted to a great extent, the authorities in Great Britain might consider the provisions of the Government of Ireland Act as to discrimination were infringed.[77]

Hall-Thompson was unique amongst Northern Ireland's twelve Minsters of Education in exploiting the threat from the Privy Council against his own colleagues, but his warnings failed to influence colleagues aware of the Home Office's indifference. They insisted upon 'four and two' committees.[78] Hall-Thompson was not discouraged by yet another disappointment and continued his search for a viable solution. Finally, in March 1946 the government settled their differences with the Protestant clerics, and Hall-Thompson argued for similar concessions for the Catholic authorities. William Grant remained critical, but Brooke stated:

> the main purpose of the Government's proposals was to secure the best possible educational system in the interests of the children and he feared that if the opposition on the part of the Roman Catholics was not allayed the whole scheme of reconstruction would be prejudiced.[79]

The Cabinet finally yielded to Hall-Thompson's persistence, endorsing his proposal for a sixty-five per cent grant for capital costs and sixty-five per cent grants for internal maintenance and heating, lighting and cleaning expenses without demanding 'four and two' committees.[80]

In June 1946, Hall-Thompson informed his colleagues of a settlement 'which the Roman Catholic managers find satisfactory and, I hope, concludes an argument out of which the Government do not emerge too badly, for I had expected these Managers to stand out for seventy-five per cent Exchequer grants'.[81] As Brownell explained three years later, the Education Act of 1936 allowed seventy-five per cent capital funding for most voluntary schools in England and Wales.[82] The CCMA delegates did not mention the 1936 Act in their negotiations with the Ministry, and Brownell considered this to be a major lapse. The Catholic authorities failed to exploit a convincing argument for seventy-five per cent funding for the new secondary intermediate schools.[83] The failure to couple the fate of Northern Ireland's Catholic schools to the treatment offered to voluntary schools in England and Wales must be viewed as an expensive error. The political implications of accepting a link to developments in the rest of the United Kingdom were minimal compared to the financial advantages of reducing the voluntary contribution from thirty-five per cent to just twenty-five per cent of the cost of new buildings.

The 1947 Act was not as great an advance for the Catholic authorities as the 1930 Act, but the circumstances in 1947 were less favourable. In 1930 Protestant clerics gained significant new powers on the school committees of public elementary schools, but in 1947 they lost the guarantee enshrined in the 1930 Act that teachers would provide 'simple Bible instruction'. The concessions to clerical interests in county secondary intermediate schools eased Protestant discontent, but their dissatisfaction obviously limited the scope for larger grants to Catholic schools. In 1947 the Catholic authorities secured only sixty-five per cent of capital funds and general repairs costs whilst nine years before the government offered to increase capital funding to two thirds of total costs. The 1947 Act was a modest advance on the 1930 Act, and a minor reverse compared to the offer in 1938. The Act presented severe challenges for the Catholic authorities and the Catholic community. The slow pace of voluntary school building in the 1950s, compared to the growth of county schools, offers clear evidence that the increase in the capital grant was insufficient to relieve the Catholic populace of the burdens imposed by the Act.

Akenson argues that 'the government, in increasing its grants to Roman Catholic schools, suffered the venom of the extreme Protestants while reaping precious little gratitude from the Roman Catholics'.[84] However, Catholics in Northern Ireland would feel only slightly thankful towards a government that used public monies, including the taxes of Catholics, to create a network of county secondary inter-mediate and county grammar schools while many Catholics were unable to enjoy a secondary education.

The value to the Catholic community of Hall-Thompson's tenacity is difficult to estimate, but there can be no doubt that he significantly improved the prospects for Catholic schools in the 1950s. Hall-Thompson's success in March 1946 was the greatest achievement of his six years in office, but Northern Ireland's Catholics still paid a heavy price after 1947 for maintaining the autonomy of their schools.

The fall of Hall-Thompson

The political price for the removal of the 'conscience clause' and the increase in capital funds for voluntary schools was postponed until the final weeks of 1949 when a minor dispute involving the government's decision to pay the employers' contribution for National Insurance payments for voluntary school teachers was exploited by unionist critics to force Hall-Thompson from office.[85]

Hall-Thompson was aware that his opponents were conspiring to challenge him. In October 1949 he prepared a memorandum for the Cabinet on the case of a scholarship for a Catholic boy in County Londonderry. His conclusion betrayed his unease:

> If I reverse my decision I shall be attacked by the 'strong Protestants' who are so anxious at present to find fault with my administration of the Education Act and who seem to think that the development of education in this area should enure to the benefit of Protestants alone.[86]

Political developments in the Irish Free State once again influenced education policy in Northern Ireland. In 1948 the Fianna Fáil government was displaced by a disparate alliance led by John Costello of Fine Gael. Costello sought to unite his coalition by withdrawing the Irish Free State from the British Commonwealth to become a fully sovereign republic. The Unionist leadership responded by dissolving the Northern Ireland Commons to contest an election in defence of the Union.[87]

Nationalists, aided by an election fund collected outside Catholic churches throughout Ireland, launched a vigorous campaign under the guise of the Anti-Partition League as politicians from Fianna Fáil, Fine Gael, Labour and Clann na Poblachta flooded the market squares and churchyards of Northern Ireland to support nationalist candidates.[88] The presence of so many Irish Free State politicians naturally antagonised the unionist community, and the 1949 election was the most bitter contest since the early 1920s. Community relations were left in a fragile state. In December 1949 the *Belfast Telegraph* claimed that the 1947 Act would not have been approved by the new Commons.[89]

The National Insurance crisis reached a climax in December 1949 when twelve Unionist MPs, a third of the government's strength in the Commons, opposed the Bill.[90] Brooke met with Hall-Thompson and Brownell to discuss the future for Northern Ireland's schools. He proposed abandoning the education authorities and reverting to the traditional system of explicitly denominational schools, but Brownell argued that many of the existing schools were amalgams of various denominational schools. Few Protestant clerics would allow the local county school to pass to the control of a clergyman from another denomination, or to a colleague from another parish.[91]

Brooke's despondency in December 1949 appears misplaced because the gradual assimilation of Protestant voluntary schools by the education committees begun by Lord Londonderry in 1923 was almost complete by the end of the 1940s.[92] Brooke appeared to be clutching defeat from the jaws of victory, and his proposals for reviving the National Board threatened to surrender all the Ministry's achievements of the previous thirty years. Brownell's concern that the guiding principle of the past three decades was jeopardised by the National Insurance crisis may partly account for Hall-Thompson's decision to resign the following day.

Brooke was disheartened by the course of events, and he shared his disquiet with his Cabinet colleagues:

> The hopes of the original planners that elementary schools should all come under local authority control had not been realised and the present system seemed to contain the seeds of continued trouble with the attendant risk of splitting the Unionist Party and ultimately endangering the constitutional position of Northern Ireland. He had come to the conclusion, therefore, that it should be carefully re-examined in order to see whether some alternative could not be found which, while ensuring fair treatment for all creeds and classes, would be more universally acceptable.[93]

In the Commons a few hours later, Brooke announced a major review of the education system 'to find something that will be better received, will be more popular, and perhaps will be easier worked'.[94] Brooke, so despondent in the morning, was hoping to reconcile contradictory aims by the afternoon. The National Insurance problem arose from the determination of a substantial minority within the Unionist Party to reverse the sixty-five per cent capital grant promised by the 1947 Act,[95] and Brooke could not offer a new education settlement that would allow 'fair treatment of all creeds and classes' and satisfy his critics. His promise of a review only postponed the problem for Hall-Thompson's successor. Hall-Thompson resigned because he epitomised liberalism at a time when the Unionist Party was captivated by an intolerant impulse that even Brooke was unable to resist.

Hall-Thompson ended his ministerial career with a memorandum in the final days of 1949 in which, released from the constraints of office, he was sharply critical of the treatment of Catholic schools by his Cabinet colleagues and Unionist MPs. He wrote of the suggestion by Morris May, later to serve as Minister of Education, that the government insist upon compulsory 'four and two' committees: 'thus they will gain their end – to strike at the Roman Catholics and so bring it about that a very large percentage of the community will be denied State assistance in education'.[96]

Hall-Thompson tried to fashion a fairer settlement with the Catholic authorities during his six years as Minister. He was fully entitled to claim:

> We have in Ulster a peculiar educational setup which, as I have shown, favours the Protestant as against the Roman Catholic, and such as it is I have tried to operate it fairly.[97]

A liberal Minister of Education was sacrificed to the intolerants within the Unionist Party. The Archbishop of Armagh, Cardinal John D'Alton, highlighted Catholic unease when he claimed that 'recent developments give one an uneasy feeling that sinister influences are at work with the object of undermining the agreement reached under the Act of 1947'.[98]

The question of Hall-Thompson's successor was yet another difficulty for Brooke. He wrote to Lord Glentoran on the day of Hall-Thompson's resignation to ask 'if you can think of anybody, either in the Senate or in the House of Commons, who would do Education I should appreciate it.'[99] The *Belfast Telegraph* commented that 'there will be few 'takers' for an office which has proved the graveyard of more than one political career'.[100] Brooke's search ended in the New Year when he 'surprised everyone, and appalled Catholics'[101] by appointing Harry Midgley, an avowed opponent of the Catholic authorities, as Northern Ireland's sixth Minister of Education.

HARRY MIDGLEY

Henry Cassidy Midgley was one of Northern Ireland's most controversial figures during the fifty years of devolved government.[102] His lengthy evolution from socialist opponent of partition in 1921 to Unionist minister and member of the Royal Black Preceptory and the Orange Order culminated in a seven year spell as Minister of Education from 1950 until his death in 1957. Akenson and Graham Walker both contend that Midgley, though prone to sectarian rhetorical outbursts, was a fair and efficient minister. Akenson claims Midgley 'died in office in 1957 with good intentions and competent administration to his credit',[103] and Walker offers fulsome praise:

> Midgley picked his way through this political and administrative minefield sufficiently well to give life to the ideals of the 1947 Act. That he did so was testimony to his skill in government administration. He realised that he had to be pragmatic and that compromises

had to be worked out. He was the first to compromise when he took office in 1950. From that day he knew that his own educational ideals would not constitute the policy he would be attempting to put into practice. He was aware of the problems he faced but at no time did he lose the determination to come up with a solution. His persistence in this regard, combined with a willingness to be flexible and to preside over steady, if unspectacular, progress, issued tangible achievements and warm praise at the end of the day.[104]

Walker highlights Midgley's hostile rhetoric, but he also adopted a partial and intolerant attitude towards Catholic voluntary schools and his prejudice limited the opportunities for thousands of Catholic children. Midgley supervised Northern Ireland's education system during a vital phase as the Ministry began to develop mass secondary education in the aftermath of the 1947 Act. The evidence from the PRONI archives, newspaper reports and Commons debates indicates that he did not temper his antagonism towards the Catholic clergy or Catholic voluntary schools during his years as Minister.

The Ministry of Education had been a defender, if a rather diffident one, of Catholic schools since 1922 as Ministry officials struggled to counter the influence of the education committees, the Orange Order, Unionist backbenchers and the minister's Cabinet colleagues. Brooke's choice of Midgley, however, allowed an acknowledged critic of the Catholic clergy to exercise a significant influence over Northern Ireland's Catholic schools.[105] Cardinal D'Alton was not alone in feeling unease at the course of events in the first weeks of 1950. Rumours of Midgley's appointment were, according to Shea, 'greeted with derision, then, as they persisted, with annoyance' by Ministry officials.[106]

The fall of Hall-Thompson in the final weeks of 1949 was prompted by the opposition of a substantial minority of Unionist MPs to any concessions to the Catholic minority, and Midgley appeared the most suitable candidate to reflect the new militant tone. As a member of the Cabinet between 1943 and 1945,[107] he opposed Hall-Thompson's proposals for increased funding for voluntary schools.[108] In October 1944 he drafted a memorandum for his Cabinet colleagues on the proposed White Paper opposing any increase, even for voluntary schools willing to accept a 'four and two' committee.[109] After leaving the government, Midgley frequently spoke and voted in the Commons against the government's measures for voluntary schools.[110] In November 1946 he opposed all forms of capital funding for voluntary schools, claiming 'Northern Ireland went astray' in 1930 with a 'mischievous policy' of granting fifty per cent of capital funds for voluntary schools.[111] Midgley often referred to the importance of public control of education, but he frankly admitted that the 'blunder' of 1930 was designed to aid Catholic schools, and opposed the increase on those terms.[112]

Midgley was also one of the leaders of the unionist revolt against National Insurance payments because 'he was against making life easier for schools managed by people whose attitude to the Crown and the State of Northern Ireland was less than enthusiastic'.[113] As Farren notes, by the end of the 1940s Midgley was 'still energetic, but by now quite unapologetically anti-Catholic . . . particularly prominent in the attacks on grant aid for voluntary schools, inside and outside parliament'.[114] In November 1949 Midgley was recalled to the Cabinet,[115] but he continued to oppose Hall-Thompson's plans for paying the employer's National Insurance contributions, claiming that because the number of Protestant voluntary schools was declining:

> in course of time practically the only voluntary schools would be those under Roman Catholic control. The government, by proceeding with the Bill, would be accepting a responsibility which later on would be a benefit for Roman Catholic schools alone.[116]

Thus, only weeks before he became Minister of Education, Midgley opposed a Bill simply because he suspected it would eventually aid only Catholic schools.

Walker claims Midgley 'wasted no time in dissociating himself from the people he had led in the campaign against state aid to voluntary schools' and 'he was the first to compromise when he took office in 1950'.[117] However, Midgley employed the review promised by Brooke on the day of Hall-Thompson's resignation to launch a protracted campaign against the concessions to voluntary schools contained in the 1947 Act. As Shea states: 'so far as I know he did not particularise his views on what was wrong with the system except that he felt in a general way that the voluntary schools were too well treated'.[118]

In March 1950 Midgley proposed that the sixty-five per cent capital grant should cease after five years, allowing only 'four and two' schools to retain the award. He also attempted to appease Protestant clerics by allowing the school committees of county schools to supervise denominational religious instruction and proposed that the school committee should assess teachers on 'faith and morals' – an obvious attempt to ensure teachers acceptable to the Protestant clergy.[119] Midgley's plans for county schools were the most radical departure from Londonderry's original concept, ending the notion of treating county schools as public institutions. Midgley claimed that the offer of denominational religious instruction and greater influence in teaching appointments was designed to ease Protestant clerical 'resentment' at the Catholic clergy's power to appoint teachers and control religious instruction in voluntary schools,[120] but he failed to note the severe financial burden of the voluntary contribution – the price of faith for Catholic schools. Midgley intended to grant the Protestant clergy the same managerial rights as their Catholic counterparts, but he did not demand the same exacting price for their autonomy.[121]

Brownell visited London for informal discussions with Sir Alexander Maxwell, now retired from the Home Office, to assess the potential reaction of the London government to the proposed amendments to the 1947 Act. The Home Office remained reluctant to intervene in Northern Ireland's affairs. Maxwell only advised Brownell against reducing the sixty-five per cent capital grant, and told him that the London government would probably only object to denominational teaching in county schools if teachers strongly contested the proposal.[122] Midgley's colleagues approved both measures, but the scheme was abandoned in September 1950 after the Attorney General ruled that allowing the school committee to supervise denominational religious instruction was *ultra vires*.[123] Once again, the devolved government's own law officers, rather than the Home Office in London, was frustrating efforts to construct a network of explicitly Protestant schools.

Midgley was not simply accommodating his Unionist colleagues to atone for his radical past. The Cabinet finally decided not to amend the 1947 Act in February 1951, but Midgley continued to argue for a reduction of the capital grant.[124] Walker claims that, from January 1950, Midgley 'knew that his own educational ideals would not constitute the policy he would be attempting to put into practice'.[125] However, the evidence from the PRONI archives indicates that Midgley remained a vehement opponent of the 1947 Act even after the rest of the Cabinet chose not to alter the funding conditions for voluntary schools.

St Joseph's college

After his failure to reverse the concessions contained in the 1947 Act, the first major clash between Midgley and the Catholic authorities revolved around the fate of the new teacher training college for Catholic men in Belfast. The episode was to underline his antagonism towards the Catholic authorities because he even defied Brooke to counter their claims.

Ministry officials recognised as early as March 1943 that education reform would require considerable numbers of new teachers, and the potential shortage was exacerbated by the Cabinet's decision to suspend male teacher training for the duration of the war. The Minister of Education, Robert Corkey, recommended allowing fifteen male trainees into Stranmillis college but, despite the support of the General Assembly of the Presbyterian Church, the Ulster Teachers' Union and Mageean, the Cabinet postponed any decision.[126] In June the Cabinet discussed the issue once more without reaching a conclusion. Midgley claimed that, despite Catholic children comprising nearly forty per cent of elementary pupils in 1939, the Ministry's proposal to offer a third of the places to Catholics was excessive.[127]

The problem became acute for the Catholic authorities early in 1945 when St Mary's college, London, announced that it could no longer accept male trainees from Northern Ireland. The Catholic authorities asked for the students to be sent to colleges in the Irish Free State which, in contrast to the early 1920s, were willing to accept the Ministry's conditions for teacher training.[128] Hall-Thompson needed an alternative to offer the Catholic authorities, and urged the Cabinet to withdraw Ministry of Agriculture and Admiralty officials from Stranmillis to allow for increased teacher training.[129] The Cabinet agreed not to send student teachers to the Irish Free State, but failed to offer another solution.[130]

The Cabinet's indecision left Hall-Thompson to choose between building a separate hostel for Catholic students at Stranmillis college or funding an extension to the Catholic women's college – St Mary's college in Belfast.[131] The Catholic authorities insisted upon a new men's college within the grounds of St Mary's, but the issue was submerged beneath the wider questions of education reform and the fate of capital funding for voluntary schools until 1952 when Midgley imposed a sixty-five per cent capital grant for the proposed new men's hostel at St Mary's.[132]

St Mary's was built by the British government and handed over to the Catholic authorities without charge in 1901, and after 1922 the Ministry paid tuition fees to finance the college and support a sinking fund for future capital projects.[133] The Ministry was therefore almost fully funding St Mary's during the 1920s – when there was no capital funding for voluntary schools – and the 1930s and 1940s – when Catholic voluntary schools gained only half the capital costs. The Ministry's generosity was abruptly halted by Midgley at a time when the college urgently needed substantial investment.

A deputation of Catholic clerics in February 1952 found Midgley adamant and the following month the Cabinet approved his ruling.[134]

The issue was abandoned for more than a year until May 1953 when the Catholic authorities illustrated the importance of teacher training by sending five of Northern Ireland's six bishops to visit Brooke and Midgley to discuss the problem.[135] In contrast, the Education Bill of 1930 and the White Paper of 1944 both led only two bishops to visit the Minister of Education. The five bishops and Midgley agreed that the 1947 Act was vague on the level of grant available for voluntary teacher training colleges, but they differed on the consequences of this uncertainty. Midgley argued that the Ministry should follow the general principles of the 1947 Act and grant only sixty-five per cent of the capital costs[136] while the bishops countered that St Mary's had been almost fully funded until 1952 and so the Ministry was obliged to offer a generous rate for the new college.[137]

Brooke was sympathetic to the Catholic authorities' problems when the Cabinet discussed the issue in July and August 1953, but the majority of the Cabinet, led by the former Parliamentary Secretary to the Ministry of Education Dehra Parker, insisted upon a sixty-five per cent grant and offered only a loan to pay for the remainder of the costs.[138] The Catholic authorities may have been aware of Brooke's concern for their case, because in December 1953 D'Alton contacted Brooke to ask him to see Mageean. A few days later the Secretary to the Cabinet, Robert Gransden, told Brownell that 'he believed that the Prime Minister was anxious to help the RC Church in this matter, but as I know the Cabinet had already turned it down' and asked him to approach Parker to fashion a compromise.[139]

The Catholic authorities usually negotiated with either the Minister of Education or his officials, but their relations with Midgley were too strained to allow for constructive discussions. As D'Alton told Brooke in September 1953 'we did not expect any concessions from your Minister of Education, who seems to lose few opportunities of reviling Catholics, and especially the Catholic bishops'.[140] The evidence in the PRONI archives is unclear as to whether Midgley was aware of Gransden's approach to Brownell, which must be viewed as an initiative by Brooke, but his determination not to allow an increased grant for the proposed college may partly be explained by Brooke's intervention in the Ministry of Education affairs.

Brooke also asked Midgley to explore ways of easing the problem,[141] but Midgley refused to offer any concessions. He solicited a ruling from the Attorney General that the 1947 Act did not command the government to provide any money for new voluntary teacher training colleges,[142] and the absence of an obligation was enough for Midgley and most of his Cabinet colleagues. The following day Brooke informed Mageean there was no possibility of a compromise.[143]

The decision to deny a higher rate of capital funding to the new Catholic men's college was taken by the entire Cabinet. However, the 1947 Act allowed the Minister of Education to set the rate of capital funding, and Midgley offered less than his own Prime Minister was willing to grant to the Catholic authorities. The Minister of Education was usually struggling against some of his Cabinet colleagues to defend the interests of Catholic schools, but Midgley was unique in challenging his Prime Minister to insist upon less money for Catholic education.[144]

'Sectarian utterances'

Lord Londonderry, Lord Charlemont, Robb and Hall-Thompson all enjoyed a measure of personal respect from Nationalist politicians. They were criticised for failing to defend Catholic schools from their less tolerant colleagues and backbench MPs, but none was accused of personal bias or prejudice against Catholics or Catholic schools. Midgley, in sharp contrast, enjoyed poor relations with nationalist MPs in the Commons. The Republican Labour MP, Harry Diamond, claimed that Midgley was a major source of conflict:

> a great deal of the trouble, friction and ill feeling that exists is due to the Minister of Education careering around the Six Counties trailing his coat and making the most truculent and, in many instances, offensive speeches regarding the administration of education and the opinions of those who differ from him.[145]

The responsibilities of office did not temper Midgley's intense animosity towards the Catholic Church, and there were a series of incidents in his final years which underlined his militant unionism. In February 1955, a speech led a Dublin newspaper to claim that Midgley was courting 'the Norman Porters and other anti-Catholic crusaders to the right of him',[146] and twelve months later a local paper claimed he called for Protestant landowners in Dungannon not to sell land for the construction of Catholic schools. The Dungannon speech provoked a debate in the Commons where Midgley explained his statement:

> I said that to me it was an outrage that a Protestant in Northern Ireland who owned land – and I repeat this in the House for what it may be worth; I do not care whom it displeases – about which there were negotiations for a school, and who knew the county education

authority was seeking it for that purpose, should shamefully violate and betray his heritage by selling that land to a Roman Catholic bishop which meant that it would never be utilised for a county school.[147]

The Minister of Education was expected, and obliged by law, to act as an impartial arbiter in conflicts between the local education authorities and voluntary schools. A politician who claimed that any Protestant selling land to the Catholic Church would 'shamefully violate and betray his heritage' could not claim to be treating voluntary and county schools as simply two differing classes of school, distinguished only by public representation on the county school's committee in exchange for greater amounts of public money.

Midgley intensified nationalist resentment in February 1957 when he stated that 'all the minority are traitors and have consistently been traitors to the Government of Northern Ireland' during a speech in Portadown.[148] Midgley displaced Hall-Thompson in January 1950 because his strident unionism captured the prevailing mood in the aftermath of the bitter 1949 election. Seven years later, only two months before his death, he still displayed a strong antipathy towards Catholic schools. Walker recognises that nationalist criticism was partly justified:

> It is to be regretted that on the vast majority of occasions in this stage of his career he took the easier option and played his own part in fortifying the cultural and political barriers which stood resolutely between Ulster's Protestants and Catholic communities.[149]

In 1953 the writer Paul Blanshard visited Northern Ireland to research material for his book *The Irish and Catholic Power*. He praised Midgley's administration of Northern Ireland's schools:

> The Unionist government had in its colourful Minister of Education, Harry Midgley, one of the most outspoken critics of Catholic educational policy in Ireland . . . He has the sagacity to attack the weakest feature of the Catholic system – the theological coercion used by the Church in maintaining that system. He contends that thousands of Catholic parents would like to send their children to schools with the children of other faiths in order that they should learn tolerance and cooperation, but that the Catholic hierarchy prevents this 'rapprochement'.[150]

Midgley may have believed that 'thousands of Catholic parents would like to send their children to schools with the children of other faiths', but he ensured that Catholic children would encounter few Catholic teachers if they were sent to 'learn tolerance and cooperation' in county schools. In April 1953, a member of the Board of Education of the Presbyterian General Assembly asked the Ministry to recognise teaching qualifications from the Irish Republic. Midgley refused, claiming 'it might, for example, increase the likelihood of applications from RC teachers in county schools'.[151] The following year he opposed any public reference to Catholic students attending Stranmillis because 'there is no doubt that there would be strong and immediate opposition from the Protestant Churches'.[152]

Protestant clerics were also hostile to practical measures likely to encourage integration, opposing Ministry officials' suggestion that they should allow Catholic primary school graduates to attend county secondary intermediate schools in areas without voluntary secondary intermediate schools.[153] The scheme was abandoned after Protestant clerical objections, and Midgley did not urge county schools to accept Catholic pupils. Clearly, the Catholic authorities were not alone in seeking to prevent any 'rapprochement'.

The Ministry's statistics indicate that Catholic schools remained popular amongst the overwhelming majority of Catholic parents in Northern Ireland. In 1957 there were only 900 Catholic county school pupils in contrast to more than 90,000 Catholics in voluntary schools,[154] and Midgley's years as Minister of Education probably underlined segregation in Northern Ireland's schools because, as Dunn notes:

> The impact on the Catholic community of a Minister of Education so powerfully and publicly opposed to their position must have been considerable and would have added greatly to the view that an independent Catholic system was necessary.[155]

Midgley's behaviour disturbed Shea who asked Brownell for a transfer. Brownell 'agreed that I had good reason to feel aggrieved and suggested that the Catholic members of the staff should get together and prepare a 'dignified protest' at the Minister's sectarian utterances'.[156] Brownell's suggestion that Catholic civil servants should protest, even if in a 'dignified' manner, against Midgley underlined the intensity of his estrangement from his own Minister. Midgley's abrasive and confrontational manner would inevitably cause friction with a senior civil servant such as Brownell dedicated to accommodation with the Catholic authorities.

Midgley's seven years as Minister emphasised the relative liberalism of the institutional viewpoint within the Ministry of Education because Midgley, although the most militant of Northern Ireland's twelve

Ministers of Education, was typical of a broad section of the Unionist Party in the 1950s.[157] Midgley's spell, however, also highlighted the limited influence of civil servants when confronted by a minister determined to undermine the Ministry's relations with Northern Ireland's Catholic schools.

'Ancient traditions'

The government and its followers constantly argued that any disadvantage suffered by Catholic schools was a consequence of their refusal to accept 'local democratic control', and that this price was also paid by voluntary Protestant schools. The fate of voluntary grammar schools after 1947 offers an interesting comparison to the treatment of secondary intermediate and primary schools, because the Ministry of Education and the Cabinet granted concessions to the voluntary grammar schools they denied to other voluntary schools. The treatment of voluntary grammar schools emphasised the government's partial attitude towards Catholic schools because most eminent grammar schools were attended by Protestants.

The classification of schools by title is an inexact science, but there are clear ethnic and religious values explicit in titles such as the Royal School, Victoria College, the Convent of the Sacred Heart and the Christian Brothers' School. Therefore, an analysis of the names of the sixty-five voluntary grammar schools in Northern Ireland in 1950 allows for a reasonably clear distinction between Protestant and Catholic voluntary grammar schools.[158] The thirty-five Protestant schools were educating 15,956 pupils whilst the thirty Catholic schools contained only 7,720 pupils, less than a third of those attending voluntary grammar schools at a time when Catholics comprised more than forty per cent of elementary school pupils.[159]

The venerable academies with distinguished and prosperous graduates were more capable than most voluntary schools to finance their development after 1947. However, grammar schools were assisted by generous grants in the form of tuition fees, and throughout the 1950s they consistently extracted more public money from the Cabinet.

The government was eager to preserve the independence of the grammar schools. As Hall-Thompson explained to his colleagues in June 1944:

> The governing bodies of the (senior) secondary schools have no wish to transfer, nor do I think that they should be encouraged or forced to do so; if they can be assured of sufficient grants for

extension they will be glad to extend and maintain the ancient traditions of their schools.[160]

The government, willing to confront the Catholic authorities' opposition to 'four and two' committees, declined to challenge the powers of the grammar school governors because 'it is clear that the voluntary schools, most of which have a long tradition of independence, would strenuously resist any attempt to bring them under the control of the education authorities'.[161] Ministers ignored the Catholic authorities' intense hostility to school committees evident since the beginning of the century but they were discouraged only by the prospect of protests from the governors of grammar schools. As Farren comments, 'it is difficult to avoid the conclusion that this exception was motivated by the fact that many of these secondary schools catered for the (Protestant) middle and upper classes and so had to be protected'.[162]

The grammar schools, the White Paper contended, 'must be specially considered for it will require a measure of financial assistance to enable it to provide places for an increased number of pupils'.[163] Catholic clerics were expected to build entirely new secondary schools aided by only half of the capital costs, but grammar school governors were thought to be unable to embark upon the less challenging task of expanding their schools without nearly two thirds of the costs coming from public funds. All voluntary schools obtained sixty-five per cent of capital costs from the 1947 Act, but voluntary primary and secondary intermediate schools only secured this rate after a prolonged struggle while the grammar schools were granted the increase in the White Paper without a contest.[164]

At the end of 1949 voluntary grammar schools were protected from the 'Orange' campaign against voluntary schools because, as the *Belfast Telegraph* explained:

> In education circles the view is expressed that since the voluntary grammar schools, many of them dating back many years, are saving public funds large sums of money, the payment of fees by the education authorities should not necessarily be followed by intrusion into the governing bodies.[165]

The *Belfast Telegraph* failed to illustrate how the voluntary grammar schools differed from other voluntary schools in saving 'large sums of money', or why an emphasis upon tradition justified preferential treatment by Unionist politicians for predominantly Protestant schools.

Midgley maintained the government's benevolence towards grammar schools. His proposal in February 1950 to reduce the rate of capital grant for voluntary schools excluded voluntary grammar schools, if they allocated one fifth of the school committee seats to the education authority.[166] Midgley initially refused to allow grammar schools to raise the voluntary contribution from the tuition fees paid by the local education authorities,[167] but the following month he was concerned that Protestant grammar schools would be unable to finance their expansion plans. He assured his colleagues, without any supporting evidence, that Catholic schools would find the necessary funds, but added that 'unless something is done I do not see from what source many of our Protestant schools can find the necessary money'.[168]

The Cabinet granted numerous concessions to 'our Protestant schools' after 1947 to ensure that more than sixty-five per cent of the costs of building work were paid from public funds. The Cabinet approved Midgley's proposal to allow an additional tuition fee, and later agreed to provide financial assistance for 'unqualified' pupils – pupils who failed or failed to sit the qualifying exam for the Ministry's scholarships.[169]

Midgley was unwilling to offer more favours to voluntary grammar schools because, as he explained to a delegation of Presbyterian clerics, 'he thought that considering his own personal background he had been exceedingly generous to the voluntary grammar schools in their present difficulties',[170] but he was not the only minister attending to the interests of voluntary grammar schools. In February 1951, Dehra Parker, the Minister of Health and Local Government and always a diligent advocate for voluntary grammar schools, argued for grammar schools to be allowed to charge an additional fee to compensate for capital costs. Midgley, initially hostile, eventually accepted her proposal.[171] The problems facing voluntary grammar schools were similar to the Catholic community's difficulties funding primary and secondary intermediate voluntary schools, but the contrasting approach offers conspicuous evidence of the attitudes of Midgley and his colleagues towards Catholic voluntary schools and the distinguished voluntary grammar schools.

In May 1957 the Unionist MP, Nathaniel Minford, sponsored a motion to reduce the capital grant for voluntary schools, but his motion did not apply to voluntary grammar schools. Martin Wallace of the *Belfast Telegraph* offered two explanations for their exclusion. The motion spared the grammar schools 'because they have a tradition and quality which justify independence, or because many of them are Protestant and have powerful friends'.[172]

The power of the friends of voluntary grammar schools had been demonstrated eight years earlier when the Cabinet discussed a proposal to build a Catholic grammar school in Maghera, County Londonderry. Ministry officials recognised the need for a grammar school,[173] but Dehra Parker, the local MP, noted the political implications of building the school when she claimed: 'the fact that the new school would draw off a number of Roman Catholic pupils from the Rainey Endowed School in Magherafelt also gave cause for much local concern, especially in view of the close link between the management of that school and the local Unionist Association'.[174] The proposed Catholic school was not built, and Catholic pupils in southern Londonderry who passed the scholarship examination were offered only a grammar stream in a secondary intermediate school.[175]

The Cabinet distorted the principles of the 1947 Act to ensure that voluntary grammar schools were not subject to the same conditions imposed on other voluntary schools, and they sanctioned a series of measures after 1947 to ease their plight. Catholic voluntary grammar schools also enjoyed these financial advantages, and some Protestant children were still attending voluntary primary schools, but grammar schools were the only schools in the voluntary sector educating a substantial number of Protestant children. The contrast with the treatment of Catholic voluntary schools serves only to highlight the antagonistic sentiment inspiring education policy in the 1950s.

In January 1945, the Association of Northern Ireland Education Committees met to discuss the previous month's White Paper. The meeting opposed the document's use of the terms 'junior secondary' and 'senior secondary' to describe secondary intermediate and grammar schools because, the Association claimed, the words 'suggest invidious distinctions'.[176] A far more invidious distinction was to dominate Northern Ireland's education system during the 1950s, and Midgley played a major role in exacerbating this difference. The 1947 Act was a partisan law, denying Catholic voluntary schools equal treatment with the county schools, but Hall-Thompson could rightly claim in his final memorandum as Minister that he attempted to operate the Act without prejudice.[177]

Midgley, in contrast, tried to alter the 1947 Act to the disadvantage of the Catholic community and, after his failure to convince his Cabinet colleagues to amend the Act, he allowed Catholics only a second-class education. The difference between the development of county and voluntary secondary intermediate schools in the 1950s greatly influenced the lives of many Catholic school children. The failure of the Catholic community to create as extensive a network of secondary schools as the local education authorities obviously impaired the employment opportunities for young Catholics.[178] As Farren notes: 'decisions were made at ministry and cabinet level which reflected a considerable degree of antagonism towards Catholic education'.[179]

Walker claims Midgley opposed any increase for voluntary schools because 'he stood for a completely comprehensive publicly funded and controlled system in line with socialist thinking in Britain and elsewhere',[180] but the evidence does not support such a conclusion.

In January 1929, during an election campaign for Belfast's city council, Midgley outlined his vision for Northern Ireland's education system:

> the broad highway of educational opportunity would be opened up to all workers, and beginning at the elementary school, they would march progressively to the secondary school, and then to the university.[181]

In November 1946, during the Second Reading of the Education Bill, he returned to the theme of the educational road:

> We want to see that highway made a broader highway upon which all children of all sections of the community can march with the God given right to the highest destiny possible for them.[182]

Three years later Midgley was given the opportunity to accomplish his ambitions. However, during his seven years as Minister of Education he condemned Northern Ireland's Catholics to endure the disadvantages of limited access to secondary education while the Ministry and the education authorities furnished Protestant primary school graduates with the advantages of secondary education. Many Catholic children found Midgley's 'broader highway' to be a narrow road.

THE NARROW ROAD

The Second World War was a stagnant interlude for Northern Ireland's education system.[183] The damage inflicted by German bombs was marginal compared to the devastation wrought against cities in England,[184] but six years without investment left both voluntary and public elementary schools in need of significant sums of public money by the late 1940s. The devolved government embraced the British government's ambitious scheme for education reform. The 1947 Act led to a dramatic growth in the number of secondary schools as the Ministry of Education and local education authorities built new secondary intermediate schools and expanded the capacity of existing voluntary grammar schools. The Ministry's Estimates rose from £3,867,914 in 1946 to £12,084,780 by 1957, when education absorbed one sixth of the government's budget.[185] The government also used local rates to finance its school building programme to raise the total amount dedicated to education to £18.5 million by 1959.[186]

The striking data should not obscure the detail that the 1947 Act intensified the financial liability of voluntary status and exacted a more profound cost upon Catholic pupils, because the contrast between the opportunities available to Protestant and Catholic primary school graduates widened throughout the 1950s. The expansion of secondary education envisaged by the Act dictated a substantial investment in new intermediate schools and improvements to existing grammar school buildings, and the rise in capital funding to sixty-five per cent only eased the additional burden for the Catholic populace.

The Ministry's statistics indicate that voluntary schools were unable to emulate the brisk rate for new buildings set by the education authorities. The voluntary contribution of thirty-five per cent of the cost of new buildings and thirty-five per cent of general maintenance costs was a liability under normal circumstances, but during the 1950s the Catholic community paid a heavy financial price to maintain clerical control of its schools. The evidence contained in the Ministry's Reports indicates that Catholic children also suffered a considerable educational disadvantage.

The acute shortage of building materials initially frustrated the education authorities' efforts, but by 1951 they intended to spend £2.5 million each year on new schools.[187] The Ministry's Report for 1951–52 admitted that 'on the voluntary side development was not so pronounced', but was confident that the disparity between voluntary and county school building would decrease:

> The expansion of the building programme of local education authorities was matched by an increase in the rate of voluntary school building and the number of major projects which reached an advanced stage of planning during the year indicated that progress in voluntary school building would be substantially accelerated in succeeding years.[188]

The Ministry's optimism proved to be misplaced. By July 1954 there were only four voluntary secondary intermediate schools compared to fourteen county secondary intermediate schools.[189] Three years later there were only eight voluntary schools while Protestant pupils were attending twenty-six county schools.[190] Four schools in three years cannot be viewed as a 'substantial acceleration' compared to twelve new county schools. Throughout the 1950s the Ministry's intentions and rhetoric never fully translated into bricks and mortar for Northern Ireland's Catholics.

The difference in the number of new places for the two classes of schools offers clear evidence of the fate of county and voluntary schools in the 1950s. The Ministry's Report for 1957–58 noted that there were 21,000 places in county secondary intermediate schools but only 5,000 places in voluntary secondary intermediate schools.[191] County secondary intermediate schools were educating more than four times as many pupils as their voluntary counterparts by the spring of 1958, and the education authorities also built eight county grammar schools for over 4,000 pupils between 1948 and 1959.[192]

County secondary intermediate schools gained more than 600 places before 1953 while graduates of voluntary primary schools waited for their first secondary intermediate school.[193] Figure 4A highlights the contrast in the number of new places created between 1953 and 1959. The Ministry's Report also admitted that county secondary intermediate schools were providing more than half the necessary places for county primary school graduates in 1958, but voluntary secondary intermediate schools could cater for less than twenty per cent of the potential demand from voluntary primary schools.[194] Also, in 1958 there were still no voluntary secondary intermediate schools in either County Londonderry or Fermanagh.[195] In October 1946 Midgley believed 'in the right of every child to enjoy secondary education',[196] yet after seven years as Minister of Education the overwhelming majority of Northern Ireland's voluntary primary school graduates were not enjoying a secondary education.

The penalty of the voluntary contribution before 1947 was largely financial, but Catholic children also suffered a clear educational disadvantage in the 1950s. A Protestant primary school graduate was twice as likely as his or her Catholic counterpart to be attending a secondary school by the end of the 1950s, and the profound impact of this contrast underlined the second-class status of Catholics within Northern Ireland. Educational qualifications are vital in determining employment opportunities, and the greater access to secondary education enjoyed by Protestants in the 1950s and 1960s (as indicated by Figure 4A) secured an obvious advantage in the labour market.

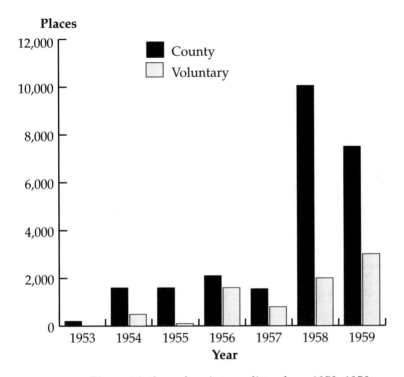

Figure 4A. Secondary intermediate places 1953–1959

Catholic primary schools also suffered a notable disadvantage in the 1950s. Public elementary schools secured £2 million of investment in the 1920s and 1930s while voluntary schools received only £160,000, yet in the 1950s Catholic voluntary schools gained a mere twenty-seven per cent of new primary school places. The education authorities provided more than 28,000 new county primary places between 1 April 1948 and 31 July 1959 while voluntary primary schools gained only 10,000 new places.[197] The differential was not simply the cause of delayed growth for Catholic schools because Figure 4B shows how the contrast between voluntary and county primary schools was increasing in the final years of the decade.

The Ministry's Reports for the years after 1947 do not provide financial statistics to allow for a direct comparison between the amounts of public money spent on the two classes of schools. However, Nationalist MPs were able to extract figures from answers to Parliamentary Questions which offer some evidence of the scale of public spending for county and voluntary schools. Primary and secondary intermediate county schools obtained nearly £10 million in

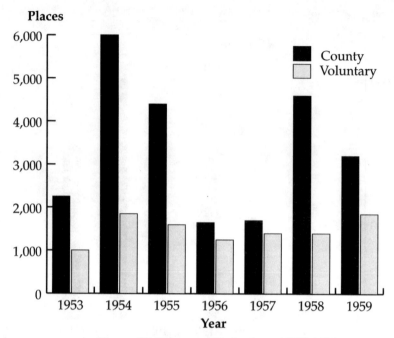

Figure 4B. Primary schools places 1953–1959

building grants during the first eight years of the Act when just over £2.5 million was spent on voluntary schools.[198] The Catholic element of the primary school population was forty-four per cent by the end of 1956 and rising steadily,[199] but between 1948 and 1956 the Catholic community paid nearly £1 million for just one fifth of the investment available for primary and secondary intermediate schools, and these figures do not include the funds dedicated to county grammar schools.

The price of voluntary status was not confined to the cost of building and maintaining voluntary primary and secondary intermediate schools. The Catholic men's teacher training college, St Joseph's, was subject to the same funding conditions as voluntary schools. The Ministry estimated in 1954 that the cost of the college would be £130,000. The voluntary contribution for St Joseph's college therefore amounted to almost £4 million in 1996 prices.[200]

The distinction between county and voluntary schools cannot be viewed as a consequence of nationalist abstention. Catholic authorities fully cooperated with the Ministry's officials when formulating their development schemes, and their proposals often coincided with the recommendations of the Ministry's inspectors.[201] The inspector for the

City of Londonderry stated that the Catholic authorities' proposals were 'sound and practicable' as early as November 1948, but progress remained slow compared to the growth of county schools.[202]

Farren claims that 'why there was this slow rate of progress is difficult to determine'.[203] However, the significant increase in the scale of building for both primary and secondary intermediate voluntary schools outlined in the next chapter underlines how political rather than administrative and financial factors explain the notable differences between the development of county and voluntary schools during the 1950s. Midgley must be viewed as the prime culprit for denying Catholic pupils the opportunities available to their Protestant counterparts. He inherited a partisan education system in 1950, but the evidence from the Ministry of Education's Reports for the 1950s and 1960s indicates that he exacerbated rather than eased the 'invidious distinctions' between Catholic and Protestant which, forty years later, still exercise a profound impact on the lives of Catholic families.

'DISLOYAL ELEMENTS'

The Gaelic language was the focus for 'Orange' criticism of Catholic schools between the wars, but after the abolition of the grants in 1933 interest in the language waned amongst Unionist politicians. After 1945 there were two major issue for Unionist critics – the fate of the National Anthem and the teaching of Northern Ireland's troubled history.

Nationalist cultural values were naturally viewed as a challenge to the dominant Protestant and Unionist ethos, and Unionist MPs were prompt in noting and condemning any evidence of defiance. After 1945 the attitude of the Catholic minority towards the National Anthem, a battle tune in Blanshard's cultural war between Ulster unionism and Irish nationalism – attracted their attention.

In 1946 a concert at the Stranmillis Summer School concluded without a rendition of the National Anthem. Hall-Thompson responded by insisting that all concerts sponsored by the Council for the Encouragement of Music and Arts (CEMA) should end with the anthem 'in accordance with the British traditions and cultural interests of Northern Ireland'.[204] The Nationalist MP Eddie McAteer later claimed that the Ministry's insistence upon the anthem was discouraging Catholics from attending CEMA's concerts, but Hall-Thompson refused to compromise.[205]

The Stranmillis episode in the late 1940s was only a prelude to the severe conflict between Unionists and Nationalists in the aftermath of the 1949 election. The assertive declaration of loyalty to the Crown and the Empire demanded by the Unionist leadership was certain to cause friction between the two communities. These tensions were exemplified by the Flags and Emblems Act of 1954 which prohibited the display of the Irish tricolour within Northern Ireland.[206]

An incident in a Belfast cinema in March 1954, when Catholic pupils remained in their seats during the playing of the anthem, allowed Midgley to offer his opinion of the purpose of education in Northern Ireland's schools:

> I think personally that the time has arrived when local education authorities should ask and expect to receive from all schools . . . a greater measure of recognition for the patriotism and loyalty of this democratically elected and administered part of the United Kingdom.[207]

Unionist MPs remained attentive to such rebellious outbursts, and the following June they exposed another episode in a Belfast cinema when the anthem was not played at all after a showing of *Julius Caesar*. MPs complained of the city's education authority 'capitulating completely to this disloyal element in the community' and Midgley promised to act.[208] However, the following year the 'Protestant Unionist' MP Norman Porter highlighted another seditious display by Catholic schoolboys at a showing of *The Dambusters*. Midgley claimed no knowledge of the incident, but Porter insisted upon a resolute response:

> If I bring this evidence before the Minister is he prepared to see that these teachers obey the law, or alternatively will the Minister see that grants are withdrawn from their schools?[209]

Minford later related yet another subversive episode in a cinema involving a group of convent girls, which provoked the comment that 'children in Roman Catholic schools are taught a hatred of everything that we hold dear in this country of ours'[210] and led Midgley's successor as Minister of Education to state that 'all children in our schools should be taught to respect Her Majesty the Queen'.[211]

These events attracted the attention of no more than a handful of Unionist MPs, but they evoked a response from a broad section of the Unionist Party. The cultural clashes of the early 1930s were motivated by the economic depression, but the conflict of the early 1950s arose directly from the political antagonism generated by the 1949 election.

The election had been a triumph for the Unionist Party against both the Nationalists and the NILP, and Unionists were reluctant to ease the tensions aroused by the 'Chapel Gate' election. The reaction to these adolescent incidents in cinemas may appear excessive, but there were clear electoral motives lurking beneath their intense sensitivity.

The intense struggle between Ulster unionism and Irish nationalism ensured that the contents of the history textbooks used in Northern Ireland's schools would be a major concern for the Ministry of Education. The Lynn committee recommended that 'no book bearing upon the subject of history should without previous official sanction be permitted to be used in any school under the Ministry'.[212] Primary and secondary intermediate, but not grammar, schools required the prior approval of the Ministry for all history and Gaelic language books. This scrutiny was more than nominal, because in 1943 the Ministry's inspectors rejected all the proposed history books for Catholic schools in the diocese of Down and Connor.[213]

The Ministry's determination to supervise the history books read in Northern Ireland's schools was highlighted by the fate of Miss Bluett, the daughter of a former Irish Lord Chief Justice, who was recommended to the Ministry by the Church of Ireland's Bishop of Down. Miss Bluett's initial submissions on Irish history were rejected, and the inspectors refused to approve her subsequent work *A Children's History of Ireland*, despite her efforts to fashion the material to suit their demands.[214] The Ministry's sensitivity later led another history book to be ruled unsuitable because of references to the Easter Rising. In contrast, *A Story of Gibraltar* was thought to be an interesting and useful book for Northern Ireland's schoolchildren.[215]

Unionist MPs also monitored the books used in Catholic schools for disloyal traits. In December 1955 Porter complained of a picture of a tricolour in a Gaelic language book used in Armagh's schools.[216] Midgley was critical of the use of the book *Cosan an Oir*, but claimed that the decision rested with the county's education authority.[217] Three months later he decided that the matter was his responsibility and banned the book because 'we are not going to subsidise this disloyalty'.[218]

Unionists were not only vigilant against subversive books in Catholic schools; they were also anxious to influence the education of Protestant pupils. A common theme in education debates during the 1940s and 1950s was the demand by Unionist MPs for compulsory Ulster history classes and an official textbook to ensure that the teaching of history conformed to a Unionist version of the past. Hall-Thompson refused to sanction compulsory history classes, but promised an approved history book in June 1946.[219] The proposed textbook was clearly not a priority for Hall-Thompson and his officials, because MPs waited nearly two years before he announced that the Ministry had commissioned the writer Hugh Shearman to prepare a draft of a textbook.[220] In March 1949, the Unionist Party conference passed a motion calling for compulsory classes and a definitive history textbook, but the following month Hall-Thompson only promised that a handbook for teachers would provide a historical background to the 'constitution' of Northern Ireland.[221]

The fall of Hall-Thompson left the problem with Midgley, who stated in March 1950 that there would be no compulsory history classes and there was still no official textbook.[222] A year later he admitted 'I cannot truthfully say that a history approved for use in the schools is forthcoming at the moment'.[223] The parliamentary silence on Shearman's book was only dispelled in April 1953 when Diamond claimed that the book had been discarded because 'the history presented so many snags for the Unionist point of view that it was decided we should be better without it'.[224]

Porter later revived the issue:

> There must be introduced into our schools a more positive history which will deal with the background of our Ulster Province so that our Protestant children might be told in a more forcible manner the historical background of the heritage of ours. The children should be educated by means of more distinctive Protestant books and literature.[225]

Porter expected Midgley to support his efforts: 'I know that I have the sympathy perhaps of the Minister of Education himself in this matter but I feel that the Minister should be keener on enforcing this than he has been in the past'.[226] Porter was a lone voice calling for a history book until he was joined by the Unionist MP Alexander Hunter who, like Porter, was only concerned with promoting the unionist and Protestant features of the region's history:

> instead of one child in 500 knowing about King William's progress in Northern Ireland and possibly one child in 10,000 knowing about Lord Carson and Lord Craigavon we will have educated children in our schools in Ulster.[227]

No MP mentioned the history textbook again until Joseph Morgan in July 1959. He demonstrated a greater regard for historical accuracy by recommending J. C. Beckett as a suitable guide for the region's history,[228] but his intervention failed to inspire a renewed challenge. By the end of the decade the history textbook campaign had faded into obscurity.

The Ministry's resistance to the concerted campaign for a definitive history book is difficult to explain without understanding the cultural implications of history teaching in Northern Ireland. Midgley's successor, Morris May, underlined the powerful bond between history teaching and national and religious identity when he claimed 'all I know of Ulster history was gained at my father's knee or from my mother. That is where children should imbibe their history and their religion'.[229] Ministry officials recognised that the sharp cultural and political clashes within Northern Ireland prevented any history book being acceptable to both Catholic and county schools, and they were wary of sanctioning an approved textbook to satisfy Unionist backbenchers that could eventually become obligatory reading in *every* school. The efforts by backbench Unionist MPs to secure an approved history textbook underlined the determination of some Unionists to establish a cultural dominance over the Catholic and Nationalist minority. However, the Ministry's success in deflecting the campaign demonstrated its capacity to secure the support of senior Unionists against the intolerant elements within the Unionist Party.

In the late 1940s Gaelic language classes once more inspired a brief spasm of hostility from unionists, with even liberal Unionists criticising Gaelic classes in schools. O'Neill asked Hall-Thompson in March 1947 'is it not a fact that for sheer waste of time there is little worse than learning Erse?'[230] Two months later Hall-Thompson admitted 'I think I had better be quite frank and say that although the Irish language may be taught at the present time it will not get much sympathy from me. I am not really in sympathy with the teaching of Irish'.[231]

The debate throughout most of the 1950s was confined to occasional Nationalist protests against the abolition of the special grants for Gaelic teaching[232] whilst Unionist backbenchers, absorbed by the antics of schoolchildren in cinemas, did not revive the Gaelic issue until Porter complained of the tricolour on the cover of *Cosan an Oir*. Gaelic in Catholic schools was a minor question, but it provoked a last intolerant tremor from the most ardent critics of Catholic schools. In March 1956, during the debate of Midgley's decision to ban *Cosan an Oir*, Porter criticised the Ministry's tolerance of Gaelic and announced he would be tabling a motion calling for a revision of the 1947 Act.[233] The motion, sponsored by Minford and Porter, asked that 'no educational grants to voluntary schools should in future exceed fifty per cent of the approved expenditure unless such voluntary schools adopt a four and two committee basis of management'.[234] Minford attempted to portray the motion as a debate on public representation, but he could not avoid the occasional descent into sectarian rhetoric:

> It is entirely wrong that we should be handing out money and should continue to hand out money to at least one section of the community who shows its discourtesy to the Government of the country year after year . . . I fail to see why we should continue to support the present system and give grants to people whose only desire is to do us all the harm they possibly can.[235]

Porter, seconding the motion, was equally blunt when he stated: 'many of the 25,000 people who voted Sinn Féin in the recent Mid Ulster election have been educated by this money . . . I take it that the Government should not approve of financing the enemies of Ulster in that way'.[236] Minford and Porter were peripheral figures within Ulster unionism, but their pursuit of sedition in all its forms within Catholic schools evoked a response from other Unionist MPs that Hall-Thompson was unable, and Midgley was unwilling, to resist.

Unionist MPs were not alone in seeking to cultivate cultural and national values within schools. Some senior Catholic clerics also wished to blend history and Gaelic language teaching to create a distinctive Catholic and nationalist account of Irish history. In July 1954 Mageean, opening a new secondary intermediate school, told his audience:

> This is an Irish school, an Irish Catholic school, and I should like it to be a school in which pupils will learn something about the history of their country, its manners, its traditions, its outlook, its language, and learn to be true and staunch Irishmen . . . I make a special appeal to the staff of this new school to see that the children under their care know something about the history and literature of our native land.[237]

Mageean's speech underlined the Catholic authorities' willingness to promote national and ethnic as well as religious values within Catholic schools. Nationality remained a 'secondary' feature compared to the 'primary' purpose of fostering religious devotion, but an appeal to nationalist sentiment was an effective means of gathering support from the Catholic laity.

CONCLUSION

The 1947 Act transformed Northern Ireland's education system. Mass secondary education was to have a profound impact upon the lives of thousands of schoolchildren, and in the 1950s reform exacerbated the disadvantages of voluntary schools. Farren is right to claim that 'it would be churlish . . . to suggest that the 1947 Act did not mark a considerable change in the educational opportunities available to young people throughout the north',[238] but the benefits of secondary education were unfairly shared between the two communities.

The Catholic authorities, as in 1930, secured a reduction in the voluntary contribution without surrendering clerical authority to a school committee, but only after two arduous years of struggle. The 'conscience clause' dispute gravely undermined the Catholic authorities' campaign for increased funding, and only the Cabinet's decision to allow Protestant clerics significant powers in the proposed secondary schools enabled them to secure a fifteen per cent increase in capital funds. The 1947 Act was not only the first major defeat for the Protestant clerics; it was to be the last occasion when the Protestant clergy would clash with the government on education issues. As Farren notes 'after 1947 religious controversy of the very acrimonious kind witnessed from 1923–1947 gradually moved to the margins of educational development in Northern Ireland'.[239]

The final settlement, though leaving the Catholic community with the burden of finding more than one third of the cost of building and maintaining its schools, was a testament to Hall-Thompson's determination to find an accommodation with the CCMA. His proposals were constantly rejected by his Cabinet colleagues, but he eventually secured a reasonable settlement.

O'Neill's comment that Brooke's defence of the concession to voluntary schools in 1946, seventeen years before his retirement, was 'his last act of political courage'[240] should not obscure the evidence that Brooke was more accommodating than many of his colleagues towards the Catholic authorities' education demands in the late 1940s and early 1950s. He was one of the first ministers to accept Hall-Thompson's proposals for improved funding for voluntary schools, and his conduct during the St Joseph's college episode indicated a willingness to address the Catholic authorities' concerns. Therefore, his choice of Midgley in 1950 can only be explained as a hasty response to the revival of political strife following the 1949 election.

Midgley was a partisan figure, the most belligerent critic of the Catholic authorities of Northern Ireland's twelve Ministers of Education. He 'lost few opportunities to give vent to his very critical views of the Catholic Church's approach to education'.[241] He tried and failed to amend the 1947 Act and, after his colleagues chose not to upset the agreement with the Catholic authorities, he denied funding to the Catholic community. The languid pace of voluntary secondary intermediate school building in the 1950s was not caused by either a reluctance to participate in education reform or the inability of the Catholic populace to provide the voluntary contribution, though the financial burden of reform should not be understated. The course of events after Midgley's death outlined in the following chapter high-lights the political rather than the financial limitations upon voluntary schools during Midgley's seven years as Minister of Education. The increased pace of building for Catholic schools in the early 1960s cannot be explained by greater prosperity within the Catholic com-munity, or by a more accommodating attitude from Catholic clerics. The Ministry of Education's own statistics indicate that Midgley was responsible for the second-class condition of voluntary secondary intermediate schools at the end of the 1950s. Farren claims that Minford and Porter's motion of June 1956 'would have had the effect of seriously delaying the provision of new secondary intermediate and additional grammar schools for the Catholic community',[242] but the evidence suggests that the Catholic community was already facing severe difficulties in developing Catholic secondary education.

Blanshard's claim that Northern Ireland's schools were the frontline trenches in a cultural war was never more appropriate than during the fifteen years after 1945. The displays of nationalist sentiment by Catholic schoolchildren in cinemas might appear trivial today, but they antagonised elements within Ulster unionism. The government deflected most of these challenges, but it was aware of the implications within the Unionist Party and in the Orange Halls of conspicuous concessions to the Catholic authorities.

CHAPTER FIVE

Stormont's last years

The end of the 1950s brought a gradual change in Northern Ireland's political mood. The failure of the IRA's campaign in the border areas only underlined the limitations of traditional republicanism, and nationalists began to look beyond the border question to address practical daily concerns. There was also evidence of change within the unionist camp, and by the early 1960s 'liberals' within the Unionist Party appeared to be more influential than at any time since partition. These prospects for change and progress were greatly enhanced in March 1963 when the elderly and indolent Brookeborough suffered a 'diplomatic' stomach ulcer,[1] and gave way to his Minister of Finance Terence Marne O'Neill.[2]

O'Neill's deeds as Prime Minister never matched his rhetoric. However, observers should not understate the importance of gestures such as the visits to Catholic schools, meetings with the Republic's premier Sean Lemass, and the message of sympathy on the death of Pope John XXIII. The reaction of sections of the Unionist Party to these modest initiatives demonstrated the limited scope for a Unionist politician seeking to foster tolerance between the two communities. O'Neill's limitations did not prevent a widespread spirit for reform developing in Northern Ireland in the 1960s, and the Nationalist Party responded to O'Neill's meeting with Lemass in 1965 by accepting the role of the official opposition.[3]

Events in Rome also encouraged hopes that Northern Ireland's politics might converge around an accommodating consensus. The Papacy embarked upon its own ambitious project of renewal when Pope John XXIII announced 'an ecumenical Council for the universal Church' in January 1959.[4] Barritt and Carter claim:

> No outside event contributed more to the improving of group relations than the liberalising influence of Pope John XXIII and the Vatican Councils. The desire of the Catholic clergy to maintain a strong hold over the activities of their flocks had not helped in breaking down the division in the community. With the wind of

change blowing from the Vatican Councils more strongly than many dared hope, the Church appeared to present a new image of cooperation.[5]

Barritt and Carter, devout Christians, probably overstate the impact of the Vatican Council, and the optimism of the early 1960s should also not be exaggerated, but the Cameron Commission in 1969 was right to note that 'traditional patterns of antagonism have at least begun to erode in recent years'.[6]

The optimism of the first half of the decade gradually dissipated as O'Neill failed to translate his rhetoric into palpable reforms. The civil rights movement provoked a hostile reaction from an influential minority of unionists, and by the summer of 1969 Northern Ireland was gripped by the most intense violence since partition. The revival of traditional conflicts led the British government to intervene in Irish affairs for the first time since the 1920s and eventually brought the collapse of the devolved government in the spring of 1972.

Although the last decade of devolved power was afflicted by mass violence and economic collapse the 1960s brought progress for Catholic schools after the struggles of the 1950s. O'Neill's government increased the scale of funding for voluntary schools in 1968, but the most significant advance for the Catholic populace came with increased spending on new schools which finally began to eradicate the effects of decades of disadvantage. Catholic schools enjoyed considerable progress in Stormont's final years.

MORRIS MAY

Harry Midgley's successor, Morris May, began his parliamentary career as an avowed opponent of Catholic schools. He entered the Northern Ireland Commons after the acrimonious election of 1949, and by the end of the year he was playing a prominent role in the National Insurance crisis. He spoke against Brooke's temporary compromise of paying the employer's contribution until the end of March 1951, which was accepted by most of the rebels on the day of Hall-Thompson's resignation,[7] and five days later he called for the government to insist upon compulsory 'four and two' committees for all voluntary schools.[8]

May lapsed into a parliamentary silence on education issues until June 1956 when Minford and Porter combined to launch an assault on the sixty-five per cent grant for voluntary schools.[9] The Cabinet, concerned by Minford's motion, drafted an amendment calling for yet another review of the grants to voluntary schools.[10] The choice of May to propose the government's amendment underlined his aversion to the 1947 Act because ministers presumably chose a professed critic of the Act to increase support for the review from discontented MPs.

May restated his opposition to the 1947 Act during the debate on Minford's motion.[11] Only three months before he succeeded Midgley he called for the elimination of the voluntary primary school:

> I believe it is in the best interests of this Province, and of those who hold varying political and religious beliefs, that the present system of primary education by which grants are given to non-transferred schools should be discontinued at the earliest possible moment.[12]

The evidence from May's backbench career suggested he would follow Midgley's fractious course, but within a fortnight of his appointment in May 1957 he noted the 'disappointing' pace of voluntary school building and defended Catholic clerical managers from insinuations of fraud.[13] A year later he paid tribute to voluntary school managers for their cooperation with Ministry officials, and the Queen's Speech for 1959 also commended voluntary schools.[14] May also attempted, without success, to convince his Cabinet colleagues to provide clerical assistants for voluntary schools.[15] The evidence may appear sparse, but May offered a more accommodating tone than Midgley's blatant animosity.

May's amendment in June 1956 called for another review of the education system,[16] and Midgley's death in April 1957 left May himself with the perplexing task of satisfying critics on the unionist backbenches without embarking upon fundamental reform. This dilemma had troubled almost all of May's predecessors, but his problems were greatly eased by a waning of interest in education issues by Unionist MPs. Porter lost his Commons seat in the spring of 1958, evidence that the influence of the intransigent right was declining within unionist ranks. When the Ministry eventually recommended maintaining the status quo there were no protests from the unionist backbenches.[17] Minford failed to mention the review until March 1959 when he vaguely recalled his motion of nearly three years before:

> I remember I raised this matter some years ago on a Motion and the then Minister of Education said that the Government desired to look into the matter at a certain time, but unfortunately the Minister passed away before that could be done.[18]

There were a few isolated outbreaks of dissent,[19] but the defeat of Porter and Minford's motion and their diminishing role in the Commons[20] allowed May to develop a more accommodating relationship with Catholic voluntary schools without significant criticism.

The Catholic authorities and their nationalist allies were less attentive to education questions, because they squandered an opportunity to argue for a ten per cent increase in the capital grant. In 1959 the British Department of Education allowed voluntary schools to claim three quarters of the cost of all capital projects rather than just claim for projects to provide the additional teaching space necessary to increase the school leaving age to fifteen.

The devolved government obviously feared a nationalist campaign linked to the changes at Westminster, but they failed to attract a response from nationalist politicians or Catholic clerics.[21] At the end of June 1959 a Unionist Senator claimed that 'the grants have recently been raised in England from fifty per cent to seventy-five per cent and immediately there is a clamour here for the same thing'.[22] However, there is no evidence from either the Commons or the Senate that nationalist politicians were planning an offensive against the 1947 Act in the autumn or winter of 1959. Also, the *Irish Catholic Directory* does not note any comment by senior Catholic clerics. Nationalist MPs mentioned the grant increases in February and December 1960,[23] but there was no coordinated campaign. In 1945 the Catholic authorities failed to exploit the advantages offered by the 1936 Act, and fifteen years later they repeated the error.

The Catholic authorities may have consciously chosen not to confront the government, preferring to foster closer ties with education officials. The *Irish Catholic Directory* editions for the 1950s are littered with references to the 'burden that is beyond our resources or that can be borne only by the most heroic efforts',[24] but by the early 1960s Catholic bishops and senior Ministry officials were clearly enjoying friendly relations. In September 1960 Mageean thanked the Ministry's officials for their efforts on behalf of Catholic schools, and twelve months later Brownell's successor, A. C. Williams, paid tribute to Mageean's diligence in providing schools in his diocese.[25] In April 1963 Mageean's successor, William Philbin, expressed his 'gratitude for all the interest, care and pains that have been taken in regard to the education of our Catholic young people' and Williams responded by complimenting the work of the Christian Brothers, the embodiment of Irish Gaelic Catholicism so despised by many Ulster Unionists.[26] The evidence from the Northern Ireland Hansard and the *Irish Catholic Directory* suggests that the Ministry of Education and the Catholic authorities were enjoying improved relations. The Ministry's own statistics confirm that this rapprochement was translated into more investment in Catholic voluntary schools.

May inherited an education system in which Catholic pupils were suffering a significant disadvantage, and he openly recognised the problems facing voluntary schools:

> I have a fear . . . that because of the difficulty of raising large sums of money for voluntary schools many of the children in this Province are being denied all the advantages of education to which they are entitled under our modern system, because it has been impossible for voluntary schools to raise sufficient money to give all the advantages which are available in State schools.[27]

> If honourable Members on the other side of the House are honest and sincere they will admit that not only are their communities suffering serious financial disadvantage by the amount of money they have to raise to pay their proportion of the costs of upkeep of such schools, but they will also recognise that the children who attend the schools are under a serious handicap and at a grave disadvantage compared to those who attend transferred schools.[28]

May's comments could be interpreted as traditional unionist criticism of the Catholic authorities' intransigence, but he appeared committed to resolving these problems. In April 1958 he announced that the Ministry expected that only fifty-five per cent of the necessary secondary places would be available for voluntary school pupils by August 1960,[29] but a few months later the Ministry's Report for 1957–58 promised places for seventy per cent of voluntary pupils by September 1961.[30] This modest growth should be viewed as evidence that May was dedicated to diminishing the contrast between county and voluntary schools.

The prolonged process of official approval for new schools, involving the assessment of the local religious demography, purchase of sites, drafting of architect's plans and sanctioning of construction estimates, meant that May's efforts were not translated into tangible benefits for Catholic parishes until the end of the decade. In Midgley's final year as Minister, the Ministry provided just 720 voluntary secondary intermediate places, but in the twelve months to the end of July 1958 voluntary secondary intermediate schools secured more than 2,000 places. The Ministry funded more than 3,000 places for each of the following two years, and in 1961 the number rose to nearly 4,000 places. Figure 5A illustrates the persistence of this preference for voluntary secondary intermediate schools throughout the 1960s, with

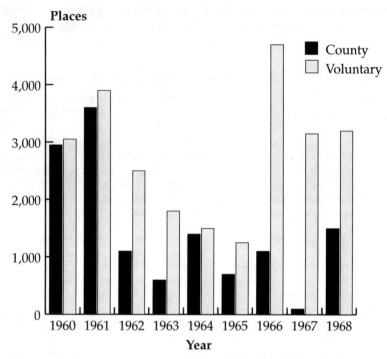

Figure 5A. Secondary intermediate places 1960–1968

voluntary schools gaining the majority of new places each year between 1960 and 1968. Voluntary secondary intermediate schools gained over 11,000 new places between the beginning of 1966 and the end of 1968, more than the number of places created in the first twelve years after the 1947 Act.[31]

May's liberalism should not be overstated as the apparent ebbing of Catholic disadvantage during the 1960s can only be partly explained by the Ministry's novel enthusiasm for investment in Catholic schools. The decline in the number of new county secondary intermediate schools accounts for the number of new voluntary places finally surpassing the county total in 1960. There was a significant increase in investment in voluntary schools in the early 1960s, but the number of new places for voluntary secondary intermediate places declined until 1965 when the Ministry funded just over 1,000 places. The scale of county secondary intermediate school building also declined during the mid 1960s, but Catholic pupils were still awaiting the investment enjoyed by their Protestant counterparts in the 1950s. There may have been an inevitable improvement for Catholic schools in the early

1960s, but, May's five years as Minister from 1957 until his death in 1962 was a key phase in the development of voluntary schools. May began to reverse decades of second-class treatment by the devolved government by dedicating significant sums to voluntary schools.

TERENCE O'NEILL

Terence Marne O'Neill remains a mystery for modern Irish historians. Nearly thirty years after his resignation, many questions surrounding his six years as Prime Minister have yet to be answered.[32] O'Neill, as his autobiography mentions,[33] gave his maiden speech early in December 1946 in support of Hall-Thompson and the Education Bill,[34] but his second intervention in education debates displayed more traditional unionist values. In March 1947 he criticised Gaelic classes in Catholic schools.[35] His only other parliamentary contribution came ten years later when he once more spoke of the futility of learning Gaelic, claiming that 'it takes up so much time of so many people here in Northern Ireland who waste all their time on it and then go over to England and get a job'.[36]

O'Neill was certainly both arrogant and naïve, and only a few days after his resignation he offered stark evidence of his condescending view of Northern Ireland's Catholics:

> It is frightfully hard to explain to a Protestant that if you give Roman Catholics a good job and a good house they will live like Protestants, because they will see neighbours with cars and TV sets. They will refuse to have eighteen children, but if the Roman Catholic is jobless and lives in a most ghastly hovel he will rear eighteen children on national assistance. It is impossible to explain this to a militant Protestant, because he is keen to deny civil rights to his Roman Catholic neighbours. He cannot understand, in fact, that if you treat Roman Catholics with due consideration and kindness they will live like Protestants in spite of the authoritarian nature of their church.[37]

Education policy during the late 1960s offers no firm clues to resolve the enigma, providing evidence both of O'Neill's liberalism and his arrogant misunderstanding of the Catholic minority. There were genuine hopes for reform in Northern Ireland during O'Neill's six years as Prime Minister, but the evidence suggests that the disadvantage of voluntary status persisted throughout the 1960s to remain a considerable liability in 1969. The problems for voluntary schools were outlined by the Ministry's Report for 1963–64:

> where the accommodation is completely inadequate, where schools
> are understaffed and classes swollen to beyond a tolerable size and
> where children are in consequence deprived of many of the benefits
> which accrue from modern methods of teaching and organisation.[38]

The inferior condition of voluntary primary schools in the 1960s was
illustrated by the number of overcrowded classes. In January 1962
only six county primary classes contained more than fifty pupils and
no county school class held more than fifty-five pupils. However, there
were ninety-six voluntary primary school classes with more than fifty
pupils, twenty-six classes with more than fifty-five pupils and three
classes with more than sixty pupils.[39]

The investment of the early 1960s brought only gradual relief for
thousands of Catholic pupils. Two years later there were only two
county school classes with more than fifty pupils, but forty-six
voluntary school classes contained more than fifty pupils, eight had
more than fifty-five pupils and in two classes teachers were still coping
with more than sixty pupils.[40] There were nearly 10,000 voluntary
pupils in classes of more than forty pupils in January 1964 while less
than 3,000 county pupils suffered a similar fate.[41]

The statistics for class size only partly reveal the second-class
condition of voluntary primary schools in the 1960s. In Belfast and
Londonderry primary schools resorted to the 'dual day' system to
educate two groups of pupils in the same school. The 'dual day' was
obviously exhausting for the teachers and unsuitable for pupils, who
spent less time in the classroom than in ordinary schools. As the
Ministry's Report for 1965 explained:

> It is the cause of a good deal of unnecessary difficulty in conducting
> the school, it imposes an unwelcome strain on many of the pupils,
> and it is a major obstacle to the introduction and development of
> modern teaching methods.[42]

The number of 'dual day' schools increased during the early 1960s
despite the gradual overall improvement for other voluntary schools.
In 1962 there were eleven 'dual day' schools and in 1965 there were
fourteen schools – all voluntary schools – educating more than 3,500
pupils.[43] The following year sixteen schools were operating the 'dual
day' system, and the Ministry accepted that the problem would persist
for many years because 'in most of these cases an alleviation of the
situation depends on building schemes which will take some time to
complete'.[44]

The Ministry's pessimism proved to be justified and the 'dual day' school was to survive until the early 1970s.[45] Population growth in Belfast and Londonderry may partly explain why Catholic schools were so overcrowded in the 1960s, but Ministry officials were expected to counter these problems. The Ministry's annual Report contained statistics that confirmed the gradual rise of the Catholic primary school population, until the Ministry decided to cease collecting this data in 1963.[46]

May's successor, Ivan Neill, pledged in April 1963 to 'remove this blot' of overcrowded classes and dedicate more funds to voluntary schools.[47] The following year's White Paper, *Educational Development in Northern Ireland*, recognised that conditions in many schools remained inadequate and acknowledged the severity of the problem of over-crowded classes:

> The main objectives in the field of primary education in the imme-diate future will be the elimination of excessively large classes and the closing of small schools which are outworn, unhygienic and ill-provided with modern amenities.[48]

A Ministry survey for the White Paper underlined the problems facing Northern Ireland's primary schools. The survey found half of the region's 1,482 primary schools had been built before 1900; 850 were without central heating; more than 450 were lacking artificial lighting; over 300 schools did not have piped water, and eighty schools had no playground.[49] The government recognised the scale of the problem, but only promised to pay greater attention to renovating decaying schools.

The White Paper of 1964, despite ignoring the implications of the voluntary contribution, renewed the impetus for additional funds for voluntary schools. The Ministry's Report for 1964 noted that the development schemes for the City of Londonderry and Fermanagh were revised by the Ministry. The following year Armagh's education authority's development scheme for voluntary schools was amended while the Ministry also discussed the provision of voluntary schools with the Londonderry City committee.[50] The Report offered no explanation for these changes, but the Ministry probably insisted the education authorities expand their plans for voluntary school projects.

The second half of the 1960s witnessed a dramatic increase in voluntary school building, prompted by the Ministry's enthusiasm for addressing the problems of voluntary schools following the 1964 White Paper. As Figure 5B indicates, voluntary primary schools enjoyed spectacular growth in the second half of the decade.

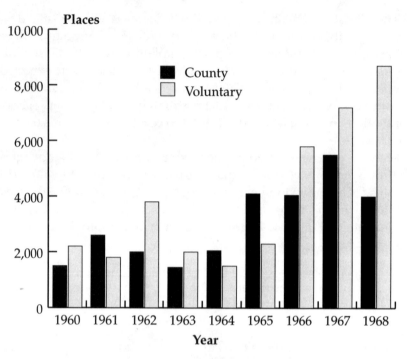

Figure 5B. Primary school places 1960–1969

The White Paper promised a five year plan to reduce the number of primary classes with more than forty pupils,[51] and after 1964 the Ministry dedicated substantial sums to finance primary school building. Voluntary schools, suffering the worst cases of overcrowding, gained most of this investment, and the number of new voluntary primary school places rose from less than 1,500 in 1963–64 to more than 8,500 places by 1968.[52]

In the seventeen years to the end of 1965, voluntary primary schools gained less than 24,000 new places, but from January 1966 to December 1968 the Ministry funded more than 21,000 new places.[53] The statistics appear impressive, but voluntary primary schools remained a quarter of a century behind the county schools. Only in 1965 did the total number of new places provided since the 1930 Act surpass the number of new places created for public elementary schools by the outbreak of war in 1939.[54]

The Ministry increased spending for Catholic schools in the 1960s, but the claims of Unionist politicians and Ministry Reports for a new generation of 'palatial schools'[55] could not obscure the detail that this investment was failing to solve the severe problems facing Catholic schools, particularly in the two major cities.[56] The central purpose of the 1947 Act was to create a network of secondary schools for all children from the age of eleven. However, the shortage of secondary intermediate schools compelled many primary schools to educate pupils beyond the age of eleven. The number of 'unreorganised' primary schools presents valuable evidence of the relative condition of Northern Ireland's county and voluntary schools in 1965 228 of the 284 'unreorganised' schools were voluntary schools.[57]

New voluntary secondary intermediate schools reduced the total number of 'unreorganised' schools to 124 by the end of 1967 when 'reorganisation' was almost complete in Belfast, the City and County of Londonderry, Down and Tyrone, but there remained 'large groups of unreorganised voluntary schools in Armagh and Fermanagh'.[58] Thousands of Catholic schoolchildren were still being denied the opportunity of a full secondary school education at the end of the 1960s. The investment in voluntary schools in the second half of the 1960s began to ease the concerns of Catholic parents that their children gained only a second-class education, but the Ministry's efforts also exacerbated the financial penalty of the voluntary contribution.

As Figure 5C shows, the voluntary contribution for capital projects almost doubled to more than £800,000 in the two years after the 1964

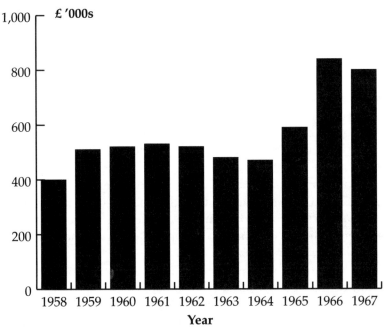

Figure 5C. Capital voluntary contribution 1958–1967

White Paper, and Northern Ireland's Catholics were paying a further £100,000 to finance heating, lighting and cleaning costs.[59] The burden was considerable by the end of the 1960s, with the Catholic community paying an annual contribution of more than £10 million in 1996 prices to develop its network of schools.

These escalating costs provoked an inevitable reaction from nationalist politicians. Harry Diamond initiated the first major debate of voluntary school funding since the late 1940s in March 1965, and the following year nationalist politicians paid greater attention to the proposed five per cent increase for voluntary schools in England and Wales than to the ten per cent rise of 1959.[60] Nationalist agitation led the Minister of Education, William Fitzsimmons, to state that a corresponding increase for Northern Ireland's schools was 'being very carefully considered' and he acknowledged that 'voluntary schools have done a very good job in Northern Ireland'.[61] The nationalist campaign secured another significant success in January 1967 when the Minister of Finance and former Minister of Education, Herbert Kirk, pledged to dedicate more public funds to voluntary schools.[62] At the end of September 1967 the government demonstrated the importance of education by appointing Robert Bradford as the first Parliamentary Secretary of the Ministry of Education since Dehra Parker's departure in the summer of 1944. Three weeks later the government published another White Paper which finally proposed increasing the rate of funding offered by the 1947 Act.

THE 1968 EDUCATION ACT

In October 1967 the Minister of Education, William Long, responded to the nationalist campaign[63] for improved funding, and the British government's decision to increase capital funding for voluntary schools in England and Wales to eighty per cent with the White Paper *Local Education Authorities and Voluntary Schools*.[64] The White Paper offered voluntary schools the chance to become 'maintained' schools and gain 80% of capital funding, the full costs of maintenance and the cost of heating, lighting and cleaning the school.[65] The government, as usual, demanded a 'four and two' committee as a condition for the additional funds.[66]

The government also maintained its tradition of offering more generous conditions to voluntary grammar schools. The White Paper argued that local education authorities were less involved in the maintenance of grammar schools than in voluntary primary and secondary intermediate schools, and therefore the proposed school committees for existing grammar schools would contain nominees of the Ministry rather than the local education authority.[67] The White Paper asserted that 'it is important to preserve the principle that a scholarship is awarded for the benefit of the pupil, not the school',[68] but grammar schools enjoyed the same transport, school meal and milk services as other voluntary schools. The government's claim that the local education authority paid the scholarship fee to the pupil rather than to the school can be dismissed as an artificial distinction. As the Catholic bishops noted in January 1968: '*All* grants are ultimately given for the benefit of the pupil and no juggling with book keeping items can eliminate this simple fact'.[69]

The White Paper also contained an element of coercion. A 'four and two' school was entitled to revert to voluntary status after two years' notice, but the White Paper proposed to abolish this right for 'maintained' schools. Also, no new school would be funded without a 'four and two' committee.[70] Thus, the White Paper presented the Catholic authorities with a stark choice between accepting 'four and two' committees or losing public funding for any new schools – a threat never imposed by either Craig or Brooke.

The Archbishop of Armagh, Cardinal William Conway, was attending a synod in Rome, but Philbin issued a swift condemnation of the White Paper on the day of publication. The proposals were 'an invasion of the established system of Catholic school management', and he was particularly concerned by the threat from the local education authorities because 'the attitudes of many of these bodies to Catholic interests is so notorious that we can only regard with dismay their direct involvement in the running of our schools'.[71] The generous terms for grammar schools also provoked criticism, and Philbin was troubled by the threat of future changes to the composition of the school committee. This fear had alarmed Mageean in the 1940s, and the following January the six northern bishops issued a statement which also echoed Mageean's concerns:

> It would obviously be much easier for legislation to give complete control of the management of voluntary schools to the State by a gradual process of changing the mixture on school committees than by depriving individual managers of their rights at one blow.[72]

The threat of discrimination from the education authorities, the loss of the right to revert to voluntary status, the danger of the government altering school committees to secure a majority for the education authorities, and the preferential treatment of voluntary grammar schools were all to be major themes of the Catholic authorities' resistance to the White Paper. However, Philbin's statement of 19 October did not attract widespread support from the Catholic community.

The *Belfast Telegraph* claimed that Bishops Farren and Eugene O'Doherty of Dromore both declined to sign Philbin's statement, preferring to await Conway's return from Rome.[73] Nationalist politicians were also reluctant to denounce the White Paper.

The Nationalist leader, Eddie McAteer, was hostile to surrendering Catholic schools to the 'unloving care' of local councils,[74] but he also viewed the White Paper as a 'welcome wee step in the right direction'.[75] The Republican Labour MP, Gerry Fitt, was even more hesitant, promising a response after discussions with his party colleagues.[76] A month later, Fitt told the Commons that he disagreed with Philbin's statement, though he qualified his remarks by claiming that he now endorsed the Catholic authorities' more compromising stance.[77] The only enthusiastic defender of Catholic schools in the Commons was Harry Diamond, who baldly stated that, because local councils were guilty of gross discrimination, they should not be involved in Catholic schools.[78] Nationalist politicians were hesitant, but Northern Ireland's Catholic teachers positively welcomed the White Paper.

The northern executive of the INTO published a statement on the same day as Philbin that pledged qualified support for the White Paper, claiming that because:

> the standards of equipment cleaning and maintenance of voluntary schools have fallen behind those of county schools . . . we believe that the Government's scheme goes a long way to eliminate present inequalities and we strongly urge voluntary school authorities to accept it, provided certain necessary safeguards are secured.[79]

The initial response of the *Irish News* was also critical, but not damning, and in the final week of October most letters to the paper's editor either supported the government's plans or suggested that the White Paper offered a basis for discussion. The influence of the Vatican Council was evident in some contributions:

> There is not a parish that is clear of debt, and though we are eternally grateful to our pastors for all they have done in the matter of our schools we must face the fact that . . . our children must do with second best.[80]

> The people at local parish level must be allowed to have their say in this matter before any out-of-hand rejection of Captain Long's proposals is even contemplated.[81]

> I think it is high time that parishioners themselves were allowed to voice their opinions on such matters as it is they who are being pushed to pay for their schools.[82]

A speaker at the Ulster Liberal Party conference was guilty of over-statement when he claimed that ninety-nine per cent of the 'informed Catholic laity' disagreed with Philbin.[83] However, his comprehensive denunciation of the government's proposals clearly did not generate the loyal support from the Catholic laity evident in previous campaigns.

Conway returned from Rome on 1 November to issue a statement which the *Belfast Telegraph* considered to be 'considerably more helpful' than Philbin's earlier condemnation,[84] but which also indicated a shift in the direction of the Catholic authorities' campaign. Conway acknowledged that elements of the White Paper were acceptable, but he underlined his opposition to the local education authorities:

> What guarantee could we have that the local authorities will use these vast new powers over our schools fairly. If they treat us unfairly in such matters as housing – as many of them do – may they not do the same thing with our schools? It is hard to see how any reasonable person can fail to recognise that we have legitimate grounds for worry here.[85]

Conway emphasised practical rather than theological reasons for opposing the White Paper, and advanced Ministry appointments for the 'four and two' committees as the central question in the education debate. His return inspired a more confident defence of clerical interests. The *Irish News* briskly followed the Cardinal's lead, condemning those who 'assert, with all the gusto of Luther penning the scurrilities of his Table Talk, that such management has produced second-class schools and, therefore, second-class education'. The editorial also opposed the campaign against segregated education by:

> those worthies who pontificate on radio, television and in the Press about educational segregation and, wanting a cause for their passionate protests about a divided community, failing all else, find one in the Church's insistence on Catholic schools.[86]

Conway's new approach also converted the principal nationalist advocates of the White Paper the INTO. The leader of the northern section of the union, Gerry Quigley, insisted that there was 'no difference' between the INTO and Conway, and quoted the final sentence of their statement of 19 October calling for 'certain necessary safeguards' which had been viewed at the time as a qualified acceptance of Long's proposal.[87]

The contrast between Conway and Philbin was a question of methods rather than objectives, and dissent within the Catholic community was never as great as claimed by a unionist press ever vigilant for signs of the Catholic laity finally revolting against what O'Neill termed the 'authoritarian nature of their church'. Conway's emphasis on the role of the local education authorities offered the Catholic authorities significant advantages by satisfying a Catholic laity acutely aware of the bias of many local councils, but who no longer appeared willing to endure the sacrifices demanded by the 1947 Act to retain the clergy's monopoly of authority within Catholic schools. Conway attempted to divert the debate from the issue of clerical authority to discrimination against the Catholic minority. He highlighted 'nationalist' fears of the local education authorities, astutely blending civil rights agitation against local Unionist councils with the Catholic authorities' defence of clerical power.

Conway's new strategy also attracted notable unionist support. The *Belfast Telegraph* recommended that the Ministry, rather than the local education authorities, appoint the two public representatives.[88] In the Commons, Robert Porter, Robert Nixon and the Prime Minister's cousin Phelim O'Neill of the Unionist Party, along with the Liberal MP Sheelagh Murnaghan, and Fred Simpson of the NILP advised Long to negotiate with Conway.[89] The Catholic authorities found a potent issue,[90] and events in Armagh strengthened their case against the local education authorities.

The education authority in Armagh refused to allow voluntary schools to use the authority's buses for educational visits. The issue had been mentioned in the Commons in April and May of 1967,[91] but the education authority twice failed to accept Long's advice to allow the voluntary schools to use the buses. The Commons discussed the problem once more on 26 October, and Long promised a third attempt to persuade the education authority.[92] The Catholic bishops and nationalist politicians were searching for an illustration of the 'unloving care' of the local education authorities, and the Ministry's impotence when confronted by an obstinate local authority. Unionists in Armagh were swift to oblige with an audacious case of petty discrimination.[93]

The Nationalist MP for East Tyrone, Austin Currie, claimed that the Cabinet was encouraged to be uncompromising by the dissension evident from the letters' page of the *Irish News*,[94] and clearly the Catholic authorities' campaign in 1967 was hindered by the cool response of the major Catholic teachers' union and senior nationalist politicians to Philbin's condemnation of the White Paper. Conway could only unify the Catholic community by abandoning absolute opposition to any form of school committee. The *Irish News* was overstating the change of mood within Catholic ranks when it claimed that the course of events had vindicated Philbin's initial condemnation,[95] but the Catholic community was finally united by the end of November.

The conspicuous displays of loyalty from Nationalist politicians in 1930 and 1946 were valuable to the Catholic authorities in their negotiations with the government. Conway's efforts to rally the Catholic community around his qualified opposition to the White Paper were vital to their hopes for a compromise. Thus, Conway waited nearly a month after the publication of the White Paper before meeting Long for discussions. He found Long in an obdurate mood, refusing to accept his two major demands of Ministry appointments for the school committees and retaining the existing powers of 'four and two' school committees.[96] Relations between the Ministry and the Catholic authorities suddenly deteriorated in the week before the Commons debate of the White Paper at the end of November 1967. The *Irish News* noted that nationalist MPs were considering a boycott of the White Paper debate, and warned that 'the Catholic community will have to face a continuance of their present school burdens unless there is a change of heart'.[97] The *Belfast Telegraph* also adopted a harsher attitude in the final week of November. On 24 November the paper's editorial urged the government to allow the Ministry to appoint the public representatives on the school committees, but four days later the editorial stated that the Catholic authorities' acceptance of the 'four and two' committee did not allow for independence from the education authority.[98] The following day the paper claimed 'unionist backbenchers are expected to make it clear that . . . there is little room for negotiation'.[99]

The prolonged Commons sessions of 29 and 30 November appeared to offer the possibility of a compromise.[100] Long thanked McAteer at the end of the two day session for his 'temperate and helpful attitude'[101] and promised:

> I shall think carefully over all that has been said in this debate. I shall examine each suggestion or compromise fairly and objectively. It may be that when the Bill is presented it will show a change here and there.[102]

Conway dampened the optimistic mood the following day by claiming that Long had not 'budged one millimetre' during their negotiations,[103] and his pessimism proved to be justified when the government published the Education Bill in the first week of 1968.

The Education Bill

The government's only significant compromise was to allow existing schools to revert to voluntary status, but only after the school returned all additional public funds provided by the 1968 Act. The bishops considered this to be 'a very minor concession' because, they argued, few schools would be able to refund the monies.[104] The Bill elaborated on the brief basic outline of the White Paper,[105] and senior Catholic clerics were particularly disappointed by the increased powers for the local education authority.

The fundamental objective of the White Paper was to increase the status of the education authority, and both the Ministry of Education and individual voluntary schools were to surrender some of their powers. Long was responding to criticism that Ministry officials enjoyed excessive influence within Northern Ireland's schools by devolving greater powers to the local authorities, but he was the victim of an unfortunate coincidence. The Ministry attempted to grant substantial powers to local councillors in the late 1960s just as civil rights activists were campaigning against many local Unionist councils.

The maintenance of school buildings and the appointment of ancillary staff offered many opportunities for discrimination by local Unionist politicians – opportunities denied in grammar schools where these powers remained with the school's governors. The Catholic clergy feared local Unionist politicians interfering in the administration of Catholic schools, and Long's reply that 'I am sure that this fear is unfounded. Education authorities which appointed unsuitable persons would be creating difficulties for themselves' was unlikely to ease their concerns.[106]

Conway, after the confusion and discord of October, secured the support of nationalist politicians in January 1968. He met senior nationalist MPs with Philbin for three hours a few days before the Second Reading debate at the end of January to discuss the nationalist campaign.[107] McAteer visited Bishop Farren with all the Catholic members of the Londonderry Corporation 'to assure His Lordship of our fullest support in the efforts of the Bishops to secure a just settlement of the schools controversy'.[108] Prayers were offered for a 'reasonable settlement' at every Sunday mass in churches throughout Northern Ireland[109] while McAteer, in another echo of 1930, asked for a meeting of every Catholic MP and Senator with O'Neill and Long because 'we have arrived at a make or break moment for the whole crusade for a better community'.[110] O'Neill had already hinted at the possibility of a compromise and the meeting of 22 January allowed O'Neill to illustrate to Catholics in Northern Ireland, and ministers in London, that he was sincerely committed to providing tangible benefits for the Catholic minority. The meeting proved to be a major disappointment to nationalist politicians and they left without a settlement.[111]

The government's wavering course during the winter of 1967 and the spring of 1968 demonstrated both the limits of O'Neill's power and his reluctance to insist upon substantial benefits for Catholic schools. The Education Bill was an examination of the government's determination to improve community relations by offering palpable assistance to thousands of Catholic families. The eighty per cent capital grant was a modest offer after the London government raised the capital grant for voluntary schools in England and Wales, yet the Act greatly increased the influence of the local education authorities within Catholic schools. Craigavon in 1930 and Brooke in 1946 never, ultimately, insisted upon 'four and two' committees in exchange for improved funding conditions, but O'Neill and Long were unyielding in the first months of 1968.

The PRONI files for the late 1960s remain closed for a few more years, but there is no evidence in the contemporary newspaper reports that O'Neill was constrained by his colleagues. Unionist MPs were quoted in the *Belfast Telegraph* to be opposed to improving the conditions offered in the White Paper in the last week of November,[112] but this followed the failure of Long and Conway to find a compromise at their meeting in Stormont Castle and should not be viewed as evidence of discontent from backbench Unionists. There are no references in the *Belfast Telegraph*, the *Irish News* or the *Belfast Newsletter* to backbench discontent during the first weeks after the White Paper, when 'Orange' MPs would be likely to protest against increased funding for Catholic schools. Craigavon in 1930 and Brooke in 1946 both alienated powerful elements within the Unionist Party to compromise with the Catholic authorities, but O'Neill did not insist upon reforms which went beyond merely fostering goodwill and creating a more sympathetic atmosphere between Protestants and Catholics in Northern Ireland.

The Education Bill was not just a test for O'Neill and his ministers. The Bill was a challenge to the Catholic authorities. O'Neill's liberalism could not be ignored by the Catholic minority without undermining his position within the Unionist Party, and the Nationalist Party responded to O'Neill's meeting with Lemass in January 1965 by accepting the status as the official opposition party. The White Paper questioned the enthusiasm of the Catholic authorities for cooperating with O'Neill. They were disappointed by their failure to alter the Education Bill, but the decision to accept maintained status for Catholic schools was a major vote of confidence in the integrity of O'Neill and his government at a pivotal moment in the history of Northern Ireland.

The failure of the meeting with the Catholic parliamentarians ended the Catholic authorities' hopes of gaining significant changes to the Education Bill. The last major initiative was McAteer's proposal for a 'four and one and one' school committee of four representatives of the trustees, one Ministry representative and one education authority representative. This appeared to be a feasible attempt to breach the difference between the Catholic authorities' demand for two Ministry appointments and the government's insistence on two representatives of the local education authority. However, Long rejected the compromise because 'to do so would be tantamount to my expressing a vote of no confidence in the local education authorities'.[113] Long, despite his conciliatory language, refused to accept any nationalist amendments during the passage of the Bill. An exchange in the Commons embodied nationalist reaction to his approach during 1967 and 1968:

> *Captain Long* I have tried as best I can to deal graciously with the criticisms of myself and of the proposals. Therefore I must ask hon. Members opposite to be equally gracious in accepting my refusal to accept this Amendment.
> *Mr McAteer* We shall graciously vote against it.[114]

The Catholic authorities and their nationalist allies were unable to modify any of the major clauses of the Education Bill, and retreated to the minor question of the right of new schools to opt out of the maintained system. The government was unwilling to offer even this meagre success to nationalist MPs and, after the Committee stage of the Bill, the Catholic authorities abandoned any hope of amending the Bill. None of the Lenten Pastorals of the six northern bishops at the end of February 1968 even mentioned the Education Bill.[115]

The 1968 Act was a modest advance for the Catholic authorities. The scale of public funding for maintained schools rose, according to government figures, to ninety-eight per cent of the total cost of educating a Catholic child,[116] but the Catholic authorities and their nationalist allies failed to emulate the grammar schools and obtain Ministry representation for the school committees. Also, the powers of the new school committees were limited compared to the responsibilities of the former 'four and two' committees or the 'maintained' grammar schools.

The Act provided some benefits for the Catholic community by reducing the voluntary contribution from more than a third to one fifth of capital costs and abolishing the voluntary contribution for maintenance. Also, the new law came at a vital moment for Catholic schools, as the quickening pace of new schools alleviated the educational price, but intensified the financial cost, of voluntary status. The Catholic authorities' scope for defending their influence within Catholic schools was limited by the reluctance of both nationalist influence politicians and Catholic teachers to offer their traditional loyalty in those vital first weeks. Conway eventually defused this discontent, but there can be no doubt that Long was encouraged to insist upon school committees by the evident disunity amongst the Catholic laity.

The end of Stormont

The grave misgivings of the Catholic authorities and nationalist politicians did not deter most Catholic schools from accepting maintained status. Long informed the Commons in December 1968 that 'the initial response by the authorities of voluntary schools to the new arrangements for increased capital grants . . . has been encouraging',[117] and by the end of 1969 sixty-four of the eighty-three voluntary secondary intermediate schools accepted 'maintained' status.[118] Some 382 primary schools, educating nearly seventy per cent of Northern Ireland's Catholic pupils, accepted the government's conditions by the end of 1970, and twelve months later eighty per cent of all Catholic schools were operating as maintained schools.[119]

The intense turmoil of the early 1970s would not encourage Catholic clerics to surrender influence within Catholic schools to Unionist politicians, and the rapid pace of transfer to maintained status emphasises the scale of the financial pressures troubling many Catholic schools in the late 1960s. The full maintenance grant rather than the increase in capital funding probably accounts for such a brisk rate of transfer, because few schools would be taking advantage of the eighty per cent capital grant so soon after the 1968 Act.

There were a number of successes for the Catholic authorities in the final years of the devolved government. In May 1969 Long announced that the two Catholic teacher training colleges would receive an eighty per cent grant with a 'four and two' committee, but with Ministry appointees as the two representatives on the colleges' committees.[120] Civil rights campaigners secured a major success in 1970 when the Macrory Report recommended profound reforms of local government in Northern Ireland. In January 1971 Long announced that the eight existing education authorities would be replaced by five area boards which would guarantee seats for representatives of maintained schools.[121] The Catholic clergy would finally gain access to the education committees where Protestant clerics had enjoyed substantial influence since the early 1930s.

The Catholic authorities waged a determined struggle to defend the clergy's monopoly of authority within Catholic schools, but local Catholic clerics did not maintain a rigid control of the 'four and two' committees of maintained schools after 1968. Long's answer to a Parliamentary Question in December 1970, asking for the names of the members of every maintained school committee in Tyrone, provides valuable evidence of the degree of clerical control of Catholic schools in the aftermath of the 1968 Act.

Thirty-four of the forty-two primary school committees in Tyrone contained six members and twenty of these thirty-four committees contained only two clerics, leaving the Catholic clergy as a minority on the school committee. One of the 'six member' committees contained a solitary cleric whilst another school committee was without any clerical representation, though these two schools were probably Protestant schools.[122] Ten of the remaining twelve 'six member' committees were equally divided between clerics and laity, and all four places were claimed by clerics on only two school committees. In the eight committees containing more than six members, clerics never held more than one third of the seats. Therefore, despite the Catholic clergy enjoying the right to appoint two thirds of the maintained school committee, in only two of the forty Catholic primary school committees did clerics hold all the trustees' seats.[123]

Tyrone's maintained secondary schools were more closely supervised by the clergy than the county's primary schools. Six of the eleven committees contained six members, and on two of these committees clerics, or nuns, held all four available seats while in the other four committees there was only one lay member and three clerics. Two committees with twelve members contained four clerics, and the other three committees contained a majority, or a significant minority, of clerics.[124] Tyrone is only one of Northern Ireland's six counties, but the findings from Tyrone were confirmed by the evidence from six schools in Newry. In June 1971, a Parliamentary Question asked Long for details of the school committees for three primary schools and three secondary schools in the city. Two of the primary schools were managed by the same committee of twelve members which was evenly divided between clerics and laity, and the third committee contained only one cleric amongst the six members. In contrast, two thirds of the seats on the secondary school committees were held by clerics or members of religious orders.[125]

Clearly, the clerics responsible for secondary schools were less willing than their primary school counterparts to accept a dilution of their authority. This contrast may be explained by differing attitudes towards the Catholic laity by the teaching religious orders, who were often responsible for Catholic secondary schools, and the secular clergy who managed most Catholic primary schools. The teaching orders often performed no tasks other than supervising their schools, and a significant lay influence might undermine their *raison d'être*. The management of the local primary school was one of many duties for parish priests, who might welcome lay members on the school committee to share the burden of management. Parish priests would also possess greater knowledge of local lay notables who might be offended by exclusion from the parish school's committee, whilst the religious orders would know few parents other than from occasional visits to the schools.

A substantial majority of Tyrone's Catholic schools were governed by a lay majority by the end of 1970, and there were only a few cases of clerics appropriating all the available places on the committees. There can be no doubt that the Catholic clergy in Northern Ireland were willing to concede an element of authority within Catholic schools to the laity. The Catholic authorities' decision to accept the formal abolition of the clerical majority on the maintained school committee in 1993[126] appears, therefore, to be a recognition of the practice in many parishes by the early 1970s.

The enhanced role of the local education authority within Catholic schools remained a major concern for Catholic clerics and nationalist politicians. A Unionist local council such as Fermanagh county council which, one Catholic MP claimed, did not employ a single Catholic amongst its sixty-four school bus drivers,[127] could clearly not be trusted with the fate of Catholic schools. In October 1969, the *Irish News* noted the presence of two members of Catholic maintained school committees on the platform of a meeting organised by militant loyalists. Two days later a letter to the paper's editor claimed that twenty-three of Belfast education authority's twenty-nine representatives on Catholic maintained school committees were Protestants, and that six of these were Protestant clerics.[128] The presence of loyalists on Catholic school committees clearly threatened the autonomy of Catholic schools. However, four years after the 1968 Act the collapse of the devolved government ended local education authority control of Northern Ireland's schools. The Minister of Education, along with the rest of the Cabinet, was displaced by the British government, and responsibility for education in Northern Ireland passed to the Home Secretary in London.

The devolved government was gone, and the education committees were going, by the spring of 1972, but a new threat was developing to the principle of clerical control of Catholic schools.

THE INTEGRATION DEBATE

Integration has been the dominant issue for Northern Ireland's education system since the late 1960s, but the belief that Northern Ireland's troubles might be eased if the two religious communities enjoyed a common education is not solely based upon developments since August 1969. As long ago as 1830 the Catholic bishop of Kildare and Leighlen, James Doyle, argued:

> I do not see how any man, wishing well to the public peace, and who looks to Ireland as his country, can think that peace can ever be permanently established, or the prosperity of the country ever well secured, if children are separated, at the commencement of life, on account of their religious opinions. I do not know any measures which would prepare the way for a better feeling in Ireland than uniting children at an early age, and bringing them up in the same school, leading them to commune with one another and to form those little intimacies and friendships which often subsist through life.[129]

Stanley's National Schools, introduced the following year, were envisaged as 'integrated' schools, but Protestant and Catholic clerics swiftly established effective control in the vast majority of Irish schools. The principle of integration remained enshrined in the National Board's regulations despite the denominational practice and in the first decades of the twentieth century many education reformers attempted to revive Stanley's original concept with a new education system that would sharply curtail the power of the clergy.

Numerous unionists portrayed denominational schools as anti-quated and divisive, but after partition the Lynn committee avoided the delicate question of integrating Protestant and Catholic schools:

> Whilst we deplore the fact that children of all denominations have not been educated together in the same schools, and believe that this separation of the pupils has been productive of great injury to the community, we think that under existing conditions no attempt to amalgamate schools under Roman Catholic and Protestant management would meet with any measure of success.[130]

The determination of Protestant and Catholic clerics to control the education of their congregations ensured the development of a segre-gated system in the nineteenth century, and the mutual trust vital for a genuine integration of Catholic and Protestant schools was impos-sible during Northern Ireland's first years. Unionist MPs called for 'shared' schools during the debates on the Education Bill, but this enthusiasm for integration was swiftly dispelled by the Protestant clergy's assault on the 1923 Act.

Integration was a peripheral issue for the next forty-five years, and the occasional appeal for integration by unionists often exposed a strong antipathy towards Irish nationalism and autonomous Catholic schools:

> In an earlier time in Irish history there was a chance of having schools built on the collective basis where children could have been educated together. Had that been accepted we might have had a different public spirit manifesting itself throughout Ireland at present.[131]

> If we had all the children going to the same type of school, being taught by the same sort of teachers, and honouring the flag of the country, I believe that the day would not be far distant when the sectarian troubles in this country would be a thing of the past.[132]

The Ministry of Education, despite the protests of 'Orange' critics, never embarked upon a concerted effort to fashion an integrated schools system after the UEC overcame Londonderry's opposition to 'simple Bible instruction' in public elementary schools. Northern Ireland's 'sound denominational education' system remained unchallenged for more than thirty years, but by the 1960s critics of segregation were no longer confined to the 'Orange' edge of the Unionist Party.

In March 1965 Harry Diamond initiated a major debate on volun-tary school funding, but the discussion failed to concentrate on the financial problems of voluntary schools.[133] An amendment from David Bleakley of the NILP calling for integrated education[134] provoked a dispute lasting nearly an hour, while the Minister of Education, Herbert Kirk, spent only five minutes dismissing nationalist calls for improved funding.[135] Fitt resorted to defending the principle of autonomous Catholic schools:

> A Catholic education is not seditious. There was a time, in the more troubled period of Irish history, when to be a Catholic meant that one was taken to be anti-Government. That is not the position now. Catholic education is concerned solely with the spiritual welfare of children and has nothing whatever to do with the political set up of this or any other country.[136]

The March 1965 debate was the first significant indication of the new threat from liberals and the NILP to denominational schools. The following year they secured a powerful ally when O'Neill attended an ecumenical conference at the Corrymeela centre in April 1966.[137] He spoke of the need to improve community relations, and mentioned the role of denominational schools:

> A major cause of division arises, some would say, from the de facto segregation of education along religious lines. This is a most delicate matter and one must respect the firm convictions from which it springs. Many people have questioned, however, whether the maintenance of two distinct educational systems side by side is not wasteful of human and financial resources and a major barrier to the promotion of communal understanding.[138]

Clerical unease at this new threat was underlined by the silence of the nationalist press and nationalist politicians[139] until Conway eventually responded to O'Neill's speech. O'Neill and the liberal advocates of inte-gration presented an awkward challenge to the Catholic authorities because, in contrast to the 'Orange' unionists, clerics and nationalists could not question their motives. Conway was compelled to accept their honesty, if not their judgement, though he noted that O'Neill did not mention the major nationalist grievance of discrimination as a source of division. Conway concluded with a warning:

> I welcome very much the appeal for good will and Christian charity and I respect the sincerity with which it was made. I am bound to say, however, that I find this continuing pressure on Catholic schools by the head of the government very surprising and, indeed, dis-quieting.[140]

Three years later the report of the special commission established by O'Neill to investigate the causes of the civil unrest troubling Northern Ireland added further impetus to the integration campaign by underlining liberal criticism of segregated schools.[141] Lord Cameron and his companions were sympathetic witnesses for the Catholic community, condemning numerous examples of unionist malpractice, but when discussing the sources of community tension they noted that 'segregated education – insisted upon by the Roman Catholic Church – also plays its part in initiating and maintaining division and differences among the young'.[142]

Unionist MPs highlighted the importance of segregated schools during the Commons debate of the Cameron Report, and some MPs offered their own advice on how to 'integrate' Northern Ireland's schools:

> This is one of the root causes of segregated life and thought in this country . . . and all their attendant consequences, including the rioting. Why has the Commission nothing to say on this vital matter?[143]

> the Roman Catholic community by means of separate and segregated education . . . has contributed greatly towards the division in this country.[144]

> voluntary schools . . . could and should respect the Constitution of the country and teach their children to do so. I notice that there is one county in Northern Ireland where at schools receiving direct Government support the Union Jack is flown every day. That is the emblem of the British State of which everyone claims to be a member. If people require, ask and expect British standards they should at least be willing to accept the British flag at the same time.[145]

> Would it not be a good gesture and a step in the right direction if at the official opening of a new Roman Catholic school to which a substantial grant has been given the Union Jack were flown on the building on that occasion or on other occasions? Surely that would be a step in the right direction.[146]

Critics of segregation exhibited traditional unionist sentiments, but nationalist MPs were unusually reluctant to defend the principle of denominational schools. Fitt and the Nationalist MP James O'Reilly spoke for Catholic schools on the second day of the debate,[147] but the reference to segregation was one of the few sentences from the Cameron Report to be quoted more often by unionists than nationalists. The Catholic authorities also encountered problems from a new power in Northern Ireland politics, one which was playing an ever greater role in the course of events.

The British Home Secretary, James Callaghan, addressed the Labour Party Conference only days before the Cameron Report debate. He attempted to ease unionist fears by following a condemnation of discrimination with criticism of the Catholic authorities' insistence upon denominational schools:

> I find it *equally offensive* if it is separate education that is advanced as an unshakeable principle. This will separate the community almost from infancy and certainly from the time they begin their schooling. That is *equally as offensive* as a decision by a group in power which denies a man a house because of his religion and because he is in a minority.[148]

Catholic clerics were accustomed to unionist criticism of Catholic schools, but the hostility of the British government and the Cameron Commission – both sympathetic to nationalist complaints against the devolved government – posed a severe problem for the Catholic authorities.

Nationalist politicians were reluctant to support clerical interests, but the INTO swiftly endorsed the Catholic authorities' opposition to integrated schools. The INTO leadership wrote to Callaghan's deputy, Lord Stonham, less than a fortnight after the Cameron Report debate. Segregation, they argued, existed because the overwhelming majority of Catholic parents wished to guarantee a Catholic religious education for their children. The INTO emphasised their fears of discrimination in teaching appointments, questioned the integrity of Protestant clerical claims to support integration and highlighted the concerns of Catholic parents that their children might be taught by members of the Orange Order.[149]

The Cameron Commission confirmed nationalist claims of discrimination by many unionist councils and the INTO, as the major trade union representing Catholic teachers, was obviously concerned that the education authorities would be partisan in their appointment of teachers. The teaching profession was, and remains, an important source of employment for educated Catholics, and the fear of 'Orange' education committees has been a significant factor accounting for the support of the INTO for Catholic schools.

The *Irish News* also, eventually, responded to Callaghan's critique of Catholic schools:

> There are still too many people rushing to subscribe to the view that a cure from the distemper in our society lies in integrated education.

> This seems as plaintive a bit of whistling in the dark as one can recall . . . It is time people stopped using segregated education as a stick to beat the Catholic community and as a way of apportioning blame for the present situation.[150]

The support of the INTO and the *Irish News* was a minor compensation for the silence of nationalist politicians. The reluctance of nationalists to endorse the Catholic authorities' opposition to integrated schools persists to this day. Integration remains the major issue for the Catholic authorities in Northern Ireland, and the loss of their traditional allies has greatly hindered their efforts to repulse the most significant challenge to Catholic schools since the creation of Northern Ireland.

There was a clear and genuine change from the antagonism troubling Northern Ireland's politics in the 1950s, and this 'thaw' was evident in the treatment of such sensitive 'national' issues as the role of the Union Flag in schools and the Gaelic language. Minford and Porter's motion of June 1956 was the last serious assault by Unionist MPs against Catholic schools. The gradual ebbing of antagonism evident by the late 1950s led to dwindling interest amongst both Nationalist and Unionist MPs in the 'national' aspects of Catholic schools.

In 1962, the Unionist MP Robert Burns failed to convince the Commons to demand the Union Flag fly over every voluntary school,[151] and the following December, Hunter, veteran of the vain struggle for an Ulster history book in the 1950s, called for a review of the Ministry's policy towards Gaelic teaching,[152] but these were isolated protests. Gaelic in Catholic schools was no longer a crucial problem for most unionists, and few were willing to insist upon a display of loyalty from Northern Ireland's voluntary schools.

In June 1967, Minford's nephew and successor as MP for Antrim argued for the Ministry to demand that all county schools fly the Union Flag during teaching days, because the flag was 'the only symbol that can guarantee them the British way of life and secure for them a free and honourable future'.[153] Burns once more argued that the flag should be flown from voluntary schools, but Minford emphasised that he was only calling upon county schools to fly the flag.[154] The flag issue was not exploited to provoke a confrontation with the nationalist minority, only as a symbol of the Union for Protestant pupils in 'their' schools. The Cameron Commission aroused a brief spasm of unionist criticism of autonomous Catholic schools and their failure to honour the Union Flag,[155] but such 'national' questions disappeared as issues for Unionist MPs during the 1960s. The only politician to emphasise cultural and 'national' issues in the late 1960s was the Protestant civil rights MP, Ivan Cooper, who consistently argued for the Ministry to promote Irish history teaching.[156] The outbreak of severe communal violence in the summer of 1969 also did not revive the interest of Unionist MPs in either Gaelic in Catholic schools or the history taught to Catholic children.

The fate of Gaelic was also an insignificant issue for most nationalist politicians and voters in the 1960s, and this disinterest was confirmed by a Parliamentary Question in December 1970. Only one eighth of Catholic primary pupils, and less than a quarter of secondary inter-mediate pupils, were studying the language. Clearly many teachers and clerical managers were indifferent to the fate of the language, and only Catholic grammar schools displayed any enthusiasm by teaching Gaelic to more than half of their pupils.[157]

CONCLUSION

In 1957, shortly after his appointment, May claimed that the financial burden of voluntary status was damaging the education of Catholic pupils, but the increases in voluntary school building during his five years as Minister of Education exacerbated the Catholic community's problems. In the years after his death they were to find that May's generosity created problems as severe as those he attempted to solve. In January 1968 the six northern bishops claimed that the cost of maintaining Catholic schools since the 1947 Act amounted to £20 million.[158] The evidence contained in the Ministry's Reports and answers to Parliamentary Questions allows for a crude calculation of the voluntary contribution in the two decades after the Second World War, and this does not confirm the bishops' claims. The voluntary contribution for the 21 years between 1947 and 1968 amounted in 1968 prices to just over £12 million. The burden may not have been as grievous as the bishops claimed, but it translates to more than £90 million in 1996 prices.

The striking progress for Catholic schools in the 1960s underlined the importance of political rather than financial factors in explaining the failure of Catholic voluntary schools to develop during the 1950s. Once the Ministry of Education chose to invest in voluntary schools, money was available for capital projects. The Ministry's statistics also underline the resurgence of investment in county schools, indicating that Ministry officials were not simply investing in Catholic schools to preserve their budget. The increase in capital spending for voluntary schools certainly eased the educational burden of voluntary status, but the evidence for both overcrowded classes and 'unreorganised' schools in the 1960s indicates that the scale of the disadvantage afflicting Catholic schools at the end of the 1950s required sustained investment for many years.

The 1968 Act was a partial defeat for the Catholic authorities, but the acceptance of 'four and two' committees was an inevitable consequence of the cool response to Philbin's strident opposition to the White Paper. Conway was fortunate to be in Rome when the Ministry published its proposals, allowing him to adopt a more accommodating tone once Philbin's adamant stance proved to be unpopular. The notable absence of opposition from 'Orange' unionists or the Protestant clergy to the White Paper allowed O'Neill and Long considerable scope for compromise in the first weeks of 1968, but they refused to offer any significant concessions. The evidence suggests that O'Neill was less accommodating towards the Catholic authorities than either Craig or Brooke.

The absence of any corresponding concessions to the Protestant clergy may partly account for the government's adamant stance. In 1930 the Protestant clergy gained effective control of public elementary schools, and in 1947 the government granted them similar powers in the proposed county secondary intermediate schools. In 1968 there were simply no new powers available to the Protestant clergy.

The events of 1967 and 1968 illustrated the importance of political factors in the Catholic authorities' opposition to an influence for education committees rather than universal, theological motives. Canon Law does not distinguish between local and regional governments, but this question was the main issue during the first phase of the education debate. The importance the Catholic authorities attached to Ministry appointments for the 'four and two' committees in 1968 underlines the confidence of senior Catholic clerics that Ministry officials would not abuse their powers.

The central issue for the Catholic authorities in Stormont's final years was the developing campaign for integrated schools. Callaghan's speech to the Labour Party conference indicated that integration was finding favour with influential forces guiding Northern Ireland's education system. After 1969 the Catholic authorities were to find the integration issue to be their gravest problem.

CHAPTER SIX

British rule

The mass unrest of the late 1960s was swiftly followed by a prolonged era of chronic paramilitary violence and political stalemate. The Provisional IRA emerged at the end of 1969 to pursue a ruthless campaign of bombings and shootings which eventually led to the suspension of the devolved government in the spring of 1972. Labour and Conservative governments then attempted a series of constitutional initiatives such as the Executive of 1974, the Constitutional Convention of 1975 and the Northern Ireland Assembly of 1982, all of which failed to generate the confidence necessary to create a lasting settlement.

The intensity of the conflict was exacerbated by the hunger strikes of 1981 which brought significant electoral successes for Sinn Féin in the early 1980s. The Irish government responded with the New Ireland Forum in 1983, but the most significant shift came in November 1985 when the British and Irish governments signed an accord allowing the Irish government an advisory role in Northern Ireland's affairs. The Anglo-Irish Agreement provoked widespread and often violent opposition from the unionist majority, but the British government was determined to incorporate the Irish government into its search for a solution.

The British government's pursuit of a constitutional settlement was combined with efforts to reform Northern Ireland and alleviate the disadvantages faced by the nationalist minority. The Anglo-Irish Agreement has survived the unionist assault, but the practical benefits appear to have been marginal because the depressed economic climate has severely limited the scope for a profound change in the social structure of Northern Ireland. The only significant success for the Agreement has been the decline in support for Sinn Féin.

The early 1990s witnessed a revival of loyalist paramilitary violence and a renewed cycle of atrocities which culminated in the Shankill bomb in the autumn of 1993 and the inevitable brutal loyalist reaction. The threat of a renewed loyalist campaign, and the waning of Sinn Féin, epitomised by the defeat of Gerry Adams in the April 1992 election, encouraged republicans to negotiate an end to the violence. A series of confidential discussions between republicans and representatives of both the British and Irish governments eventually led to an IRA ceasefire at the end of August 1994 and a loyalist ceasefire a few months later. The optimism of 1994 proved to be misplaced as delays and disagreements eventually led to a renewed bombing campaign by the Provisional IRA in February 1996. A second ceasefire renewed the efforts for a constitutional settlement which, at the time of writing, remains intact despite sporadic episodes of sectarian violence.

The Education and Library Board Order of 1972 was as significant a change as the abolition of the devolved government for Northern Ireland's education system. The Order replaced the eight education authorities with five Education and Library Boards and diminished the role of the Boards in supervising the region's schools by enhancing the powers of the new Department of Education for Northern Ireland (DENI). The Department has been administered by a succession of British ministers with limited experience of Northern Ireland's distinctive education system. They also supervise other departments. So, with a minister who is invariably an outsider and who holds a number of other posts, the influence of DENI officials has probably increased in recent years.

Two education topics have attracted increasing interest from the Catholic community in the last twenty-five years; the campaign for integrated schools, and the role of the Gaelic language in maintained schools. The Catholic authorities have found these issues to be a major diversion from the defence of their 'clerical' interests.

THE FINAL COMPROMISE

The suspension of the Northern Ireland Parliament in March 1972 left the Westminster Parliament as the only constitutional means of expressing Catholic and nationalist discontent. The principal device available to MPs to highlight an issue, extract information, petition the government and demonstrate their industry to constituents is a Parliamentary Question to the relevant minister. The evidence from Hansard indicates that nationalist MPs have been reluctant to exploit these opportunities to raise education issues compared to their Unionist counterparts, and their predecessors at Stormont.

Gerry Fitt was MP for West Belfast between 1966 and 1983, and during his seventeen years at Westminster he intervened only once in support of Catholic schools. In 1978 he, briefly, outlined the problems facing maintained schools finding additional land when Unionist MPs opposed the Education and Libraries (Northern Ireland) Order allowing the Education and Library Boards to purchase land for building maintained schools.[1] Fitt spoke in other debates on education in the 1960s and 1970s, but he rarely addressed the Catholic authorities' concerns. His maiden speech as an MP came in a debate on 'Education and Technology' in April 1966, but he did not mention the problems facing Catholic schools in Northern Ireland, despite the significant parliamentary campaign by nationalists in the Northern Ireland Commons which eventually led to the 1968 Education Act. Fitt's contribution to the debate on the important Education and Libraries (Northern Ireland) Order of July 1972 was to argue with Paisley on the treatment of detained rioters.[2]

In December 1975 the Education (Northern Ireland) Order slightly increased the capital grant for maintained schools from eighty per cent to eighty-five per cent. The Order allowed Fitt the opportunity to underline the continuing burden of the voluntary contribution, but he discussed only the problem of school uniforms and free meals for poor children.[3] The cost of uniforms and school meals may have been a serious problem for many of Fitt's constituents in West Belfast, but the 1975 Order still left Northern Ireland's Catholics to find nearly one sixth of the total cost of building new schools. Fitt never asked an education Parliamentary Question in seventeen years at Westminster.

Fitt was reluctant to support clerical interests, but his nationalist colleague during the early 1970s, Bernadette Devlin, was actually hostile to clerical authority within Catholic schools. In July 1972 she spoke against the principle of segregated schools:

> We have systematically to set about bringing in a coherent policy for integrated education. My belief is that integrated, comprehensive education is the only way forward, but it is not something that will happen by accident. We must recognise the role of religion as a prejudicial factor in Northern Ireland and legislate to remove it.[4]

The third nationalist MP, the independent MP for Fermanagh and South Tyrone Frank Maguire, shared his colleagues' reluctance to discuss education. He asked only two minor questions during his seven years as an MP.[5] The Catholic authorities lacked an energetic advocate at Westminster, in contrast to the band of Nationalists MPs in the Northern Ireland Commons who consistently defended clerical interests during the fifty years of devolved power.

In 1983 Fitt lost his seat to Gerry Adams of Sinn Féin, but his successor as leader of the SDLP, John Hume, was elected for the Foyle seat in Londonderry on the same day. Hume, a former teacher, showed only slight interest in education issues during most of the 1980s, and he promoted 'nationalist' concerns such as the fate of the Gaelic language in Catholic schools rather than the Catholic authorities' fears for the preservation of clerical authority within Catholic schools.[6] The majority of Hume's education Parliamentary Questions concerned higher education.[7]

The Catholic authorities' problems persisted until the late 1980s, when SDLP MPs finally began to discuss the funding problems of Catholic maintained schools. In December 1988 Hume asked for the number of pupils at, and the public monies available to, secondary intermediate and grammar schools.[8] The following February he asked for the funding details for individual schools and a schedule of all the major capital projects approved by the DENI since 1985. He also demanded an explanation of the government's funding policy for grammar schools. The Northern Ireland Office (NIO) minister for education, Dr Brian Mawhinney, admitted that funds were granted on the basis of 'historic patterns of expenditure', but promised a new formula from the DENI which would place greater emphasis upon the number of pupils in each school.[9] Hume's efforts in the final weeks of 1988 and the first two months of 1989 provided useful information for the Catholic authorities, but he remained reluctant to speak in most education debates or to support the Catholic authorities's defence of denominational schools.

Seamus Mallon, SDLP MP for Newry and South Armagh since 1986 and a teacher for twenty years before his election,[10] has concentrated on the fortunes of the Gaelic language and rarely emphasised the Catholic authorities' concerns.[11] In April 1989 Mallon intervened during a Parliamentary Question asking the DENI to promote integrated schools to complain that many secondary schools in his constituency were using mobile classrooms. He called for improved capital grants 'so that the children who are being educated in those mobile classrooms may be integrated into the rest of the school'.[12] Mallon's contribution may have been witty, but it was also unique. He shares his leader's reluctance to defend clerical interests in Catholic schools or to urge the government to improve the funding conditions for maintained schools.

Eddie McGrady, SDLP MP for South Down since 1987, has asked numerous education Parliamentary Questions at Westminster, and has discussed funding issues. He revealed the preferential funding terms for Stranmillis compared to St Mary's college with a series of

Parliamentary Questions in January and February 1989, and obtained further details in June 1991 which showed that the advantage – though diminished – persisted into the 1990s.[13] St Mary's college remains a major concern for the Catholic authorities, and McGrady's questions yielded vital information for their negotiations with the DENI. McGrady also responded on the day of the publication by the Standing Advisory Commission on Human Rights (SACHR) of a report claiming that maintained Catholic schools suffered a financial disadvantage; he called for immediate action from the British government.[14]

McGrady was the only nationalist MP to confront the integration campaign in the late 1980s. He defended the principle of segregated education during a Commons exchange in December 1987, and the following July he claimed that school trustees 'will have their school properties confiscated without compensation or consultation, if governors and parents elect to apply for grant maintained status'.[15] McGrady's comments were the only criticism by any nationalist MP of the DENI's initial proposals for education reform. The fourth SDLP MP, Dr Joe Hendron of West Belfast, was largely silent on education issues.

The small number of nationalist MPs at Westminster may partly account for nationalist politicians not vigorously supporting Catholic schools. After the 1987 election the three SDLP MPs were more conspicuous during education debates. Also, the Catholic authorities have not launched a concerted campaign against the voluntary contribution. There is no evidence in the *Irish Catholic Directory*, which faithfully printed countless speeches and messages by senior Catholic clerics in the 1970s and 1980s, of any clerical agitation. The reluctance of the Catholic authorities to argue for improved funding may partly explain the silence of the nationalist MPs. However, in the early 1980s the clerical majority on maintained school committees and the future of the two Catholic teacher training colleges were threatened by two official committees. The Catholic authorities offered stern resistance, but they gained no parliamentary support from nationalist MPs.

The Astin Committee

In June 1977 the NIO minister for education, Lord Melchett, established a committee chaired by Professor Alan Astin 'to consider the arrangements for the management of schools in Northern Ireland, with particular regard to the re-organisation of secondary education and the Government's wish to ensure that integration, where desired, should be facilitated and not impeded'.[16]

The Astin committee eventually proposed that parents, teachers, clerics and either the Education and Library Board or the DENI should each hold a quarter of the seats on the school committee. The report claimed that the Catholic 'ethos' would survive in Catholic schools without a clerical majority on the school committees because these values were shared by Catholic parents and Catholic teachers, but the terms of reference instructed the committee to remove obstacles to integration. The Catholic authorities were naturally reluctant to dilute the authority of the Catholic clergy within maintained schools. The avowed intention to promote integration also accounts for their strident reaction to the committee's recommendation for a significant reduction in clerical power within Northern Ireland's schools.[17]

Parents and teachers in primary and secondary intermediate schools were to be trusted with the traditions and character of their schools, but parents and teachers in grammar schools were not thought to be so reliable by the Astin committee. Preferential treatment for grammar schools was a constant theme of the education policy of the devolved government, and this custom survived the advent of direct rule. The Astin committee, though willing to promote a radical review of the management structures of primary and secondary intermediate schools, preserved the distinctive character of grammar schools by allowing the founders of the school to retain half of the seats of the board of governors.[18]

The Catholic authorities led the struggle against the Astin committee, but the Protestant clergy were also determined to preserve their influence within controlled schools. The General Assembly of the Presbyterian Church rejected the Astin committee's report and the Church of Ireland was also reluctant to surrender any authority to parents and teachers.[19] The Astin committee's proposals posed a particularly severe problem for the Protestant clergy as the committee was influenced by the failure of the 1978 Education (Northern Ireland) Act to develop controlled integrated schools.[20] Catholic schools were unlikely to be enticed into the controlled sector, especially without the offer of more public funds. However, many controlled schools would be attracted by transfer to controlled integrated status if integration could augment declining pupil rolls and rescue the school from closure. A quarter of the school committee seats might prove insufficient to prevent a ballot by parents fearful of losing their local school.[21]

The combined efforts of the Catholic authorities and Protestant clerics prompted a retreat by the DENI. In the spring of 1981 Melchett's

successor, Lord Elton, announced that the majority of the school committee seats for maintained schools would be retained by the trustees –
the Catholic clergy – and in controlled schools the representatives of
the transferers – the Protestant clergy – would remain the largest single
interest on the school committee.[22] The Ulster Unionist MP, Harold
McCusker, and the Conservative MP, John Biggs Davison, urged the NIO
to accept the Astin committee's report,[23] but the Education (Northern
Ireland) Order of 1984 was a mild version of the committee's radical
proposals.

The Catholic clergy preserved their majority on the school committee
with six trustees among the ten members. The Education and Library
Board retained the two seats secured by the 1968 Education Act, leaving
parents and teachers with a solitary seat each on the school committees.[24]
The Catholic authorities may have been concerned by the decline in
clerical representation, but the 1984, Order also reduced 'public' representation from one third to just one fifth of the committee.

The 1984 Order was a minor defeat for the Catholic authorities as it
weakened clerical influence within Catholic schools without offering
any financial compensation. In 1968 the Catholic authorities had gained
improved funding conditions for accepting 'four and two' committees,
but the 1984 Order maintained the existing scale of the voluntary
contribution. Mageean's fears in 1946 of 'scarcely perceptible pressure'
to dilute clerical control appeared to be justified by the events of 1984,
when the NIO insisted that parents and teachers were entitled to a role
in the management of maintained schools. After 1984 the major threat
to clerical authority came from within the Catholic community, from
teachers and parents, but the Catholic laity had been represented on
many maintained school committees since the 1968 Act. Therefore, the
reality of clerical power within Northern Ireland's Catholic schools may
not have been profoundly threatened by the 1984 Order. However, the
second official committee to report in the early 1980s was to pose a
more potent threat to clerical control.

Sir Henry Chilver

In February 1979 the Higher Education Review Group, chaired by Sir
Henry Chilver, began the task of advising on the development of
higher education in the 1980s and 1990s. Falling pupils rolls and the
government's determination to restrain public spending ensured that the
committee's primary task was to identify potential savings. Teacher
training was an obvious target as the DENI's annual requirement for 620

new teachers was only one seventh of the capacity of Northern Ireland's seven teaching colleges.[25]

A rationalisation of teacher training appeared inevitable, but in June 1980 the Chilver committee recommended that the two Catholic teaching colleges – St Mary's and St Joseph's – be amalgamated and transferred to Stranmillis to form the Belfast Centre for Teacher Education.[26] The committee presented its plans as a merger of the Catholic and state colleges, but its proposals called for the closure of two Catholic colleges and the displaced students to attend a Protestant institute weakly disguised as a non-denominational college.

The Catholic authorities prepared for a resolute defence of their teaching colleges as early as the first week of June, when sermons were read at every Sunday Mass warning of the approaching threat.[27] The *Irish News* also alerted its readers to the potential consequences:

> We must face that there has always been a powerful prejudice against the Catholic school . . . Unless they stand firm, Catholic parents may lose much of the precious heritage of Catholic education.[28]

The publication of the committee's report led the Archbishop of Armagh, Cardinal Tomas O'Fiaich, to threaten 'very strong resistance' to the DENI. He noted that the committee recommended the closure of the two Catholic colleges but none of the other five teaching colleges were to be closed, and he also complained of the lack of a Catholic quota for the proposed Belfast Centre for Teacher Education.[29] O'Fiaich's intervention emphasised the importance of the fate of the colleges to the Catholic authorities because, in contrast to his predecessor Conway and his colleagues Philbin and Cahal Daly, he rarely discussed education issues. Dunn claims the Chilver report provoked an 'almost hysterical campaign' from the Catholic clergy,[30] and the issue was certainly vitally important for their control of Catholic schools. The teaching colleges guaranteed a reliable supply of Catholic teachers vital to the preservation of the distinctive religious character of Catholic schools.[31] A shortage of Catholic teachers was a greater threat than the presence of local Unionist politicians on the school committees. The Catholic authorities insisted upon a quota for Catholic teachers in the proposed new college. However, the DENI could not guarantee forty per cent of the places at the proposed new college because the government's equal opportunities legislation would not allow separate standards for Catholic and Protestant applicants.

The *Irish News* loyally followed the course set by the Catholic authorities, but there were severe difficulties securing the support of Catholic teachers and the students in the teaching colleges. The INTO accepted a reduction in the scale of teacher training to protect the employment prospects of their members, and the promise of closer relations with Queen's University for the proposed Belfast Centre for Teacher Education also enhanced the status of the teaching profession.[32] Therefore, the INTO was hesitant, and the Catholic authorities faced an even more critical problem with the next generation of Catholic teachers.

The student committees of both St Mary's and St Joseph's dutifully endorsed the Catholic authorities' policy in 1967 and 1968, but by the end of the 1970s student teachers were less accommodating. The representatives from St Joseph's proposed an integrationist motion at the Union of Students of Ireland (USI) conference in January 1979. The teaching staff at the college resorted to visiting classes after the conference to convince their own students of the importance of autonomous Catholic colleges. The deputy president of the USI, a former pupil of St Mary's, later claimed that the principal of St Joseph's, Michael Dallat, underlined the determination of the college's management to silence discontent amongst students by drafting a motion opposing integration for the following year's conference.[33] The Catholic authorities eventually convinced the student representation committees to support the denominational principle, and by 1982 they were lobbying British ministers to insist upon a Catholic college.[34] The campaign for the Catholic colleges exposed severe discord amongst Catholic teachers.

The Catholic authorities were struggling to maintain the support of Catholic teachers, and Fitt was unwilling to defend the colleges in the Commons at Westminster, but this acute lack of allies could not prevent the Catholic authorities preserving an autonomous Catholic teacher training college. The role of the Protestant clergy was probably vital in dampening the British government's initial enthusiasm for reform. The NIO minister for education, Nicholas Scott, announced the end of their efforts to transfer the colleges in April 1982 when he promised that 'no steps will be taken which would be detrimental to their denominational ethos'.[35] The hunger strikes and the intense alienation caused by the deaths of the republican prisoners may have discouraged the NIO from offending an authoritative interest group at such a vital moment, but, the attitude of the Protestant clergy may also explain why the Chilver committee's proposals were abandoned.

The initial reaction of the Protestant clergy and Unionist politicians to the Chilver report was favourable. The Church of Ireland Synod welcomed the plan[36] and the *Belfast Telegraph* wrote before the official statement that 'obviously the two Roman Catholic training colleges with only 800 students between them must be the first in line for amalgamation'.[37] Unionist MPs joined the Protestant clergy in urging the government to implement the Chilver committee's recommendations. Peter Robinson and James Kilfedder urged the government to act during the summer of 1980,[38] but the following year no Unionist MP questioned the government on the fate of the Catholic colleges.

The ebbing of unionist interest in the amalgamation of Stranmillis and the Catholic colleges probably arose from assurances offered by the DENI to the Catholic authorities. The DENI was unable to accept a quota for Catholic students, but it could not hope to overcome clerical opposition without promising a distinctive role for the Catholic authorities within the proposed college. Thus, Catholic clerics would enjoy an influence in the training of Protestant teachers for controlled schools which would be unacceptable to many unionists and Protestant clerics. In February 1982 the Church of Ireland Synod, possibly responding to these threats, urged the DENI to preserve 'the traditional identity, ethos and moral and spiritual values of Stranmillis College of Education'.[39] The Protestant clergy were clearly determined to maintain Stranmillis college as a distinctive Protestant institution, but this would greatly hinder the DENI's efforts to integrate the Catholic colleges.

The Chilver committee was the most notable example of official indifference towards Catholic and nationalist education interests since the Lockwood committee recommended siting Northern Ireland's second university at Coleraine in 1965. The Catholic proportion of Northern Ireland's schoolchildren was increasing throughout the 1970s and 1980s. However, the DENI proposed closing both Catholic colleges to strengthen the state college with students who would probably never be more than Catholic tenants in a Protestant academy with a branch of the Democratic Unionist Party and its own lodge of the Orange Order.[40] St Joseph's and St Mary's merged in September 1985[41] and by the end of the decade the new St Mary's college was training more teachers than Stranmillis.[42]

The Astin and Chilver committees threatened the Catholic clergy's traditional powers within the Catholic schools system. The Astin committee led to the 1984 Order, and Chilver's report was to lead to the amalgamation of the two Catholic colleges. These were minor reverses compared to both committees' initial intentions, and in 1987 the Catholic authorities secured a major success when the DENI profoundly altered its relations with the Catholic schools system.

The Council for Catholic Maintained Schools

One of the few recommendations of the Astin committee endorsed by the Catholic authorities was the suggestion for a coordinating body for all Catholic schools in Northern Ireland. This was to ease the administrative problems of the DENI and the Education and Library Boards which was dealing with more than five hundred schools employing over seven thousand teachers.[43] Five years of inaction followed before Scott established a working party of DENI officials and representatives of the Irish Episcopal Conference to fashion a proposal in 1985.

Two years of negotiations finally yielded the Council for Catholic Maintained Schools (CCMS) in July 1987.[44] The initial scheme envisaged a Council of thirty-six members with twenty representatives of the schools' trustees, eight appointees of the DENI, four teachers and four representatives of Catholic parents.[45] The Council's structures closely mirrored the maintained school committees established by the 1984 Order by granting nearly, but not quite, half of the seats to the DENI, teachers and parents. The 1987 agreement between O'Fiaich and Mawhinney outlined the extensive tasks of the Council:

> The Council will, in consultation with the Department of Education and the Education and Library Boards, negotiate, establish and implement policy both in general educational matters and in areas of management of the Catholic maintained sector in accordance with the Statement of Aims of Catholic Schools.[46]

Reaction to the CCMS divided along political lines. The *Belfast Telegraph* claimed that 'strengthening the existing system does nothing to diminish the sectarian divisions in Ulster's schools'[47] whilst the *Irish News* termed it 'a landmark in the history of the Northern Ireland education system'.[48] The DENI acknowledged that education in Northern Ireland was, with a few notable exceptions, a denominational system. The education laws viewed voluntary and maintained schools as simply independent enterprises managed by private individuals, but the creation of the CCMS recognised that the Catholic schools system was a distinctive element requiring unique treatment. The emphasis for education policy in England and Wales during the 1980s was to devolve powers to individual schools. In Northern Ireland the DENI reversed this trend to create a potentially powerful instrument that provided the Catholic authorities with a forum for negotiations with the DENI and better prospects of success than attempting to motivate Catholic electors or nationalist politicians who no longer appeared willing to defend clerical interests.

The advantage of the CCMS for the DENI was not solely administrative convenience. The Council incorporated the Catholic authorities within the DENI's decision-making apparatus. The CCMS provided greater access into the policy process for senior Catholic clerics, but they were also obliged to address awkward questions arising from school rationalisation and the allocation of resources. After 1987 the Catholic authorities were implicated in many of the decisions effecting individual Catholic schools.

The status of the Catholic clergy within the Catholic school and the future of autonomous Catholic teacher training had been preserved by the mid 1980s, but the advent of education reform in England and Wales evoked a response from the DENI which once more challenged clerical authority within Catholic schools. The Catholic authorities resented the apparent dilution of the CCMS's authority outlined in the DENI's consultative document of March 1988 and the following October's White Paper. They complained that 'the *raison d'être* of the Council has been disregarded, its role has been negated'.[49] The 1987 agreement differed sharply from the British government's education reforms in England and Wales, where the Education Reform Act of 1988 devolved greater powers to individual schools. The Education Reform Order of 1989 appeared to dilute this contrast, drawing Northern Ireland's education system closer to the English and Welsh pattern.

In the aftermath of the agreement with O'Fiaich, Mawhinney sought to ease the fears of the Education and Library Boards that the CCMS would act as a sixth board, controlling half of Northern Ireland's schools. He insisted that the Education and Library Boards retain a significant influence within Catholic maintained schools.[50] The White Paper and the draft Order-in-Council of the following year appeared to address the Boards' concerns, challenging the Catholic authorities' interpretation of the role of the CCMS. The Education and Library Boards no longer provoked unease for the Catholic authorities, but they were not alone in wishing to avoid 'interference' from the Boards. In June 1995 the Ulster Unionist MP, Dr Martin Smyth, complained that voluntary grammar schools were to become accountable to the Education and Library Boards for grants for recurrent spending, despite the objections of numerous boards of governors.[51] The governors of voluntary grammar schools also valued their autonomy from the Education and Library Boards. The CCMS attempted to reverse these apparent changes, but the Order was presented to Parliament in December 1989 without substantial amendment. The loss of status for the CCMS does not appear to have been as significant as the Catholic authorities contended, but the 1989 Order reversed some of the advantages secured by the 1987 agreement.

The 1989 Order initiated the most significant reform of Northern Ireland's education system since the 1947 Act with the introduction of the core curriculum, the preference for integrated schools and greater autonomy for individual schools. The Order offered Catholic schools no financial assistance to satisfy the demands created by the core curriculum, but the Catholic authorities appeared indifferent to the burden of the voluntary contribution. They launched their first legal challenge to Northern Ireland's education laws in 1990, but this was provoked by the preference for integrated schools rather than the threat of massive voluntary contribution payments. The voluntary contribution appeared to be an enduring feature of Northern Ireland's education system until a dramatic change was imposed upon the British government by an independent investigation which found substantial evidence of conspicuous differences between Catholic and Protestant schools. The voluntary contribution suddenly became the central issue in education for the first time since 1968.

The SACHR Inquiry

In the late 1980s the Standing Advisory Commission on Human Rights (SACHR) launched an extensive study of the social ramifications of the education system after a SACHR report on fair employment found Catholics were more likely to leave school without any qualifications, and less likely to secure 'A' Levels, than Protestants.[52] The SACHR inquiry provides the most extensive analysis of the impact of the voluntary contribution upon Catholic schools. It investigated three aspects of the education system; curriculum differences between the two school systems, access to grammar schools and the financial arrangements for controlled and maintained schools.[53]

John D'Arcy and Anne E. Sutherland studied curriculum provision 'to examine the extent to which the Northern Ireland education system reflects, exacerbates or ameliorates differences by reason of sex, religion or social class'.[54] They found Protestant pupils in both secondary intermediate and grammar schools were more likely than Catholic pupils to study science 'A' levels. They also noted that the distinction between the two denominations was closing in recent years, the difference between grammar and secondary intermediate schools was more significant than between maintained and controlled schools, and gender was a more significant factor than religion in determining

whether a pupil studied science and technology courses.[55] These qualifications should not obscure the finding that Protestants were gaining
an advantage by studying subjects considered to be valuable in the
labour market.

The differential between Catholic and Protestant pupils was partly
caused by Catholic schools teaching the Gaelic language and dedicating a greater part of the school day to religious education.[56] However,
the traditional Catholic preference for humanities was judged to be a
consequence of differential funding. D'Arcy and Sutherland noted that
Catholic schools in Scotland, which have enjoyed equal treatment with
state schools since 1918, showed no variation in their curriculum from
other Scottish schools.[57] Also, the statistics for special education rooms
indicated that Protestant pupils were able to study a wider range of
subjects than those available to Catholic pupils.[58] A number of these
rooms were music rooms, but many were language laboratories or
craft and technology rooms which allowed controlled school pupils to
collect useful qualifications.

In the early 1980s, after more than a decade of direct rule by British
ministers, thirty-five per cent of Protestants were attending grammar
schools in contrast to only twenty-six per cent of Catholics.[59]
Livingstone's 1987 study offered three major reasons to explain this
difference argued that a small minority of Catholic parents preferred
to send their children to Protestant grammar schools, Catholics were
more likely to refuse the opportunity of a grammar education and
Protestants showed a greater willingness to pay fees.[60]

Firstly, the preference for Protestant grammar schools by a minority
of Catholic parents may be explained by the evidence collected by the
SACHR inquiry that Protestant grammar schools received more than
their fair share of funds for recurrent spending. Protestant schools
would, therefore, probably offer better facilities than their Catholic
counterparts. Also, Catholic parents might be influenced by the
general perception of Catholic grammar schools as 'arts' rather than
'science' schools – which D'Arcy and Sutherland judged to be a
consequence of the voluntary contribution – and by the prospect of
their children making influential 'connections' within the affluent
Protestant community which might prove useful in later years. Also,
decades of rhetoric by nationalist politicians and Catholic clerics on
the 'crushing burden' of the voluntary contribution may have convinced some parents that Catholic schools were second-class schools
compared to the Protestant voluntary grammar schools and controlled
schools. Finally, the greater willingness of Protestant parents to pay

grammar school fees may be explained by the social contrast between Catholic and Protestant parents – a distinction the education system perpetuated after the 1925 Act.

The difference in the prospects for a grammar school education between the two communities was viewed as a major factor in explaining the attainment differential between Catholic and Protestant pupils. The Commission recommended that the DENI fund an expansion of Catholic grammar schools.[61] Mawhinney's successor, Jeremy Hanley, announced shortly after the publication of the SACHR report that the DENI would fund an additional 1,470 places in Catholic grammar schools.[62]

The most significant study for the SACHR inquiry was undertaken by Robert Cormack, Anthony Gallagher and Robert Osborne. Their study, *Religious Affiliation and Educational Attainment: The Financing of Schools in Northern Ireland*,[63] formed the basis of the SACHR's calls for reform of the funding arrangements for maintained schools. The authors found notable variations in both capital and recurrent spending between controlled and maintained schools.

A DENI survey of Northern Ireland's schools found a quarter of controlled secondary intermediate schools, but half the maintained secondary intermediate schools, to be in an unsatisfactory condition.[64] The authors concluded that maintained schools were overcrowded because the voluntary contribution discouraged Catholic parishes from building large schools which could cater for an increasing number of pupils.[65] They viewed the voluntary contribution, rather than any increase in the Catholic populace, as the primary factor explaining this disparity. They also warned that the obligations arising from the core curriculum imposed by the 1989 Order would increase the investment needs of many Catholic schools and exacerbate the burden of maintained status. They concluded that 'there is a strong case for a new examination of the voluntary contribution with a view to a decrease from its current level of fifteen per cent'.[66] The Commission noted that Mawhinney's speech during the debate of the 1989 Order proposed discussions to increase capital funding if the Catholic authorities reduced their management role within Catholic schools, and recommended that the DENI should initiate discussions with the CCMS.[67]

The study also found that recurrent expenditure, which since 1968 had officially been awarded in equal measure to maintained and controlled schools, favoured controlled schools. Controlled primary schools received £177 for every pupil while maintained primary schools gained only £143 – just eighty per cent of the controlled average – and the secondary school figures were £350 and £312 – a ten per cent difference.[68] Recurrent spending patterns for voluntary grammar schools showed a similar trend, though the report acknowledged that the funding differentials between Catholic and Protestant grammar schools were partly caused by the presence of clerical teachers in Catholic schools in previous decades and lower fees in Catholic schools before the 1947 Act.[69] The authors recognised that declining numbers of Protestant pupils might also partly account for these discrepancies, but they judged that 'a consistent pattern of differentials in recurrent expenditure existed to the disadvantage of the Catholic school system'.[70]

The former deputy director of the CCMS, Paddy McCavera, calculated the amount of public funds that maintained and controlled schools *would have* received during the late 1980s if the monies for recurrent spending were allocated simply according to pupil numbers. He compared these figures to the *actual* amounts dedicated to recurrent costs. McCavera estimated that maintained schools received nearly £2.2 million less each year than their share under this simple formula, and controlled schools received an excess of more than £2.2 million.[71] The government anticipated such criticism in February 1989 when Mawhinney announced that the formula for allocating funds for recurrent spending to grammar schools was to be amended to place greater emphasis upon student numbers rather than the 'historic patterns of expenditure'.[72]

The SACHR inquiry revived the question of the voluntary contribution by presenting evidence of disadvantages for Catholic schools and a consistent preference for controlled and Protestant grammar schools. The Commission's findings, and the threat that the 1989 Order would widen the inequalities between Catholic and Protestant schools unless the Catholic populace paid millions of pounds each year to finance reform, compelled the DENI to reconsider the funding conditions for Catholic schools. The outcome was the Education Order of October 1993 which finally abolished the voluntary contribution.

The 1993 Order

The DENI initiated negotiations with representatives of the Catholic authorities, led by Bishop Edward Daly of Derry, shortly after the publication of the SACHR report. By the end of 1992 they agreed a settlement which granted Catholic maintained schools full public funding in exchange for the Catholic clergy surrendering their majority on the school committees.[73] The new school committee would consist of four trustees, two members appointed by the Education and Library Board and a single member representing the DENI, parents and teachers.[74] The agreement ensured that six of the nine members of the school committee would be Catholics, and the Northern Ireland Secretary, Sir Patrick Mayhew, promised that the DENI representative would be appointed following consultations with the CCMS.[75]

The DENI's agreement with the Catholic authorities provoked a hostile reaction from unionist politicians. The Democratic Unionist Party condemned the proposal as a 'total disgrace' and further evidence of the influence of the Dublin government in Northern Ireland's affairs. The DUP's spokesman on education, Sammy Wilson, also claimed that the additional money for Catholic schools would come from funds promised to controlled schools.[76] Wilson's fears were probably justified. The Commission urged the British government to finance the abolition of the voluntary contribution with additional funds, but greater investment for maintained schools has certainly influenced the budget available for controlled schools in recent years. The Commons debate of the Education (Northern Ireland) Order underlined unionist discontent, with Kilfedder asking if the Protestant churches supported the Order and Smyth urging the government not to use the Order to discriminate against controlled schools.[77] Paisley also called for a revival of the founding principles of the National Schools of religious instruction being provided by the various denominations.[78]

The 1993 Order arose almost entirely from the initiative of the Commission, with the Catholic authorities and nationalist politicians appearing to play a minor role.[79] Cormack, Gallagher and Osborne found the Catholic authorities' representatives, in a notable repetition of the debate amongst senior Catholic clerics in the spring of 1930, reluctant to abandon the principle of the voluntary contribution[80] while the four SDLP MPs were notable by their absence during the debate on the 1993 Order. The Catholic authorities and the SDLP leadership appeared apathetic, despite the Order finally relieving the Catholic community of the burden of finding nearly one sixth of the cost of new schools.

The 1993 Order does not appear to alter the practice in many Catholic schools. The 1968 Act granted the education committees one third of the school committee's seats and the 1993 Order provides the Education and Library Board and the DENI with three of nine seats. The presence of a DENI representative appointed in consultation with the CCMS obviously dilutes the potential disruption from intransigent unionists, but the Boards have attracted few complaints from Catholic clerics or nationalist politicians in the last two decades.

Also, the evidence from maintained schools in Tyrone and Newry in the early 1970s indicated that the Catholic clergy in many parishes involved the Catholic laity in the management of their schools.[81] The liberal ethos encouraged by the Vatican Council, and the declining number of vocations, has enhanced lay influence within Catholic schools without the encouragement of the DENI. The abolition of the voluntary contribution in exchange for the loss of the clerical majority was an overdue compromise that neither the DENI nor the Catholic authorities appeared eager to pursue until the SACHR inquiry.

The 1993 Order almost resolves the vexed question of the voluntary contribution, and ends the official disadvantage suffered by Catholic schools since 1925. The SACHR report indicates that Catholic schools suffered discrimination in the allocation of grants for recurrent spending, and the Commission advised the DENI to monitor the 1993 Order to ensure fair treatment for all schools. The DENI will not be alone when studying the application of the Order, because the history of Catholic education in Northern Ireland has amply demonstrated the Catholic authorities' determination to defend their interests.

SHARED SCHOOLS

Callaghan's speech to the Labour Party conference in the autumn of 1969 appeared to indicate British antipathy towards segregated education, but the British government swiftly sacrificed the principle of integration to its wider objectives. British ministers employed the Catholic authorities, in the absence of a credible political leadership, to communicate with the nationalist community.[82] The formation of the SDLP in August 1970 diminished the political role of senior Catholic clerics, but the Home Office continued to view clerical support as a valuable means of influencing the nationalist electorate.

In March 1973 the British government tried to fashion a new constitutional settlement with a White Paper, *Northern Ireland Constitutional Proposals*. The document contained a sympathetic assessment of denominational schools.[83] The White Paper began by emphasising the need to eradicate intolerance and claimed that 'one of the obvious factors in the situation is the high degree of educational segregation'.[84] This ominous tone was soon dispelled as the text, betraying the signs of many compromises and numerous drafts, continued by defending the principle of denominational schools and casting doubts on alleged Protestant support for integration:

> The importance which, in the United Kingdom and in many other countries, certain of the Churches place upon their own school systems stems from deep conviction about the need for an underlying religious basis to all teaching. While, in Northern Ireland, it is the Roman Catholic Church which maintains a separate system, it is by no means to be assumed that, in practice, all Protestant parents would be happy to see a completely integrated school system, involving as it would the teaching of Protestant children by Roman Catholic teachers, some of them members of religious orders.[85]

The White Paper recognised the underlying reluctance of many Protestants to contemplate a genuine integration of Catholic and controlled schools. The following year a delegate to the annual conference of the Ulster Teachers' Union outlined his conditions for integration:

> Lay Roman Catholic teachers we will accept, but on certain conditions, and I cannot see the Protestant people in the city of Belfast accepting nuns and Christian Brothers as teachers of their children.[86]

The Catholic authorities have consistently emphasised the importance of a Catholic 'atmosphere' in Catholic schools,[87] and the presence of members of religious orders in the classroom has been viewed as a vital means of maintaining this religious climate. The decline in vocations has diminished the role of religious orders within Catholic schools, but clerical teachers remain an important feature of Catholic secondary schools which the Catholic authorities fiercely defend.

The White Paper's answer was to encourage greater contact between Catholic and Protestant pupils attending their own schools rather than attempt to fuse Catholic and Protestant pupils together in 'shared' schools:

> There are, however, some encouraging indications of a new consciousness of the need to promote real and continuing points of contact and mutual interest between all the children of Northern Ireland . . . it will be a vital task of government in the future to facilitate, to encourage and to promote these points of contact. Unless, in the future, a greater sense of community can be fostered amongst the young people of Northern Ireland, it is difficult to see how this mutual distrust can be broken down.[88]

The White Paper concluded with a sentence which has been frequently quoted by Catholic clerics during the last twenty years: 'to make the educational system itself the scapegoat of all the ills of Northern Ireland would obscure problems whose origins are of a much more complex character'.[89]

The White Paper of 1973 led, eventually, to the brief experiment in power sharing known as the Northern Ireland Executive. The Executive was to govern Northern Ireland for less than five months in 1974, but this temporary revival of devolved power produced the most significant threat to Catholic schools since the early 1950s.

Basil McIvor

In April 1974 the Executive's Minister of Education, Basil McIvor, announced a radical proposal for school committees involving both Protestant and Catholic clerics. The initial plan only envisaged joint committees for nursery schools and sixth form colleges, but McIvor stated that he hoped to extend the committees to every school in Northern Ireland.[90] His proposal was no more than 'a suggestion',[91] and his speech to the Northern Ireland Assembly offered an optimistic assessment of the potential problems:

> If the main groups of churches are involved together in the management of a school they will between them have sufficient goodwill to agree what should be done and to make arrangements which enable the children who are members of their faith in the school to be suitably instructed in the particular tenets of that church.[92]

The initial response of SDLP members in the Assembly was sharply critical. Mallon called the speech 'a statement which is inaccurate in its claims, superficial in its approach to a highly sensitive area of community life and that draws facile conclusions about a scheme that does not even exist'.[93] Paddy O'Donoghue was also sceptical, but only insisted upon careful consideration of any scheme.[94] Curiously, clerical reaction was less strident. Canon Padraig Murphy of Ballymurphy condemned McIvor's scheme as 'quite naïve and quite ill-informed'[95] on the day of the speech, but he was a lone clerical voice in the first week of May 1974. A spokesman for Cardinal Conway claimed on the night of McIvor's speech that the only information available to the Cardinal came from radio bulletins,[96] but a lack of consultation had not prevented Philbin condemning the White Paper in October 1967.

Protestant and unionist reaction was less equivocal. The three major Protestant churches welcomed McIvor's speech, along with Archbishop Michael Ramsey of Canterbury, and both the Ulster Teachers' Union and the National Association of Schoolmasters.[97] The unionist parties supported McIvor, though a *Belfast Telegraph* editorial less than a fortnight before his announcement claimed that 'more professional influence and less clerical influence should be the aim for the future'.[98] A number of unionist politicians were unable to resist the opportunity to criticise the Catholic authorities' education policy. Dr Smyth claimed 'the greatest tragedy has been the unwillingness of the Roman Catholic authorities from the very beginning to cooperate within the State system. I hope that the sectarian approach taken by Canon Murphy is not typical of the attitudes held by all Roman Catholics'.[99] However, he later tarnished his integrationist credentials by claiming that controlled schools, being available to every child in Northern Ireland, were truly integrated schools.[100] Another unionist member of the Assembly, Brigadier Ron Broadhurst of South Down, declared 'those who seek to build a community in Northern Ireland are disgusted and revolted by such Church intransigence'.[101]

Smyth's hopes that Canon Murphy's remarks were an isolated opinion within Catholic ranks were not dispelled in the weeks following McIvor's speech. Clerics were silent while nationalist politicians were notably less hostile. Mallon, initially critical, later called the scheme 'the best proposals that the Minister could have come up with',[102] and in the Irish Republic the leader of the opposition Fianna Fáil party welcomed McIvor's offer.[103] The SDLP was committed by the Executive's policy document *Steps Towards a Better Tomorrow* to 'pilot experiments . . . in integrated education',[104] and they could not easily retreat from an agreed commitment.

Nationalist reluctance to condemn McIvor's proposals may have been influenced by the fragile state of community relations in the spring of 1974. Unionist opponents of the Executive won eleven of Northern Ireland's twelve Westminster seats in the February 1974 election, and the Ulster Workers' Council was preparing the general strike which would eventually destroy the Executive. McAllister is correct to note that 'the SDLP has been less than enthusiastic about integrated education, and it is thus an open question whether the SDLP ministers would have supported Executive policy in the event of a major conflict with the Catholic hierarchy'.[105] However, there was also no guarantee that the SDLP ministers would confront the unionist majority on the Executive and threaten the survival of power sharing to protect segregation. The SDLP's leadership may have judged the first week of May 1974 to be an inopportune moment to insist upon clerical control of Catholic schools.

The Catholic authorities' silence in May 1974 may also have been motivated by their assumption that McIvor's scheme was both unrealistic and unlikely, in practice, to appeal to the Protestant clergy.[106] McIvor did not settle the vital question of teaching appointments or state whether teachers would be allowed to provide denominational religious instruction. His proposal also failed to confront the national and ethnic implications of 'shared' schools. The problems surrounding Gaelic games, the Gaelic language, the Union Flag and the National Anthem were never explained to the Northern Ireland Assembly or the public.

McIvor was attempting to revive Lord Stanley's scheme of 1831, but the National Board's preference for joint applications from Protestant and Catholic clerics failed to prevent the development of a denominational system by the middle of the nineteenth century. A policy which failed during the relative calm of Ireland in the 1830s and 1840s was unlikely to be more successful in the turmoil of Northern Ireland in the 1970s.

McIvor also never explained how Protestant clerics in former Catholic schools, or Catholic priests in former Protestant schools, would ease community tensions, nor did he offer a solution to the severe practical problems arising from combining children in 'shared' schools. *The Times Educational Supplement* article on McIvor's plans was entitled 'Armour Plated Bussing',[107] and Cahal Daly later emphasised the practical difficulties of transferring children across the various 'peace lines' to their new schools:

> even those who believe in the value of integrated education must recognise that their solution would affect very few. It could not, for long established historical and geographical reasons, be realised between, say, the Falls Road and the Shankill Road other than by some process of bussing which would expose young children to real physical danger, intimidation, threats to which no parents would willingly subject their children.[108]

Government ministers also mentioned the risks of attempting to integrate schools when countering accusations of indifference to integration. In May 1980 Lord Elton claimed:

> If you actually look at the map where the communities live and where the schools are, even if you were to have instant integration you could only do so by bussing, which has proven to be disastrous for instance in the States, and has magnified all the tensions it is designed to relieve.[109]

McIvor was attempting an administrative rather than a social and cultural integration and, while sectarian violence persisted, there was no prospect of McIvor's 'shared' schools containing more than an isolated and vulnerable minority. McIvor's scheme was a bold attempt to rescue Northern Ireland's next generation from the bitter antagonisms which were inflicting so much violence in the spring of 1974. The collapse of the Executive denied McIvor the opportunity to develop his ideas. The approaching clash with the loyalists may have prompted McIvor to announce his scheme, but he was unlikely to ease the fears of Catholic and Protestant clerics in the troubled months before, during and after the fall of the Executive.

The practical problems were severe, but McIvor broached awkward questions for the Catholic authorities until their plight was eased by the Ulster Workers' Council's strike and the collapse of the Executive. The events of April and May 1974 also underlined the growing detachment of constitutional nationalists from senior Catholic clerics when the Catholic authorities' education interests appeared to clash with the SDLP's political objectives. The Catholic authorities' problems were about to increase, because they soon faced an alarming threat from within the Catholic community.

All Children Together

The most intense challenge to the principle of segregated schools since the fall of the devolved government has come from the organisation All Children Together (ACT). ACT began in the early months of 1972 as an informal grouping of Catholic parents in North Down who were sending their children to controlled schools.[110] The parents' motives varied from a principled belief in the merits of integration to an assumption that controlled schools provided a higher standard of education.[111] The initial aim of ACT members was simply to ensure their children received Catholic religious instruction, but Philbin's refusal to perform the sacrament of Confirmation for pupils from controlled schools, or to discuss their predicament, led the group to publicise its difficulties in the *Belfast Telegraph* in April 1974.[112]

The Catholic authorities refused to engage in a public debate with the leaders of ACT. The *Irish News* for April 1974 contains no references to ACT, despite the article receiving extensive coverage in the *Belfast Telegraph* and provoking a significant response in the letters page from both Catholic and Protestant parents.[113] Unionist criticism could be dismissed as prejudice, but the first leaders of ACT were

Catholics, and many devoutly practised their faith. The Catholic authorities' silence was ample testimony to the unease caused by such a profound challenge from lay Catholics.

Philbin's colleagues were less adamantly opposed to the Confirmation of controlled school pupils. In October 1977 O'Fiaich agreed to the Confirmation of the children if they attended a series of preparation classes supervised by the local priest.[114] O'Fiaich's attempt to defuse the controversy failed to prevent ACT from developing beyond the concerns of liberal Catholics in North Down into a campaign to undermine segregation. The following year they scored an apparent success when Parliament passed the Education (Northern Ireland) Act. The purpose of the 1978 Act was 'to facilitate the establishment in Northern Ireland of schools likely to be attended by pupils of different religious affiliations or cultural traditions'[115] by allowing a school to be treated as an integrated school if a ballot initiated by the school committee found seventy-five per cent of the parents in favour of a change to integrated status.[116]

The clerical majority on the school committees ensured that few maintained schools would initiate ballots, but the Act's authors hoped the school committees of controlled schools would consider balloting parents. The major Protestant denominations had pledged at succe- ssive annual assemblies to support integrated education. The Church of Ireland approved an integration motion at its 1970 Synod, and the Church's education committee published papers recommending integration in 1974, 1975 and 1978. The General Assembly of the Presbyterian Church passed resolutions in 1971 and 1974 affirming its support for the principle of integrated schools.[117]

The ACT leadership realised the Protestant clergy would be slow to respond to the new Act, but by May 1980 only one school, scheduled for closure by Belfast's Education and Library Board, applied for a ballot.[118] Senior Protestant clerics claimed that any attempt to initiate trial schemes would undermine relations with the Catholic authorities,[119] but the Protestant clergy were reluctant to surrender their power and influence within controlled schools. The Catholic authorities presented a principled defence of denominational schools while the Protestant churches adopted a more accommodating approach, without facing the prospect of translating their pledges into practical measures until the 1978 Act. The practical problems of integrating schools without the cooperation of the Catholic authorities should not be understated, but there was no genuine challenge to segregation from the Protestant clergy after 1978.

The integration movement responded to the disappointment of the 1978 Act by attempting to create its own network of 'shared' schools. However, it found the DENI's conditions for funding new schools to be a major obstacle. An integrated school would not receive any public funds until the DENI was convinced the school could ensure a viable number of pupils. Dunn claims that this process, which could last two years for primary schools and longer for secondary schools, was a severe impediment to the integration movement,[120] but the difficulties did not provoke a sympathetic response from the British government.

The 1978 Act was passed by Parliament without the explicit approval of the British government. The NIO and the DENI drafted various Orders and other forms of statutory legislation to implement the Act, but British ministers were studiously neutral. In May 1980 Lord Elton emphasised that the government remained sceptical that integration was a feasible possibility for most children in Northern Ireland:

> to the outsider it is a perfectly simple object to integrate education: but both in practical and philosophical terms it is anything but a simple question. The first thing is that people's emotions and loyalties are very deeply committed indeed and no solution will work that is not accepted. Therefore there is no question of imposing or forcing an integrated system upon the province against the resistance of the people.[121]

Seven years later there was no fundamental change in government policy. In May 1987 Mawhinney outlined the DENI's funding conditions for integrated schools:

> Independent integrated schools seeking recognition as grant aided maintained schools must prove over a period that they are able to attract enough pupils to make them potentially viable. When they are recognised as maintained schools they are funded in the same way as maintained schools.[122]

The British government remained sceptical, but a series of opinion polls since the late 1960s have demonstrated popular support for integration. A poll conducted for *Fortnight* magazine in May 1973 found sixty-four per cent of Catholics and fifty-nine per cent of Protestants supporting integration,[123] and another poll in 1980 confirmed the general trend of Catholic support, with sixty-two per cent supporting and twenty-two per cent opposing the idea.[124] Eight years later an opinion poll conducted in Belfast in April 1988 poll also showed increasing support for integration, with sixty-seven per cent in favour and only twenty per cent opposed to greater government assistance for integrated schools.[125]

The evidence of popular support for integration is clear, but the principle has proved more popular than practical integration measures. The 1980 poll found only thirty-three per cent of Catholics favoured amalgamating the Catholic teacher training colleges with Stranmillis college and forty-two per cent, nearly twice the number opposing integration in principle, were hostile to integrating teacher training colleges.[126] The 1988 poll found that only twenty per cent of parents with children of school age opposed additional public monies to promote integration, but thirty-seven per cent of parents also preferred to send their child to a denominational school.[127]

Poll evidence also indicates that the areas suffering the most intense political violence – working-class urban districts – have displayed least enthusiasm for integration. The 1973 poll found 'the only people strongly against the idea were the supporters of Ian Paisley and of the Provisional IRA',[128] and the 1980 poll also revealed greater opposition amongst working-class Catholics and Protestants than their respective middle classes.[129] The 1988 Belfast poll appears to contradict the widespread assumption that integration is a middle-class issue, claiming that working-class voters in the west and the north of the city were as sympathetic as their more middle-class counterparts in south Belfast,[130] but few of the twenty-eight integrated schools operating in the autumn of 1995 were based in poor or disturbed areas.[131]

There remains a notable discrepancy between the ecumenical statements of the electorate and their denominational deeds, but there can be no doubt that a substantial number of Catholic parents wish to send their children to integrated schools, and many accept the assertion that denominational schools fortify sectarian attitudes. The Catholic laity share many common convictions and prejudices with their clergy, but education is one of the few issues to reveal a substantial difference of opinion between Catholic clerics and their congregations.

Gerald McElroy conducted a survey of Northern Ireland's Catholic clergy in March and April 1986 which found integration to be the only significant issue separating clerics from the views of the majority of the Catholic populace. A majority of the survey sample of 232 priests and members of religious orders disputed the claim that 'if Protestant and Catholic children were educated in the same schools, some of the problems in Northern Ireland would be reduced' while less than a third of all respondents, and only one seventh of parish priests, supported the statement.[132]

McElroy's study also revealed that over half of the survey sample were opposed in principle to integrated schools and nearly sixty per cent of the rest felt, despite the merits of integration, 'under the present circumstances in Northern Ireland nothing can be done to change the present schools system except to increase contacts between children attending Catholic and Protestant schools'. Only ten per cent of the sample believed 'the Church and State ought to launch a campaign for integrated education in Northern Ireland'. McElroy noted that clerics educated in Northern Ireland's Catholic schools were more sceptical of integration than outsiders – even those educated in Catholic schools in the Irish Republic. He also found a majority of the comments offered by the participants at the end of the questionnaire mentioned integration, though this may partly be explained by the survey form concluding with the education questions.[133]

The defence of denominational education is a central issue for the Catholic authorities, yet opinion polls indicate that support for integration is stronger amongst Catholic than Protestant voters, and the majority of pupils attending integrated schools are Catholics.[134] The Catholic authorities, despite the avowed wishes of the Catholic laity and the ambivalence of nationalist politicians, have never wavered in their determination to oppose integration. Denominational schools form one topic where the Catholic clergy and the laity must simply agree to disagree.

Unionists and integration

Unionist MPs were enthusiastic advocates of integration during the first decade of direct rule. The most diligent champion of integrated schools was James Kilfedder, Unionist MP for North Down from 1970 to 1995.[135] Kilfedder tirelessly exhorted the British government to integrate Northern Ireland's schools, and he rarely squandered an opportunity to argue for 'shared' schools. In 1989 Mawhinney claimed that 'the people of the Province owe him a great debt' for his efforts to promote integrated schools.[136] Hansard evidence also illustrates that Kilfedder was a strident opponent of Catholic schools.

Kilfedder questioned the honesty of maintained school committees submitting estimates to the Education and Library Boards, protested at the use of maintained schools for political meetings and the presence of republican slogans on the walls of maintained schools, and he even objected to the DENI funding youth work projects in maintained schools.[137] None of these questions involved segregation or the power of the Catholic clergy within Catholic schools, but were motivated by a traditional antipathy towards autonomous Catholic schools. In 1978 Kilfedder claimed 'I have always been a staunch advocate of ending religious apartheid between schools', but only moments before he opposed the 1978 Education (Northern Ireland) Order because it granted voluntary and maintained schools equal rights with controlled schools to acquire land for new schools. Kilfedder failed to dispel the suspicion that some unionist advocates of integration were hoping to undermine Catholic schools rather than seeking to ease community tensions.

The Ulster Unionist MP, Enoch Powell, defended segregated schools,[138] but he was an exception amongst Unionist MPs. Powell's colleagues invariably endorsed calls for integrated schools, and criticised the Catholic authorities for obstructing integration. In June 1984 the Ulster Unionist MP, Harold McCusker, complained:

> It will not happen because the Roman Catholic hierarchy has a system of education that it controls, which is financed from public funds and which is probably as good a system as it is ever likely to get, and at no time is it likely to relinquish its hold.[139]

Unionist politicians were critical of the Catholic authorities' hostility to integration, but no Unionist MP mentioned the 1978 Act which allowed any controlled school to convert to an integrated school. Unionist MPs asked ministers to initiate discussions with the Catholic authorities, but none asked for similar talks with the Protestant clergy or encouraged the school committees of controlled schools to apply the 1978 Act.

The tone of unionist criticism of Catholic schools also changed in the 1970s and 1980s. The 1968 Act granted education authorities one third of the seats of maintained school committees, so Unionist MPs no longer complained of a lack of 'local democratic control' within Catholic schools. The problem with Catholic schools in the 1980s became their divisive impact upon community relations. Unionist politicians, discounting nationalist complaints of alienation and discrimination, emphasised segregation as a major factor fostering the conflict, and they found numerous allies amongst English, Scottish and Welsh MPs.

The new integration campaign gathered support beyond the usual coterie of unionists on the Conservative backbenches.[140] Liberals such as Alan Beith, the Catholic MP David Alton and Labour's shadow minister for education, Neil Kinnock, all called for integration initiatives in the 1970s and early 1980s.[141] In contrast, there were few MPs beyond the government front bench to defend denominational schools. In April 1988 Kilfedder claimed 'I know that the SDLP disagrees with my wish to see the bringing together of Protestant and Roman Catholic'.[142] Hume and Mallon were both present in the Commons, but neither responded to his challenge.[143]

Unionists were enthusiastic advocates of integration in the 1960s and 1970s, but their enthusiasm has waned in recent years as they have found the potential impact of integrated schools less enticing than the principle of integration. The prospect of a substantial network of integrated schools has exposed the problems facing the Protestant community's controlled schools. A study of Northern Ireland's schools, commissioned by SACHR in 1989, found the pupil rolls of controlled primary schools were significantly smaller than those of maintained schools. A quarter of all controlled schools contained less than fifty-five pupils,[144] and the number of pupils in Belfast's controlled schools fell by fifteen per cent between 1979 and 1983 while the city's maintained schools suffered only a two per cent decline.[145] Therefore, integrated schools threaten many controlled schools, and these fears partly account for growing unionist disquiet. The Ulster Teacher's Union underlined the changing attitudes within the Protestant community when the Union's annual conference passed a motion in April 1987 claiming that an 'artificial balancing of numbers' was unnecessary for controlled schools to be treated as integrated schools.[146]

Kilfedder continued to encourage the government to support integrated schools but, by the late 1980s, most of the questions recommending government initiatives to promote integration came from Liberal and Conservative MPs.[147] In March 1984 Dr Smyth complained that Lagan College, the new integrated secondary school in south Belfast, was undermining the prospects of controlled schools in the area and his criticisms were supported by Paisley.[148] The 1989 Reform Order was severely criticised by a succession of Unionist MPs. In June 1994 the Ulster Unionist MP for Fermanagh and South Tyrone, Ken Maginess, criticised 'profligate' spending by the DENI on an integrated secondary school in Fermanagh.[149]

The Ulster Unionist Party's manifesto for the 1992 election failed to mention integrated education,[150] but five years later the party's manifesto recognised 'that many parents wish to have their children educated in integrated schools'.[151] The manifesto then displayed recent Unionist concerns when it continued 'we oppose funding from already scarce educational resources to develop a third system of integrated schools at post primary level in Northern Ireland when surplus accommodation for post primary pupils already exists in the controlled and maintained sectors'.[152] The manifesto recommended 'a policy of transformation to controlled integrated status where appropriate'.[153] The Unionist Party appears only to favour bringing Catholic pupils into overwhelmingly Protestant schools. The DUP was less subtle, declaring that 'we are opposed to priority being given to integrated and maintained schools to the detriment of schools in the State sector. Churches . . . who may wish to have separate schools should pay for them'.[154] Unionist disquiet about integration has even led the Free Presbyterian Church to explore the possibilities of developing a network of completely independent schools to safeguard the religious development of the children of Free Presbyterians.

The advocates of integrated schools lost the support of Ulster's Unionists during the 1980s, but by the end of the decade they secured a more influential ally.

The 1989 Order

The British government maintained the policy outlined by Elton in May 1980 that 'all the government would express its intention of doing is assisting any authority which wishes to introduce integration voluntarily to the best of its powers'[155] until the arrival of Mawhinney at the Northern Ireland Office in January 1986. He led a gradual change from approval tempered by scepticism to an explicit commitment to assist integration.

In May 1987 Mawhinney, an Ulster Protestant, underlined a more positive approach when he stated 'it is the Government's policy to encourage integrated education, if that is what the parents wish'.[156] The contrast was subtle, and with only three integrated schools receiving grants from the DENI by the end of 1987,[157] Mawhinney opted for a more assertive strategy. He exploited the opportunity presented by education reform in England and Wales to provide substantial assistance for integrated schools.

In March 1988 the DENI published a consultative document entitled *Education in Northern Ireland – Proposals for Reform* which proposed significant advantages for integrated schools. Firstly, the paper promised preference for integrated schools in allocating public funds for building projects. The consultative document was unclear how the DENI would award this preference, but the following month Mawhinney announced that the government intended to pay all the bills for grant maintained integrated schools.[158]

Secondly, the DENI hoped to encourage the growth of controlled integrated schools by reducing the necessary ratio of parents supporting transfer from seventy-five per cent to a simple majority, and removing the school committee's veto enshrined in the 1978 Act.[159] The DENI hoped the Order would revive the integration campaign amongst controlled schools after the failure of the 1978 Act which, the *Belfast Telegraph* claimed, 'never worked because it could only be triggered by the Churches, none of which have been keen on integrated education in principle'.[160]

Thirdly, the consultative document recommended that integrated schools should be allowed to apply for funds to expand their capacity whilst controlled and maintained schools would only be allowed to replace existing buildings.[161] The restriction on the potential growth of denominational schools was a particularly severe problem for Catholic maintained schools because, during the 1980s, the number of maintained school pupils consistently increased while the number of pupils in controlled schools suffered a steady decline.[162]

Finally, the DENI proposed that a school should be treated as an integrated school if only one fifth of the pupils practised a different religion.[163] This qualification was later abandoned after SACHR questioned the legality of a religious quota for the allocation of public funds.[164] The October 1988 White Paper *Education in Northern Ireland: The Way Forward* only insisted that integrated schools should 'demonstrate commitment to and progress towards integration'.[165]

The Catholic authorities' reaction to the March 1988 paper was predictably hostile,[166] but nationalist politicians were less critical. The SDLP spokesman for education, Paddy O'Donoghue, did not mention integration in his response while the *Irish News* accepted the sincerity of integrated education's advocates:

> Dr Mawhinney's proposal to provide a positive incentive to the establishment of integrated schools will be welcomed by many. While the sincerely held view of the Catholic Church and many Protestants on the issue of separate schooling must be respected, it is only fair that the facility is available to those who may wish to avail of it.[167]

The DENI addressed the 'national' issues raised by the consultative document. However, the preference for integrated schools emerged as the focal point for clerical opposition after the White Paper stated 'building projects for the provision of additional places will receive priority within the schools' capital programme'.[168] The Catholic authorities' dissatisfaction with the White Paper was shared by unionist politicians and Protestant clerics. Paisley was typically forthright:

> Dr Mawhinney sees integrated education as a means of destroying Ulster's resistance to the Anglo-Irish agreement and a united Ireland and, therefore, something which can be profitably engaged in even though it will lead to the closing down of State schools and making State school teachers redundant.[169]

Unionists were dissatisfied with the DENI's proposals, but they secured a significant victory during the summer of 1988. The consultative document intended to allow controlled and maintained schools to opt for grant maintained status, thus enjoying direct relations with the DENI. However, this measure was abandoned in the White Paper after sustained opposition from unionists and the Education and Library Boards. Unionist politicians and the Boards' officials feared that widespread defections by controlled schools would lead to the virtual disintegration of the Boards, leaving the rest of Northern Ireland's controlled schools without an effective advocate.[170] The unionists saved the Boards, but they were unable to deflect Mawhinney and the DENI from their promise to promote integration.

An exchange at Westminster in June 1989 underlined the government's determination to assist integrated schools. In reply to a complaint from Eddie McGrady that 'many schools in the voluntary and state sectors have been waiting for capital and development programmes for almost a decade, whereas the integrated school system that he favours seems to be privileged', Mawhinney stated that, after sixty-five years of denominational education, 'it seems to the Government a matter of justice that, for a few years, a degree of preference should be given to integrated schools' capital programmes to help to redress the balance'.[171]

Mawhinney was willing to 'redress the balance' for integrated schools, but not for maintained schools. The 1989 Order did not alleviate the burden of the voluntary contribution for maintained schools. This left the Catholic community to find one sixth of the total cost of any additional building work to fulfill the new responsibilities imposed by the core curriculum. The CCMS claimed that forty-four major projects and nearly one hundred minor projects for Catholic schools were awaiting DENI approval, and more than fifty projects approved by the Department were still overdue more than two years later.[172] However, the DENI would only assist integrated schools.

The Education Reform (Northern Ireland) Order was discussed at Westminster in December 1989, and the debate concentrated on the terms for integrated schools. Nationalist and Unionist MPs were reluctant to criticise the principle of integration, and chose to concentrate on the preferential treatment for grant maintained integrated schools. Mallon, who claimed to have supported pilot schemes for integration since 1973,[173] stated 'this debate is not about integrated education. It is about whether any sector should take financial preference over other sectors and be able to jump the capital expenditure queue'.[174] He quoted an *Irish News* editorial:

> Whatever about the merits of integrated education, there can be no justification for diverting much needed resources away from disadvantaged schools and pupils to underwrite the choice of a minority . . . the present Minister seems bent on re-opening old wounds by promoting legislation which flagrantly discriminates in favour of a sector with a specific religious ethos – that of 'integration'.[175]

Unionists joined the nationalists to oppose the Order. Paisley complained 'is it not a fact that the Order discriminates in favour of what the Minister calls integrated education and will mean the reduction of money to other schools which have previously achieved good work in the education system'.[176] He later claimed that the DENI closed a school, refurbished the building and opened the same school as an integrated school and that Lagan College had been built without the permission of Belfast City Council.[177] The Ulster Unionist Roy Beggs echoed Paisley's concerns for the rest of Northern Ireland's schools.[178]

The concerted efforts of the SDLP and the Unionists failed to influence the government during three hours of debate – a prolonged discussion by the brusque standards of most Northern Ireland debates at Westminster – and the Order was passed by eighty-eight votes to eighteen. The voting list provides a rare example of collaboration between Unionists and nationalists. Eddie McGrady and the Ulster Unionist William Ross acted as tellers for the 'noes' which included Mallon, Paisley, the Ulster Unionist leader James Molyneaux, the 'nationalist' Labour MP Kevin McNamara and the deputy leader of the Democratic Unionist Party, Peter Robinson.[179]

In the final speech on the night of 13 December, McNamara warned Mawhinney that the Catholic authorities might view the Order as discrimination under the Northern Ireland Constitution Act of 1973.[180] In the summer of 1990, dissatisfied both by the preference for integrated schools and the DENI's interpretation of the role of the CCMS, they challenged the 1989 Order in the High Court. The Catholic authorities asserted that the preference for integrated education constituted discrimination against parents wishing to educate their children in Catholic schools. The High Court rejected the appeal in October 1990 because both Catholic and Protestant schools were facing a relative disadvantage, and the Order could not, therefore, be viewed as religious discrimination.[181]

The 1989 Order not only granted integrated schools full capital and maintenance funding, it also established an official body – the Northern Ireland Council for Integrated Education (NICIE) – to promote integration through public information and advice to potential school governors. The DENI devoted more than £378,000 to the NICIE in 1996[182] and provided a special grant of £1 million in 1994 to develop the organisation.[183] The 1989 Order has also led to substantial investment in integrated schools. By 1997 the British government was dedicated to spending £28m on new integrated schools in the next three years. This compares with an annual budget for maintained and controlled schools of just £27 million (UK Commons Sixth Series 301 955 26 November 1997 307 439 2 March 1998).

The efforts of the DENI, the NICIE and groups such as All Children Together have prompted significant advances, yet integrated schools are still educating a small minority of Northern Ireland's school children today. Integration has been one of the devices employed by the British government to ease tensions, but another education issue has been revived since the upheavals of 1969. The quest for a more 'Gaelic' education for Northern Ireland's nationalist community now provokes more interest for many nationalists than the fate of the voluntary contribution, the powers of the Catholic clergy or integrated schools.

'ONE NATIONAL CONSCIOUSNESS'

The Catholic authorities and Irish republicans enjoy an uneasy relationship. Senior Catholic clerics in Northern Ireland have frequently condemned republican violence, whilst republicans often criticise the Catholic authorities' accommodating attitude towards the British government. The traditional republican antipathy towards clerical control of education dating from Wolfe Tone and Thomas Davis has occasionally influenced republican education policy.[185] The Official IRA condemned segregation in the 1970s and Sinn Féin criticised Philbin's decision not to confirm Catholic pupils attending controlled schools,[186] but the major republican criticism of clerical control has been the neglect of the Gaelic language and Irish history.[187] Republican discontent has not translated into overt opposition to clerical control of Catholic schools for two reasons; because the Catholic authorities retain an influence within the nationalist community which they would be unwise to challenge, and because Catholic schools have promoted a Gaelic ethos in contrast to the cultural and national values of loyalty to the Crown and the Union cultivated in Northern Ireland's controlled schools.

Republicans are troubled by the close ties between religious identity and nationalist aspirations, but they have been unwilling to challenge clerical education interests. In 1971 republicans published a policy document, *Eire Nua*, outlining their perspectives on the future for Northern Ireland. The education proposals underlined their reluctance to advance beyond a vague support for integrated education common amongst Northern Ireland's political parties. *Eire Nua* promised an education system which would educate children:

> so that they will become God fearing and responsible citizens of a free and independent nation. The rights of the family as the primary and natural educator of the child and the spiritual interests of the various religious denominations shall be acknowledged within the framework of an educational system whose philosophy shall be to unify the people with one national consciousness.[188]

The document addressed the Catholic authorities' concerns by promising to uphold their 'spiritual interests' and accepting that the family was 'the primary and natural educator', a phrase lifted almost verbatim from previous statements by Catholic bishops. The republican vision for Northern Ireland's schools appears broadly similar to the practice in the Irish Free State and the Republic, an energetic development of the Gaelic language combined with deference for clerical control.

In 1974 republicans underlined their caution by opposing McIvor's proposals for 'shared' schools. They defended their denominational stance by claiming that they were determined to integrate Northern Ireland's schools, but only after the British withdrew from Ireland.[189] In 1980 attempts to close the two Catholic teacher training college provoked a similar response from Sinn Féin.[190] The occasional protest at the failure of clerics to pay greater attention to Gaelic games and the Gaelic language should not be viewed as a significant threat to the principle of denominational schools. Sinn Féin is fully aware of the political implications of challenging clerical authority within Northern Ireland's schools, and has avoided confrontation by declining to endorse integration.

Farrell criticises the Catholic authorities for tolerating partition in 1923 for the sake of their schools, but, as Sinn Féin explained in 1982, 'in the North the separate identity of the Catholic Schools and their policy of teaching Irish history and language have contributed towards keeping alive the flames of Nationalism'.[191] Republicans support clerical authority because they realise that their cultural and political traditions were sustained in Catholic schools during the fifty years of devolved government.

Loyalist paramilitaries have also noticed the 'national' implications of Catholic schools. In March 1975 the newspaper of the Ulster Defence Association (UDA), the *Ulster Loyalist*, asserted:

> Few who have read Irish history as taught in RC schools, would fail to recognise the anti British trends. Such patriotic writings do much to develop the young men and women who make and plant the bombs and murder with impunity. There is no doubt that the bulk of IRA activists have received their sectarian beliefs through the bigoted teachings of their RC schools.[192]

A leading member of the UDA explained to two American academics 'the Hierarchy has a hell of a lot of responsibility for the conflict since they have created the whole Catholic education system which indoctrinates children',[193] and some unionist politicians share these sentiments. Dr Smyth, who is not only an Ulster Unionist MP but also the Grand Master of the Orange Order, exemplified unionist hostility towards autonomous Catholic schools:

> They are responsible for segregated education. Forty years ago there were national schools where Catholics and Protestants went to school together. Now Sinn Féin opposes it (integration) for political reasons. And at Catholic schools they never fly the British flag even though they are financed by the British government; this shows the attitude of those who run Catholic schools.[194]

Unionist MPs may view Catholic schools as republican academies, drawing no distinction between Sinn Féin and the Catholic clergy, but republicans enjoy minimal influence within Catholic schools. A senior republican recently claimed that Sinn Féin councillors were not chosen by the Catholic authorities to sit on the committees of maintained schools or the board of governors of Catholic grammar schools, but SDLP councillors and party members were regularly invited to join these committees.[195]

Republicans remain critical of the clergy's failure to emphasise nationalism within Catholic schools. However, they support clerical authority because the alternatives of alienating a powerful interest group within the nationalist community or allowing British ministers to supervise the education of Catholic children appear less attractive than the preservation of the clerical status quo.

The one area where republicans have influenced education policy has been in the development of the bunscoil – primary schools where almost all subjects are taught in the Gaelic language. Bunscoils have become increasingly popular during the 1980s, and the first success came in 1984 when the DENI granted public funds for a bunscoil in west Belfast after fifteen years of struggle by parents and nationalists.[196]

The Gaelic language groups failed to convince the Belfast Education and Library Board to fund a Gaelic secondary school,[197] but by 1989 there were four primary schools teaching nearly six hundred children in Belfast, along with nine nursery schools and a further five nursery schools in Londonderry, where Her Majesty's Inspectorate noted the pupils' 'ardour for learning' and the commitment shown by parents and teachers.[198] The Catholic clergy have been less enthusiastic advocates for the language, and Cardinal Conway's windows were allegedly broken by Gaelic enthusiasts dissatisfied by his hesitant response.[199] The bunscoils are managed as standard maintained schools with the full cooperation of the Catholic authorities, but the Catholic authorities prefer to maintain a low profile on the Gaelic language issue.

The bunscoils have become a divisive issue in education policy, with unionists arguing without success for similar treatment for 'Ulster Scots',[200] but the DENI has responded to the Gaelic campaigns. The opinions of the republican electorate in west Belfast and Londonderry exercise a profound impact upon the course of events in Northern Ireland, and the NIO probably views conciliating the Gaelic campaigners to be an effective means of gratifying 'republican' voters. The British government was not alone in paying greater attention to the fate of the Gaelic language in the 1980s.

The SDLP and Catholic schools

The rise of Sinn Féin in the aftermath of the hunger strikes, culminating in Gerry Adams' victory in the 1983 election, indicated that Catholic voters were distinctly more 'nationalist' by the early 1980s. Gaelic suddenly became an important issue for constitutional nationalists, and the SDLP attempted to counter the republican challenge by emphasising the party's commitment to the language.

After 1983 Hume swiftly showed he was more willing to discuss 'national' issues such as the Gaelic language than his predecessor as party leader, Gerry Fitt. In 1984 he called for the language to be granted similar status to the Welsh language in Wales, and in 1987 he demanded improved funding for Gaelic nursery schools.[201] Mallon also highlighted the fate of the language. In July 1986 and January 1987 he called for more money and improved conditions for teaching Gaelic, and in June 1988 he asked for Gaelic to be included as a foundation course in the proposed core curriculum for all schools.[202]

McGrady was also diligent in tabling Parliamentary Questions. In May and June 1988, shortly after the DENI published a consultative document in which the language appeared to nationalists to have been granted a peripheral role, he asked sixteen questions on the provision for Gaelic training for trainee teachers, relations between the DENI and Gaelic groups, and the scale of Gaelic language study in Northern Ireland's schools.[203] Gaelic aroused considerable attention from nationalist MPs and the Irish government in the 1980s,[204] in contrast to the persistent burden of the voluntary contribution and the campaign for integrated schools.

The Catholic authorities have also exploited the Gaelic issue. The CCMS's reply to the DENI's first set of reform proposals in March 1988 emphasised the importance of Gaelic in Catholic schools. The Council called for the DENI to increase the scope for Gaelic within the curriculum, and a canvass of the opinions of teachers and school committees echoed their concerns for the future of the language.[205] The White Paper of October 1988 admitted that the DENI received many comments on the role of Gaelic. The Department staged a rare retreat, stating that 'the government fully recognises the importance of the Gaelic language to many people in Northern Ireland'.[206]

The DENI allowed primary schools converting to bunscoils to remain as maintained schools, granted Gaelic a similar status to Welsh in Welsh schools and allowed children to learn Gaelic instead of one of the major European Community languages such as French, German or Spanish.[207] The DENI has been particularly sensitive to nationalist criticism of its treatment of Gaelic, and the enhanced role for the language was one of the few changes to the initial proposals for education reform.

After the 1989 Order Gaelic was once more a minor education issue, and the only MP to argue for improved facilities for Gaelic at Westminster in recent years has been the Labour MP for West Newport, Paul Flynn. He asked a succession of questions after 1995 on the role of the DENI in promoting the language, training Gaelic teachers and providing adult education courses, but his efforts evoked no response from the SDLP MPs.[208]

The British government will remain attentive to the fate of the language[209] because Gaelic is an important issue for a significant constituency within the Catholic community.[210] Republicans have effectively exploited the issue, compelling the DENI to be generous with public monies for both Gaelic language courses and Gaelic language schools. The Education (Northern Ireland) Order of 1998 was passed as a consequence of the Good Friday Agreement and provides a "Statutory duty to encourage and facilitate Irish medium education." Reference UK Commons Sixth Series 314 254, 17 June 1998. The 1998 Order provoked a spasm of interest from Labour MPs, but the SDLP MPs remained silent on the Gaelic language question (UK Commons Sixth Series 301 955, 26 November 1997, 307 439 2 March 1998, 318 319 28 October 1998, 323 893 20 January 1999, 324 57 25 January 1999, 328 283 24 March 1999, 329 363 16 April 1999.) The only Northern Ireland MPs to discuss Gaelic have been Unionist MPs calling, without success, for DENI recognition of 'Ulster Scots' as a distinctive ethnic language.[211]

The DENI has sought to ease communal tensions by respecting and accommodating the nationalist minority's cultural values, and another official scheme has also emphasised the quest for the respect of diversity.

Education for mutual understanding

The potential for education to ease communal tensions has been noted by politicians and commentators since the late 1960s. When the Department of Community Relations was absorbed by the DENI on 1 April 1975, education officials became responsible for any significant initiatives to improve community relations in schools. These obvious opportunities were neglected for seven years until the DENI published a circular entitled *The Improvement of Community Relations: The Contribution of Schools* in June 1982. The circular outlined the DENI's strategy:

> Our educational system has clearly a vital role to play in the task of fostering improved relationships between the two communities in Northern Ireland. Every teacher, every school manager, Board member and trustee, and every educational administrator within the system has a responsibility for helping children to learn to understand and respect each other, and their differing customs and traditions, and of preparing them to live together in harmony in adult life.[212]

The DENI sponsored the Northern Ireland Council for Educational Development (NICED) to supervise a series of studies, but the NICED was not alone in exploring the possibilities for improving community relations in schools. SACHR also decided to investigate 'whether enough is being done in our schools to educate for diversity and to encourage the trust, tolerance and mutual respect between our young people which must in the long term be the healing influence in our community'.[213] SACHR appointed Clem McCartney, a research officer at the University of Ulster, to study the efforts of teachers, lecturers, officers of the Education and Library Boards and DENI officials to promote 'mutual understanding'.

McCartney found many individual teachers and schools striving to promote contacts with other schools, but often without a clear understanding of either methods or objectives. He also noted apathy, even hostility, towards community relations issues amongst some education officials.[214] The Commission's report noted the lack of resources available for community relations projects in contrast to schemes in Canada, Australia and New Zealand,[215] and called for systematic initiatives by the DENI and the Education and Library Boards:

> Both communities have a right to maintain and promote their traditions and beliefs but also an obligation to respect those of others. From an early age children can be taught positive attitudes to enable them to transcend the barriers of our respective heritages and appreciate the life styles that are valued by others. We believe that more needs to be done to give our children that appreciation and an understanding of our similarities as well as our differences.[216]

In September 1987 Mawhinney responded to SACHR's findings and the report of the NICED by introducing the education for mutual understanding programme (EMU) to ensure a more cohesive approach to the DENI's efforts. The EMU project was the first concerted attempt to implement the ideas contained in the White Paper of March 1973 to 'promote real and continuing points of contact and mutual interest between all the children of Northern Ireland'.[217]

The scheme, naturally, was welcomed by the Catholic authorities because EMU 'recognises the reality of segregated education for most children, and works within existing structures'.[218] They view EMU as a potential alternative to integration, demonstrating the denominational system's ability to accommodate diverse traditions without major structural and managerial change. EMU also allows the Catholic authorities to illustrate their commitment to easing community tensions, deflecting unionist criticism of their insistence upon segregation.

The Catholic authorities argue that supporters of integration have abandoned existing schools – which still educate nearly ninety-seven per cent of all pupils – without exploring the possibilities for encouraging contact and harmony within the current system. In February 1984 a delegation from the Irish Episcopal Conference appeared before the New Ireland Forum (the Irish government's attempt to bolster constitutional nationalism in the aftermath of Sinn Féin's success in the 1983 elections). Cahal Daly argued for exploiting the potential for improving community relations within segregated structures:

> Surely it is much better to invite a Protestant clergyman from the Shankill or wherever to come to a school on the Falls Road and talk to the children there and to ask a priest or head teacher to go to a school in the Shankill or East Belfast and talk about his tradition to the children there than it is to be content with a few isolated experiments.[219]

Unionist politicians, so strident in their condemnation of segregated education, have responded cautiously to the EMU project. Paisley complained that children were attending EMU courses without the knowledge or permission of their parents.[220] Dr Smyth also underlined the persistence of traditional unionist views of the influence of Catholic schools when he claimed 'joint community education imposes tremendous responsibility on the voluntary school system to teach civics, which would allow us to move together as a people and as a nation, rather than have two separate identities'.[221] Smyth obviously misunderstood the principles guiding 'mutual understanding'. Firstly, he viewed Catholic pupils in voluntary schools to be in greater need of tolerance and understanding than their Protestant counterparts in controlled schools. Secondly, the purpose of the EMU programme was to cultivate respect for both traditions within Northern Ireland rather than constructing uniformity around the concept of 'civics', a phrase employed in the 1930s by advocates of flying Union Flags over Northern Ireland's schools.

Unionist politicians were hesitant, but many controlled schools participated in the EMU programme. Nearly 250 schools applied for funds by June 1988, usually on the basis of joint projects with other schools. Therefore, within nine months of Mawhinney's announcement, more than 120 controlled schools were fostering links with Catholic schools.[222] The DENI underlined their ambitions by recommending in the White Paper of October 1988 that EMU courses and 'cultural heritage' classes should be compulsory for all schools.[223] A further ninety schools applied for funds in the twelve months after June 1988, and Mawhinney increased the initial EMU budget of £200,000 to £650,000 to encourage further interest.[224] This initial enthusiasm should not understate the problems encountered by advocates of greater contact between the two communities. Only a quarter of all schoolchildren in Northern Ireland were involved in EMU projects by the summer of 1989, and in recent years the number of secondary schools receiving grants has declined, despite the 1989 Order including both EMU and cultural heritage classes in the core curriculum.[225] Northern Ireland's voters consistently tell pollsters they favour integrated schools, but the evidence from the EMU scheme underlines the reluctance of both communities to confront the antagonisms which still trouble Northern Ireland. Blanshard's 'cultural war' persists today, and probably rages more fiercely than at any time since early 1930s.

MAINTAINED SCHOOLS

The 1968 Act increased the capital grant to eighty per cent and abolished the voluntary contribution towards maintenance costs for voluntary schools converting to maintained status. After 1968 one fifth of capital costs became the sole financial liability for maintained schools. These improved conditions were to prove vital to the Catholic community, because the sustained growth of the late 1960s persisted into the following decade. Maintained schools enjoyed substantial investment in the decade after the 1968 Act, with the majority of the new primary school places provided in the thirty years after 1947 coming in the nine years after 1968.[226]

In the 1960s voluntary primary schools secured more than half of the total number of new places.[227] In the nine years after the 1968 Act maintained primary schools gained more than three fifths of the total number of new places. By the end of 1972, the final year of devolved government, the number of new maintained primary school places provided since the 1947 Act finally surpassed the total for controlled primary schools.[228] The considerable advantage amassed by public elementary schools in the 1920s and 1930s was not erased, but Catholic education enjoyed substantial progress in the final years of devolved power. The Northern Ireland government was floundering in the early 1970s but, as Figure 6A shows, Catholic schools secured substantial improvements from the Ministry of Education during its final years.

The scale of the educational disadvantage of maintained status was clearly diminishing throughout the 1970s. The Ministry of Education and the DENI financed nearly 100,000 places for voluntary primary schools in the thirty years to the end of 1977, in contrast to just 86,000 places for controlled schools and their county school predecessors.

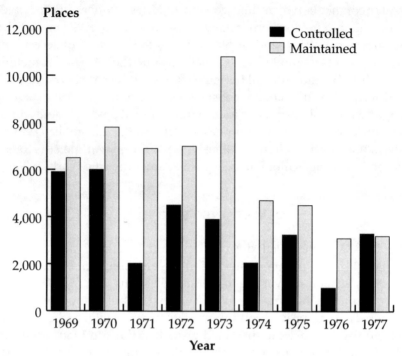

Figure 6A. Primary school places 1969–1977

Maintained secondary intermediate schools gained more than sixty per cent of the total number of new places in the nine years after the 1968 Act. Once again, the 1970s witnessed a dramatic improvement for maintained schools as nearly 29,000 new places (more than the number provided in the twenty years between 1947 and the end of 1966) were built in contrast to less than 20,000 places for controlled secondary intermediate schools.

These figures should not obscure the significant advantages for the Protestant community provided by the county grammar schools. The number of secondary intermediate pupils surpassed the grammar total in 1958, but grammar schools were still educating more than forty per cent of Northern Ireland's secondary school pupils in 1967.[229] The voluntary grammar schools were the only voluntary schools to secure more places than their county counterparts, with almost 41,000 places compared to the county schools' 15,000 places by the end of 1970,[230] but nearly a third of all new grammar school places were provided in county schools. The county grammar schools widened the scope for a grammar school education for graduates of controlled schools – opportunities denied to the Catholic graduates of maintained schools.[231]

The DENI statistics do not allow for an estimate of the financial liability of maintained status in the 1970s. However, the figures provided by the Ministry of Education in the 1960s allow for a crude calculation of the cost of the voluntary contribution. Secondary intermediate places were more expensive to provide than primary places, and a simple combination of the two classes will not provide an accurate assessment of the overall cost. Fortunately, the number of maintained secondary intermediate places provided in 1967 compared to the number of maintained primary places is strikingly similar to the secondary intermediate share of the total number of maintained school places provided between the end of 1968 and the end of 1975, when the voluntary contribution was further reduced to fifteen per cent of capital costs.[232]

The statistics available indicate that the total cost of maintained school places, in 1967 prices, was £14.6 million during these seven years. The voluntary contribution of a fifth of capital costs during this period therefore amounted to nearly £3 million. The cost of the 7,800 secondary and the 6,100 primary places provided in 1976 and 1977 can only be estimated, in 1967 prices, to be roughly £2 million for each year. Therefore, the voluntary contribution for the first nine years after

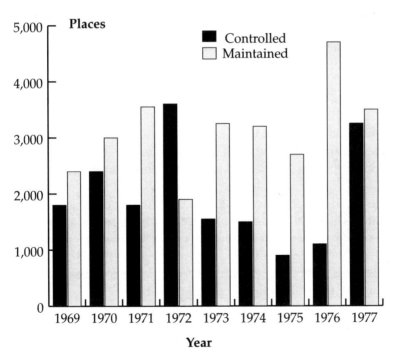

Figure 6B. Secondary intermediate places 1969–1977

the 1968 Act cost the Catholic community, in 1996 prices, nearly £36 million. The costs were clearly substantial, but the Catholic populace would have faced a charge in excess of £50 million if the Catholic authorities had refused to accept the conditions of the 1968 Act.

One area where controlled schools enjoyed a notable and enduring advantage was in the provision of nursery schools. The 1947 Act encouraged education authorities to provide nursery schools. However, by January 1965 there were only eighteen county nursery schools educating less than 600 pupils. Voluntary nursery schools were even more scarce, with just seventy children in two voluntary nursery schools.[233] Nine years later more than 1,000 children were attending county nursery schools, but there were still only two voluntary schools educating just eighty-seven pupils.[234] The contrast between controlled and maintained nursery schools has diminished in the last two decades, but in 1994 there were only 1,332 pupils in maintained nursery schools compared to 3,878 pupils in controlled nursery schools.[235]

The failure of the Catholic minority to develop an extensive network of nursery schools should not be viewed as evidence of discrimination by the DENI and the Education and Library Boards. The Catholic authorities opposed the principle of nursery schools during their discussions with Hall-Thompson in 1944, when a senior Catholic cleric 'referred to the growing tendency on the part of some young mothers to disregard their responsibilities towards their own children and accept employment when their husbands were already receiving adequate wages'.[236] The Catholic clergy's conservative social values, rather than the impact of the voluntary contribution, accounts for the lack of nursery provision for Catholic children. Catholic clerics have tempered their opposition in recent years, but the reluctance of the Catholic authorities to sponsor nursery education is underlined by the absence of any nursery schools in the Western Education and Library Board area – the one Board where nationalists enjoy a predominant influence.[237]

The DENI is less forthcoming than the Ministry of Education with its statistics. The DENI ceased to provide an annual report after 1975, and Parliamentary Questions became the most effective means of extracting data from the Department. The course of events is often difficult to trace, but there are a few clues which allow for tentative conclusions and crude estimates of the scale of the voluntary contribution.

As Figures 6A and 6B indicate, the advantage enjoyed by maintained schools in the first years of direct rule was drawing to a close in 1977, when the number of new controlled primary places surpassed the maintained total for the first time since 1966. The DENI's funding policy in the early 1980s sustained this trend, with controlled schools once more securing the majority of capital funds between 1978–79 and 1983–84. The statistics, contained in an answer to a Parliamentary Question in December 1983, do not allow for an estimate of the number of places created during these six years, but they show that controlled schools obtained more than £12 million whilst just over £10.5 million was spent on maintained schools.[238]

Critics of the devolved government may wish to note that Catholic schools secured a greater share of capital funding in the final years of unionist rule than in the first years of direct rule from Westminster. British ministers were not as accommodating towards the Catholic authorities as their Ministry of Education predecessors. However, the most striking feature of Figure 6C is the dramatic decline in the overall scale of capital projects in the early 1980s. The DENI intended to spend just over £1 million in 1983–84 compared to more than £5 million in 1980–81.[239] The extensive projects of the previous decade, for both controlled and maintained schools, may partly account for the decrease, but by the end of the 1970s the British government was determined to limit public spending. The DENI's building programme was an obvious choice for spending cuts.

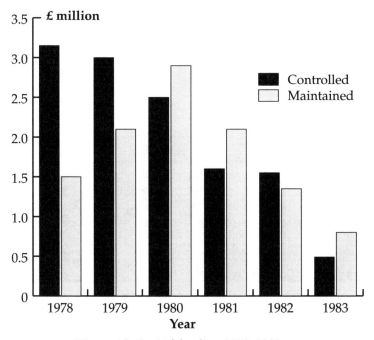

Figure 6C. Capital funding 1978–1983

The course of events is obscured for the next eight years until a Parliamentary Question in January 1992 extracted more relevant statistics. The DENI's figures for the years 1986–87 to 1990–91 indicate a marginal advantage for controlled schools at the end of the 1980s. The pace of school building accelerated in the second half of the decade. During the five years from 1986–87 the DENI sanctioned £66.4 million of capital investment in controlled schools and £57.8 million for maintained schools, £49.1 million in grants and a voluntary contribution of £8.6 million.[240]

The statistics contained in Figure 6D indicate that the DENI secured a significant increase in investment for Northern Ireland's schools. The revival of the capital spending programme in the 1980s improved the quality of education for Northern Ireland's Catholics, but the escalating cost of new schools exacerbated the financial penalty of maintained status. The Catholic community spent more than £4 million in 1990–91, and this rising tide of spending combined with the SACHR inquiry prompted a last increase in capital funding which finally abolished the voluntary contribution.

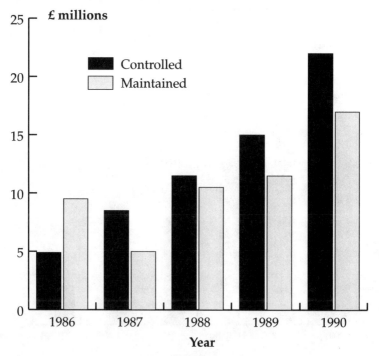

Figure 6D. Capital funding 1986–1990

CONCLUSION

The twenty five years after the 1968 Act brought only a modest five per cent decrease in the voluntary contribution, and the 1975 Order was prompted by a similar measure for voluntary schools in England and Wales rather than any campaign in Northern Ireland. The struggle against the integration campaign was a major distraction, but the Catholic authorities' recent attempts to ease the financial cost to their laity have been timid compared to the achievements of their predecessors. MacRory and Mageean secured half of the costs of building new schools from Craigavon, Andrews, and Pollock, whilst Mageean and Farren wrested a further fifteen per cent from Brooke, Midgley, Grant and Parker. In contrast, the Catholic authorities gained only five per cent of the cost of building new schools from the succession of British ministers governing Northern Ireland's education system since 1972.

There have been a number of achievements for the Catholic authorities, the most notable being the Council for Catholic Maintained Schools. The Council employed thirty-seven staff at a cost of more than £1.6 million to the DENI by the summer of 1996.[241] It has attracted the envy of many Protestant clerics who no longer view the Boards as effective vehicles for influencing DENI policy.[242]

One of the major reasons for the failure of the Catholic authorities to alleviate the burden of the voluntary contribution has been the decline in clerical authority. The Astin and the Chilver committees both posed a significant threat to clerical control, but the major challenge has come from the advocates of 'shared schools'.

Integration cannot be dismissed as simply a unionist ploy to 'capture' Catholic schools because devout Catholics have been leading figures in the campaign and successive opinion polls have demonstrated significant and enduring support amongst Catholics for integrated schools.

Protestant clerics and unionist politicians may be wary of the practical impact of integration, but the central conflict remains a dispute between the advocates of integration and the Catholic authorities. This tenacious defence of Catholic schools has been exploited by unionist politicians to depict the Catholic clergy as intransigent opponents of compromise. The response of nationalist politicians has also undermined the Catholic authorities' cause. One of the most notable features of education public policy during the last twenty years has been the reluctance of nationalist politicians to defend the Catholic authorities' role within Catholic schools. Nationalist MPs in the Northern Ireland

Commons were assiduous questioners and debaters, but since 1972 nationalists at Westminster have rarely spoken in favour of clerical control of Catholic schools. Segregation remains a sensitive issue for both constitutional nationalists and republicans.

The most significant development since 1972 has been the change of course by the British government. The White Paper of 1973 endorsed denominational schools and, as late as the early 1980s, British ministers emphasised the problems rather than highlighted the potential advantages of integration. The arrival of Mawhinney in 1986 brought a more assertive policy of encouraging, and financing, integrated schools. The British government now fully funds grant maintained integrated schools and allows integrated schools preferential access to capital funds, but integration remains a minority interest. Eight thousand of Northern Ireland's three hundred and fifty thousand pupils attend integrated schools.[243]

The enthusiasm of the British government also appears to be waning as the financial cost of satisfying parental demand for a network of new integrated schools becomes apparent. In February 1997 the Northern Ireland Office minister for education, Michael Ancram, announced that the DENI was refusing permission for a new integrated secondary school in Newtownards because the Department did not expect the school to secure a reasonable religious balance amongst the proposed 500 pupils.[244]

The Archbishop of Armagh, Cardinal Cahal Daly, in an interview in 1991 with the editor of *Fortnight* magazine, Robin Wilson, explained the Catholic authorities' position:

> Our case has never been one of opposing integrated education, but of saying that it should not be promoted to the detriment of other forms of education. And well, the government does encourage integrated education: integrated education has now an opportunity to demonstrate its capacity to deliver its ideals. I'm quite happy to await the results.[245]

The events of the past twenty-five years do not fully endorse the Cardinal's claim that the Catholic authorities never opposed integration, but he is probably wise to await developments. The integration campaign will struggle to overcome 'sound denominational education' in the coming decades.

The rise of Sinn Féin in the early 1980s provoked a response from the SDLP which emphasised the significance of the Gaelic aspects of Catholic schools. The Catholic authorities now employ the defence of the Gaelic language and Gaelic cultural identity to justify Catholic schools to a nationalist electorate seemingly reluctant to pay the price of clerical control. The importance of these cultural dimensions of Catholic schools in recent years even secures the conditional support of Sinn Féin for clerical control of Catholic schools, because they sustain 'the flames of Nationalism'[246] amongst young Catholics.

In recent years a more formidable challenge to Gaelic cultural values within Catholic schools has emerged from within the Catholic community. Fionnuala O'Connor's study *In Search of a State: Catholics in Northern Ireland* found many middle-class and aspiring middle-class Catholics hostile to the language as a diversion from the major objective of securing useful examination qualifications.[247] These concerns were confirmed by the SACHR study of the early 1990s which found that one of the most significant factors accounting for the differences between the qualifications obtained by Catholics and Protestants was the emphasis in many schools upon religious education and the Gaelic language. There appears to be a class dimension to the Gaelic language issue within the Catholic community, with working-class republicans favouring the language while middle-class Catholics view Gaelic as an obstacle to a university education. Unionist politicians may not be alone in viewing Gaelic classes as 'useless work'.

Conclusion

The history of Catholic education in Northern Ireland for the last seventy years has been a chronicle of gradual success for the Catholic authorities. The education laws of 1930, 1947, 1968, 1975 and 1993 steadily relieved the Catholic community of the financial liability of voluntary status imposed by the 1923 Act. The central issue for the Catholic authorities since the advent of the devolved government in 1921 was their determination not to surrender control to the education committees or the Ministry of Education. This conflict dominated their negotiations with the Ministry of Education in 1930, 1947 and 1968, and the link between clerical power and public funds dominated the discussions between the British government and senior Catholic clerics in 1993. The 1993 Order finally eliminated the voluntary contribution, but this final triumph was tempered by the failure to preserve the Catholic priest as the dominant authority within Catholic schools.

Education policy and the relative success of each major contest between the Catholic authorities and the devolved government was determined by two significant factors – the impact of the Protestant clergy and the enthusiasm of nationalist politicians. The influence of the Minister of Education within the Cabinet, the role of the Prime Minister and the state of community relations also influenced the course of events.

In 1930 the imposition of 'simple Bible instruction' in all public elementary schools, the compulsion of teachers to provide these Bible classes and the guarantee of one quarter of the seats on the education committees, and half of the seats on the school committees for the Protestant clergy, provided an enormous advantage for the Catholic authorities. In 1947, in contrast, the removal of the promise of 1930 to ensure that every teacher in public elementary schools provided 'simple Bible instruction' undermined the Catholic campaign. Hall-Thompson only secured sixty-five per cent of capital and maintenance costs for voluntary schools after the Cabinet allowed the Protestant clergy similar management rights in the proposed secondary intermediate schools to those they already enjoyed in public elementary schools. This close link between the treatment of Protestant and Catholic clerical interests was underlined in March 1946 when ministers agreed the compromises with both sets of clerics at the same Cabinet meeting.

Protestant clerics played a peripheral role in the events of 1968 and 1993, and their absence must be viewed as a significant factor accounting for the relative failure of the Catholic authorities in recent years to improve the funding terms for Catholic schools without a dilution of their authority.

The Catholic authorities' failure to achieve their objectives in recent decades partly arises from a lack of confidence in their ability to motivate the Catholic laity. In 1920 Cardinal Logue declared that Catholic children were to be educated 'under the care and direction of their pastors, whose strict right and leading duty it is to watch over, direct and safeguard the religious education of the lambs of their flocks'.[1] The Catholic clergy does not display such arrogance today and the last few decades have witnessed a significant weakening of lay support for clerical control of Catholic schools.

In the first half of the twentieth century the Catholic authorities enjoyed the diligent allegiance of both Catholic teachers and nationalist politicians, and they played an important role in securing improved conditions for Catholic schools without diminishing clerical influence. In 1930 Devlin led an enthusiastic parliamentary campaign on behalf of the Catholic authorities while Catholic teachers were also emphatic in their support for clerical control. Every nationalist MP and Senator attended the delegation to Charlemont led by O'Kane in April 1930, the Second Reading of the Education Bill brought a record number of MPs to the Commons and the Bill provoked the longest debate of the first decade of devolved government. Seventeen years later, nationalist politicians and Catholic teachers also strengthened the Catholic authorities' case by their unconditional opposition to 'four and two' school committees.

The events of the last thirty years indicate that the Catholic laity is no longer willing to endure the sacrifices of voluntary status simply to retain clerical authority. The reluctance of nationalist politicians to endorse Philbin's implacable rejection of the White Paper of October 1967, and the tepid response of the laity evident in the letters pages of the *Irish news*, were the first hints that the Catholic authorities could no longer rely upon political notables and Catholic voters for absolute loyalty. This initial hesitation, though tempered by approval for Conway's more measured approach, was the main reason for the Catholic authorities' acceptance of 'four and two' committees in 1968. The next twenty-five years were to confirm the Catholic authorities' increasing isolation.

The two dominant forces in nationalist politics since the collapse of the Nationalist Party in 1969 – the SDLP and Sinn Féin, both highlight their autonomy from clerical influence. The SDLP, though heirs to the Nationalist Party's constitutional nationalist tradition, have consciously distanced themselves from the Catholic clergy. The failure of the Catholic authorities to achieve a significant decrease in the voluntary contribution until the early 1990s is partly explained by the SDLP's aversion to binding the party to clerical education interests.

Nationalist politicians have highlighted other education issues. The emphasis for SDLP MPs since the rise of Sinn Féin in the early 1980s has been the defence of 'nationalist' rather than Catholic values within Catholic schools. In the late 1980s the Catholic authorities themselves resorted to underlining the 'national' implications of autonomous Catholic schools to maintain support from the nationalist electorate. In the first decades of devolved power, the Catholic authorities could rely upon the unconditional loyalty of nationalist politicians and the Catholic laity, but today they must justify their control of Catholic schools.

The decline of lay support in recent decades has raised major problems for the Catholic authorities by undermining clerical confidence. Since 1972 they have sought to defend the status quo inherited from the devolved government rather than pursue further reforms from the British government. This defence of their interests has ultimately proved successful. They have retained control of the training of Catholic teachers, prevented the creation of an extensive network of integrated schools, and there have also been a number of successes since 1972 such as the Council for Catholic Maintained Schools, the improved conditions for Gaelic teaching and the eventual abolition of the voluntary contribution.

The education committees may have been unacceptable to the Catholic authorities, but the Minister of Education and his officials enjoyed the trust and confidence of senior Catholic clerics. The Catholic authorities and the Ministry of Education were never irreconcilable adversaries, even during the traumatic early years of the devolved government. The fate of Catholic teachers refusing to recognise the

Ministry in 1922 was swiftly resolved without embarrassment to either the teachers or the clerical managers, and in the spring of 1925 Londonderry and Cardinal O'Donnell amicably settled the problem of male Catholic teacher training.

Northern Ireland's Minister of Education was usually one of the most tolerant and liberal members of the devolved government. Londonderry, Charlemont and Robb were all aware of the problems facing Catholic schools and argued for concessions from their Cabinet colleagues, but the most liberal of Northern Ireland's twelve Ministers of Education was Hall-Thompson. He could justly claim to have governed fairly within the constraints imposed by Northern Ireland's education laws. Hall-Thompson's six years as minister also underlined the limited scope for the Ministry of Education. He only secured the sixty-five per cent capital and maintenance grant for voluntary schools after a prolonged contest with his Cabinet colleagues, despite gaining the support of Brooke.

The disadvantages of relying upon the good intentions of politicians were highlighted in 1950 when Hall-Thompson was replaced by Harry Midgley, one of the most vociferous critics of the Catholic clergy within the Unionist Party. Midgley was committed to removing the concessions contained in the 1947 Act, and only the Cabinet's fear of renewing the bitter education conflicts of the late 1940s rescued the Catholic community from the grievous burden of finding half of the costs of new Catholic secondary intermediate schools.

Midgley's seven years as minister did not eradicate the Catholic authorities' confidence in the Ministry of Education, and by the end of the decade there was clear evidence of improved relations with Ministry officials. In 1968 the key issue was whether the Ministry or the education committees would appoint the two public representatives for the 'four and two' committees, underlining the Catholic authorities' confidence in the integrity of Ministry officials.

The Ministry of Education was notable within the devolved government as the only ministry to be led by a Catholic civil servant. Bonaparte Wyse was Secretary of the Ministry from 1927 until his retirement in 1939. He favoured accepting the Christian Brothers' schools in 1926, advised Charlemont and Craigavon in 1930 to allow the Ministry to provide the capital grants for voluntary schools and opposed the abolition of the grants for Gaelic classes. Wyse's successor, Brownell, worked closely with Hall-Thompson to fashion a compromise in 1945 and 1946, and his memorandum of October 1945 illustrated his distaste for the partisan structure of the education system. In the 1950s he frequently clashed with Midgley, and even encouraged Shea to protest at his sectarian outbursts. Shea chose to leave, but he returned in 1969 as Secretary, only the second Catholic civil servant to lead a ministry.

The Catholic authorities, despite friendly relations with individual ministers and Ministry officials, would not entrust Catholic schools to Unionist politicians who were vulnerable to sporadic 'Orange' outbursts. The evidence in the PRONI archives indicates that the Minister and his officials often vigorously presented the case for Catholic schools, but could not always convince the Cabinet to resist backbench agitation. The campaign by the UEC in the 1920s and the elimination of the special grants for Gaelic classes in 1933 highlighted their weakness when confronted by a sustained unionist campaign.

The role of the Prime Minister was another significant influence upon the course of events, because no Minister could expect to convince his Cabinet colleagues to compromise with the Catholic authorities without the support of the Prime Minister. The evidence suggests that Craig rejected Londonderry' proposals for the boundaries of the education committees in 1922 because the scheme envisaged a number of 'Catholic' education committees. Three years later Craig, rather than Londonderry led the negotiations with the UEC. Craig was more accommodating towards the Protestant clergy than Londonderry or Charlemont, but in 1930 he challenged the more intolerant members of his party by personally announcing the concession of fifty per cent of capital costs to voluntary schools to a meeting of the County Down Committee of the Orange Order. He was also willing to consider further increases for voluntary schools in 1938.

Basil Brooke is not fondly remembered by Northern Ireland's nationalists, but the evidence in the PRONI archives indicates that he was more liberal than most of his Cabinet colleagues towards the Catholic authorities. He appointed the most liberal of Northern Ireland's twelve Ministers of Education in 1944, and his opinions of the Protestant clergy were often as scathing as Hall-Thompson's during 1945 and 1946. Also, Brooke was one of the first ministers to convert to Hall-Thompson's compromising policy during the negotiations leading to the 1947 Act, and his support was vital in eventually securing the fifteen per cent increase in the 1947 Act. Brooke challenged Midgley's intractable opposition to the Catholic minority after 1950, leading the efforts to find a compromise with Cardinal D'Alton on the scale of public funding for the proposed Catholic men's teacher training college.

O'Neill offers an interesting contrast to his predecessors.[2] The heightened interest of the British government and the absence of a notable 'Orange' agitation against the initial offer of eighty per cent of capital and full maintenance costs allowed O'Neill greater scope for compromise in 1968. O'Neill spurned the opportunity, refusing to offer any significant changes to the Catholic authorities, even after they accepted the 'four and two' committee for maintained schools. Numerous commentators have emphasised how O'Neill's rhetoric was more liberal than his deeds, and the evidence from 1968 supports these claims.

The British government's influence upon education policy during the fifty years of devolved government was notable by its absence. In 1925 the Governor informed Craig that the Home Office was disturbed by the Education Act, but five years later the Home Secretary, Clynes, rejected Devlin's invitation to study the 1930 Act. In 1945 Home Office officials vigorously encouraged Brooke and his colleagues not to disturb the 1930 settlement.

The collapse of the devolved government in 1972 was viewed as a major success for the nationalist minority, but the evidence indicates that the advent of direct rule brought only marginal benefits for Northern Ireland's Catholic schools. The scale of investment for both controlled and maintained schools diminished in the first years of direct rule compared to the final years of the devolved government. Also, the DENI's statistics indicate that controlled schools, in contrast to the 1960s and early 1970s, gained most of the investment in new schools in the late 1970s and 1980s.

The Astin and Chilver committees were both significant threats to clerical authority within Catholic schools. The Astin committee's strategy for reducing clerical influence to just one quarter of the school committee was eventually abandoned, but Protestant clerics also resisted forfeiting their influence within controlled schools. The 1984 Education Order diminished clerical influence within Catholic schools without offering any relief from the voluntary contribution, a feat never attempted by the devolved government.

The Chilver committee's recommendation in 1982 to close the two Catholic teacher training colleges – and only the two Catholic colleges – was the most significant threat to clerical power within Catholic schools since the advent of direct rule. The Catholic authorities' 'almost hysterical'[3] response underlined the importance they attached to teacher training. The impact of the committee was eventually diluted, but St Joseph's teacher training college was amalgamated in 1985 to reduce costs while no other teacher training college suffered closure.

The threats to the clerical majority on the maintained school committee and the future of Catholic denominational teacher training were severe challenges, but the promotion of integrated schools by British government since the mid 1980s has posed the most significant threat to the future of Catholic schools. The 1989 Order offer attractive conditions for founders of integrated schools, and the DENI has provided substantial public funds to establish these schools. ACT initiated the campaign for integrated schools, but since 1989 the main impetus has come from the British government. This conspicuous preference for integrated schools provoked a legal challenge to the DENI's education policy in the summer of 1990 – a threat contemplated but never employed in 1930 and 1947 against the devolved government.

The fate of the voluntary contribution has also highlighted the limited advantages of direct rule. The 1993 Order abolished the voluntary contribution, but the first twenty years after the collapse of the devolved government brought only a five per cent increase in capital funding, and this was due to a corresponding increase in capital grants for voluntary schools in England and Wales.

THE 'FOUR AND TWO' COMMITTEES

Unionist ministers and MPs persistently called for the Catholic authorities to accept 'four and two' committees. Lynn unwittingly justified their fears of the education committees in May 1923 when he stated that 'the Catholic Regional Committees will act tyrannically in their appointments to schools attended by a large majority of Protestant children'.[4] Unionist politicians and Protestant clerics expected protection for Protestant schools from 'Catholic' education committees, but Catholic schools were to be governed by education committees whose boundaries were manufactured to protect Protestant clerical interests and encourage the transfer of Protestant denominational schools.

The Catholic authorities were intensely suspicious of the education committees, and they struggled for more than forty years to limit their influence within Catholic schools. The evidence from five decades of devolved government suggests they were wise to be wary of the education committees. The payments for heating, lighting and cleaning voluntary schools were a constant source of conflict between Catholic clerical managers and the education committees, but Protestant managers faced few problems collecting their grants. In the 1950s the awards for grammar school scholarships was also causing major problems for Catholics.[5] After 1968 Belfast's education committee appointed loyalist politicians and Protestant clerics as members of maintained school committees. The Cabinet eased the concerns of Protestant clerics with the manipulation of the education committee boundaries in 1923 and the education laws of 1925 and 1930, but Catholic clerics were to place their trust in the goodwill of the local unionists and the determination of Ministry officials to prohibit abuses. Ministry officials were unable to censure the education committees because they were so closely tied to the local councils who exercised a powerful influence upon the devolved government. Therefore, the education committees, despite the formal legal powers of the Ministry, enjoyed considerable autonomy.

The Cabinet recognised Catholic clerical suspicions of the education committees in 1930 when they allowed voluntary school managers to collect the fifty per cent capital grant from the Ministry of Education rather than the education committees. As Wyse explained to Mageean in 1938, 'if it depended on the goodwill of the Regional Committee they would get none'.[6] In contrast, in 1968 Long and O'Neill refused to accept criticism of the education authorities, despite the extensive evidence gathered by civil rights activists that many local councils were guilty of abuses.

The Catholic authorities' opposition to the 'four and two' committees was primarily motivated by their fear of losing control of teaching appointments. Mageean's proposal of April 1930 expressly maintained clerical control of the appointment of teachers, and the Catholic authorities were also determined to maintain control of teacher training. The creation of denominational teacher training colleges in 1883 was one of their most important successes in the nineteenth century because, as Corcoran noted, 'the most essential issue in the Catholic nature of Catholic Schools is full Catholic control of the choice of teachers'.[7] The Catholic authorities viewed the preservation of denominational teacher training college as a 'vitally important question'[8] in the 1920s, the fate of St Joseph's college brought five of Northern Ireland's six bishops to see Brookeborough, and the Chilver report of 1982 provoked the most passionate clerical campaign since the 1968 Education Act.

Teaching appointments were also important to the Protestant clergy. Lynn emphasised teaching appointments when he depicted the threat to Protestant schools from 'Catholic' education committees. The struggle between the devolved government and the UEC in the late 1920s was only resolved when the government finally guaranteed Protestant teachers for Protestant children in 1930 by allowing the school committee a significant influence in teaching appointments. Also, Protestant clerics insisted upon a major role in the management of Stranmillis college, the state teacher training college.

The 'four and two' committee was a potential trojan horse for Catholic schools. However, the Catholic authorities, despite their profound misgivings, were willing to compromise on the 'four and two' question as early as 1930. Mageean's proposed school committees were to be concerned solely with the issues financed by the voluntary contribution, but the Cabinet chose to deflect the challenge by granting half of capital costs to prevent a possible Protestant and Catholic clerical alliance undermining education reform. The Catholic authorities appeared intransigent and distrustful, but the government spurned opportunities to alleviate clerical fears and strengthen the case for those senior Catholic clerics who were advocating compromise. The manipulation of the boundaries of the education committees in 1923, the inability of the Ministry to protect Catholic schools from abuses in the allocation of heating, lighting and cleaning grants and the appointment of loyalist politicians to maintained school committees after 1968 did not encourage confidence in the education committees.

The 1993 Order may therefore appear as a bitter defeat, evidence that the sacrifices of the past have ultimately proved to be futile, but the school committees created by the 1993 Order differ greatly from the 'four and two' committees envisaged by the authors of the 1923 Act. The 1993 Order allows the Education and Library Boards (less 'unionist' and less powerful than their predecessors), only two of the nine seats on maintained school committees. Catholic clerics have surrendered power within Catholic schools, but to Catholic parents, Catholic teachers and DENI officials rather than to unionist politicians. The 1993 Order may finally end these fears, but the Catholic authorities will remain cautious, alert to any 'scarcely perceptible pressure', for many years.

In April 1930, only days before the vital Second Reading of the Education Bill, Devlin told Charlemont that 'the Catholics did not wish to repeat the fiasco of 1923; they wished to establish peace in educational matters'.[9] Akenson, Bardon and Buckland all view the failure of the Catholic authorities to attend the Lynn committee as a major error and a lost opportunity,[10] but there was no viable alternative available for either the Ministry or the Catholic authorities in the early 1920s. The intense antagonism between unionists and nationalists dominating Northern Ireland's first years prevented the Catholic authorities and senior Ministry officials from accomplishing what everyone else on the island of Ireland had failed to achieve – a just resolution of their differences. The options available to the Catholic authorities were limited, because Sinn Féin was the dominant political force in Irish nationalist politics in 1921, despite the Nationalists abandoning their traditional policy of participation.

The Nationalist abstention from the first Northern Ireland Parliament cannot be viewed as the principal reason for the failure of the Catholic authorities to secure improved conditions for their schools in 1923. The absence of Nationalist MPs ensured that the debates of the Education Bill emphasised the defence of Protestant values, but the basic features of education reform had been discussed by unionists and reformers since the beginning of the century. Also, the evidence of fifty years of devolved government suggests that neither Nationalist MPs in the Commons nor the four proposed Catholic representatives on the Lynn committee were likely to deflect the unionist majority from their set course.

THE PRICE OF CATHOLIC SCHOOLS

The 1923 Act imposed a financial liability upon voluntary schools which was to last for more than seventy years. The calculations are necessarily crude, but they offer a plausible estimate of the scale of the voluntary contribution over the past seven decades. The rate of inflation has been calculated from the year before the places were provided, which probably understates the value of the voluntary contribution because the monies for new schools would be collected for a number of years before the beginning of the project.

The total cost of the voluntary contribution for Catholic schools during the past seventy years amounted, in 1996 prices, to nearly £200 million. As Dunn states 'the response of the Catholic community to the challenge is something of which they are rightly proud'.[11] The educational penalty of the voluntary contribution was also considerable, with limited access to secondary education during the 1950s and 1960s and second-class schools since 1923. The seven decades between the 1923 Act and the 1993 Order can be separated into four distinct phases, each differing in the scale and character of the price of voluntary status.

The first phase lasted from 1925 until 1947. The most significant feature of this era was the widening distinction between Catholic voluntary schools and public elementary schools. The education committees spent more than £1.8 million by the outbreak of war in

1939 providing 42,000 new places for nearly half of all public elementary pupils while voluntary schools gained £160,000 – just one twelfth of total capital spending for less than 8,000 places.[12]

The problems afflicting the most decrepit Catholic schools were eased after the 1930 Act, and the 8,000 new places for voluntary schools matched the Ministry's estimate of the number of pupils in 'unsuitable' schools in April 1930.[13] The evidence from the PRONI archives and the Ministry's Reports indicates that the Ministry was attempting to maintain, though not to improve, Catholic schools during the 1920s and 1930s. The underlying themes of these decades were Catholic stagnation and Protestant progress. The lack of investment in voluntary primary schools left thousands of Catholic pupils in decaying schools whilst 'in nearly every case in which schools have been transferred the committees have done or are doing a great deal towards rendering the accommodation and equipment adequate and suitable'.[14]

The educational damage caused by the voluntary contribution in the 1920s and 1930s is difficult to assess without clear evidence of variations in the performance of voluntary and public elementary school pupils, and the Ministry's statistics do not allow for any comparative analysis of examination results. Therefore, the only basis for speculation comes from the numerous quotes in the Ministry of Education's reports extolling the benefits of modernisation and amalgamation. The Ministry's reports were partisan accounts, aimed to encourage wary Protestant clerics to transfer their schools, but there is no evidence to suggest that the Catholic authorities or Nationalist politicians disputed the Ministry's claims for the educational advantages of rationalisation and capital investment.

The second phase, which lasted from the late 1940s to the end of the 1950s, witnessed the most severe disadvantage for voluntary schools. Catholic primary schools continued to suffer a feeble pace of development and renewal, with only 10,000 new places between 1947 and 1959 while the education committees provided new accommodation for more than 28,000 Protestant pupils.[15] Disadvantage persisted for voluntary primary schools, but the most significant feature of the first decade of the 1950s was the contrast between the development of county and voluntary secondary education. The education committees supplied 30,000 secondary intermediate school places, and a further 4,000 places in the new county grammar schools for Protestant pupils, but Catholics gained only 8,000 places. Also, the Ministry provided generous subsidies to the predominantly Protestant voluntary grammar schools. This contrast granted a substantial advantage to thousands of

Protestant children, and continues to effect Catholic employment prospects in Northern Ireland today. The CCMA fully cooperated with Ministry officials in the late 1940s and the Catholic authorities prepared their development schemes for voluntary schools before most education authorities presented their proposals for county schools.[16] However, throughout the 1950s Catholic parishes failed to secure the grants which would allow them to match the growth of county secondary schools.

The end of the 1950s witnessed the first signs of the third phase – an era of comparative advantage for Catholic schools. The Catholic populace gained the majority of capital funding and began to finally close the gap between the opportunities available to Catholic and Protestant pupils. The 1964 White Paper generated a dramatic increase in the scale of voluntary school building, and the number of new primary and secondary intermediate voluntary school places doubled in the next ten years.[17]

The statistics for the 1960s underline the political rather than the financial restrictions upon Catholic education in the 1950s. The surge of investment of the late 1950s arose from the determination of May to diminish the contrast between county and voluntary schools following Midgley's years as Minister of Education. The increased investment of the late 1960s was a recognition of the scale of the problems facing Catholic schools. The rapid progress of the late 1960s lessened the educational disadvantages, but exacerbated the financial costs of voluntary status. The voluntary contribution nearly doubled in the late 1960s,[18] and by 1967 the Catholic community was paying, in 1996 prices, more than £10 million each year for their schools. The 1968 Act greatly eased the burden during a time of substantial investment in Catholic schools.

The abolition of the devolved government in March 1972, and the replacement of the local education authorities by the Education and Library Boards the following July, did not lead to significant improvements for Catholic schools, because the reduction of the voluntary contribution to just fifteen per cent of capital costs at the end of 1975 coincided with the beginning of the fourth and final phase of the history of the voluntary contribution. Catholic schools appeared to suffer a slight disadvantage in the allocation of capital funds in the decade after 1977, but the most notable feature of the late 1970s and early 1980s was the dramatic decline in spending for both controlled and maintained schools.

In 1988 the DENI initiated the most significant reform of the education system since 1947, and these changes required substantial capital investment. By 1991 Catholics were paying £4 million each year for their schools. The Catholic authorities appeared to accept such a sum as a fair price for the autonomy of their schools, and it was the SACHR inquiry, rather than the opposition of the Catholic authorities or nationalist politicians, which finally persuaded the DENI to discuss the possibility of abolishing the voluntary contribution.

The cost of voluntary Catholic schools has not been confined to the intense burden of paying the voluntary contribution and the delay in the construction of secondary schools, though these were substantial penalties. May claimed in 1957 that voluntary school pupils suffered 'under a serious handicap and at a grave disadvantage compared to those who attend transferred schools',[19] and the SACHR study found that Catholic pupils gained fewer qualifications and lower grades than Protestant students.[20]

The SACHR study noted that Catholic maintained schools were smaller than the controlled schools, and concluded that the voluntary contribution encouraged the Catholic authorities to commission the cheapest available design.[21] In the 1960s, Catholic schools were more likely to contain overcrowded classrooms, and some Catholic schools operated the 'dual day' system to accommodate all their pupils. Inferior schools were often the only option for Catholic parishes because, even in 1969 when the intensity of Catholic disadvantage appeared to be diminishing, the average sum spent on providing a child in the voluntary system with a new place was only half the amount spent on behalf of a county school pupil.[22]

The SACHR inquiry also found Catholic schools contained fewer special teaching rooms for technology, craft and design classes, and Protestant grammar schools obtained larger grants than Catholic grammar schools, despite both sets of schools enjoying similar legal rights to funding grants. Protestant pupils also enjoyed greater access to grammar schools, with thirty-one per cent of Protestants attending grammar schools in contrast to just twenty-six per cent of Catholics in the 1980s. The 15,000 places in county grammar schools gave Protestant pupils an advantage that could not be eradicated by increased spending on voluntary secondary intermediate schools.

The anecdotal evidence collected by Dominic Murray may indicate that maintained schools were not as enterprising as controlled schools in bidding for funds from the DENI and the Education and Library Boards.[23] However, the experience of fifty years of devolved government depressed Catholic expectations of fair treatment from the education committees or the Boards. Also, the SACHR investigation found notable patterns of disadvantage against Catholic schools by the DENI and the Boards twenty-five years after the 1968 Act granted maintained schools full funding of recurrent spending. Clearly, the financial cost of autonomous Catholic schools did not arise solely from the legal penalties of voluntary status.

The evidence of the significant educational and financial penalty of the voluntary contribution should not obscure the important fact that this liability was imposed upon the Catholic laity by both the devolved government and the Catholic authorities. The debate amongst senior Catholic clerics in the spring of 1930 on the implications of complete state funding was echoed more than sixty years later when Catholic bishops expressed their concerns for the implications of abolishing the voluntary contribution to researchers from the SACHR inquiry. The abortive discussions surrounding the Education Act of 1938 also underlined the willingness of senior Catholic clerics to insist upon sacrifices from the laity to preserve clerical control. The Catholic authorities cannot escape some of the responsibility for the price paid by the Catholic laity for the maintenance of autonomous Catholic schools.

The impact of the voluntary contribution upon the lives of every Catholic in Northern Ireland over the past seventy years, with second-class schools and the delayed development of secondary education, has been immense. The consequences will persist for many years.

'NATIONAL' SCHOOLS

Education in the 'narrow ground' of Northern Ireland was destined to lead to conflict between a unionist majority dedicated to creating a new state based upon the principles of loyalty to the Union and a nationalist minority determined to preserve its distinct Gaelic and Irish identity. As Osborne, Cormack and Gallagher explain:

> in a society which is intolerant and inequitable, it should come as no surprise that ethnic and religious minorities will seek to defend their identity and traditions, and that one of the routes they will follow is to demand the right to their own schools.[24]

The Gaelic language was a sensitive issue after 1921, but the most notable feature of the 1920s was the relative moderation of the

Ministry's language policy. The Gaelic language was not only tolerated, but the Ministry also financed the special grants inherited from the National Board and created a post for promoting the language.

The loss of these special grants in 1933, and the fact that no-one was appointed as Organiser of the Irish Language before the post was abolished, should not diminish the significance of the government's decision to allow Gaelic to be taught in Catholic schools. The Ministry restricted the amount of time allocated to Gaelic, but resisted efforts to prohibit the language. Also, the Cabinet's decision to abolish the grants in 1933 was partly influenced by the absence of Nationalist MPs. The devolved government may have offered sterner resistance to opponents of the grants if Nationalist MPs themselves had been willing to defend the payments.

Gaelic annoyed virtually every Unionist, and even liberals such as Hall-Thompson and O'Neill expressed their dislike of the language, but only a handful of Unionist MPs pursued the issue in the Commons. 'Orange' Unionist MPs never posed a genuine threat to the language, and by the end of the 1950s even their minor campaign withered from lack of support on the Unionist backbenches. Unionist MPs, both in Stormont and Westminster, have remained largely silent on the language issue for the last thirty years, and have even resorted in recent years to highlighting the claims for 'Ulster Scots' to be treated as a distinct ethnic language.

The ability to determine the collective understanding of the past is a valuable asset for any government, but in Northern Ireland the region's history was a matter of profound dispute between the two cultural traditions. Ministry officials closely studied the history books used in Catholic schools, but they vehemently resisted the sustained efforts of Unionist MPs during the 1950s for compulsory courses on 'Ulster' history with a definitive textbook that would inevitably present the views of the Protestant majority. The Ministry was not opposed to the principle of teaching 'Ulster' history in county schools, but they were unwilling to provoke a confrontation by proposing a textbook which would be unacceptable to most nationalist MPs and Catholic clerics. The textbook issue was pursued by the same MPs who criticised the government for tolerating the Gaelic language, and even with Midgley as Minister of Education they failed to persuade the government to prepare a book. The majority of Unionist MPs were not prepared to translate their hostility towards the 'nationalist' features of Catholic schools into a direct challenge.

Many Catholic clerics were ardent Irish nationalists and enthusiastic champions of the Gaelic cultural tradition, but the cultural dimensions of Catholic schools have been secondary issues for the Catholic authorities compared to the major struggles with the Ministry of Education surrounding the voluntary contribution and clerical authority. The teaching of Gaelic was never widespread in Catholic schools, with no more than one sixth of all pupils studying the language, and the *Schools Apart* study found a significant minority of Catholic schools did not play Gaelic games. Catholic schools lost their grants for Gaelic classes in 1933 without significant clerical protest, but plans to amalgamate adjacent boys' and girls' elementary schools the following year provoked the most intense clerical campaign since the 1930 Act.[25] Blanshard's 'cultural war' in Northern Ireland's schools was not a vigorous struggle for many Irish nationalists or Ulster unionists.

The outbreak of mass violence in 1969 and the revival of militant republicanism has led nationalist politicians to emphasise the cultural and ethnic features of autonomous Catholic schools. The SDLP's MPs asked numerous questions on the fate of the Gaelic language at Westminster in the 1980s, and the growth of bunscoil schools has demonstrated the importance of Gaelic culture to many of Northern Ireland's Catholics. The schools function as typical Catholic maintained schools, but the initiative for these schools has come from republican elements within the nationalist community. The Catholic authorities have not resisted the development of bunscoil schools, but they are unlikely to welcome schools where the formative influence appears to be Irish nationalism rather than Catholicism.

The Catholic authorities have responded to the republican challenge by placing a greater emphasis upon Gaelic in Catholic schools. The CCMS's pamphlet of 1988 outlining the Council's objections to the DENI's reform proposals dedicated three pages to the Gaelic issue. The enhanced role for the language in the final version of the 1989 Order was one of the few successes for nationalists during the education reform debate. O'Connor argues that amongst middle-class Catholics, the 'nationalist' features of Catholic schools no longer appeal, and there appears to be a distinct class contrast within the Catholic community between middle-class 'liberals' and working-class 'nationalists'. The increasing influence of the Catholic laity and the provisions of the 1998 Order which places a "Statutory duty" on the DENI to promote the language will probably lead to many Catholic schools, particularly in 'republican' areas, placing a greater emphasis upon Irish history and the Gaelic language in future years.

PROTESTANT SCHOOLS

The tale of Catholic schools in Northern Ireland cannot be told without recognising the importance of the devolved government's relations with the Protestant clergy in determining the outcome of the major contests surrounding education policy since 1921. The 1923 Act was designed to encourage rather than coerce Protestant clerical managers to abandon voluntary status, though also ensuring that the distinction between voluntary and public elementary schools was sufficient to attract Protestant clerics.

The 1947 Act was the last major conflict between the Protestant clergy and the government because the 1947 settlement proved, in practice, to be as acceptable as the 1930 Act.[26] The Protestant clergy's role in education public policy since 1950, especially the events surrounding the reforms of 1968 and 1993, was peripheral. This absence of Protestant clerical agitation partly accounts for the lack of significant progress by the Catholic authorities in easing the penalties of voluntary status since the 1950s.

A principal contention of this book has been that the treatment of Northern Ireland's Catholic schools must be contrasted with the fate of controlled 'Protestant' schools. Therefore, it is notable that the future for Catholic schools appears promising compared to the prospects for Northern Ireland's controlled schools.

The Church of Ireland Archbishop of Armagh, Dr Robert Eames, spoke in Dublin in 1992 of his concerns for the future of Protestant education in Northern Ireland:

> the system of educational administration in Northern Ireland had been radically altered to the disadvantage of controlled schools which serve the Protestant community . . . The education report . . . says the future of the present five boards as effective agencies catering for the ethos and identity of state, mainly Protestant, schools is highly suspect.[27]

The 1989 Order, following the trend set by the Education Reform Act 1988 for England and Wales, has greatly increased the authority of the DENI and the autonomy of individual schools at the expense of the Education and Library Boards. Also, the Order formally recognised the CCMS as the representative body for all Catholic schools and created the Northern Ireland Council for Integrated Education to promote the growth of integrated schools. Some Protestant clerics are now calling for their own denominational council similar to the CCMS to replace the 'redundant' Boards which no longer appear capable of defending Protestant interests.[28] Protestant clerics will probably need such a body to represent their concerns as controlled schools face many problems in the years ahead.

A consistent feature of Northern Ireland's education system has been the steady decline in the number of primary schools. In 1923 there were more than 2,000 elementary schools, but by 1992 the number had fallen to just 964 schools.[29] The impact of these changes has been most keenly felt amongst rural and controlled schools. The number of Protestant schools has more than halved in the past seventy years whereas Catholics have lost only one third of their schools. In 1964 there were 450 schools with less than fifty pupils, but by 1992 only 143 such schools remained. The DENI will probably attempt to close many of these schools in the coming decade, especially as the DENI estimates that 20,500 of the 94,000 places in controlled schools were not filled in the spring of 1998. (Reference UK Commons Sixth Series 308 252 11 March 1998).[30]

The SACHR study found a significant numbers of small controlled schools, and the fear that integrated schools will lure children away from controlled schools probably accounts for the diminishing enthusiasm for integration amongst Protestant clerics and unionist politicians. Integration now poses a greater threat to the viability of many controlled schools than the network of Catholic schools, and this may also explain the higher numbers of Catholic pupils in integrated primary schools. In the years ahead, Protestant clerics and unionist politicians may emerge as opponents of the cause they championed so fervently in the 1970s and 1980s.

THE FUTURE FOR CATHOLIC SCHOOLS

In May 1906 the Nationalist MP T. M. Healy offered his view of the fundamental argument for Catholic schools:

> I would rather have my children learn to say 'Our Father' than to learn the use of globes. I would rather they understood their religion in the provision for the eternity which is to come than they should become rich and prosperous, and educated in the things of the world.[31]

Healy may have overstated the spiritual and understated the temporal aspects, but Catholic education in Ireland is inspired and motivated by the Catholic faith. The political consequences of autonomous schools and the cultural features of Catholic maintained schools are important, and have grown more important for many Catholics in recent years, but they remain secondary issues for the Catholic authorities. Elemental religious convictions guide their defence of Catholic schools, and these convictions are shared by many Catholics throughout the world:

> the belief that our children, whatever be their distresses, whatever be their misfortunes, whatever be their poverty in this world, if they have listened to the teaching of the Church, will reap a rich reward in putting into practice the lessons of Christianity which they receive in the Catholic schools.[32]

The Catholic authorities may dismiss, and even resent, the importance of Gaelic culture within Catholic schools, but the impact of autonomous Catholic schools in sustaining Irish Gaelic sentiment should not be understated. The Catholic minority in Northern Ireland survived as a coherent community after 1921 because it sustained its identity, and the local Catholic school was vital to the preservation of each parish. Farrell criticises the Catholic authorities when he claims: 'if the bishops had to choose between accepting the Northern state and losing their schools then they were going to keep their schools'.[33] The evidence of the last seventy years suggests that Logue and his colleagues, un-wittingly, chose the right option for many republicans in the autumn of 1923.

The education system was, once more, 'as denominational almost as we could desire' for the Catholic authorities by the end of 1993. Catholic schools were educating more than 160,000 pupils in thirty grammar schools, eighty-two secondary intermediate schools, four hundred and fifty-three primary schools, twenty-five nursery schools and two special schools. Catholic schools now educate the majority of Northern Ireland's primary and secondary intermediate pupils,[34] and though opinion polls show most Catholics support the principle of integration few Catholic parents send their children to integrated, schools.

Also, the Catholic authorities' contention that 'religious education should be woven into the curriculum'[35] appears to be justified by the scale of church attendance by Northern Ireland's Catholics throughout the twentieth century.[36] The Catholic school must be viewed as one of the major factors accounting for such intense religious devotion. The rewards for the Catholic authorities have clearly been considerable, but for the Catholic laity the cost of autonomous schools has been a notable financial and educational penalty for the past seventy years. The Catholic authorities wrested vast sums of money from the Catholic laity during the last seventy years to finance their control of Catholic schools, but the Catholic authorities now appear willing to accept the right of Catholic teachers and parents to a role in the education of Catholic children.

The autonomy of Catholic teacher training has been secured, the Council for Catholic Maintained Schools offers the Catholic authorities privileged access to the DENI and the NIO, and the cultural features of Catholic schools, so important to an influential minority within the Catholic community, have been guaranteed by the 1989 Order. The long-term future for clerical control of Catholic schools appears safe in Northern Ireland today.

The 1993 Order will, in the years ahead, relieve the Catholic community of the damage caused by the unequal funding of Catholic schools. The legacy of the voluntary contribution will persist, but some day soon Catholics in Northern Ireland will no longer pay the price of their faith.

Notes

1 The term 'Catholic authorities' is employed to define the leadership of the Catholic Church in Northern Ireland. The term 'the Catholic bishops' is slightly misleading. The bishops of the six dioceses covering Northern Ireland – Armagh, Down and Connor, Derry, Clogher, Kilmore and Dromore – would occasionally issue joint statements, but the Church's education policy appears to have been developed by the bishops of Armagh, Down and Connor and Derry. Also, senior Catholic clerics in these dioceses played a leading role in formulating the Church's strategy
2 Farren (1989), p. 8
3 Studies June 1930, No. 74, p. 67
4 The term 'elementary schools' corresponds broadly to the modern version of the primary school, but until the creation of an extensive network of secondary schools in the aftermath of the Second World War, many elementary schools were educating children to the age of fifteen. In some schools this practice continued until the late 1950s, and this book will demonstrate that the overwhelming majority of these schools were Catholic schools
5 See Chapter 2 for a definition of 'voluntary' schools
6 In December 1988 and February 1989, John Hume asked a number of Parliamentary Questions on the level of funding for secondary intermediate and grammar schools which led to the Northern Ireland Office minister responsible for education, Dr Brian Mawhinney, to promise a revision of government policy. UK Commons Sixth Series Vol. 143 Column 746 and 144 37 and 146 626, 717, 16, 19 December 1988 and 7, 8 February 1989. See Chapter 6
7 Murray, (1985), p. 116
8 NI Commons XVII 1324, 9 April 1935
9 Osborne, Cormack and Gallagher (1993), p. 5
10 Dunn (1990), p. 50
11 NI Commons Vol. XV Column 773, 9 March 1933
12 NI Commons XL 1941, 12 June 1956
13 NI Commons XLIV 671, 11 March 1959
14 NI Commons XLVI 1933, 9 June 1960
15 Only five Cardinals – Michael Logue, Joseph O'Donnell, Joseph MacRory, John D'Alton and William Conway – served as leaders of the Irish

Catholic Church during the fifty years of devolved government, whilst both Down and Connor and Derry were served by only three bishops
16 See Chapter 2
17 See Chapters 2 and 3
18 See Chapters 5 and 6
19 See Chapters 2 and 3
20 See Chapter 4
21 The Public Record Office in London does not contain any files relevant to this book
22 See Chapter 3
23 NI Commons LXVII 2462, 30 November 1967
24 *The Roman Catholic Church and the Foundation of the Northern Irish State 1912–1930* (Oxford 1994). *The Politics of Irish Education 1920–1965* (Belfast 1995)
25 Cormack, Gallagher and Osborne (1991), p. 141

CHAPTER TWO

1 *Irish Ecclesiastical Record December* 1900 p. 552
2 Akenson (1970), p. 390
3 Coolahan (1981), pp. 12–13
4 See Auchmuty (1937), Corcoran (1928) and Dowling (1935) for the most comprehensive discussion of 'Bible societies'
5 The two Catholic representatives were Archbishop Murray of Dublin and Antony Blake, the Treasury Remembrancer and an archetypal 'Castle' Catholic. The Presbyterians were also granted only two seats. Corcoran (1928) p. xxix
6 Akenson (1970), p. 117
7 Auchmuty (1937), p. 146
8 Akenson (1970), p. 49
9 Ibid., p. 53
10 Dowling (1971), p. 144
11 Titley (1983), p. 4
12 Akenson (1970), p. 204
13 Ibid
14 Corish (1959), p. 394
15 Coolahan (1981), p. 17
16 The 1841 ruling was only employed in the archdiocese of Tuam to orchestrate a boycott of the National Schools. On his death in 1893 a senior colleague claimed that MacHale's archdiocese contained the worst schools in Ireland. Dowling (1971), p. 120
17 Akenson (1970), p. 255
18 Atkinson (1969), p. 128
19 Hislop p. 65
20 The evidence from the fifty years of devolved government indicates that these concerns were to prove to be unfounded
21 Akenson (1970), p. 190

22 Ibid., p. 190

23 Ibid., p. 199

24 Atkinson (1969), p. 95

25 Akenson (1970), p. 198. In its evidence to the Powis Commission, the Church Education Society claimed to have educated as many as 46,000 Catholics. O'Buachalla (1988), p. 22

26 Akenson (1970), p. 290

27 By 1896 the Society was responsible for a mere 5,000 pupils. Ibid., p. 371

28 Batterbury (1940), p. 552

29 Akenson (1970), p. 179 and 180

30 Batterbury (1940), p. 555

31 Akenson (1970), p. 309

32 Ibid., p. 304

33 O'Buachalla (1988), p. 24

34 The Catholic clergy were particularly eager to safeguard clerical control of Catholic schools. Eighty-five per cent of Catholic schools were supervised by clerical managers, in contrast to sixty per cent of Presbyterian schools and only a third of Church of Ireland schools. Akenson (1970), p. 215

35 The exact figures were 57.4% and 25%. Farren (1995), p. 8

36 The delay was also probably caused by Protestant reaction to the authoritarian declarations of the Vatican Council of 1870 rather than the financial implications of segregated schools and separate teacher training colleges

37 Gladstone's efforts ultimately proved to be futile, because in 1886 the Cabinet and the party split irrevocably on the Home Rule question. The Liberals were to enjoy only three years of power during the next two decades

38 Auchmuty (1937), p. 149

39 Coolahan (1981), p. 32

40 See Chapters 2 and 4 for a more detailed examination of the efforts of the Catholic authorities to retain control of teacher training in Northern Ireland

41 Atkinson (1969), p. 114

42 The figures for 1881 were 12,064 Catholics and 12,629 Protestants. By 1911 there were 31,742 Catholics and 11,395 Protestants attending intermediate schools. Titley (1983), p. 8

43 O'Buachalla (1988), p. 31

44 Auchmuty (1937), p. 150

45 Titley (1983), p. 3

46 Akenson (1970), p. 9

47 The exact figures were 14,181 out of 17,614 schools and 46% of pupils. Akenson (1970), p. 10. Kenneth Wald's *Crosses on the Ballot* (1983) provides a stimulating analysis of the electoral implications of the decline of denominational schools in England and Wales

48 Akenson (1970), p. 348

49 The bishops also offered a concession to intermediate teachers with a clarification of the dismissal procedures. No teacher was to be dismissed without the approval of the local bishop. *Irish Ecclesiastical Record* (July 1898), pp. 75–78

50 Starkie was 'probably the most knowledgeable and certainly the most powerful of Irish professional educators'. Akenson (1975), p. 5. He was

also on poor terms with the senior Catholic clergy. In the summer of 1901 Archbishop Walsh of Dublin resigned from the National Board following a disagreement with Starkie. *Irish Catholic Directory* (1902), p. 494

51 Starkie (1902), pp. 37–38

52 *Irish Ecclesiastical Record* (1902), p. 460

53 In October 1902 a meeting of Catholic managers challenged Starkie's allegations, and six months later another gathering of Catholic clerical managers in Armagh called on Starkie to resign because 'we regard his continuance in office as a grave danger to Catholic education.' *Irish Catholic Directory* (1903), p. 454 and (1904), p. 439. The Armagh managers refused to abandon the struggle, renewing their call for Starkie's resignation in January 1905. *Irish Catholic Directory* (1906), p. 447

54 Titley (1983), p. 19

55 The government was officially a 'unionist' government, but the term would only cause confusion with the Ulster Unionists

56 *Irish Catholic Directory* (1907), p. 451. O'Dwyer's criticisms were notably similar to the objections of Protestant clerics to Northern Ireland's Education Act of 1923

57 Titley (1983), p. 26

58 Ibid., p. 69

59 *Irish Catholic Directory* (1908), p. 456

60 Titley (1983), p. 55

61 Ibid., p. 60

62 Ibid., p. 61

63 Holmes (1970), p. 28

64 *Irish Ecclesiastical Record* (December 1919), p. 505

65 Titley is a severe critic of the Catholic Church's role in Irish education, but he notes 'the response to Cardinal Logue's Passion Sunday protest call was considerable . . . public opinion in the country, apart from the north-west region, was firmly behind the bishops in their demand for its withdrawal'. Titley (1983), p. 68

66 Ibid., p. 70

67 Holmes (1970), p. 3

68 Farren (1995), p. 25

69 Erskine Holmes' excellent MA dissertation remains the clearest analysis of the issues surrounding education reform in the first decades of this century

70 The association changed its title from the Association for the Promotion of Educational Reform in Ireland. PRONI D 3316/3

71 Holmes (1970), p. 3. The formation of the Association may have been in response to Starkie's speech in the city the previous September

72 McKeown (1993), pp. 6 and 13

73 *Secular Control of Secular Education.* Educational Reform Association (Belfast 1903)

74 Holmes (1970), p. 8

75 Harris (1994), p. 23

76 Holmes (1970), p. 21

77 Akenson (1973), p. 49

78 Wyse to Blackmore, 5 January 1929. PRONI CAB 9D/1/6

79 *Irish Ecclesiastical Record* December (1919), p. 504. Quoted in Titley (1983), p. 62
80 Harris (1994), p. 24
81 The 1901 figures were 19.1% of Catholics, 9.8% of Church of Ireland followers and 5% Presbyterians. The 1911 figures were 14.7%, 6.1% and 2.8% respectively. Rafferty (1994), p. 171
82 Holmes (1970), p. 9
83 In the 1980s advocates of integrated education were also misled by statements from Protestant clerics favouring integration. The reality, as illustrated by the fate of the 1978 Education Act, was notably different. See Chapter 6
84 Harris (1994), p. 196
85 Cmd 6, p. 5
86 Akenson (1973), p. 49. The conference did not contain any representative Catholics, but as Akenson observes 'to note that the Belfast conference represented chiefly the viewpoint of Protestant educators would be an accurate observation, but not an argument against its having been influential'
87 Ibid., pp. 49–50
88 Farren (1995), p. 39
89 Londonderry to Logue, 29 August 1921. PRONI CAB 4/18. Londonderry asked the Cardinal to nominate one representative each for clerical, lay, primary and secondary interests. Logue may have been offended by Londonderry's limitations on his choice of possible Catholic representatives
90 Logue to Londonderry, 2 September 1921. PRONI CAB 4/18
91 Buckland refers to Londonderry as 'a very sensitive Minister of Education'. Buckland (1979), p. 249
92 Londonderry to Fitzalan, 4 September 1921. PRONI CAB 4/18
93 Dunn (1993), p. 17
94 Farren (1995), p. 27
95 In the spring of 1925 Londonderry visited Cardinal O'Donnell for lunch at Armagh. There is no evidence of any other Minister of Education dining with senior Catholic clerics. PRONI ED 32/B/1/2/62
96 Cmd 6, p. 9
97 Akenson (1973), p. 52. The only Catholic amongst the thirty-two members of the Lynn committee was Bonaparte Wyse, a former National Board civil servant responsible for elementary education. Wyse was to demonstrate his cultural origins when he drafted Craigavon's speech for the Second Reading debate of the 1930 Education Act and referred throughout to the Catholic Church. Craigavon inserted the word 'Roman' before every mention in the text. PRONI CAB 9D/1/8
98 Buckland (1981), p. 52
99 Farren (1995), p. 45
100 Logue to Londonderry, 2 September 1921. PRONI CAB 4/18
101 Dunn (1993), p. 17
102 Farren is correct to raise the question of whether a delay by the Ministry of Education until the middle of the 1920s might have led to Catholic involvement. Farren (1995), p. 45
103 Rafferty (1994), p. 210

104 Akenson (1973), p. 51
105 Farren (1995), p. 46
106 NI Commons III 360, 17 April 1923
107 NI Commons III 1620, 25 October 1923
108 Bishop O'Donnell of Raphoe sat on the Molony committee and Professor Timothy Corcoran of University College Dublin was a member of the Kilanin committee. Titley (1983), p. 55
109 *Irish News* 9, 21, 28, 29, 30 November and 11 December 1918. *Irish Times* 26 and 27 November 1918. The only bishop to favour abstention in 1918 was Dr Fogarty of Killaloe. *Irish News* 30 November 1918. The elimination of the Nationalists and their displacement by Sinn Féin was viewed as inevitable even before the election campaign. The *Irish News* estimated that Sinn Féin would win sixty of Ireland's one hundred and five seats, and by the end of November 1918 thirty Nationalist MPs had already withdrawn from the approaching contest. Every seat in Cork, the largest county in Ireland, was surrendered to Sinn Féin without a struggle. *Irish News* 28 November 1918
110 *Irish News* 9 May 1921
111 Elliott (1973), pp. 2, 4, 6, 8, 10, 12, 14, 16 and 18
112 *Irish News* 14 May 1921. The Nationalists continued to enjoy some clerical support. Nationalists in West Belfast, East Belfast, North Belfast and South Belfast were all nominated by priests. The 1921 elections were conducted using proportional representation, and there was no need for the Nationalists and Sinn Féin to reach an electoral pact to protect 'nationalist' seats from Unionists
113 Buckland (1981), p. 35
114 The Ministry of Education Report stated that 270 of 740 schools were not submitting payment claims to the Ministry. Cmd 16 p. 3
115 Akenson (1973), p. 46
116 Buckland (1981), p. 35
117 Akenson (1973), p. 44
118 *Irish News* 27 February 1922
119 PRONI T 2886
120 McQuibban to Londonderry, 15 September 1922. PRONI ED 32/B/1/2/8
121 McQuibban to Londonderry, 15 September 1922. PRONI ED 32/B/1/2/8. The Catholic authorities' caution proved to be a wise decision when the boycott was abandoned after the Dublin government, facing the huge expenses arising from the republican insurgency, suspended payments to the teachers in September 1922. PRONI T 2886
122 The 'National' in the union's title did not possess any political implications. The union was simply for teachers in National Schools
123 Farren (1995), pp. 32 and 33
124 *Irish News* 26 March 1923
125 *Irish News* 26 March 1923
126 *Irish News* 26 March 1923
127 PRONI CAB 9D/45/1
128 Craig to Londonderry, 19 September 1922. PRONI CAB 9D/45/1
129 PRONI CAB 4/48

130 PRONI ED 32/B/1/2/62

131 See Chapter 3

132 Cmd 6 p. 34

133 As Londonderry bluntly explained during the First Reading of the Education Bill 'beyond giving opportunities for denominational instruction the State cannot go'. NI Commons III 125, 14 March 1923. He provided a more ambiguous interpretation of the role of religious instruction in the proposed public elementary schools the following month during the Second Reading debate. NI Commons III 351–352, 17 April 1923

134 Lynn to Londonderry, 20 February 1923. PRONI CAB 9D/1/1

135 NI Commons XXVII 2846, 25 January 1945

136 Akenson (1973), p. 71

137 NI Commons III 1628, 25 October 1923

138 Cabinet Conclusions, 15 December 1922. PRONI CAB 4/61

139 Akenson (1973), p. 67

140 In 1913 a delegation of senior Protestant clerics only insisted upon the right of access to schools. There was no mention of teachers providing religious instruction. Farren (1995), p. 27

141 Lynn would have been one of the first to know that the Bill would not follow his committee's advice, and he did not protest until February 1923

142 NI Commons I 948–1216, 10 October 1922

143 NI Commons III 125, 14 March 1923. Londonderry was the Leader of the Senate, but the Government of Ireland Act allowed ministers to speak in either chamber. Akenson (1973), p. 43

144 NI Commons III 18, 27 February 1923

145 Ibid., 1616, 25 October 1923

146 Ibid., 29, 27 February 1923

147 Ibid., 388, 17 April 1923

148 Ibid., 131, 14 March 1923. Lynn's reference to the 'simple principles of the Bible' once more underlined his essentially Protestant understanding of religion within Northern Ireland's elementary schools

149 NI Commons III 360, 17 April 1923

150 The Act contained 111 sections and six schedules. Londonderry (1924), p. 328

151 The Lynn committee adopted the terms Class One, Class Two and Class Three to describe the three varieties of schools, but this wording did not appear in the final version of the Education Bill. Some politicians and administrators referred to elementary schools controlled by the education authorities as provided and transferred schools, but public elementary schools appears to be the most convenient phrase

152 Akenson (1973), p. 68

153 See Chapter 5

154 A dozen Catholic clerical managers accepted 'four and two' status in the 1920s. Wyse to Blackmore, 5 January 1929. PRONI CAB 9D/1/6

155 Wyse informed Craig that only six Catholic 'four and two' schools were receiving capital grants. Wyse to Craig, 8 April 1930. PRONI CAB 9D/1/8

156 The 1923 Act termed both Class Two and Class Three schools as 'voluntary' schools, but this book will refer to the former as 'four and two' schools and the latter simply as 'voluntary' schools

157 Cmd 6, p. 32
158 Akenson (1973), p. 55
159 HC 80 p. 7
160 The exact figures were 629,038 pupils and 3,623 schools in Scotland and 478,224 pupils and 8,684 schools in Ireland. *Belfast Telegraph* 17 April 1902. The article was quoted in Dr William McKeown's *National Education in Ireland* PRONI D 3316/2
161 NI Commons XI 656, 18 June 1929
162 Akenson (1975), p. 8
163 Cmd 6, p. 42
164 Cmd 6, p. 74. The wording in the main text on page 42 reads 'the Roman Catholic and Protestant committees', but the summary of the recommendations on page 74 reads 'the Roman Catholic and Protestant communities'
165 *Irish Ecclesiastical Record* (March 1920), pp. 252–253
166 *Irish News* 28 March 1923
167 Farrell (1980), p. 84
168 Akenson (1973), p. 34
169 *Irish Catholic Directory* (1924), p. 605
170 PRONI CAB 9D/1/1. The unionists were slightly unfortunate with the initial plan. The Catholic majorities were often marginal, but almost all the Protestant committees were heavily Protestant
171 PRONI CAB 9D/1/1
172 '. . . the exact delineation of their areas of control is . . . a matter of detail affecting only the localities themselves'. NI Commons III 347, 17 April 1923
173 Londonderry (1924), p. 329
174 HC 154 p. 53
175 Akenson (1973), p. 60
176 Corkey to Spender, 30 June 1923. PRONI CAB 9D/1/1
177 D'Arcy to Craig, 24 April 1923. PRONI CAB 9D/1/1
178 Lynn to Londonderry, 7 May 1923. PRONI CAB 9D/1/2
179 Farren (1995), p. 68
180 Garret found the Protestant clergy in Dungannon, Fermanagh, Magherafelt, Omagh, Strabane and the city of Londonderry reluctant to transfer. Garrett to Wyse, 26 March 1928. PRONI ED 32/B/2/1
181 PRONI ED 32/B/2/1
182 Cmd 6, p. 42
183 PRONI CAB 9D/1/1
184 The issue only emerged after the education committee passed a resolution in September 1934 calling for secondary school teaching applicants to also state their religion. PRONI ED 13/1/318
185 Auchmuty (1937), p. 42
186 The proportion of Ireland's population able to speak Irish was only 23.3% by 1851, and fell to just 15.1% in 1871. Akenson (1970), p. 378
187 Ibid., p. 381
188 Farren (1995), p. 13
189 Ibid., p. 13
190 Akenson (1970), p. 381
191 Ibid., p. 382

192 *Irish Catholic Directory* (1902), pp. 411 and 496
193 The exact figure was 3,047 schools. *Irish Catholic Directory* (1910), p. 495
194 Titley (1983), pp. 78 and 80
195 Akenson's 1975 study and Farren's book both offer an excellent analysis of education in independent Ireland
196 Report of National Programme Conference 5 (Dublin 1922)
197 Professor William Corkey's pamphlet *The Church of Rome and Irish unrest: how hatred of Britain is taught in Irish schools* exemplified the attitudes of many unionists. Farren (1995), p. 43
198 Ibid., p. 103
199 Cmd 15 p. 49
200 Cmd 15 p. 83
201 NI Commons III 663, 2 May 1923
202 NI Commons I 520, 9 December 1921
203 Ibid., 527, 17 May 1922
204 NI Commons II 525, 17 May 1922
205 Farren (1995), p. 49
206 Ibid., p. 50
207 PRONI CAB 9D/44/1
208 HC 54 p. 31
209 HC 154 p. 112
210 NI Commons IV 46, 11 March 1924
211 Akenson (1973), p. 67. The willingness of other ministers, including Craig, to discuss educational issues with Protestant clerics would have irritated a less temperamental man than Londonderry
212 Buckland (1979), p. 251
213 Farren (1995), p. 70
214 Akenson (1973), p. 80
215 Cabinet Conclusions, 2 October 1923. PRONI CAB 4/88
216 NI Commons III 1643, 25 October 1923
217 Londonderry to Craig, 8 December 1924. PRONI CAB 9D/1/4
218 PRONI CAB 9D/1/4
219 Farren (1995), p. 62
220 Akenson (1973), p. 83
221 Farren (1995), p. 61
222 In March 1923 he was willing to allow religious instruction during the hours of compulsory attendance and the following month his attempts to compromise with the Education Act's critics were repulsed by the majority of the Cabinet. In September he proposed that the teachers in public elementary schools should be of the same denomination as the transferrers of the school. Farren (1995), pp. 64 and 74
223 Farren (1995), p. 74
224 Craig to Londonderry, 6 March 1925. PRONI CAB 9D/1/4
225 Londonderry to Craig, 6 March 1925. PRONI CAB 9D/1/4
226 NI Commons V 86–91, 12 March 1925
227 Londonderry (1924), p. 328
228 Ibid., p. 333
229 Ibid., p. 334

230 Harris (1994), p. 198
231 Akenson (1973), p. 58
232 Farren (1989), p. 155
233 Abercorn to Craig, 13 March 1925. PRONI CAB 9D/1/4
234 Buckland (1979), p. 254. The letter from McQuibban to the education committees was dated 4 July 1925, to ensure that the compromise would be known before the 'Twelfth' celebrations. HC 107 p. 8
235 Londonderry to James Cooper, 23 February 1925. PRONI ED 32/A/1/31
236 The second UEC campaign was provoked by the refusal of Armagh's education committee in 1928 to include a pledge to continue 'simple Bible instruction' in the deeds of transfer for Protestant schools. Corkey to Craigavon, 23 March 1928. PRONI CAB 9D/1/6
237 Corcoran (1916), p. 141
238 Farren (1995), p. 5
239 Akenson (1973), p. 58
240 The Leech Commission and the manipulation of the borders of the committees rescued the Catholic authorities from the perplexing question of a Catholic education committee. This was to remain a hypothetical issue until the creation of the Education and Library Boards in 1972
241 Farren (1995), p. 34
242 Farren (1989), p. 207. Quoted in Harris (1994), p. 228
243 Akenson (1973), p. 58
244 Farren (1995), p. 78
245 Buckland (1981), p. 77
246 Akenson (1973), p. 87
247 Farren (1989), p. 156

CHAPTER THREE

1 The depression followed a slightly different course from events in Great Britain and the rest of Europe. Britain suffered the nadir of the depression in 1932, and enjoyed a gradual recovery tainted only by a minor recession in 1936 until the Second World War. In Northern Ireland the rate of unemployment remained constantly high until the mid 1930s, and then rose to peak at over 30% in 1938. The annual rate of unemployment in Northern Ireland did not fall below the peak level for Great Britain until 1940. Isles and Cuthbert (1957), p. 21
2 Farrell (1980), p. 90
3 In May 1943, Brooke displaced Craig's successor, John Andrews, and served as Prime Minister for twenty years before making way for Terence O'Neill
4 The phrase was used by Sean Lemass, deputy leader of Fianna Fáil, in the Dáil in March 1928. Lyons (1973), p. 495
5 The limits of de Valera's commitment to actively pursuing the cause of Irish unity were evident by the end of the 1930s, when IRA insurgents were interned and the Fianna Fáil government executed nine republicans. Lyons (1973), p. 557. The Northern Ireland government was unwilling, or

unable, to recognise the distance between the rhetoric and the reality in de Valera's policy. The Irish Free State remained a diabolic figure in unionist politics until the advent of O'Neill in the 1960s. The intransigence of Fianna Fáil exacerbated, but did not generate, unionist hostility to the Irish Free State

6 Farrell (1980), p. 136
7 Buckland (1981), p. 71
8 Elliott (1973), pp. 96 and 98
9 *Irish News* 13 October 1923. Harris highlights the strident Unionist reaction to the statement, and the bellicose speeches of senior Catholic clerics at the subsequent public meetings. Harris (1994), pp. 155 and 156. However, the purpose of the bishops' statement was to encourage nationalists to abandon abstention
10 Farrell (1980), p. 101
11 *Irish News* 21, 23, 24, 26 and 30 March 1925
12 *Irish News* 24 March 1925
13 McVeigh (1989), p. 43
14 *Irish News* 25 March 1925
15 *Irish News* 27 March 1925. My emphasis
16 Elliott (1973), pp. 3, 5, 7, 9, 11, 13, 15, 17 and 19. In 1921 the Nationalists and Sinn Féin both won six seats
17 Buckland (1981), p. 57
18 The Catholic authorities in the Irish Free State also endorsed the moderates of Cummann na nGaedheal against the republican insurgents in the civil war. The August 1923 election witnessed considerable clerical support for the government party. *Irish Times* 11, 13, 16, 20, 22 and 25 August 1923
19 NI Commons III 355–356, 17 April 1923
20 *Irish News* 28 March 1923
21 *Irish Catholic Directory* (1924), pp. 558 and (1925), pp. 562–563
22 *Irish Catholic Directory* (1926), p. 561
23 Titley (1983), p. 59
24 PRONI ED 13/1/989
25 Akenson (1973), p. 122
26 Farren (1988), p. 29
27 PRONI ED 13/1/35
28 NI Commons III 356, 17 April 1923. Harris notes an error by Londonderry. He quotes 172 Catholics from a total of 420 applicants whilst Harris observes that the combined figures of 113 women and 46 men gives a total of only 159 students. Harris (1994), p. 214
29 Harris (1994), p. 214
30 Spender to McQuibban, 22 and 27 February 1924. PRONI CAB 9D/1/3. A third of the applicants in 1923 for Stranmillis may have been Catholics, but only twenty-five Catholics were training at the college in 1924. Harris (1994), p. 217
31 HC 107 p. 40
32 NI Commons VI 172–174, 23 April 1925
33 NI Commons VI 231, 28 April 1925
34 Wyse to Blackmore, 5 January 1929. PRONI ED 32/A/1/58. Quoted in Harris (1994), p. 221

35 Akenson provides a comprehensive account of the UEC's second campaign. Akenson (1973), pp. 89–118. The government also published its own version of the events leading to the Education Act, which highlighted the government's efforts to avoid a confrontation with the Protestant clergy. Cmd 84
36 Akenson (1973), p. 103. The government later allowed the transferrers – the Protestant clergy – half of the seats on the education committees
37 Charlemont had not even acknowledged Tierney's letter by the end of November. Tierney to Mageean, 21 November 1929. Down and Connor Diocesan Archives (DCDA) ED 11/30. Tierney's letter did not warrant a reply, but was the subject of a memorandum for the Cabinet by Charlemont at the end of October in which he rejected Tierney's call for two thirds of the capital costs. Charlemont Memorandum, 30 October 1929. PRONI CAB 9D/1/8
38 *Irish Catholic Directory* (1931), pp. 575–576
39 'As long as our schools are giving efficiently the public education which the State has a right to demand they are entitled to share equally with all other schools in all public grants for education. If they are denied their equal share they are treated unjustly'. *Irish Independent* 22 February 1930
40 Akenson (1973), p. 107
41 Ibid.
42 NI Commons VI 430–434, 6 May 1925
43 NI Commons VII 1241–1248, 13 May 1926
44 The motion stated 'that in the opinion of this House it is desirable to place schools which have not been, and will not be, transferred under the Education Act (Northern Ireland) 1923 in a similar position with respect to grants of public monies as they were prior to the passing of that Act'. NI Commons VIII 543, 30 March 1927
45 The debate covered more than thirty columns of Hansard and occupied the House for more than three quarters of the day's session. NI Commons VIII 531–578, 30 March 1927
46 NI Commons VIII 1458–1463, 17 May 1927
47 NI Commons IX 1325–1332, 3 May 1928
48 NI Commons X 780, 785–786, 795–797 and 811–814, 13 March 1929
49 NI Commons XI 621, 18 June 1929
50 NI Commons XII 716, 9 April 1930 and *Irish News* 10 April 1930. Devlin began his speech during the Second Reading: 'the first thought that would strike the mind of the stranger who came into this assembly today would be to wonder why the House is so crowded by Members. I might almost call this a regimental meeting of the House so large is the attendance'. NI Commons XII 709, 9 April 1930
51 *Belfast Newsletter* 9 April 1930
52 NI Commons XII 71 and 721, 12 March and 9 April 1930
53 PRONI ED 32/A/1/81
54 Akenson (1973), p. 109. Akenson appears to be excessively critical of the *Irish News*. There is no evidence from the editions for March, April and May 1930 of 'a torrent of propaganda'. The paper was assertive on behalf of the Catholic authorities, but never resorted to 'sheer invective'
55 Ibid., p. 102

56 PRONI ED 32/A/1/81
57 *Irish News* 23 April 1930
58 The three laws which raised the scale of capital grant for Catholic schools after 1923 – the Education Acts of 1930, 1947 and 1968 – were all passed while Labour ministers governed in London. Any historian of twentieth-century British history will note that this was an unusual coincidence, and would have been a grave misfortune for the Unionists if Labour ministers had shown a greater willingness to fulfil their obligations under the Government of Ireland Act
59 The Labour Party relied upon Catholic votes in many seats, particularly in Scotland, and was therefore unlikely to be sympathetic to the Unionist government
60 Anderson Memorandum, 26 November 1929. PRONI CAB 9D/1/8
61 PRONI ED 32/A/1/81
62 *Irish Catholic Directory* (1931), p. 594
63 Wilson (1989), pp. 138 and 139
64 Clynes to Devlin, 15 April 1930. DCDA ED 11/30. Clynes was probably guilty of a minor error in quoting Section 51 rather than Section 5 (1) of the 1920 Act. The Act allowed the Governor General or the British Home Secretary to send any law passed by the Northern Ireland Parliament to the Judicial Committee. The presence of the letter in the Down and Connor Diocesan Archives underlines the close cooperation between Nationalist politicians and the Catholic authorities
65 Charlemont Memorandum, 30 October 1929 and 19 February 1930. PRONI CAB 4/239 and CAB 9D/1/8
66 Charlemont may have outlined his proposals in greater detail to the Catholic authorities' representatives, but the PRONI archives offer no clear evidence of the Ministry's specific recommendations
67 PRONI CAB 9D/1/8
68 *Irish News* 23 April 1930
69 *Irish News* 6 May 1930
70 Akenson's book, nearly twenty five years after publication, remains the most incisive and informative account of the conflict between the devolved government and the Protestant clergy for the control of Northern Ireland's schools
71 PRONI ED 32/B/1/2/64. The clerics' efforts were to be unsuccessful
72 *Irish News* 6, 7 and 8 May 1930
73 Craigavon announced the concession himself at a meeting of the County Down Grand Orange Lodge. *Irish News* 9 May 1930
74 Akenson (1973), p. 109
75 MacRory to Mageean, 19 April 1930. DCDA ED 11/30
76 Tierney to Mageean, 16 May 1930. DCDA ED 11/30
77 Cabinet Conclusions, 7 May 1930. PRONI CAB 4/260
78 In late 1934 and early 1935 public meetings in every diocese in Down and Connor in support of segregated boys' and girls' elementary schools failed to influence the Ministry of Education. DCDA ED 11/33–35
79 'We are gravely disappointed'. *Irish News* 9 May 1930
80 Charlemont Memorandum, 19 March 1930. PRONI CAB 9D/1/8. The education committees were not, as Charlemont suggested, bound to be

predominantly Protestant. The Leech Commission and the Cabinet ensured that Protestants secured a majority on all eighteen education committees

81 The exact figures were 79 'unsuitable' schools with 7,737 pupils, and 14,238 pupils in 196 'fairly suitable' schools. The total for 'unsuitable' schools was estimated to be £232,110 with another £427,140 for the 'fairly suitable' schools. Charlemont Memorandum, 26 April 1930. PRONI CAB 4/259

82 The exact figures were £127,505 and £37,082. HC 211, HC 242, HC 269, HC 294, HC 315, HC 349, HC 383, HC 410, HC 440 and HC 483

83 NI Commons XII 1165, 13 May 1930

84 Raymond Burke to Mageean, 22 May 1930. DCDA ED 11/30. The civil servant is not named in the letter, but he was a Scottish Presbyterian and, probably, Lewis McQuibban. McQuibban was the former Secretary of the Ministry of Education, and the Assistant Secretary to the Cabinet in 1930. Akenson (1973), p. 43

85 *Irish News* 15 May 1930. The twelve MPs included Craigavon, four Cabinet ministers, the Attorney General and two junior ministers. The two votes against the clause were cast by John Beattie and Patrick O'Neill of the Northern Ireland Labour Party. NI Commons XII 1251, 14 May 1930

86 NI Commons XII 716, 9 April 1930

87 NI Commons XII 93, 12 March 1930

88 NI Commons XIV 1098, 28 April 1932

89 *Irish News* 3 April 1930

90 NI Commons XII 17, 11 March 1930

91 Ibid., 815, 10 April 1930

92 Akenson (1973), pp. 115 and 116

93 Ibid., p. 117

94 The Memorandum is unsigned, but the handwriting is similar to other examples of Mageean's work in the diocesan archives. The document is contained in the diocesan files for 1946

95 DCDA ED 11/44

96 Akenson (1973), p. 117

97 See Chapter 6

98 Akenson (1973), p. 115

99 The episode in 1927 of the Catholic manager in Fermanagh who was denied adequate refunds for the costs of heating, lighting and cleaning his schools was only one example in the Ministry of Education's archives. The Ministry insisted that the Fermanagh education committee provide the necessary funds and, following press coverage of the case, the education committee reversed their decision. PRONI ED 16/6/9

100 Brownell Memorandum, 1 October 1945. PRONI CAB 9D/1/12

101 Cmd 226 p. 9. The Lynn committee initially recommended that the Ministry of Education be responsible for payments to voluntary schools, but the 1923 Act granted these powers to the education committees. Akenson (1973), pp. 54 and 61

102 Mageean to Tierney, 20 October 1938. DCDA ED 11/38

103 Akenson (1973), p. 116

104 NI Commons XII 90, 12 March 1930

105 *Irish Catholic Directory* (1924), p. 607
106 Cabinet Conclusions, 26 March 1929. PRONI CAB 4/229
107 *Irish News* 1 November 1933
108 Buckland (1979), p. 263
109 Akenson (1973), p. 113
110 Buckland (1979), p. 262
111 The Education Act of 1930 obliged the education committee to provide religious instruction at the request of the parents of ten children attending the school. NI Commons XII 703, 9 April 1930
112 Candidates for teaching appointments in public elementary schools often canvassed the committee members for posts. Akenson (1973), p. 138
113 Ibid., p. 108
114 *Irish Catholic Directory* (1931), pp. 575–576
115 Tierney to Mageean, 21 November 1929. DCDA ED 11/30
116 Tierney to Charlemont, 6 August 1929. DCDA ED 11/30
117 MacCaffrey to Mageean, 17 April 1930. DCDA ED 11/30
118 NI Commons X 1487, 27 March 1929 and XII 717, 9 April 1930
119 NI Commons VIII 531–578, 30 March 1927
120 Tierney to Mageean, 16 May 1930. DCDA ED 11/30
121 Northern Ireland Senate XIII 247, 30 April 1931
122 *Irish Independent* 9 June 1930
123 Mageean to Charlemont, 6 December 1934. PRONI ED 32/A/1/96
124 HC 54 p. 7
125 The education committees spent £193,259 on 198 transferred schools. The exact figure for provided schools was 17,712 places for £544,215. HC 269 p. 57
126 HC 80 p. 7
127 Provided schools were entirely new schools built by the education committees
128 HC 269 p. 49
129 Cmd 226 p. 11
130 HC 54 p. 32
131 HC 131 p. 5
132 HC 54 p. 32 and HC 131 p. 5
133 The exact figures were £343,803 and 10,014 places and £200,412 and 7,698 places respectively. HC 269 p. 57
134 Atkinson (1969), p. 177
135 Cmd 6 p. 38
136 Buckland (1979), p. 251
137 HC 54 p. 7
138 HC 154 p. 9. At the end of 1927 36,304 of 127,417 Protestant pupils, a quarter of the total, were attending public elementary schools. HC 242 pp. 52 and 53
139 HC 154 p. 9
140 HC 180 pp. 10 and 11
141 HC 211 pp. 8 and 9
142 Appendices B and C
143 NI Commons XII 725, 9 April 1930
144 Akenson also states that the 1930 Act did not accelerate the pace of transfers. Akenson (1973), p. 140

145 HC 131 p. 10 and HC 154 p. 9. The number of transfers in 1927 is not explicitly stated, but the Report notes that the total number of transfers had more than doubled to 242 during the year
146 HC 180 p. 9, HC 211 p. 8 and HC 242 p. 9. Eighty-one schools transferred in 1928, but the following year's Report only states that the education committees were responsible for an additional eighty-seven provided and transferred schools
147 HC 242 p. 9 and HC 269 p. 17
148 HC 269 p. 17, HC 294 p. 11 and HC 315 p. 10
149 HC 349 p. 8, HC 383 p. 10 and HC 410 p. 10
150 Appendices C and D
151 HC 294 p. 12
152 HC 107 p. 9
153 Akenson (1973) pp. 115 and 117
154 HC 294 pp. 30 and 33
155 There were only eleven non-Catholic voluntary schools in the city by the end of the 1930s. Farren (1995), p. 134
156 Holmes (1970), p. 20
157 Cabinet Conclusions, 28 February 1923. PRONI CAB 4/72
158 Holmes (1970), p. 28
159 The Ministry of Education funded 550 places for 'four and two' schools between 1923 and the end of 1931 at a cost of less than £7,000. The Ministry also provided a further £10,000 for improvements to existing 'four and two' schools. Appendix F
160 The education committees were educating 22,090 of 128,811 Protestant pupils in provided schools at the end of December 1930. HC 242 p. 39. The exact figures were £680,290 and £236,663. HC 294 p. 36
161 The exact figures were 3,226 places and £49,572. HC 294 p. 37
162 The exact figures were 19,064 public elementary school places and 4,757 voluntary school places. Appendices F and H
163 71,789 of 191,862 pupils. HC 483 p. 43
164 The exact figures were 444 and 5,520. Appendices F and H
165 The exact figures were £1,815,363 for public elementary schools and £164,587 for voluntary schools. Appendices F and H
166 The exact figures were £120,282 of £142,989 and £4,980 of £19,940. NI Commons XVIII 1257 and 1258, 5 May 1936
167 NI Commons XXII 1059, 20 April 1939
168 The exact figures were £898,410 and £105,015. Appendices F and H
169 Charlemont Memorandum, 26 April 1930. PRONI CAB 4/259
170 Appendix H
171 Campbell asked Robb in July 1935 for the numbers, but Robb claimed that the information was not available. NI Commons XVII 2387, 10 July 1935
172 *Irish News* 1 November 1933
173 Brownell Memorandum, 1 October 1945. PRONI CAB 9D/1/12
174 Cmd 226 p. 9
175 The National League was formed in 1928 to unite moderate nationalists in Northern Ireland for the 1929 Northern Ireland elections. The label was to disappear in subsequent polls, but the basic organisation survived until the 1960s

176 *Irish News* 20 February 1930
177 *Irish Independent* 9 April 1930. In September 1930 Mageean contradicted his earlier statement when he stated: 'people who know the school conditions in our city ask me why we are not making some effort to build our schools. I wish to say now, publicly, that if there has been a delay we are not responsible for it'. *Irish News* 18 September 1930
178 *Irish Independent* 9 June 1930
179 NI Commons XVII 2387, 10 July 1935
180 Robb Memorandum, 15 May 1939. PRONI CAB 4/417
181 At the end of 1938 there were 91,510 pupils in voluntary schools, with a further 6,873 pupils in 'four and two' schools, whilst there were 71,789 Catholic pupils in elementary schools. HC 483 pp. 38 and 43
182 Cmd 15 p. 55
183 William Coote, Unionist MP for Fermanagh and Tyrone. NI Commons III 30, 27 February 1923
184 Captain Henry Mulholland, Unionist MP for Down. NI Commons III 672, 2 May 1923
185 Robert Crawford, Unionist MP for Antrim. NI Commons III 673, 2 May 1923
186 Dr Hugh Morrison, Unionist MP for Queen's University, Belfast. NI Commons III 674, 2 May 1923
187 NI Commons III 1092, 29 May 1923
188 PRONI ED 13/1/12
189 Cmd 15 p. 83
190 PRONI ED 13/1/12
191 PRONI ED 13/1/12
192 PRONI ED 13/1/54
193 PRONI ED 13/1/12
194 PRONI ED 13/1/12
195 Bardon (1992), p. 528
196 There is no evidence of criticism in either Hansard or the *Irish Catholic Directory*
197 Akenson (1973), p. 135
198 The Ministry estimated that the Order would require £15,000 to maintain its eight schools. McQuibban to Londonderry, 20 October 1925. PRONI ED 13/1/565
199 PRONI ED 13/1/565
200 Wyse Memorandum, 13 October 1925. PRONI ED 13/1/565
201 McQuibban to Charlemont, 26 March 1926. PRONI ED 13/1/565
202 *Irish News* 30 April 1927
203 PRONI ED 13/1/819
204 *Studies* (June 1930), No. 74 p. 67
205 Murray (1985), p. 114
206 The League was 'a Society where membership is confined solely to men and women of British race and blood, which will work primarily for the benefit of that race, its Country and its Empire and which recognises, to obtain this end, alien races must be eliminated from all our Councils and National Institutions'. PRONI CAB 9D/44/1
207 Edward Clarke to Craigavon, 10 July 1928. PRONI CAB 9D/44/1

208 Wyse to Blackmore, 20 June 1928. PRONI CAB 9D/44/1
209 NI Commons XV 959 and 1082, 21 March and 25 April 1933
210 NI Commons XV 773, 9 March 1933
211 Buckland (1981), p. 70
212 Charlemont Memorandum, 21 April 1933. PRONI CAB 9D/44/1
213 Charlemont to Craigavon, 22 April 1933. PRONI CAB 9D/44/1
214 Farren (1989), p. 277
215 NI Commons XV 1078 and 1087, 25 April 1933
216 Farren (1995), p. 138
217 Buckland (1980), p. 105
218 Spender to Blackmore, 30 December 1927. PRONI CAB 9D/136. Quoted in Buckland (1980), p. 107
219 The exact figures were 10,602 pupils in 140 schools. NI Commons XVII 466, 11 December 1934
220 At the end of 1933 there were 682 Catholic schools educating 73,969 pupils. NI Commons XVI 2713, 13 November 1934
221 At the end of 1936, 9,358 elementary school pupils were examined in Gaelic. The following year the figure rose slightly to 9,391 pupils. NI Commons XIX 676 and XXII 411, 23 March 1937 and 9 March 1939
222 NI Commons XVII 335, 4 December 1934
223 The abolition of the grant also provoked a decline in the number of pupils offering to be examined in Gaelic, and by the end of 1936 the figure had fallen to 922 pupils before rising slightly to 931 pupils at the end of 1937. NI Commons XIX 676 and XXII 411, 23 March 1937 and 9 March 1939
224 Wyse to Blackmore, 5 January 1929. PRONI ED 32/A/1/58. Quoted in Harris (1994), p. 221
225 NI Commons XIX 677, 23 March 1937. No candidates for graduation at Stranmillis college opted for Gaelic as a subject
226 NI Commons XVIII 567, XIX 676 and XXII 411, 12 March 1936, 23 March 1937 and 9 March 1939
227 The *Irish Catholic Directory* contains no references to the loss of the language grants
228 NI Commons XVI 2734–2748, 13 November 1934. PRONI ED 13/1/865. DCDA ED 11/33–35
229 NI Commons XXV 619 and XXVII 780, 12 March 1942 and 22 March 1944
230 Robb to Andrews, 7 January 1943. PRONI CAB 9D/44/1
231 Akenson has highlighted the exemptions and concessions weaved into the Act. Akenson (1973), p. 145
232 Minutes of meeting of 27 July 1938. PRONI ED 13/1/1685
233 NI Commons XXI 1529 and 1530, 12 October 1938
234 Simon (1991), p. 218
235 Robb Memorandum, 4 May 1939. PRONI CAB 4/417
236 Robb Memorandum, 4 May 1939. PRONI CAB 4/417
237 Cabinet Conclusions, 15 May 1939. PRONI CAB 4/417
238 HC 783 p. 16
239 Farren (1995), p. 161
240 NI Commons XXV 1706, 30 June 1942
241 *Irish News* 3 February 1932

242 Farren (1995), p. 104

243 See Chapter 4

244 Catholics comprised 73,838 of 200,607 pupils, 36.8% of the total, at the end of 1935 and 42.7% of the schools on the 'condemned' list. HC 384 p. 37 and PRONI ED 13/1/1761

245 *Irish Catholic Directory* (1931), pp. 575–576

CHAPTER FOUR

1 Elliott (1973), p. 117

2 Cmd 226

3 *Belfast Telegraph* 16 December 1949

4 As late as June 1956 critics of the government's education policy were calling for the repeal of the grant increases for voluntary schools contained in the 1947 Education Act. NI Commons XL 1922, 12 June 1956

5 Farren (1981), p. 244

6 Secondary intermediate schools were designed to offer a less 'academic' education than grammar schools. They could be viewed as Northern Ireland's equivalent of the British 'secondary modern' school

7 Akenson (1973), p. 16

8 NI Commons I 106, 21 September 1921

9 The exact figure was 14,557 pupils. Cmd 226 p. 7

10 Cmd 226 p. 21. The White Paper used the terms 'junior secondary' and 'senior secondary' schools to describe the two categories which later became secondary intermediate and grammar schools, but the wording was abandoned before the publication of the Education Bill. The latter terms will be employed when discussing the White Paper to avoid unnecessary confusion

11 Cmd 226 p. 15

12 The eight education authorities were created by the 1923 Act, but the Act allowed for the partition of the county between education committees. See Chapter 2

13 Wyse Memorandum, 31 January 1933. PRONI ED 13/1/1637 and 1638

14 Hall-Thompson Memorandum, 25 July 1944. PRONI CAB 4/594

15 There is no evidence in the protracted debates surrounding the Education Bill of opposition from Unionist MPs but, in the autumn of 1950, Antrim's county council sought to create two education committees. Midgley opposed the idea, and the proposal was eventually abandoned. NI Commons XXXIV 2029, 12 December 1950 and XXXV 105, 22 February 1951

16 Cmd 226 p. 27

17 The 1947 Act fused the provided and transferred categories to create the 'county' school

18 O'Neill (1972), p. 28

19 Hall-Thompson Memorandum, 25 May 1944. PRONI CAB 9D/1/10

20 In March 1942 a delegation including Professor Corkey of the UEC, the Church of Ireland Primate and the eminent historian J. C. Beckett of the

Royal Academy visited Robb to demand religious instruction in secondary schools. Robb offered them only a circular to the boards of governors of secondary schools urging them to pay greater attention to religious instruction. Minutes of meeting of 4 March 1942. Robb Circular, 18 May 1942. PRONI CAB 9D/1/10

21 Farren (1995), p. 157 and *Irish News* 1 November 1944

22 Hall-Thompson Memorandum, 25 May 1944. PRONI CAB 4/586

23 The Attorney General was obliged to certify that all Acts of the Northern Ireland Parliament were *inter vires* under the terms of the Government of Ireland Act

24 Cabinet Conclusions, 20 July 1944. PRONI CAB 4/593

25 Hall-Thompson Memorandum, Cabinet Conclusions 20 July 1944. PRONI CAB 4/593

26 Lowry Memorandum, 15 November 1944. PRONI CAB 4/606. As Home Secretary, in May 1944 Lowry opposed the compulsion of teachers in public elementary schools on the grounds that it would weaken the case against increased funding for Catholic schools. Cabinet Conclusions, 30 May 1944. PRONI CAB 4/587

27 In February 1929 the Attorney General, Anthony Babington, advised against the proposals later contained in the Education Bill for compulsory Bible instruction in public elementary schools, but three months later he changed his opinion and sanctioned the Bill. Brownell Memorandum, 2 March 1950. PRONI CAB 9D/1/20

28 Cmd 226 pp. 24 and 25

29 Hall-Thompson wrote to Chancellor Quinn the following day to confirm the Cabinet's decision to pursue an amendment to the 1920 Act. Hall-Thompson to Chancellor Quinn, 21 July 1944. PRONI ED 32/B/1/9/91

30 Cabinet Conclusions, 18 January 1945. PRONI CAB 4/611

31 Hall-Thompson Memorandum, 13 October 1944. PRONI CAB 9D/1/10

32 Minutes of meeting of 11 January 1945. PRONI CAB 9D/1/10. Somervell's contentions were directly challenged by Lowry when he claimed in his Northern Ireland Commons speech that the Free State Agreement Act of 1923 also did not allow for denominational teaching. NI Commons XXVII 2850, 25 January 1945

33 Hall-Thompson Memorandum, 20 July 1944. PRONI CAB 4/593. Two representatives of the Ulster Teachers' Union claimed there was no evidence of a reluctance by public elementary school teachers to teach religious instruction between 1923 and 1930. *Belfast Telegraph* 24 January 1945

34 *Irish News* 9 February 1945. In May 1945 Hall-Thompson assured the Northern Ireland Commons that 'Protestant teachers will be provided for Protestant schools'. NI Commons XXVIII 841, 16 May 1945

35 The leading Nationalist MP, Thomas Campbell, even stated that the prohibition against obliging teachers to teach religious instruction in public elementary schools hindered any possible transfer of Catholic schools. NI Commons XXVII 2797, 24 January 1945. Campbell may have been overstating the Catholic clergy's willingness to transfer their schools simply to disconcert the government, but the Catholic authorities were not seeking an amendment to the 1930 Act

36 A Labour MP raised the question of religious instruction in public elementary schools in the United Kingdom Commons, but the Home Secretary, Herbert Morrison, stated that the issue was a matter for the government in Northern Ireland. John Nixon, Unionist MP for Woolvale in Belfast, claimed that Herbert Morrison would not interfere with education policy in Northern Ireland. NI Commons XXVIII 394, 14 March 1945

37 Cabinet Conclusions, 18 January 1945. PRONI CAB 4/611

38 *Irish News* 26 January 1945. The editorial continued with a joke in very poor taste at the expense of the thousands of Londoners suffering death and injury from German V rockets when it commented 'since the Attorney General is relying chiefly on the first part of Section 5 of the Government of Ireland Act, it is not without interest that it is a Constitutional V–1 which has rocked the Government and its education measure to the foundation'

39 NI Commons XVII 2852 and 2853, 25 January 1945 and Akenson (1973), p. 171

40 The Cabinet envisaged parents, representatives of the education committee and Protestant clerics each comprising one third of the school committee. Cabinet Conclusions, 10 December 1945. PRONI CAB 4/647

41 The Cabinet confirmed Brooke's opposition to the UEC. Cabinet Conclusions, 15 October 1945. PRONI CAB 4/637

42 Cabinet Conclusions, 28 March 1946. PRONI CAB 4/662. In the spring of 1950 the Secretary of the Ministry of Education, Reginald Brownell, visited London to see Sir Alexander Maxwell, former Permanent Secretary at the Home Office, to discuss possible changes to the 1947 Act following the resignation of Hall-Thompson in December 1949. Maxwell claimed that the Protestant clergy's insistence upon an effective majority on the school committees of the new secondary intermediate schools was the most unacceptable feature of the 1947 Act. Brownell to Midgley, 3 April 1950. PRONI ED 32/1/9/153

43 NI Commons XXXVIII 2087, 13 May 1954

44 Cabinet Conclusions, 28 March 1946. PRONI CAB 4/662. Brownell claimed that the concessions to the Protestant clergy allowing effective control of the school committees of the new secondary intermediate schools was the primary reason for the government allowing an unconditional sixty-five per cent grant for voluntary schools. Brownell Memorandum, 20 February 1950. PRONI CAB 9D/1/20

45 *Irish Catholic Directory* (1945), p. 670

46 In November 1945 Strabane regional education committee discussed a motion to postpone the proposed Education Bill for ten years, and Farren wrote to Mageean that 'if we could encourage that generally it might solve our present difficulties'. Farren to Mageean, 23 November 1945. DCDA ED 11/44

47 Hall-Thompson lost his seat for the Clifton constituency of Belfast at the 1953 election to Norman Porter of the National Union of Protestants. Porter won 4,747 votes to Hall-Thompson's 4,402. Elliott 38. Sixteen years later, Hall-Thompson's son, standing as a 'liberal' Unionist, recovered his father's seat. O'Neill (1972), p. 122

48 Hall-Thompson believed he was pursuing constructive discussions with the Catholic authorities. In August 1945 he wrote to the Nationalist MP T. J. Campbell of his cordial meetings with 'the selected representatives of your Church'. Hall-Thompson to Campbell, 31 August 1945. PRONI CAB 9D/1/13

In contrast, by December 1945 Hall-Thompson was exasperated by the attitude of the UEC, complaining to his colleagues that further negotiations were futile. He offered the Cabinet the alternatives of either ignoring the UEC's agitation or abandoning educational reconstruction. Hall-Thompson Memorandum, 5 December 1945. PRONI CAB 4/647

49 'Dean MacDonald referred to the growing tendency on the part of some young mothers to disregard their responsibilities towards their own children and accept employment when their husbands were already receiving adequate wages'. Minutes of meeting of 22 May 1944. PRONI ED 13/1/2129

50 Minutes of meeting of 5 June 1944. PRONI ED 13/1/2129

51 The Catholic clerics also sought exemption from local rates and full funding for the costs of heating, lighting and cleaning schools. Minutes of meeting of 5 June 1944. PRONI ED 13/1/2129

52 Hall-Thompson Memorandum, 25 July 1944. PRONI CAB 4/594

53 Cabinet Conclusions, 25 July 1944. PRONI CAB 4/594. Brooke's apprehensions appeared excessive. By 1946 there were less than 11,000 Protestant pupils attending voluntary schools. HC 822 pp. 29 and 32

54 Hall-Thompson Memorandum, 9 October 1944. Cabinet Conclusions, 12 October 1944. PRONI CAB 4/601. The divisions within the Cabinet may have encouraged the wealthy Fermanagh Catholic, Sir Shane Leslie, to act as an intermediary for Cardinal MacRory during the winter of 1944. Farren (1995), p. 174

55 Minutes of meeting of 25 October 1944. PRONI ED 13/1/2129

56 Akenson (1973), p. 162. Shea also writes of Hall-Thompson as 'no intellectual heavyweight, but a fair-minded man'. Shea (1981), p. 160

57 *Irish News* 28 March 1945

58 *Irish News* 12 February 1945

59 *Irish News* 12 February 1945

60 *Irish News* 29 March 1945

61 *Irish News* 29 March 1945

62 Brownell Memorandum, 29 March 1945. PRONI CAB 9D/1/11

63 Hendricks to Londonderry, 27 January 1926. PRONI D 3099/5/14/4

64 Shea (1981), p. 159

65 Ibid., p. 160

66 Walker (1985), p. 212

67 Shea (1981), p. 165. Shea also mentions that Brownell only once called him by his first name; during their final meeting the day before Brownell retired. Brownell may have been reserved, but he told Shea that he was unlikely to be promoted because he was a Catholic. Ibid., p. 177

68 Ibid., p. 160

69 Ibid.

70 Chuter Ede was not only a former teacher, but had previously served as 'Rab' Butler's deputy at the British Ministry of Education. *Irish News* 12 December 1944

71 *Irish News* 4 November 1944
72 Brownell to Hall-Thompson, 1 October 1944. PRONI CAB 9D/1/12
73 Brownell Memorandum, 4 March 1946. PRONI CAB 9D/1/16
74 PRONI CAB 9D/1/16
75 Hall-Thompson Memorandum, 5 October 1945. PRONI CAB 9D/1/13
76 Hall-Thompson Memorandum, 5 October 1945. PRONI CAB 9D/1/13
77 Cabinet Conclusions, 15 October 1945. PRONI CAB 4/637
78 Ibid.
79 Cabinet Conclusions, 28 March 1946. PRONI CAB 4/662
80 Ibid.
81 Hall-Thompson Memorandum, 14 June 1946. PRONI CAB 4/675
82 The Act allowed voluntary schools to claim seventy-five per cent of the capital expenses for additional work needed to educate children beyond the age of fourteen, but an astute clerical manager would be able to convince most education authorities that any major project was necessary to implement the Act. The law was due to take effect from 1 September 1939, but Britain's war with Germany began the following day and postponed all investment in schools
83 Brownell Memorandum, 20 February 1950. PRONI ED 32/B/1/2/5
84 Akenson (1973), p. 180
85 Animosity towards Catholic schools was not the only issue for critics of Hall-Thompson's proposals. The Bill intended to impose the burden of funding the National Insurance contributions upon ratepayers rather taxpayers. Akenson (1973), p. 187. Farren, though, is correct to note that 'the controversy was quite unnecessary and, because of its sectarian overtones, quite nasty'. Farren (1995), p. 212
86 Hall-Thompson Memorandum, 24 October 1949. PRONI CAB 4/797. The issue of boarding scholarships for Catholic pupils was a constant problem for the Ministry of Education. Brownell's memorandum to Hall-Thompson of 1 October 1945 quoted this as one of the most significant abuses of the education system. The White Paper of December 1944 favoured 'the choice of school in each individual case being left so far as possible to the parents and the school concerned'. Cmd 226 p. 21. Some education authorities refused to provide scholarships for Catholic grammar schools, insisting that the nearest county grammar school, where the teachers were chosen by the local Protestant clergy, was a suitable school for Catholic pupils
87 The election also allowed the Unionists to overwhelm the NILP after their successes in the 1945 elections. The NILP lost all four MPs, and their vote fell from more than 66,000 votes to just 26,000 votes. The independent labour vote also fell from over 47,000 votes in 1945 to less than 8,000 votes in 1949. The NILP was to remain without any MPs until 1958. Elliott (1973), p. 116
88 The Nationalists did not seek to exploit the restoration of the primacy of the constitutional issue in the 1949 election to overthrow the two nationalist 'Labour' MPs in the Belfast's two 'Catholic' seats – Central and Falls. Frank Hanna and Harry Diamond were both returned unopposed in 1949. Elliott (1973), pp. 37 and 42

89 *Belfast Telegraph* 29 December 1949

90 Akenson (1973), p. 187

91 Brownell Memorandum, 14 December 1949. PRONI ED 32/B/1/2/5

92 By the early 1950s less than 3,000 Protestant pupils attended voluntary schools compared to over 100,000 pupils in county schools. Cmd 351 p. 29

93 Cabinet Conclusions, 15 December 1949. PRONI CAB 4/803

94 NI Commons XXXIII 2276, 15 December 1949

95 Lee is incorrect to claim that Hall-Thompson was the victim of a clerical vendetta in 1949. Lee (1989), p. 412. The 1949 crisis was orchestrated by Unionist politicians rather than Protestant clerics, and the Presbyterian education committee supported Hall-Thompson's proposals. Akenson (1973), p. 187

96 Hall-Thompson Memorandum, 23 December 1949. PRONI CAB 9D/1/20

97 Hall-Thompson Memorandum, 23 December 1949. PRONI CAB 9D/1/20

98 *Irish News* 2 January 1950

99 Brooke to Glentoran, 15 December 1949. PRONI CAB 9D/1/17. Brooke's comments may have been a subtle invitation, because the *Belfast Telegraph* quoted Glentoran as a possible candidate for the vacancy. *Belfast Telegraph* 16 December 1949

    Brooke may have considered Glentoran as a possibility, but he would have soon faced the problem of finding a new Minister of Education because Glentoran died the following July. NI Commons XXXIV 1432, 25 July 1950

100 *Belfast Telegraph* 16 December 1949. Shea wrote of Brooke's choice: 'he had, indeed, seemed an unlikely candidate for Education. People asked if Brookeborough was mad. Others, remembering that every previous Minister of Education had to leave because of a disagreement with his Cabinet colleagues or a clash with some of the powerful influences concerned with education, wondered if the Prime Minister was hoping that Education would rid him of his turbulent convert'. Shea (1981), p. 162

101 Dunn (1990), p. 22

102 Graham Walker provides an able account of Midgley's political career in his sympathetic biography *The Politics of Frustration: Harry Midgley and the Failure of Labour in Northern Ireland* (Manchester, 1985)

103 Akenson (1973), p. 191

104 Walker (1985), p. 211

105 Edward McAteer, Nationalist MP for Mid Londonderry, claimed that the Orange Order had been involved in the replacement of Hall-Thompson by Midgley. NI Commons XXXIII 2369–2370, 17 January 1950

106 Shea (1981), p. 162

107 Midgley joined the Unionist government as Minister of Public Security in May 1943 after John Andrews was ousted as Prime Minister by Sir Basil Brooke. He moved to the Ministry of Labour in June 1944, where he remained until he left the government in the summer of 1945 to lead the Commonwealth Labour Party in the Westminster and Northern Ireland elections. Walker (1985), pp. 148, 156 and 166

108 Cabinet Conclusions, 25 July 1944. PRONI CAB 4/594

109 PRONI CAB 9D/1/10

110 Walker states that Midgley 'rarely wasted an opportunity to make life uncomfortable for Hall-Thompson', and Akenson refers to Midgley being 'dogged in his opposition' to the increase in capital funding for Catholic schools. Walker (1985), p. 192 and Akenson (1973), p. 179
111 NI Commons XXX 2671, 14 November 1946
112 NI Commons XXX 2677 and 2674, 14 November 1946
113 Shea (1981), p. 161
114 Farren (1995), p. 211
115 Walker (1985), p. 191
116 Cabinet Conclusions, 18 November 1949. PRONI CAB 9D/1/17
117 Walker (1985), pp. 198 and 211
118 Shea (1981), p. 166
119 Midgley Memorandum, 22 March 1950 and 16 January 1951. PRONI CAB 9D/1/20 and CAB 4/837
120 Midgley Memorandum, 16 January 1951. PRONI CAB 4/837
121 The Cabinet approved both measures, but the scheme was abandoned after the Attorney General ruled that allowing the school committee to supervise religious instruction contravened the Government of Ireland Act of 1920. Midgley Memorandum, 11 September 1950. PRONI CAB 9D/1/20
122 Brownell to Midgley, 3 April 1950. PRONI ED 32/1/9/153. A few days earlier Midgley informed his colleagues that the British government would only object to his proposals if there was opposition from MPs in Westminster. Midgley Memorandum, 28 March 1950. PRONI ED 32/B/1/2/5
123 Midgley Memorandum, 11 September 1950. PRONI CAB 9D/1/20
124 PRONI CAB 9D/1/20
125 Walker (1985), p. 211
126 Cabinet Conclusions, 2 March 1943. PRONI CAB 4/533
127 Corkey Memorandum, 23 June 1943 and Cabinet Conclusions, 29 June 1943. PRONI CAB 4/548
128 PRONI ED 13/1/35
129 Hall-Thompson Memorandum, 30 March 1945. PRONI CAB 4/621
      Hall-Thompson was also concerned by the threat of the Church of Ireland's bishops asking for trainees to attend their teacher training college in Kildare Place, Dublin.
130 Cabinet Conclusions, 12 April 1945. PRONI CAB 4/621
131 The Ministry of Education estimated that the Catholic men's hostel would cost £130,000. Midgley Memorandum, 2 July 1954. PRONI CAB 4/943
132 Midgley Memorandum, 19 March 1952. PRONI CAB 4/870
133 Minute of meeting of 1 February 1952, PRONI CAB ED 32/B/1/9/13
134 Cabinet Conclusions, 26 March 1952. PRONI CAB 4/870
135 The five bishops were D'Alton of Armagh, Mageean of Down and Connor, Farren of Derry, O'Callaghan of Clogher and O'Doherty of Dromore. The only absentee was Bishop Quinn of Kilmore. PRONI ED/B/1/9/24
136 Midgley Memorandum, 19 March 1952. PRONI CAB 4/870

137 Minutes of meeting of 20 May 1953. PRONI ED 32/B/1/9/24

138 Cabinet Conclusions, 24 July 1953 and 19 August 1953. PRONI CAB 4/912 and CAB 4/913

139 Brownell Memorandum, 8 December 1953. PRONI ED/32/B/1/9/24

140 D'Alton to Brooke, 7 September 1953. PRONI ED 32/B/1/9/24

141 PRONI ED 32/B/1/9/24

142 Midgley Memorandum, 8 January 1954. PRONI CAB 4/925

143 Brooke to Mageean, 15 January 1954. PRONI ED 32/B/1/9/24

144 The episode reached an unsatisfactory conclusion for the Catholic authorities in September 1955 when Mageean proposed Trench House as the site for the men's hostel, and accepted the sixty-five per cent grant from the Ministry. Midgley Memorandum, 5 August 1955. PRONI CAB 4/980

145 NI Commons XXXX 530–531, 7 March 1956

146 Porter was viewed as the champion of the ultra Protestant elements within Ulster unionism. *Irish Press* 5 February 1955. Quoted in Walker (1985), p. 205

147 NI Commons XXXX 544, 7 March 1956

148 Brooke and Midgley both claimed that Midgley was only quoting from Blanshard's *The Irish and Catholic Power*, and that his remarks were misquoted by a newspaper reporter who was considered 'suspect' by Portadown Unionists. NI Commons XLI 484–506, 28 February 1957

149 Walker (1985), p. 205

150 Blanshard (1954), pp. 233 and 234. Quoted in Walker (1985), p. 208

151 Midgley to Dr McIlroy, 15 April 1953. PRONI CAB 9D/1/20

152 Midgley Memorandum, 4 August 1954. PRONI CAB 4/944

153 PRONI CAB 9D/59/2

154 The official figures were 904 county pupils and 90,679 voluntary pupils. Cmd 392 33

155 Dunn (1993), p. 22

156 Shea (1981), p. 172

157 Hall-Thompson's predecessor, Robert Corkey, may have proved to be as militant a Minister of Education as Midgley, but he was Minister for less than a year

158 The only potential confusion arises from the presence of three St Patrick's colleges which, possibly, were Protestant establishments. These, however, have been counted as Catholic schools

159 Cmd 322 pp. 37, 50, 51 and 52

160 Hall-Thompson Memorandum, 14 June 1944. PRONI CAB 9D/1/12

161 Cmd 226 p. 21

162 Farren (1995), p. 170

163 Cmd 226 p. 28

164 The only concession required of the grammar schools was to pledge to allow eighty per cent of the pupils to be selected from pupils passing the scholarship examination. Cmd 226 p. 21

165 *Belfast Telegraph* 19 December 1949

166 Midgley Memorandum, 22 March 1950. PRONI ED 32/B/1/2/5

167 Midgley Memorandum, 15 February 1950. PRONI CAB 4/809

168 Midgley Memorandum, 7 March 1950. PRONI CAB 4/813. Midgley's private concerns for the fate of grammar schools contrasted with his public statement in the Northern Ireland Commons only three weeks later that the thirty-five per cent voluntary contribution for grammar schools could only be paid by private funds. NI Commons XXXIV 2064, 12 December 1950

169 Cabinet Conclusions, 27 March 1950. PRONI CAB 4/813

170 Minutes of meeting of 19 June 1950. PRONI ED 32/B/1/9/13

171 Cabinet Conclusions, 15 February 1951. PRONI CAB 4/838
    In October 1952 the Cabinet discussed further financial assistance for 'unqualified' pupils and Parker once again argued the grammar schools' case. Midgley and the Minister of Finance, John Sinclair, asserted that money pledged to grammar schools was slowing the growth of the secondary intermediate schools, but the Cabinet granted yet more public funds to the voluntary grammar schools. Cabinet Conclusions, 29 October 1952. PRONI CAB 4/886

172 *Belfast Telegraph* 10 May 1957. PRONI ED 32/B/1/9/61. The motion was not discussed, and there is no reliable means of confirming the contents

173 Farren (1995), p. 214

174 Cabinet Conclusions, 18 November 1949. PRONI CAB 4/799

175 Cabinet Conclusions, 18 November 1949. PRONI CAB 4/799

176 *Belfast Telegraph* 22 January 1945. The Association was not antagonistic to all distinctions. The meeting opposed the Catholic authorities' calls for improved funding for voluntary schools, and criticised Hall-Thompson for failing to reach an accommodation with the Protestant churches on the 'conscience clause'

177 Hall-Thompson Memorandum, 23 December 1949. PRONI CAB 9D/1/20

178 SACHR (1989), pp. 43 and 142

179 Farren (1995), p. 214

180 Walker (1985), p. 165. Shea also claims that Midgley was opposed to increased aid for voluntary schools because it was 'an attitude which was in accordance with his former Socialist affiliations'. Shea (1981), p. 162

181 Walker (1985), p. 53

182 NI Commons XXX 2761, 14 November 1946

183 The number of pupils attending provided public elementary schools only increased from 38,621 at the end of 1938 to 39,930 at the end of 1945. HC 483 p. 38 and HC 783 p. 35

184 The few German raids against Belfast in 1941 did cause extensive damage to the city. Bardon (1992), pp. 564–574

185 NI Commons XXX 1131, 6 June 1946 and XLI 1351, 30 May 1957

186 NI Commons XLIV 733, 19 March 1959

187 HC 883 p. 7 and Cmd 313 p. 9

188 Cmd 322 pp. 9 and 14

189 Cmd 338 p. 6

190 Cmd 380 p. 9

191 Cmd 392 p. 5

192 Appendix I. The Ministry of Education's statistics do not allow for a comparison of the scale of development of Protestant and Catholic

voluntary grammar schools. Therefore these schools have not been included in the overall calculations of the financial cost of the voluntary contribution. Also, Protestant voluntary grammar schools faced the same financial penalties as Catholic voluntary grammar schools

193 Appendices I and J
194 Cmd 392 p. 5
195 NI Commons XLII 412, 30 April 1958
196 NI Commons XXX 2096, 16 October 1946
197 The exact statistics were 28,546 places for county schools and 10,735 places for voluntary schools. Appendices I and J
198 The figures quoted in the Northern Ireland Commons were £9,800,000 and £2,671,000. NI Commons XL 2097 20 June 1956
199 Cmd 380 p. 39
200 There is also evidence of notable differences in the public funding for Stranmillis and St Mary's as recently as the early 1990s, with St Mary's training more students whilst receiving a smaller grant from the DENI than Stranmillis. UK Commons Sixth Series 192 592 and 593, 12 June 1991. The exact figures were as follows:

		1988–89	*1989–90*	*1990–91*
Pupils	Stranmillis	736	782	756
	St Mary's	766	796	781
Grant	Stranmillis	£3.544m	£3.836m	£4.117m
	St Mary's	£3.345m	£4.032m	£4.032m

201 PRONI ED 13/1/2463, ED 13/1/2466 and ED 13/1/2468
202 PRONI ED 13/1/2463. Farren also notes that the Catholic dioceses prepared their development plans before most education authorities offered their schemes. Farren (1995), p. 217
203 Farren (1995), p. 217
204 NI Commons XXX 2718 and 4354, 20 November 1946 and 25 February 1947. The incident at Stranmillis was only raised in November 1946, during the controversy surrounding the Education Bill
205 NI Commons XXX 4720, 11 March 1947
206 The Act was partly motivated by the Unionist government's efforts to sustain the constitutional issue after losing votes in the 1953 elections. Elliott (1973), pp. 92 and 93
207 NI Commons XXXVIII 1169, 4 March 1954
208 NI Commons XXXVIII 2451 and 2452, 2 June 1954
209 NI Commons XXXIX 2747, 4 May 1955
210 NI Commons XLIV 671 and 781, 19 March 1959 and XLVI 1933, 9 June 1960.
211 NI Commons XLVI 1935, 9 June 1960
212 Farren (1995), p. 49
213 Mageean to Brownell, 15 March 1943. PRONI ED 13/1/327A
214 PRONI ED 13/1/327A

215 PRONI ED 13/1/327A
216 NI Commons XXXIX 2989, 13 December 1955
217 NI Commons XXXIX 3153, 25 January 1956
218 NI Commons XXXX 396, 410, 425 and 441, 1 March 1956. 531, 7 March
    1956. 1049 and 1143, 3 and 9 May 1956
219 NI Commons XXX 1165, 6 June 1946
220 NI Commons XXXII 1705, 26 May 1948
221 NI Commons XXXIII 244 and 556, 14 March and 5 April 1949
222 NI Commons XXXIV 86, 7 March 1950
223 NI Commons XXXV 1227, 23 May 1951
224 NI Commons XXXVII 602, 1 April 1953
225 NI Commons XXXVIII 2087, 13 May 1954
226 Ibid.
227 NI Commons XLI 1348 and 1392, 30 May 1957. Northern Ireland's
    schoolchildren would have been grievously misled if they were taught
    that 'Northern Ireland' existed in 1690
228 NI Commons LXI 1601 and XLIV 2130, 12 June 1957 and 9 July 1959
229 NI Commons XLI 1392, 30 May 1957
230 NI Commons XXX 4750, 13 March 1947
231 NI Commons XXXI 463–464, 15 May 1947
232 NI Commons XXXVII 855 and 871, 16 April 1953. XXXIX 1196, 4 May
    1955. XXXXI 1606, 12 June 1957
233 NI Commons XXXX 428, 1 March 1956
234 NI Commons XL 1922, 12 June 1956
235 NI Commons XL 1923 and 1933, 12 June 1956
236 NI Commons XL 1941, 12 June 1956
237 *Irish Catholic Directory* (1955), p. 639
238 Farren (1995), p. 221
239 Farren (1995), p. 186
240 O'Neill (1972), p. 47
241 Farren (1995), p. 215
242 Ibid., p. 215

CHAPTER FIVE

1 Farrell (1980), p. 228
2 The second name was in honour of the Allied success at the River Marne
  in the summer of 1914
3 NI Commons LIX 128, 2 February 1965
4 *Irish Ecclesiastical Record* XCIV (July 1960), p. 1
5 Barritt and Carter (1962), xi
6 Cmd 532 p. 15
7 NI Commons XXXIII 2280, 15 December 1949
8 NI Commons XXXIII 2323, 20 December 1949
9 NI Commons XL 1922, 12 June 1956

10 Cabinet Conclusions, 22 and 31 May 1956. PRONI CAB 4/1009 and 1011
11 NI Commons XL 1943, 12 June 1956
12 NI Commons XLI 71, 6 February 1957. May probably mentioned only voluntary primary schools to avoid any fears that voluntary grammar schools would be threatened with control by the education authorities
13 NI Commons XLI 1357 and 1360, 30 May 1957
14 NI Commons XLII 399, 30 April 1958 and XLIV 8, 10 February 1959
15 Farren (1995), p. 217
16 The successful amendment stated 'the system under which voluntary schools are given substantial grants from public funds without accepting a measure of public representation on their various administrative bodies should receive further consideration in regard to the amount of such grants and the terms and conditions upon which they are made; and that the Minister of Education be asked to consider and submit recommendations to the House when the new school leaving age has come into operation'. NI Commons XL 1943, 12 June 1956
17 Cabinet Conclusions, 26 March 1958. PRONI CAB 4/1061
18 NI Commons XLIV 780, 19 March 1959
19 NI Commons XLIV 780, 19 March 1959
20 The list of Minford's speeches in the Northern Ireland Commons index were notably shorter by the late 1950s
21 UK Commons Fifth Series Volume 606 1186–1191, 11 June 1959
22 Senate XLIII 456, 30 June 1959
23 NI Commons XLVI 418, 24 February 1960 and XLVII 1149, 14 December 1960
24 Cardinal D'Alton in Magherafelt 10 December 1953 *Irish Catholic Directory* (1955), p. 620. See also (1954), p. 704, 718 and 739, (1955), p. 642, (1956), p. 628 and (1960), p. 657
25 *Irish Catholic Directory* (1961), p. 701 and (1962), p. 723
26 *Irish Catholic Directory* (1964), pp. 714 and 715
27 NI Commons XL 1946, 12 June 1956
28 NI Commons XLI 71–72, 6 February 1957
29 NI Commons XLII 412, 30 April 1958
30 Cmd 392 p. 5
31 The exact figures were 11,215 and 10,920. Appendix J
32 A reading of O'Neill's autobiography, a work with the rather vapid title of *The Autobiography of Terence O'Neill*, fails to offer any firm conclusions. Farrell simply dismisses O'Neill as 'a colourless figure who was largely a mouthpiece for technocrats in the civil service . . . and regarded the Orange Order with snobbish disdain'. Farrell (1980), p. 228
33 O'Neill (1972), p. 29
34 NI Commons XXX 3119–3121, 3 December 1946
35 NI Commons XXX 4750, 13 March 1947
36 NI Commons XLI 1608, 12 June 1957. O'Neill spent only the first and final year of his Parliamentary career on the backbenches. He was elected for Bannside in November 1946, and was appointed Parliamentary Secretary to the Ministry of Finance in February 1948. He resigned as Prime Minister in May 1969, and left the Northern Ireland Commons for the House of Lords in January 1970

37 *Belfast Telegraph* 5 May 1969. Quoted in Hepburn (1980), p. 182
38 Cmd 476 p. 13. Two years previously the Ministry's Report stated: 'There is . . . a considerable amount of mostly slight overcrowding in county schools in Belfast and County Antrim, and a great deal more, and more serious, overcrowding in voluntary schools in most areas'. Cmd 450 p. 10
39 Cmd 450 p. 10
40 Cmd 476 p. 13
41 In January 1965 150 of 181 classes with more than forty-five pupils were in voluntary schools. Cmd 492 p. 10
42 Cmd 492 p. 11
43 Ibid., p. 10
44 Cmd 506 p. 11
45 After 1967 the number of 'dual day' schools declined slowly to a solitary school in 1973. Cmd 585 p. 8
46 Appendix D
47 NI Commons LIV 166, 24 April 1963 and LV 1066, 20 November 1963
48 Cmd 470 p. 8
49 Ibid., p. 7
50 Cmd 492 p. 17
51 Cmd 470 p. 27
52 Appendix J
53 The exact figure was 21,731 places. Appendix J
54 Appendices F and J
55 NI Commons XLVI 416, 24 February 1960
56 Northern Ireland's major two cities, Belfast and Londonderry, contained thirteen of the fifteen 'dual day' schools in 1965. Cmd 492 p. 10
57 Cmd 492 p. 10
58 Cmd 520 p. 12 and Cmd 527 p. 8
59 The 1947 Act also obliged voluntary schools to find thirty-five per cent of the costs of heating, lighting and cleaning their schools. By 1966–67 the voluntary contribution towards these costs had risen to £120,982. NI Commons LXVII 1220, 31 October 1967
60 NI Commons LXII 1047, 16 February 1966. The mention of the increased grants for voluntary schools in England and Wales by Diamond was ruled to be out of order by the Deputy Speaker
61 NI Commons LXIII 1001 and 1005, 11 May 1966
62 NI Commons LXV 404, 18 January 1967
63 NI Commons LVI 459, 1383 and 1865, 6 February, 3 March and 18 March 1964. LIX 1276–1316, 2 March 1965. LXII 1047, 16 February 1966
64 Cmd 513
65 The title of 'maintained' schools was adopted, the White Paper explained, because 'it is proposed that local education authorities should become responsible for the maintenance of their premises and their equipment'. Cmd 513 p. 10
66 Cmd 513 p. 4
67 Ibid., p. 7
68 Ibid., p. 7
69 *Irish News* 20 January 1968

70 Cmd 513 p. 5
71 *Irish News* 20 October 1967
72 *Irish News* 20 January 1968
73 *Belfast Telegraph* 20 October 1967
74 *Irish News* 20 October 1967
75 *Belfast Telegraph* 20 October 1967
76 *Belfast Telegraph* 20 October 1967
77 NI Commons LXVII 2485, 30 November 1967
78 *Irish News* 20 October 1967. Diamond confirmed his status as the most enthusiastic defender of Catholic schools during the debate on the White Paper at the end of November when he spoke for nearly fifty minutes. NI Commons LXVII 2289–2303, 29 November 1967
79 *Irish News* 20 October 1967
80 *Irish News* 23 October 1967
81 'Catholic Parent' *Irish News* 24 October 1967
82 'Weekly Subscriber' *Irish News* 25 October 1967
83 Anthony Cinnamond at the Ulster Liberal Party conference. The conference later passed a motion calling on the government to grant one hundred per cent funding for voluntary schools, but also urged the Catholic authorities to integrate their schools into the public system. *Belfast Telegraph* 30 October 1967
84 *Belfast Telegraph* 2 November 1967
85 *Irish News* 2 November 1967. The *Belfast Telegraph* accepted that the behaviour of the local councils and local education authorities gave the Catholic authorities genuine cause for concern. *Belfast Telegraph* 2 November 1967
86 *Irish News* 2 November 1967
87 *Irish News* 9 November 1967
88 *Belfast Telegraph* 24 November 1967
89 NI Commons LXVII 2317, 2329 and 2356, 29 November 1967. Murnaghan had suggested Ministry appointments to the 'four and two' committees as early as March 1965. NI Commons LIX 1324, 2 March 1965
90 The *Belfast Telegraph* urged Long to reform the education authorities before Conway's statement of 1 November. *Belfast Telegraph* 25 October 1967
91 Long's answer to the first question promised only to inform the education authority that the school buses could be used to take voluntary school children for educational visits, creating the misleading impression that the education authority thought that allowing voluntary schools to use the buses would violate the 1947 Education Act. NI Commons LXVI 585–586, 25 April 1967.

   Long's answer to the second question was more assertive, stating 'it is my Ministry's view that the same criteria should apply to pupils in county and in voluntary schools'. Edward Richardson, Nationalist MP for South Armagh, considered Long's answer to be a 'very satisfactory reply', but Long failed to alter the education authority's initial decision. NI Commons LXVI 1603–1604, 31 May 1967
92 NI Commons XLVII 1161–1165, 26 October 1967
93 The issue was exploited by the St Malachy's Old Boys Association in its statement of 29 October. *Irish News* 30 October 1967

94 NI Commons LXVII 2462, 30 November 1967

95 *Irish News* 9 November 1967

96 *Irish News* 28 November 1967

97 *Belfast Telegraph* 28 November 1967 and *Irish News* 29 November 1967

98 *Belfast Telegraph* 28 November 1967

99 *Belfast Telegraph* 29 November 1967

100 The first day's debate began at 3.23 p.m. and lasted until 8.45 p.m. while the second day's debate began at 5.48 p.m. and lasted until 8.30 p.m. NI Commons LXVII 2269–2372 and 2448–2498, 29 and 30 November 1967

101 NI Commons LXVII 2494, 30 November 1967

102 Ibid., p. 2498

103 *Belfast Telegraph* 2 December 1967

104 *Irish News* 6 January 1968

105 The White Paper contained only twenty-four paragraphs in its ten pages. Cmd 513

106 NI Commons LXVII 2307, 29 November 1967. Long had earlier hinted that he was considering reforming the local education authorities, but he offered no specific proposals. *Irish News* 25 October 1967

107 *Irish News* 23 January 1968 and *Belfast Telegraph* 22 January 1968

108 *Irish News* 22 January 1968

109 *Belfast Telegraph* 22 January 1968

110 *Irish News* 22 January 1968

111 *Belfast Telegraph* 23 January 1968

112 *Belfast Telegraph* 29 November 1967

113 NI Commons LXVIII 358, 24 January 1968

114 NI Commons LXVIII 1267–1268, 14 February 1968

115 *Irish News* 26 February 1968

116 NI Commons LXVIII 512, 4 June 1968

117 NI Commons LXXI 9, 17 December 1968

118 Cmd 542 p. 9

119 554 of 676 schools. NI Commons LXXIII 1350, 16 December 1971

120 NI Commons LXXIII 231, 8 May 1969

121 NI Commons LXXVIII 619, 20 January 1971

122 The first committee comprised R. H. Beattie, Rev. George C. Curry, David Graham, Charles Knox, A. J. Kyle and Leslie McCaffrey. The second committee comprised James Adams, J. Gallagher, Commander Claud A. Herdman, William Keery, Robert McNeill and J. Stewart MBE. NI Commons LXXVIII 7, 8 December 1970. The use of surnames to establish religious denomination in Northern Ireland is an inexact science, but the presence of a military officer and an MBE suggests a Protestant committee

123 NI Commons LXXVIII 7, 8 December 1970

124 Ibid.

125 NI Commons LXXXI 13–15, 8 June 1971

126 See Chapter 6

127 NI Commons LXVII 2360, 29 November 1967

128 *Irish News* 2 and 4 October 1969

129 Akenson (1970), p. 92

130 Cmd 6 p. 42

131 NI Commons XL 542, 7 March 1956
132 NI Commons LI 304, 21 March 1962
133 NI Commons LIX 1276–1328, 2 March 1965. The motion read 'that in the opinion of this House an urgent and favourable review of the State grants for the building and maintenance of voluntary schools should take place'. Fitt seconded the motion. NI Commons LIX 1284, 2 March 1965
134 The *Irish News* referred to Bleakley as a 'Six County Labour' MP. *Irish News* 3 March 1965. The amendment attempted to add to the Motion 'and this House also believes that, at the same time, every possible step should be taken towards the integration of the county and voluntary school systems of education'. NI Commons LIX 1290, 2 March 1965
135 The debate on Bleakley's amendment lasted from 4.08 pm until 5.03 pm while Kirk spoke from 5.03 pm to 5.08 pm. NI Commons LIX 1290–1308 and 1308–1310, 2 March 1965
136 NI Commons LIX 1287, 2 March 1965
137 The conference took place over the Easter weekend, while the Irish Republic was celebrating the fiftieth anniversary of the Easter Rising. Critics of O'Neill's timidity should note his willingness to talk of greater community dialogue at such a delicate moment
138 *Belfast Telegraph* 9 April 1966
139 The *Irish News* editions for the rest of April 1966 contain no evidence of a response from nationalist politicians
140 *Irish News* 21 April 1966
141 Cmd 532
142 Cmd 532 p. 14
143 Dr Norman Laird, Unionist MP for St Anne's Belfast. NI Commons LXXIV 35, 30 September 1969
144 Commander Anderson Albert Anderson, Unionist MP for the City of Londonderry. NI Commons LXXIV 49, 30 September 1969
145 Captain Robert Mitchell, Unionist MP for North Armagh. NI Commons LXXVI 114, 1 October 1969
146 Joshua Cardwell, Unionist MP for Pottinger Belfast. NI Commons LXXIV 166, 1 October 1969
147 NI Commons LXXIV 90 and 171, 1 October 1969
148 *Belfast Telegraph* 30 September 1969. My italics
149 *Irish News* 15 October 1969
150 *Irish News* 6 October 1969
151 NI Commons LI 304, 21 March 1962
152 NI Commons LV 1462, 10 December 1963
153 NI Commons LXVII 27, 13 June 1967
154 Ibid., 29, 13 June 1967
155 NI Commons LXXIV 35, 49, 114 and 166, 30 September and 1 October 1969
156 NI Commons LXXIII 263, 8 May 1969. LXXIV 258, 7 October 1969. LXXV 230, 12 February 1970 and LXXVI 176, 7 May 1970
157 NI Commons LXXVII 9–18, 8 December 1970
158 *Irish News* 20 January 1968

CHAPTER SIX

1 UK Commons Fifth Series 954 987, 20 July 1978. The Order granted the
   Education and Library Boards compulsory powers to purchase land on
   behalf of voluntary and maintained schools – powers they already
   enjoyed on behalf of controlled schools.
     The 1978 Education (Northern Ireland) Order led to the most divisive
   debate on Northern Ireland's education system since the abolition of the
   devolved government. The Labour MP for Bermondsey, Bob Mellish,
   claimed that Paisley and Kilfedder had 'based their argument solely and
   simply on a detestation . . . of the Roman Catholic faith'. Kilfedder protested that 'the main purpose of the article was to facilitate the furtherance
   of sectarian education by enabling maintained schools – not just voluntary
   schools which do not wish to have this power – to expand by getting the
   Department of Education to vest adjoining property'. Paisley also complained that the Order would aid only Catholic schools, and claimed that
   the Gaelic Athletic Association would be allowed to use the playing fields.
   Fitt intervened during this debate, but he played a secondary role –
   leaving the defence of the Order to other MPs. UK Commons Fifth Series
   954 979, 990 and 996–997.
     The debate was not only bitter, it was also slightly pointless, because
   eight years later no land had been vested on behalf of voluntary or
   maintained schools. UK Commons Sixth Series 87 117, 19 November 1985
2 UK Commons Fifth Series 727 437–446, 25 April 1966 and 840 2093–2097,
   14 July 1972
3 UK Commons Fifth Series 901 1881, 3 December 1975
4 UK Commons Fifth Series 840 2064, 14 July 1972
5 In March 1976 he asked for scholarship awards to be notified at an earlier
   date, and the following month he called for greater road safety measures
   for school buses. UK Commons Fifth Series 907 257 and 909 254, 10 March
   and 8 April 1976
6 UK Commons Sixth Series 70 213, 19 December 1984 and 110 447, 12
   February 1987
7 UK Commons Sixth Series 61 92–95, 4 June 1984. 72 441, 4 February 1985.
   106 420, 27 November 1986. 114 364, 9 April 1987. 124 797, 18 December
   1987. 127 396, 12 February 1988. 144 451, 22 December 1988. 144 557, 10
   January 1989. 166 339, 1 February 1990. 166 527, 5 February 1990. 186 598,
   28 February 1991. 186 638, 1 March 1991
8 UK Commons Sixth Series 143 746 and 144 37, 16 and 19 December 1988
9 UK Commons Sixth Series 146 626 and 717, 7 and 8 February 1989
10 UK Commons Sixth Series 163 1120, 13 December 1989
11 UK Commons Sixth Series 102 486 and 661, 24 and 25 July 1986. 108 584
    and 641, 21 and 22 January 1987. 136 515, 30 June 1988
12 UK Commons Sixth Series 151 451, 20 April 1989
13 UK Commons Sixth Series 145 600–602, 25 January 1989. 146 236, 1
    February 1989. 192 592–593, 12 June 1991
14 UK Commons Sixth Series 192 1025, 13 June 1991

15 UK Commons Sixth Series 124 571, 10 December 1987 and 136 722, 7 July 1988
16 House of Lords Fifth Series 387 1053, 24 November 1977
17 The composition of the Astin committee may not have encouraged the Catholic authorities to be sympathetic to their recommendations. The committee comprised two professors from Queen's University Belfast, two education authority officials and a journalist from the unionist *Belfast Telegraph*. DENI 1979
18 *Belfast Telegraph* 28 June 1979
19 *Belfast Telegraph* 2 and 30 June 1980
20 See below
21 Alan Astin refers to his critics' 'unsubtle preoccupation with numbers'. Astin (1987), p. 261
22 *Fortnight* (May–June 1981), No. 181, p. 7
23 UK Commons Sixth Series 3 461, 30 April 1981
24 UK Commons Sixth Series 62 929, 26 June 1984. The evidence from Tyrone in the aftermath of the 1968 Act indicates that lay Catholics were already enjoying influence on many maintained school committees. See Chapter 5
25 *Fortnight* (July–August 1980), No. 177, p. 5
26 *Belfast Telegraph* 23 March 1982
27 *Belfast Telegraph* 9 June 1980
28 *Irish News* 9 June 1980
29 *Belfast Telegraph* 24 June 1980
30 Dunn (1990), p. 88
31 The importance to the Catholic authorities of retaining control of the training of prospective Catholic teachers was underlined in the 1950s by the resolute campaign by Cardinal D'Alton and his bishops to improve the funding arrangements for the proposed St Joseph's college. See Chapter 4
32 *Irish News* 24 June 1980
33 *Belfast Telegraph* 16 June 1980
34 *Irish News* 25 March 1982
35 UK Commons Sixth Series 21 492, 8 April 1982
36 *Irish News* 26 June 1980
37 *Belfast Telegraph* 17 June 1980
38 UK Commons Fifth Series 984 173, 7 May 1980 and 987 218, 25 June 1980
39 *Belfast Telegraph* 25 February 1982. Quoted in Dunn (1993), p. 28
40 Davis (1994), p. 184
41 UK Commons Sixth Series 165 703, 24 January 1990
42 In 1988–89 St Mary's contained 692 full-time and 450 part-time students whilst Stranmillis was training only 663 full-time and 246 part-time students. UK Commons Sixth Series 165 702, 24 January 1990
43 *Belfast Telegraph* 30 July 1987
44 *Irish News* 31 July 1987
45 *Belfast Telegraph* 30 July 1987
46 CCMS (1989), p. 8
47 *Belfast Telegraph* 31 July 1987
48 *Irish News* 31 July 1987

49 CCMS (1989), p. 8
50 *Belfast Telegraph* 30 July 1987
51 UK Commons 262 407 and 1073, 26 and 29 June 1995
52 The failure rate for Catholics in 1985–86 was twenty-five per cent and for Protestants nineteen per cent. These figures were an improvement on the statistics for 1975 which revealed that forty-five per cent of Catholic pupils left school without any qualifications in comparison to forty per cent of Protestant pupils. Twenty-five per cent of Protestants left school with A levels in contrast to twenty-two per cent of Catholics. SACHR 1989 43 and 142
53 SACHR (1991), p. 121
54 SACHR (1990), p. 98
55 Ibid., p. 111
56 Catholics were twice as likely to be examined in Religious Education as Protestants. SACHR (1990), p. 125
57 SACHR (1990), p. 127
58 In 1959 there were 1,100 special educational rooms in county schools compared to 513 in voluntary schools. By 1975 the figures had almost converged, with 2,444 and 2,024 rooms. *Education Statistics* No. 7, pp. 88 and 89, No. 23, pp. 106 and 107
59 Livingstone (1987), p. 44
60 Ibid., pp. 48 and 49
61 SACHR (1992), p. 85
62 SACHR (1993), p. 58
63 SACHR (1991), pp. 118–212
64 Ibid., p. 133
65 SACHR (1992), p. 130
66 SACHR (1991), p. 131
67 Ibid., p. 12
68 Ibid., p. 145
69 Ibid., pp. 139 and 140
70 Ibid., p. 141
71 McCavera (1993), p. 71. The exact figures were a £85,079 surplus for controlled primary schools and a £2,143,392 surplus for secondary schools. Maintained primary schools suffered a £2,228,471 deficit and secondary schools enjoyed a £315,841 surplus
72 UK Commons Sixth Series 146 717, 8 February 1989
73 *The Times Educational Supplement* 13 November 1992. The Education and Libraries Order of 1986 termed all school committees as boards of governors. This term has been employed throughout this book for the school committees of voluntary grammar schools, and will be retained at this late stage to avoid unnecessary confusion
74 SACHR (1993), p. 298
75 UK Commons Sixth Series 213 242, 4 November 1992. The NIO minister responsible for education, Michael Ancram, repeated the promise during the UK Commons debate on the Order in October 1993. UK Commons Sixth Series 230 750, 26 October 1993
76 *Belfast Telegraph* 5 November 1992
77 UK Commons Sixth Series 230 749 and 752, 26 October 1993

78 UK Commons Sixth Series 230 756 and 757, 26 October 1993
79 The SDLP manifesto for 1992 called for the abolition of the voluntary contribution, but this came after the SACHR Report. SDLP (1992), p. 12
80 SACHR (1991), p. 131
81 See Chapter 5
82 McElroy (1991), pp. 27–31
83 Cmnd 5259
84 Ibid., p. 7
85 Ibid.
86 The conference later emphasised the union's hostility to Catholic schools by calling for the Department of Education of Northern Ireland (DENI) not to fund any school except controlled schools. *Belfast Telegraph* 20 April 1974
87 Conway (1973), p. 10
88 Cmnd 5259 p. 7
89 Ibid.
90 Northern Ireland Assembly Vol. 3, p. 312, 30 April 1974
91 Ibid., p. 298, 30 April 1974
92 Ibid., p. 299, 30 April 1974
93 Ibid., p. 302, 30 April 1974
94 'I trust that we will not have any sudden and instant solutions to a very complex and complicated problem'. NI Assembly Vol. 3, p. 305, 30 April 1974
95 *Belfast Telegraph* 1 May 1974
96 *Irish News* 1 May 1974. Rumours circulated throughout the spring of 1974 that McIvor was contemplating a major initiative, but the first tangible evidence appeared only a week before his speech in the Northern Ireland Assembly. The *Belfast Telegraph* reported that a major announcement was imminent, and also noted that McIvor visited London the previous week to discuss his proposals with the Northern Ireland Office minister Reg Prentice. *Belfast Telegraph* 24 April 1974
97 *Belfast Telegraph* 1 May 1974
98 *Belfast Telegraph* 18 April 1974
99 *Belfast Telegraph* 1 May 1974
100 *Belfast Telegraph* 8 May 1974
101 *Belfast Telegraph* 1 May 1974.
102 *Irish News* 9 May 1974
103 *Belfast Telegraph* 6 May 1974
104 McAllister (1977), p. 135
105 Ibid., p. 136
106 McIvor did not offer a clear view on the role of the school committee or on the procedures for the appointment of teachers, claiming that he would be canvassing opinion on these questions. *Irish News* 4 May 1974
107 *Times Educational Supplement* 10 May 1974
108 *New Ireland Forum: Report of Proceedings* Vol. 12, p. 31
109 *Fortnight* May 1980, No. 176, p. 14
110 *Belfast Telegraph* 20 April 1974
111 *Belfast Telegraph* 9 April 1974

112 *Belfast Telegraph* 9 April 1974
113 Mark (1978), p. 8
114 Ibid., p. 20
115 House of Lords Fifth Series 387 277, 10 November 1977
116 During the Committee Stage of the Bill, a peer attempted to replace the requirement for a three to one majority in favour of integration with a simple majority rule, and a colleague suggested a two thirds majority which Dunleath appeared to accept during the debate. The Act retained the original conditions. Lords Fifth Series 388 243–246, 19 January 1978.
    The Bill passed through the Commons without a debate. UK Commons Fifth Series 956 242
117 Dunn (1990), p. 84
118 *Fortnight* (May 1980), No. 176, p. 9
119 Ibid.
120 *Fortnight* (September 1987), No. 254, p. 10
121 *Fortnight* (May 1980), No. 176, p. 14
122 UK Commons Sixth Series 115 391, 5 May 1987
123 *Fortnight* (21 May 1973), No. 62, p. 7
124 *Fortnight* (October–November 1980), No. 178, p. 5
125 *Fortnight* (July–August 1988), No. 264, p. 4
126 *Fortnight* (October–November 1980), No. 178, p. 5
127 *Fortnight* (July–August 1988), No. 264, p. 4
128 *Fortnight* (21 May 1973), No. 62, p. 7
129 *Fortnight* (October–November 1980), No. 178, p. 5
130 *Fortnight* (July–August 1988), No. 264, p. 4
131 UK Commons Sixth Series 269 795, 19 January 1996
132 McElroy (1991), pp. 86–88
133 Ibid., p. 206
134 In the autumn of 1995 there were 977 Catholic children and 816 Protestant children attending grant maintained integrated primary schools. The contrast was more notable in Northern Ireland's five grant maintained integrated secondary schools, with a 1,035 to 737 majority of Catholic pupils. UK Commons Sixth Series 269 797, 19 January 1996
135 Kilfedder was the victor in the bitter West Belfast contest in 1964, a victory for which he thanked Paisley and his followers. Bardon (1992), p. 632. Two years later he lost the seat to Fitt. He was elected as an Ulster Unionist MP for North Down in 1970, but in 1980 he formed the Ulster Popular Unionist Party and defended his seat from other Unionist candidates until his death in the spring of 1995
136 UK Commons Sixth Series 132 496, 28 April 1988
137 UK Commons Fifth Series 835 40 and 41, 17 April 1972, 835 83, 18 April 1972, 853 177, 22 March 1973 and 930 58, 19 April 1977
138 UK Commons Fifth Series 994 561, 27 November 1980 and Sixth Series 4 877, 14 May 1981
139 UK Commons 62 938, 26 June 1984
140 John Biggs Davison, Conservative MP for Epping Forest, was the most persistent advocate of integration on the Conservative benches. UK Commons Fifth Series 901 1878, 3 December 1975. 952 421, 20 June 1978.

Sixth Series 21 492, 8 April 1982. There were other Tory MPs, such as Sir Nigel Fisher for Kingston upon Thames, who were also prepared to urge the Labour government to promote integration. 903 562, 22 January 1976. 916 851, 29 July 1976. 927 1617, 10 March 1977. John Farr, MP for Harborough, claimed that progress could only be made if the intransigence of the *Ne Temere* decree was abandoned by the Catholic Church. 916 853, 29 July 1976. After 1979 Conservative MPs were less enthusiastic in their support for integration, and only Cyril Townsend and Nicholas Winterton consistently urged their own ministers to assist the integration movement. Fifth Series 927 1617, 10 March 1977. 980 336, 6 March 1980 Sixth Series 8 1379, 16 July 1981. 13 101, 17 November 1981

141 UK Commons Fifth Series 901 1879, 3 December 1975. 916 851, 29 July 1976. 901 1879, 3 December 1975. Sixth Series 115 391, 5 May 1987. Kinnock asked one question in May 1980, but he did not pursue the issue in later years. UK Commons Fifth Series 984 173, 7 May 1980

142 UK Commons Sixth Series 132 496, 28 April 1988

143 They both spoke later in the same debate. UK Commons Sixth Series 132 498 and 491, 28 April 1988

144 SACHR (1989), p. 128

145 *Fortnight* (March 1983), No. 192, p. 10. In March 1996 there were 15,000 surplus primary school and 17,000 surplus secondary school places, and the following January the DENI announced that the number of primary school pupils was expected to fall by 12,000 while demand for secondary school places would increase by 4,000. UK Commons Sixth Series 273 633 12 March 1996 and 288 556, 21 January 1997

146 *Fortnight* (September 1987), No. 264, p. 10

147 Anthony Favell, UK Commons Sixth Series 112 448, 12 March 1987. Timothy Yeo, 120 351, 23 July 1987. Virginia Bottomley, 114 358, 14 December 1987. David Alton, 128 187, 24 February 1988

148 Kilfedder defended Lagan College from his Unionist allies. UK Commons Sixth Series 56 1168 and 1169, 22 March 1984

149 UK Commons Sixth Series 244 747, 16 June 1994

150 Ulster Unionist Party (1992)

151 Ulster Unionist Party (1997), p. 16

152 Ibid., pp. 16 and 17

153 Ibid., p. 17

154 Democratic Unionist Party (1992), p. 4

155 *Fortnight* (May 1980), No. 176, p. 14

156 UK Commons Sixth Series 120 474, 23 July 1987

157 UK Commons Sixth Series 124 358, 14 December 1987

158 UK Commons Sixth Series 132 265, 28 April 1988

159 *Belfast Telegraph* 30 March 1988

160 *Belfast Telegraph* 5 October 1988

161 *Belfast Telegraph* 30 March 1988

162 The number of pupils in maintained schools rose from 89,936 in 1984–85 to 95,436 in 1989–90 whilst the number of pupils in controlled schools fell from 91,670 to 90,764. UK Commons Sixth Series 259 333, 5 May 1995

163 *Irish News* 31 March 1988

164 SACHR (1990), p. 6
165 *Education in Northern Ireland: The Way Forward* DENI (1988), p. 15
166 The director of the Council for Catholic Maintained Schools, Colm McCaughan, claimed that an integrated society rather than integrated schools should be the priority for the government, comments that were condemned as 'disgraceful, negative and churlish' by the Alliance Party. *Irish News* 31 March and 1 April 1988
167 *Irish News* 31 March 1988
168 DENI (1988), p. 16
169 *Belfast Telegraph* 6 October 1988
170 DENI (1988), p. 1
171 UK Commons Sixth Series 155 487, 22 June 1989
172 CCMS (1989), p. 20
173 UK Commons Sixth Series 163 1122, 13 December 1989
174 UK Commons Sixth Series 163 1098, 13 December 1989
175 Quoted by Mallon. UK Commons Sixth Series 163 1124, 13 December 1989
176 UK Commons Sixth Series 163 1091, 13 December 1989
177 UK Commons Sixth Series 163 1108 and 1114, 13 December 1989
178 Ibid., pp. 1092 and 1109, 13 December 1989
179 UK Commons Sixth Series 163 1129, 13 December 1989. No MP from Northern Ireland voted for the Order. Kilfedder was a notable absentee
180 UK Commons Sixth Series 163 1126, 13 December 1989
181 *Fortnight* (November 1990), No. 289, p. 8
182 UK Commons Sixth Series 282 72, 22 July 1996
183 UK Commons Sixth Series 244 650, 14 June 1994
184 UK Commons Sixth Series 269 797, 19 January 1996
185 Davis (1994), p. 163
186 Ibid., p. 176
187 Ibid., p. 178
188 Ibid., pp. 179 and 180
189 Ibid., p. 180
190 Ibid., p. 183
191 *Irish News* 18 January 1982. Quoted in Davis (1994), p. 183
192 *Ulster Loyalist* March 1975. Quoted in Davis (1994), p. 172
193 Galliher and DeGregory p. 75
194 Ibid.
195 O'Connor (1993), p. 67
196 *Fortnight* (November 1986), No. 245, p. 15
197 *Fortnight* (July–August 1987), No. 253, p. 4
198 *The Times Educational Supplement* 26 May 1989
199 *Fortnight* (November 1986), No. 245, p. 15
200 UK Commons Sixth Series 271 524, 13 February 1996
201 UK Commons Sixth Series 70 213, 19 December 1984 and 110 447, 12 February 1987
202 UK Commons Sixth Series 102 486 and 661, 24 and 25 July 1986. 108 584 and 641, 21 and 22 January 1987. 136 515, 30 June 1988
203 UK Commons Sixth Series 133 566 and 595, 19 and 20 May 1988. 134 30 and 332, 23 and 26 May 1988. 135 754, 24 May 1988. 136 92, 278 and 722, 27 and 29 June and 7 July 1988

204 In May 1988 Mawhinney admitted that the fate of the Gaelic language had been discussed at a meeting of the Anglo-Irish Inter Governmental Conference. UK Commons Sixth Series 135 754, 24 May 1988

205 CCMS (1988), pp. 13, 22 and 29

206 DENI (1988), pp. 2 and 7

207 DENI (1988), p. 7 and UK Commons Sixth Series 163 1093, 13 December 1989. All secondary schools were still obliged to offer an EC language to their pupils

208 UK Commons Sixth Series 254 46, 6 February 1995. 247 486, 27 March 1995. 258 678, 27 April 1995. 260 748, 25 May 1995. 285 345, 14 November 1996. 287 350, 12 December 1996

209 In 1995–96 the DENI spent £2.5 million promoting the language. UK Commons Sixth Series 288 57, 14 January 1997

210 The returns for the 1991 census indicate that 9.5% of Northern Ireland's population claim a knowledge of Gaelic, and 3% claim to use the language on a daily basis. UK Commons Sixth Series 268 318, 6 December 1996

211 317 274 29 July 1998, UK Commons Sixth Series 271 524, 13 February 1996. 319 460 17 November 1998, 291 100, 24 February 1997

212 DENI Circular 1982/21, 1 June 1982

213 SACHR (1989), p. 33

214 Ibid., p. 115

215 Ibid., p. 34

216 Ibid., p. 36

217 Cmnd 5259 p. 7

218 The Catholic authorities in Down and Connor launched their own project for educational integration with the Roman Catholic Committee for Ecumenical Cooperation in Schools in 1983, though without any discernible effect. NICED (1988), p. 10

219 *New Ireland Forum: Report of Proceedings* Vol. 12, p. 31

220 UK Commons Sixth Series 124 570, 10 December 1987

221 UK Commons Sixth Series 124 569, 10 December 1987

222 UK Commons Sixth Series 135 624, 22 June 1988

223 DENI (1988), p. 6

224 UK Commons Sixth Series 155 487, 22 June 1989. The budget for cross community contact schemes rose to £1.5 million by 1994–95. UK Commons Sixth Series 274 756, 29 March 1996

225 UK Commons Sixth Series 274 756, 29 March 1996

226 Maintained primary schools secured more than 53,000 new places in contrast to 45,690 places for voluntary primary schools after 1947

227 The figures were 23,305 county places and 26,349 voluntary places. Appendices I and J

228 The figures were 73,290 places for maintained schools and 73,170 for controlled schools

229 Appendices I and J

230 Ibid.

231 In 1981 Osborne found thirty-five per cent of Protestant school leavers were graduates of grammar schools in contrast to just twenty-six per cent of Catholics. Livingstone (1987), p. 44

232 In 1967 there were 7,294 voluntary primary school places and 3,220 secondary intermediate places – 2.265 primary places for every secondary intermediate place. The figures for the seven years after 1968 were 47,200 and 20,900 – 2.258 primary places for every secondary intermediate place

233 *Education Statistics* No. 1, p. 13. The exact figure for controlled nursery schools was 559 pupils

234 *Education Statistics* No. 19, p. 14

235 UK Commons Sixth Series 240 665, 29 March 1994

236 Minutes of meeting of 22 May 1944. ED 13/1/2129

237 UK Commons Sixth Series 240 665, 29 March 1994

238 The exact figures were £12.185 million and £10.57 million. UK Commons Sixth Series 50 556, 15 December 1983

239 The exact figures were £1.1 million and £5.332 million. UK Commons Sixth Series 50 556, 15 December 1983. The figures for 1983–84 were estimates

240 UK Commons Sixth Series 202 153, 21 January 1992. The minister's answer provided only the amount of public grant for maintained schools. The numbers are calculated by adding the voluntary contribution to the public grant

241 UK Commons Sixth Series 259 334, 5 May 1995

242 Dunn (1993), p. 29. The CCMS has also attracted the attention of Unionist politicians such as the Ulster Unionist leader, David Trimble. UK Commons Sixth Series 291 336, 27 February 1997 and 291 441, 3 March 1997

243 The exact figures are 3846 primary and 4308 secondary pupils. UK Commans Sixth Series 315 421 7 July 1998

244 UK Commons Sixth Series 291 95, 24 February 1997

245 *Fortnight* (September 1991), No. 298, p. 13

246 Davis (1994), p. 183

247 O'Connor (1993), p. 318

CHAPTER SEVEN

1 *Irish Ecclesiastical Record* (March 1920), pp. 252 and 253

2 John Andrews' brief tenure as Prime Minister (1940–1943) did not leave any notable impression upon education policy

3 Dunn (1990), p. 88

4 Lynn to Londonderry, 7 May 1923. PRONI CAB 9D/1/2

5 PRONI CAB 9D/78/1

6 Mageean to Tierney, 20 October 1938. DCDA ED 11/38

7 Titley (1983), p. 59

8 *Irish Catholic Directory* (1926), p. 561

9 PRONI ED 32/A/1/81

10 Akenson (1973), p. 52, Buckland (1981), p. 52 and Bardon (1992), p. 622

11 Dunn (1990), p. 75

12 The exact figures were £1,815,363 for public elementary schools, and £164,587 for voluntary schools. At the end of 1938 there were 38,261 pupils in provided schools, and 57,348 pupils in transferred schools. HC 483 p. 38

13 The exact figures were 79 'unsuitable' schools with 7,737 pupils and 14,238 pupils in 196 'fairly suitable' schools. Charlemont Memorandum, 26 April 1930. PRONI CAB 4/259

14 HC 180 p. 10

15 The exact statistics were 28,546 places for county schools and 10,735 places for voluntary schools. Appendices I and J

16 PRONI ED 13/1/2463, 2464 and 2465

17 Appendix J

18 NI Commons LXVII 1220, 31 October 1967

19 NI Commons XLI 71–72, 6 February 1957

20 SACHR (1989), pp. 142–144

21 SACHR (1991), pp. 139 and 140

22 The average figures were £11.16 for county school pupils and £5.92 for voluntary school pupils. NI Commons LXXIV 890, 4 November 1969

23 Murray (1993), pp. 209–220

24 Osborne, Cormack and Gallagher (1993), p. 191

25 NI Commons XVI 2734–2748, 13 November 1934. PRONI ED 13/1/865. DCDA ED 11/33–35

26 Akenson's decision to conclude his impressive study of the education controversies between the Protestant clergy and the devolved government with the fall of Hall-Thompson in 1950 was an appropriate choice

27 *Belfast Telegraph* 19 May 1992. Quoted in Dunn (1993), p. 15

28 Dunn (1993), p. 29 Unionist politicians have also cast envious glances at the CCMS. In December 1997 David Trimble called for the government to provide arrangements for controlled schools "analogous to the arrangements available to the CCMS". UK Commons Sixth Series 303 297 18 December 1997

29 DENI Education Statistics Leaflet 1994

30 UK Commons Sixth Series 273 644 13 March 1996 and 288 556, 21 January 1997

31 UK Commons Fourth Series 156 1533, 10 May 1906

32 UK Commons Fourth Series 156 1533, 10 May 1906

33 Farrell (1980), p. 101

34 Maintained schools educate 54% of all school children while 44% attend controlled schools and the remaining 2% are pupils of integrated schools. UK Commons Sixth Series 307 439 2 March 1998

35 Buckland (1981), p. 77

36 A survey in 1968 found that ninety-five per cent of Northern Ireland's Catholics claimed to attend Mass at least once a week, treble the rate of attendance in France and Austria. McGarry and O'Leary (1995), pp. 173 and 174

Appendix A

Lord Londonderry	June 1921–January 1926
Lord Charlemont	January 1926–October 1937
John Robb	October 1937–May 1943
Robert Corkey	May 1943–March 1944
Samuel Hall-Thompson	March 1944–December 1949
Harry Midgley	January 1950–April 1957
Morris May	May 1957–March 1962
Ivan Neill	March 1962–July 1964
Herbert Kirk	July 1964–April 1965
William Fitzsimmons	April 1965–October 1966
William Long	October 1966–December 1968
William Fitzsimmons	December 1968–March 1969
Phelim O'Neill	March 1969–May 1969
William Long	May 1969–March 1972

PARLIAMENTARY SECRETARY

Robert McKeown	June 1921–April 1925
John Robb	April 1925–October 1937
Dehra Parker	October 1937–March 1944
Robert Bradford	September 1967–September 1968

NORTHERN IRELAND OFFICE MINISTER

Roland Moyle	October 1974–September 1976
Lord Melchett	September 1976–May 1979
Lord Elton	May 1979–September 1981
Nicholas Scott	September 1981–January 1986
Brian Mawhinney	January 1986–April 1992
Jeremy Hanley	April 1992–May 1993
Michael Ancram	May 1993–May 1997
Tony Worthington	May 199–July 1998
John McFall	July 1998

Appendix B

STATUS OF ELEMENTARY SCHOOLS

Year	Schools	Provided	Transferred	'4 and 2'	Voluntary
1925	2,006	2	10		1,994
1926	1,970	6	75 (4)*	88 (5)	1,801 (91)
1927	1,948	10	194 (10)	108 (5)	1,636 (84)
1928	1,933	13	323 (12)	109 (6)	1,488 (77)
1929	1,920	21 (1)	403 (21)	93 (5)	1,403 (73)
1930	1,893	33 (2)	440 (23)	99 (5)	1,321 (70)
1931	1,868	63 (3)	448 (24)	78 (4)	1,279 (68)
1932	1,837	79 (4)	474 (26)	81 (4)	1,203 (65)
1933	1,814	93 (5)	498 (27)	76 (4)	1,147 (63)
1934	1,790	109 (6)	508 (28)	66 (4)	1,107 (62)
1935	1,775	117 (6)	509 (29)	65 (4)	1,084 (61)
1936	1,753	129 (7)	512 (29)	63 (4)	1,049 (60)
1937	1,727	142 (8)	511 (29)	55 (3)	1,019 (59)
1938	1,700	166 (10)	489 (29)	54 (3)	991 (58)
1939	1,691	188 (11)	479 (28)		1,024 (60)**
1940	1,686	193 (11)	478 (28)		1,015 (60)
1941	1,681	193 (11)	483 (29)		1,005 (60)
1942	1,673	194 (11)	483 (29)		996 (60)
1943	1,667	195 (11)	485 (29)		987 (60)
1944	1,665	195 (11)	490 (29)		980 (60)
1945	1,661	196 (11)	493 (29)	48 (3)	924 (56)
1946	1,660	201 (12)	495 (30)	52 (3)	912 (55)
1947	1,653	200 (12)	497 (30)	51 (3)	905 (55)

Year	Schools	County	'4 and 2'	Voluntary
1948	1,635	690 (42)	72 (4)	873 (53)
1949	1,632	699 (43)	92 (5)	841 (51)
1950	1,631	713 (44)	105 (6)	813 (50)
1951	1,629	719 (44)	158 (9)	752 (46)
1952	1,626	730 (45)	169 (10)	727 (45)
1953	1,619	742 (46)	165 (10)	712 (44)
1954	1,606	750 (47)	150 (9)	706 (44)
1955	1,601	759 (47)	139 (9)	703 (44)
1956	1,599	764 (48)	134 (8)	701 (44)
1957	1,576	754 (48)	125 (8)	697 (44)
1958	1,558	747 (48)	115 (7)	696 (45)
1959	1,545	746 (48)	107 (7)	692 (45)
1960	1,529	752 (49)	91 (6)	686 (45)
1961	1,510	747 (49)	79 (5)	684 (45)
1962	1,485	741 (50)	70 (5)	674 (45)
1963	1,463	733 (50)	64 (4)	666 (45)
1964	1,442	727 (50)	59 (4)	656 (45)
1965	1,400	712 (50)	49 (4)	639 (45)
1966	1,369	697 (51)	47 (3)	625 (45)
1967	1,332	680 (51)	41 (3)	611 (46)
1968	1,292	662 (51)	57 (4)	573 (44)
1969	1,256	643 (51)	200 (16)	413 (33)
1970	1,216	624 (51)	382 (31)	210 (17)
1971	1,201	621 (52)	580 (48)	

NOTES TO THE TABLES

* Figures in parenthesis represent the percentage of the total number of schools
** The figures for '4 and 2' and Voluntary Schools are sometimes merged because some of the Ministry of Education's Reports failed to distinguish between these two categories of schools

Appendix C

PUPIL NUMBERS

Year	Provided	Transferred	'4 and 2'	Voluntary
1926	2,584 (1)*	13,132 (5)	11,048 (5)	175,734 (87)
1927	4,056 (2)	32,248 (16)	13,493 (7)	151,891 (75)
1928	4,786 (2)	46,606 (23)	12,653 (6)	136,874 (68)
1929	6,844 (3)	53,816 (27)	10,665 (5)	129,375 (64)
1930	10,964 (5)	71,529 (35)	11,176 (5)	107,402 (53)
1931	17,440 (8)	60,235 (30)	9,734 (5)	116,068 (57)
1932	23,023 (11)	62,522 (30)	10,425 (5)	109,660 (53)
1933	25,455 (12)	70,397 (34)	9,255 (4)	103,214 (49)
1934	27,155 (13)	66,128 (32)	9,283 (4)	100,984 (50)
1935	29,708 (14)	64,250 (32)	8,902 (4)	100,465 (49)
1936	31,562 (16)	62,165 (31)	8,569 (4)	97,446 (49)
1937	33,889 (17)	61,078 (31)	7,509 (4)	94,363 (48)
1938	38,261 (20)	57,348 (30)	6,873 (4)	91,510 (47)
1939–44	N/A	N/A	N/A	N/A
1945	39,930 (21)	54,744 (29)	5,653 (3)	85,613 (46)
1946	41,127 (22)	55,023 (29)	5,925 (3)	85,528 (46)
1947	40,918 (22)	54,716 (29)	5,866 (3)	85,092 (46)

Year	County	'4 and 2'	Voluntary
1948	92,988 (50)	6,932 (4)	84,338 (46)
1949	94,529 (50)	7,480 (4)	84,413 (45)
1950	98,047 (52)	8,208 (4)	81,736 (43)
1951	98,760 (51)	10,568 (5)	83,408 (43)
1952	102,275 (51)	11,393 (6)	84,722 (43)
1953	104,464 (51)	11,490 (6)	86,287 (43)
1954	105,249 (52)	10,478 (5)	87,328 (43)
1955	106,978 (52)	9,637 (4)	89,097 (43)
1956	105,864 (51)	9,320 (4)	90,643 (44)
1957	102,942 (50)	8,428 (4)	92,687 (45)
1958	100,258 (50)	7,610 (4)	93,233 (46)

→

cont.

Year	County	'4 and 2'	Voluntary
1959	97,899 (50)	6,823 (4)	90,344 (46)
1960	98,801 (51)	5,422 (3)	89,730 (46)
1961	96,619 (51)	5,000 (3)	87,991 (46)
1962	96,846 (51)	4,565 (3)	88,075 (46)
1963	97,510 (51)	4,329 (2)	88,426 (46)
1964	97,566 (51)	4,027 (2)	88,057 (46)
1965	99,030 (51)	3,599 (2)	88,960 (46)
1966	101,374 (52)	3,692 (2)	89,725 (46)
1967	103,831 (52)	3,514 (2)	91,423 (46)
1968	106,171 (52)	5,918 (3)	91,719 (45)
1969	108,474 (52)	45,961 (22)	53,567 (26)
1970	111,004 (52)	69,683 (33)	31,372 (15)
1971	112,577 (52)	101,694 (47)**	

*   Figures in parenthesis are percentages of the total number of pupils
** Ministry of Education Report did not distinguish between '4 and 2' and
     Voluntary Schools

Appendix D

Year	Catholics	%	Total	County	'4 and 2'	Voluntary
1922	68,959	34.8	198,385			
1923	67,925	34.7	196,015			
1924	69,166	34.8	198,593			
1925	70,232	35.0	200,287			
1926	N/A	N/A	N/A			
1927	72,143	36.1	199,560			
1928	71,998	36.1	199,511			
1929	72,068	36.1	199,560			
1930	72,872	36.1	201,683			
1931	73,291	35.8	204,400			
1932	74,443	36.0	206,736			
1933	75,150	36.3	206,834			
1934	74,517	36.5	203,943			
1935	73,838	36.8	200,607			
1936	72,964	37.0	197,353			
1937	72,259	37.2	194,347			
1938	71,789	37.4	191,862			
1939	72,797	38.0	191,734			
1940	72,082	38.6	186,333			
1941	70,988	38.4	184,858			
1942	71,200	38.5	184,755			
1943	72,246	39.0	185,542			
1944	72,759	39.2	185,621			
1945	73,242	39.5	185,470			
1946	74,369	39.7	187,261			
1947	73,814	39.8	185,418			
1948	75,083	41.0	183,445			
1949	76,335	41.1	185,712			
1950	77653	41.3	187,991			
1951	79958	41.5	192,736			
1952*	82,688	41.7	198,390	983	1,209	80,496
1953	85,120	42.1	202,241	1,025	1,243	82,852

$\longrightarrow$

cont.

Year	Catholics	%	Total	County	'4 and 2'	Voluntary
1954	86,843	42.8	203,055	1,023	1,302	84,518
1955	88,918	43.2	205,712	1,033	1,282	86,603
1956	90,617	44.0	205,827	981	1,299	88,337
1957	92,873	45.5	204,057	904	1,290	90,679
1958	93,564	46.5	201,101	879	1,291	91,394
1959	90,760	46.5	195,066	807	1,171	88,782
1960	90,386	46.6	193,953	879	1,049	88,458
1961	88,651	46.7	189,610	820	1,016	86,815
1962	88,713	46.8	189,486	806	922	86,985
1963**	89,181	46.9	190,265	837	905	87,439

* The subdivision of the figures is made possible for 1952 onwards because these statistics were made available by the Ministry of Education

** The Ministry of Education ceased publishing data on the religious composition of pupils after 1963

Appendix E

Year	Pupils	Schools
1925	8,460	69
1926	9,012	70
1927	9,913	71
1928	10,611	72
1929	11,618	74
1930	12,094	73
1931	12,267	73
1932	12,339	72
1933	12,710	73
1934	12,974	74
1935	13,165	73
1936	13,440	73
1937	13,683	76
1938	14,083	76
1939	14,557	75
1940	14,493	75
1941	14,772	75
1942	16,023	75
1943	17,535	76
1944	18,854	76
1945	19,861	76
1946	21,021	76
1947	21,973	77

→

cont.

	GRAMMAR		INTERMEDIATE	
	Pupils	*Schools*	*Pupils*	*Schools*
1948	24,418 (84)*	77	4,793 (16)	10
1949	26,735 (82)	79	5,904 (18)	11
1950	28,386 (81)	79	6,696 (19)	12
1951	29,536 (81)	80	6,785 (19)	12
1952	30,065 (80)	80	7,497 (20)	13
1953	30,332 (79)	81	8,240 (21)	18
1954	30,899 (75)	81	10,652 (25)	23
1955	31,817 (71)	81	12,961 (29)	31
1956	32,526 (68)	81	15,166 (32)	34
1957	34,232 (59)	81	23,991 (41)	56
1958	35,577 (50)	81	35,968 (50)	73
1959	36,611 (47)	81	42,364 (53)	89
1960	37,485 (44)	81	47,173 (56)	100
1961	37,996 (41)	81	54,192 (59)	116
1962	40,160 (42)	82	55,820 (58)	122
1963	41,468 (42)	81	58,102 (58)	129
1964	42,960 (42)	81	60,673 (58)	137
1965	44,821 (42)	81	63,690 (58)	143
1966	45,980 (41)	80	67,950 (59)	152
1967	47,955 (40)	81	74,118 (60)	157
1968	49,783 (39)	81	77,676 (61)	164
1969	50,818 (38)	81	80,876 (61)	168
1970	51,542 (38)	81	84,543 (62)	171

* Figures in parenthesis are percentages of the total number of pupils attending grammar and secondary intermediate schools

Appendix F

CLASS ONE SCHOOL BUILDING

	Year	New Buildings		Cost	Improvements Cost	Total Cost
		Schools	Places			
To	1931	55	17,712	£544,215	£200,303	£744,518
	1932	18	4,378	£136,075	£36,360	£172,435
	1933	12	2,019	£73,517	£68,732	£142,249
	1934	14	2,523	£73,888	£43,639	£117,527
	1935	7	2,686	£81,884	£48,084	£129,968
	1936	15	2,942	£79,848	£29,317	£109,165
	1937	17	3,374	£126,646	£28,654	£155,300
	1938	27	5,520	£198,517	£45,684	£244,201
	1939	N/A	N/A	N/A	N/A	N/A
	TOTALS	**165**	**41,154**	**£1,314,590**	**£500,773**	**£1,815,363**

Appendix G

CLASS TWO SCHOOL BUILDING

	Year	New buildings Schools	New buildings Places	Cost	Improvements Cost	Total Cost
To	1931	5	550	£6,900	£2,871	£9,771
	1932	2	193	£7,600	–	£7,600
	1933	3	392	£9,672	–	£9,672
	1934–37	–	–		–	–
	1938	2	110	£3,149	–	£3,149
	1939	N/A	N/A	N/A	N/A	N/A
	TOTALS	**12**	**£1,245**	**£27,321**	**£2,871**	**£30,192**

Appendix H

CLASS THREE SCHOOL BUILDING

	Year	New buildings		Improvements		Total
		Schools	Places	Cost	Cost	cost
To	31.3.33	8	3,226	£45,206	£4,366	£49,572
	1933–34	7	724	£9,952	£13,255	£23,207
	1934–35	3	232	£3,595	£2,563	£6,058
	1935–36	4	958	£15,568	£4,188	£19,756
	1936–37	6	1,595	£28,672	£9,922	£38,594
	1937–38	4	804	£16,980	£934	£17,914
	1938–39	5	444	£7,532	£1,854	£9,386
	1939–40	N/A	N/A	N/A	N/A	N/A
	TOTALS	**37**	**7,983**	**£127,505**	**£37,082**	**£164,587**

Appendix I

Year ending	Primary		Intermediate		Grammar	
	Schools	Places	Schools	Places	Schools	Places
1.4.48						
to						
31.7.52	11	4,378	–	380	2	1,490
31.7.53	7	2,240	–	260	–	350
31.7.54	20	5,938	3	1,440	–	480
31.7.55	15	4,440	4	1,500	1	300
31.7.56	2	1,760	5	2,210	1	175
31.7.57	8	1,840	3	1,220	1	200
31.7.58	14	4,690	19	10,220	2	880
31.7.59	19	3,260	16	7,660	1	750
31.7.60	9	1,670	6	2,910	1	470
31.7.61	9	2,640	7	3,640	–	–
31.7.62	11	1,970	2	1,120	3	1,450
31.7.63	2	1,288	1	580	1	770
30.6.64	5	2,020	3	1,400	–	290
31.12.65	14	4,141	1	700	–	170
31.12.66	18	4,038	1	1,180	1	840
31.12.67	12	5,538	–	140	–	485
31.12.68	9	3,919	1	1,570	–	470
31.12.69	N/A	5,900	N/A	1,800	N/A	–
31.12.70		6,000		2,400		–
31.12.71		2,100		1,800		400
31.12.72		4,400		3,700		1,400
31.12.73		3,800		1,600		700
31.12.74		2,100		1,500		400
31.12.75		3,200		900		1,900
31.12.76		900		1,100		300
31.12.77		3,300		3,300		–
31.12.78		N/A		N/A		N/A
TOTALS	185	55,770	72	56,230	14	9,570

Appendix J

VOLUNTARY SCHOOLS

Year Ending	Primary places	Intermediate places	Grammar places
1.4.48 to			
31.7.52	275	–	1745
31.7.53	1,023	–	470
31.7.54	1,917	400	1,870
31.7.55	1,650	150	190
31.7.56	1,210	1,500	1,220
31.7.57	1,360	720	510
31.7.58	1,340	20,40	1,020
31.7.59	1,960	3,070	1,040
31.7.60	2,210	3,040	210
31.7.61	1,815	3,940	510
31.7.62	3,615	2,240	1,080
31.7.63	1,936	1,820	660
30.6.64	1,364	1,560	1,270
31.12.65	2,284	1,225	2,180
31.12.66	5,831	4,725	2,420
31.12.67	7,294	3,220	3,100
31.12.68	8,606	3,270	5,224
31.12.69	6,400	2,400	1,600
31.12.70	7,600	3,000	1,300
31.12.71	6,700	3,600	1,600
31.12.72	6,900	1,900	2,300
31.12.73	10,600	4,100	3,400
31.12.74	4,600	3,200	1,400
31.12.75	4,400	2,700	1,200
31.12.76	3,000	4,300	1,600
31.12.77	3,100	3,500	1,800
31.12.78	N/A	N/A	N/A
TOTALS	**98,990**	**61,620**	**40,919**

Bibliography

PRIMARY SOURCES

Northern Ireland Cabinet Papers 1921–1957

CAB 4	Cabinet Conclusions
CAB 9D	Cabinet Education Papers
ED 13/16	Ministry of Education Policy Papers
ED 30/31/32	Local Education Authority Papers
T 2886	John Duffin Papers
D 3099	Londonderry Papers

Down and Connor Diocesan Archives 1928–1948

ED 11/30	ED 11/44
ED 11/31	ED 11/45
ED 11/33–35	ED 11/46
ED 11/38	ED 11/47
ED 11/39	ED 11/48

Ministry of Education Reports 1921–1973

1.4.22–31.3.23	Cmd 16	1.4.35–31.3.36	HC 383
1.4.23–31.3.24	HC 54	1.4.36–31.3.37	HC 410
1.4.24–31.3.25	HC 80	1.4.37–31.3.38	HC 440
1.4.25–31.3.26	HC 107	1.4.38–31.3.39	HC 483
1.4.26–31.3.27	HC 131	1.4.39–31.3.45	N/A
1.4.27–31.3.28	HC 154	1.4.45–31.3.46	HC 783
1.4.28–31.3.29	HC 180	1.4.46–31.3.47	HC 822
1.4.29–31.3.30	HC 211	1.4.47–31.3.48	HC 883
1.4.30–31.3.31	HC 242	1.4.48–31.3.49	HC 970
1.4.31–31.3.32	HC 269	1.4.49–31.3.50	Cmd 307
1.4.32–31.3.33	HC 294	1.4.50–31.3.51	Cmd 313
1.4.33–31.3.34	HC 315	1.4.51–31.3.52	Cmd 322
1.4.34–31.3.35	HC 349	1.4.52–31.3.53	Cmd 333

1.4.53–31.3.54	Cmd 338	1.8.63–31.7.64	Cmd 476
1.8.54–31.7.55	Cmd 351	1.1.65–31.12.65	Cmd 492
1.8.55–31.7.56	Cmd 368	1.1.66–31.12.66	Cmd 506
1.8.56–31.7.57	Cmd 380	1.1.67–21.12.67	Cmd 520
1.8.57–31.7.58	Cmd 392	1.1.68–31.12.68	Cmd 527
1.8.58–31.7.59	Cmd 409	1.1.69–21.12.69	Cmd 542
1.8.59–31.7.60	Cmd 423	1.1.70–31.12.70	Cmd 559
1.8.60–31.7.61	Cmd 435	1.1.71–31.12.71	Cmd 573
1.8.61–31.7.62	Cmd 450	1.1.72–31.12.72	Cmd 580
1.8.62–31.7.63	Cmd 463	1.1.72–31.12.73	Cmd 585

Cmd 6 (1922)	*Interim report of the Committee on Educational Services*
Cmd 15 (1923)	*Report (final) of the Committee on Educational Services*
Cmd 84 (1928)	*Correspondence between the Ministry of Education and the Armagh Regional Education Committee on the subject of Bible instruction in transferred schools*
Cmd 226 (1944)	*Educational reconstruction in Northern Ireland*
Cmd 470 (1964)	*Education in Northern Ireland in 1964*
Cmd 513 (1967)	*Local education authorities and voluntary schools*
Cmd 532 (1969)	*Disturbances in Northern Ireland: report of the Commission appointed by the Governor of Northern Ireland*
DENI (1979)	*Report of the working party on the management of schools in Northern Ireland*
DENI (1988)	*Education: the way forward*
NICED (1988)	*Education for mutual understanding: a guide*
CCMS (1988)	*Responses to the consultative document 'Education in Northern Ireland – proposals for reform'*
CCMS (1989)	*Response to proposal for a draft order-in-council*
SACHR (1989)	*Fifteenth report – HC 394*
SACHR (1990)	*Sixteenth report – HC 459*
SACHR (1991)	*Seventeenth report – HC 488*
SACHR (1992)	*Eighteenth report – HC 54*
SACHR (1993)	*Nineteenth report – HC 739*
Cmnd 5259 (1973)	*Northern Ireland Consitutional Proposals* (London)

Newspapers

Irish News
Belfast Telegraph
Belfast Newsletter

Journals

Irish Catholic Directory 1900–1994
Irish Ecclesiastical Record 1900–1968
Studies 1912–1994
Irish Educational Studies 1981–1994

SECONDARY SOURCES

Akenson, Donald (1970) *The Irish education experiment: the national system of education in the nineteenth century* (London)
Akenson, Donald (1973) *Education and enmity: the control of schooling in Northern Ireland 1920-50* (London)
Akenson, Donald (1975) *A mirror to Kathleen's face: education in independent Ireland 1922–1960* (Montreal)
Astin, Alan (1987) 'The management of schools in Northern Ireland: reflections on the Astin Report' in *Education and policy in Northern Ireland*, pp. 257–266
Atkinson, Norman (1969) *Irish education: a history of educational institutions* (Dublin)
Auchmuty, James (1937) *Irish education, a historical survey* (London and Dublin)
Bardon, Jonathan (1992) *A history of Ulster* (Belfast)
Barritt, Denis and Carter, Charles (1962) *The Northern Ireland problem: a study in group relations* (Oxford)
Barry, P. (1959) 'The Holy See and the Irish National Schools' in *Irish Ecclesiastical Record*, July 1959, pp. 88–105
Batterbury, Richard (1940) 'The Synod of Ulster and the National Board' in *Irish Ecclesiastical Record*, December 1940, pp. 548–561
Batterbury, Richard (1941) 'The Synod of Ulster and the National Board – II' in *Irish Ecclesiastical Record*, July 1941, pp. 16–28
Batterbury, Richard (1942) 'The Synod of Ulster and the National Board – III' in *Irish Ecclesiastical Record*, January 1942, pp. 61–73
Blanshard, Paul (1954) *The Irish and Catholic power* (London)
Buckland, Patrick (1979) *The factory of grievances: devolved government in Northern Ireland 1921–1939* (Dublin)

Buckland, Patrick (1980) *James Craig, Lord Craigavon* (Dublin)

Buckland, Patrick (1981) *A history of Northern Ireland* (Dublin)

Cahill, Edward (1939) 'English education in Ireland during the penal era (1691–1800)' in *Irish Ecclesiastical Record*, December 1939, pp. 627–43

Cairns, Ed; Dunn, Seamus and Giles, Melanie (1993)'Surveys of integrated education in Northern Ireland: A review' in *After the reforms: education and policy in Northern Ireland*, pp. 143–160

Campbell, J. J. (1962) *Catholic schools: a survey of a Northern Ireland problem* (Belfast)

Campbell, T. J. (1941) *Fifty years of Ulster* (Belfast)

Connolly, Michael (1993) 'The financing of education in Northern Ireland' in *After the reforms: education and policy in Northern Ireland*, pp. 33–44

Conway, William (1971) *Catholic Schools* (Belfast)

Coolahan, John (1981) *Irish Education: its history and structure* (Dublin)

Corcoran, Timothy (1916) *State policy in Irish education* (Dublin)

Corcoran, Timothy (1928) *Education systems in Ireland, from the close of the middle ages* (Dublin)

Corish, Patrick (1959) 'Cardinal Cullen and Archbishop MacHale' in *Irish Ecclesiastical Record*, June 1959, pp. 393–408

Cormack, Robert; Gallagher, Anthony and Osborne, Robert (1991) 'Religious affiliation and educational attainment in Northern Ireland: the financing of schools in Northern Ireland' SACHR 1991, pp. 118–212

D'Arcy, John and Sutherland, Anne (1990) 'System inequalities in curriculum provision and educational attainment in Northern Ireland' SACHR 1990, pp. 98–129

Davis, Richard (1994) *Mirror hate: the convergent ideology of Northern Ireland paramilitaries, 1966–1992* (Aldershot)

Democratic Union Party (1997) *Raise the standard: Democratic Unionist Party manifesto* (Belfast)

Dowling, Patrick (1935) *The hedge schools of Ireland* (Dublin)

Dowling, Patrick (1971) *A history of Irish education: a study in conflicting loyalties* (Dublin)

Dunn, Seamus (1990) 'A short history of education in Northern Ireland 1920–1990' SACHR 1990, pp. 50–95.

Dunn, Seamus (1993) 'A historical context to education and church-state relations in Northern Ireland' in *After the reforms: education and policy in Northern Ireland*, pp. 15–32

Elliott, Sydney (1973) *Northern Ireland parliamentary election results 1921–1972* (Chichester)

Farrell, Michael (1980) *Northern Ireland: the Orange state* (London)

Farren, Sean (1981) 'Curricular developments in Ireland, North and South, in the period 1945–1960: a study in contrasts' *Irish Educational Studies*, Vol. 1, pp. 243–258

Farren, Sean (1995) *The politics of Irish education 1920–65* (Belfast)

Foster, Roy (1988) *Ireland 1600–1972* (London)

Fulton, John (1991) *The tragedy of belief: division, politics and religion in Ireland* (Oxford)

Gallagher, Anthony; Osborne, Robert and Cormack, Robert (1993) 'Community relations, equality and education' in *After the reforms: education and policy in Northern Ireland*, pp. 177–196

Gallagher, Eric and Worrall, Stanley (1982) *Christians in Ulster 1968–1980* (Oxford)

Galliher, John and De Gregory, Jerry (1985) *Violence in Northern Ireland: understanding Protestant perspectives* (New York)

Harris, Mary (1994) *The Catholic Church and the foundation of the Northern Irish state* (Oxford)

Hepburn, A. C. (1980) *The conflict of nationality in modern Ireland* (London)

Hickey, John (1984) *Religion and the Northern Ireland problem* (Dublin)

Hislop, Harold (1992) 'The Management of the Kildare Place school system 1811–1831' *Irish Educational Studies*, Vol. 11, 1992, pp. 52–71

Hoban, James (1983) 'The survival of the hedge schools – a local study' *Irish Educational Studies*, Vol. 3, No. 2, pp. 21–36

Irish Department of Education (1922) *Report of the National Programme Conference* (Dublin)

Isles, K. S., and Cuthbert, N. (1957) *An economic survey of Northern Ireland* (Belfast)

Lee J. J. (1989) *Ireland 1912–1985: politics and society* (Cambridge)

Livingstone, J. (1987) 'Equality of opportunity in education in Northern Ireland' in *Education and policy in Northern Ireland*, pp. 43–54

Londonderry, Lord (1924) 'Public education in Northern Ireland: the new system' in *Nineteenth century and after* Vol. XCV, March 1924, pp. 328–34

Lyons, F. S. L. (1973) *Ireland since the Famine* (London)

McAllister, Ian (1977) *The Northern Ireland Social Democratic and Labour Party: political opposition in a divided society* (London)

McCavera, Paddy (1993) 'The role of the Council for Catholic Maintained Schools in education in Northern Ireland' in *After the reforms: education and policy in Northern Ireland*, pp. 65–74

McElligott, T. (1966) *Education in Ireland* (Dublin)

McElroy, Gerald (1991) *The Catholic Church and the Northern Ireland crisis 1968–1986* (Dublin)

McEwen, Alex and Salters, John (1993) 'Integrated education: the views of parents' in *After the reforms: education and policy in Northern Ireland*, pp. 161–176

McGarry, John and O'Leary, Brendan (1995) *Explaining Northern Ireland* (London)

McKeown, Penny (1993) 'The introduction of formula funding and local management of schools in Northern Ireland' in *After the reforms: education and policy in Northern Ireland*, pp. 79–104

McVeigh, Joseph (1989) *A wounded church: religion, politics and justice in Ireland* (Cork)

Menendez, Albert (1973) *The bitter harvest: church and state in Northern Ireland* (New York)

Mescal, John (1957) *Religion in the Irish system of education* (London and Dublin)

Milne, Kenneth (1984) 'The Irish charter schools: the grand design in principle and practice' *Irish Educational Studies*, Vol. 4, pp. 35–53

Moxon-Browne, Edward (1983) *Nation, class and creed in Northern Ireland*

Murray, Dominic (1985) *Worlds apart: segregated schools in Northern Ireland* (Belfast)

Murray, Dominic (1993) 'Science and funding in Northern Ireland grammar schools' in *After the reforms: education and policy in northern Ireland*, pp. 209–220

O'Buachalla, Seamus (1988) *Education Policy in twentieth century Ireland* (Dublin)

Osborne, Robert Cormack, Robert and Gallagher, Anthony (1993) *After the reforms: education and policy in Northern Ireland*

Osborne, Robert Cormack, and Gallagher, Anthony (1993) 'Education in Northern Ireland' in *After the reforms: education and policy in Northern Ireland*, pp. 1–14

O'Boyle, Manus (1993) 'Rhetoric and reality in Northern Ireland's Catholic secondary schools' in *After the reforms: education and policy in Northern Ireland*, pp. 197–208

O'Connor, Fionnula (1993) *In search of a state: Catholics in Northern Ireland* (Belfast)

O'Neill, Terence (1972) *The autobiography of Terence O'Neill* (London)

Osborne Robert, Cormack Robert and Miller Robert (1987) *Education and policy in Northern Ireland* (Belfast)

Salters, Matthew and McEwen, Alex (1993) 'Public policy and education in Northern Ireland' in *After the reforms: education and policy in Northern Ireland*, pp. 45–59

SDLP (1992) *A new north: a new Ireland: a new Europe SDLP manifesto 1992* (Belfast)

Shea, Patrick (1981) *Voices and the sound of drums: an Irish autobiography* (Belfast)

Shuka, Jeffrey (1989) *Hearts and minds, water and fish: support for the IRA and the INLA in a northern Irish ghetto* (London)

Simon, Brian (1991) *The politics of educational reform 1920–1940* (London)

Starkie, W. J. M. (1902) *Recent reforms in Irish education* (Dublin)

Tierney, Mark (1978) *Modern Ireland* (Dublin)

Titley, E. Brian (1983) *Church, state and the control of schooling in Ireland 1900–1944* (Dublin)

Ulster Unionist Party (1992) *The people's choice: Ulster Unionist Party manifesto* (Belfast)

Ulster Unionist Party (1997) *Secure the Union, build your future: Ulster Union Party manifesto* (Belfast)

Wald, Kenneth (1983) *Crosses on the ballot: patterns of British voter alignment since 1885* (Princeton)

Walker, Graham (1985) *The politics of frustration: Harry Midgley and the failure of Labour in Northern Ireland* (Manchester)

Wilson, Tom (1989) *Ulster: conflict and consent* (Oxford)

UNPUBLISHED THESES

Farren, Sean (1989) *Culture and education in Ireland 1920–1960* PhD, University of Ulster

Holmes, Erskine (1970) *Public opinion and educational reform in the North of Ireland 1900–1954* MA, Queen's University of Belfast

McKeown, Michael (1962) *Catholic reaction to mixed elementary education in Ireland between 1831 and 1870* MA, Queen's University of Belfast

Mark, Robin (1978) *Interdenominational education: what type of movement? Theological, sociological and ecumenical reflections on the All Children Together movement* MA, Hull University

Spence, William (1959) *The growth and development of the secondary intermediate school in Northern Ireland since the Education Act of 1947* MA, Queen's University of Belfast

Index